Protestant Dissent and Controversy in Ireland 1660–1714

Protestant Dissent
and
Controversy in Ireland
1660–1714

Phil Kilroy

CORK UNIVERSITY PRESS

First published in 1994 by
Cork University Press
University College
Cork
Ireland

© Phil Kilroy 1994

British Library Cataloguing in Publication Data
A CIP catalogue record for this book is available from
the British Library.

ISBN 1 85918 003 5

Typeset by Tower Books of Ballincollig, Co. Cork
Printed by ColourBooks, Baldoyle, Co. Dublin

Contents

Acknowledgements

In the process of writing this book I have had the help of many institutions, and my thanks are due to the staffs of the following. In Dublin: Trinity College Library, the National Library of Ireland, the Historical Library of the Religious Society of Friends in Ireland, the Gilbert Library, Marsh's Library, the National Archives, the Representative Church Body Library, the Royal Irish Academy, the Unitarian Church, St Stephen's Green West. In Belfast: the Public Record Office Northern Ireland, the Queen's University Library, the Linen Hall Library, Union Theological College Library, the Presbyterian Historical Society Library. In Armagh: the Robinson Library, Armagh Public Library, Irish Reference Department, Southern Education and Library Board. In Londonderry: Magee College Library. In Cashel: the GPA–Bolton Library. In Edinburgh: the National Library of Scotland, the Public Record Office, New College Library, University of Edinburgh Library. In Oxford: the Bodleian Library. In Cambridge: the University Library, Trinity College Library. In London: the British Library, the Library of the Religious Society of Friends, Dr Williams's Library, the Congregational Library, Lambeth Palace Library, Victoria and Albert Museum Library, the Public Record Office, the Institute of Historical Research.

I have many people to thank for their interest and support while writing this book. In addition to my colleagues, my family and friends, I would like to thank those who have helped me in a particular way: John Barkley, Kevin Herlihy, James McGuire, Jane Ohlmeyer, the late Angela Campbell, the late George Otto Simms. Margaret McCurtain initiated my explorations into seventeenth-century Ireland and since then has been a constant source of help and inspiration. The suggestions and criticisms of both Toby Barnard and Raymond Gillespie have bettered the book at every stage, and to them I am extremely grateful. Aidan Clarke supervised this work first as a thesis and later advised on its transformation into a book. I have benefited greatly from his experience and insight in this process. I thank Kathleen Finn, Mary O'Brien, Aideen Kinlen, Veronica Ranaghan and Moira Donnelly for reading parts of this book; and Marie McCarthy, who read the entire work and prevented many errors remaining in the text. Finally, I thank Cork University Press, for their encouragement and interest in this work from the beginning. This book is dedicated to the memory of the historian Adèle Cahier, 1804–1885.

Phil Kilroy,
Armagh,
May, 1994

Abbreviations

The abbreviations in T. W. Moody, F. X. Martin, F. J. Byrne (eds), *A new history of Ireland*, iii (Oxford, 1976), pp xxvi-xxxvii, have been used throughout, with the following additions:

B.L.	British Library, London
Baum. Papers	Baumgartner Papers, Strype correspondence, University Library, Cambridge
F.L.D.	Friends' Library, Dublin
F.L.L.	Friends' Library, London
J.F.H.S.	*Journal of the Friends' Historical Society*
N.L.S.	National Library of Scotland, Edinburgh
U.L.C.	University Library, Cambridge

Carte Manuscripts, Bodleian Library, Oxford

All folio references in this book are from the original manuscripts and are not taken from the catalogue compiled by Edward Edwards.

Dating

All dates are given old style, except that the year is taken to begin on 1 January.

Introduction

Are we not one body as to principles and truth and the great interest of practical godliness . . . one communion as to externals of worship? . . . there is some variety in the external forms of administration and in government, yet why should the lesser wherein we differ be more effectual to divide our hearts than the greater wherein we agree are to unite us?

Nathaniel Weld, *A sermon before the Society for the Reformation of Manners in Dublin* (1698)

The advent of the Reformation in Ireland marked a break with the religious past, opening up new paths in religious thought and practice which still affect us today. This process began in May 1534 when Henry VIII ordered the Dublin government to ignore papal provisions and jurisdiction in Ireland; bishops then in office continued to be recognised by the crown, but all new appointments were made by the king. Legislators presumed that the existing Roman church could be absorbed into the reformed church. This was an impossible project, for the personnel, structures and internal organisation of the older church were caught in a web of lay rights and family control which were all in need of reform long before 1534. Therefore legislation alone could not ensure the stability and growth of the reformed church;

1

neither did the reformed church receive the necessary support from successive administrations in Ireland which could have enabled it to succeed in its task. Besides, the Reformation in Ireland originated with the colonial power, and the reformed church executed its role within that perspective. Indeed, the church progressively perceived its role as serving the colonial community in the measure that the country became planted by English and Scottish settlers. Finally, in contrast to the situation in England, there was no dissenting movement in Ireland before the Reformation which could have served as a bridge and foundation for the Established Church.

Dissent within the Established Church was introduced from England and Scotland, mainly through the personnel of the Established Church when the first generation of bishops and clergy had passed away. By virtue of necessity, therefore, the Established Church developed within narrow confines and succeeded in evolving a distinctive theology of its own. Indeed, as early as 1567 the church adopted twelve articles of religion, the broader set of Archbishop Parker rather than the Thirty-Nine Articles of the Church of England. It was a wise move at a time of great change and uncertainty and helped to avoid conflict by broadening the base of Protestantism in Ireland. At the same time it provided the context for open debate and controversy within the newly established Reformation churches in England, Scotland and Ireland. At this time all religious issues were open to scrutiny and question, and people made choices on religious issues. The matters most hotly debated were symbolic of profound changes in religious understanding and practice: the use of vestments, the Book of Common Prayer, the authority of bishops, use of signs at worship, centrality of the sermon, sitting at communion services, observance of the Sabbath. Longstanding controversies developed on the nature of authority, of ministry, church order, and lay participation in church affairs.

Episcopalians, Puritans and separatists entered into lengthy controversies with one another. While episcopalians and Puritans agreed on the doctrine expressed in the Thirty-Nine Articles, Puritans thought that ritual and ecclesiastical order and discipline

in the Church of England needed further reformation. Some of
the Puritan insights were readily accepted by the bishops and
clergy, for many in the Church of England were Calvinist in doctrine but Catholic in ritual and discipline. Indeed, episcopalians
insisted that the ceremonies of the church should be respected
and obeyed, being matters of 'indifference'. Puritans disagreed
with this judgement, believing that Christian liberty conformed
to the scriptures even in matters of 'indifference'. Separatists,
on the other hand, considered that the Church of England was
still too much influenced by Roman church practices and theology
and so could not contain within itself the possibility of true reformation. For this reason they chose to sever themselves from
the Church of England and create a truly reformed church.

Such controversies and debates found their way to Ireland in
several ways. In 1561 Adam Loftus, Archbishop of Armagh, appointed Thomas Cartwright his chaplain. Cartwright was a critic
of the Church of England, a Puritan whose views on church order
included the abolition of bishops and of lay patrons in the church;
he also promoted churches ruled by minister and elders, with
church government by local, area and national councils. When
Loftus was translated to Dublin in 1567 he nominated Cartwright
to succeed him as Archbishop of Armagh, thereby creating suspicions that Loftus himself was a Puritan.

Further Puritan influences were introduced into Ireland when
Trinity College, Dublin, was founded in 1592. The first five
Provosts, Adam Loftus, Walter Travers, Henry Alvey, William
Temple and William Bedell were known Puritans or at least were
sympathetic to Puritan ideas. Indeed, in 1613 Archbishop Abbot
of Canterbury complained that surplices were not being worn
on Sundays either in Trinity College or in the cathedral churches
in Dublin. 'His Majesty says that is no reason to suffer those
places which should be seminaries of obedience to be the ground
plot of disorder and disobedience; neither is there any reason
to be severe against the papists if His Highness [the Lord
Chancellor, Archbishop Thomas Jones] should be remiss against
the Puritans.'[1] In the same year James Ussher wrote to Dr
Challoner from London telling him that Abbot had complained
that Trinity was 'flat Puritanical'.[2]

This Puritan tradition was reflected in the Convocation of the Established Church held in 1615 when Articles of Religion were drawn up. Such articulation of belief was a theological and historical necessity, setting the Established Church in the mainstream of both the Reformation and Celtic church traditions.[3] Thus members of the Irish Convocation prepared their own credal formularies and set them out in 104 articles. Almost all the Thirty-Nine Articles were included, sometimes adapted, sometimes in full.[4] The most pointed omissions were Articles 35 and 36: 'Of Homilies' and 'Of Consecration of Bishops and Ministers'. Indeed, the tone of the entire document expressed a resistance to ceremonies, traditions and homilies; the order of bishop was completely omitted; stress was laid on the sacredness of the Sabbath. The pope was condemned as the Antichrist (Article 80), a term not used in the Thirty-Nine Articles.

The Irish Articles of 1615 marked the Established Church as a church in its own right. It was defined by its experience in Ireland and formed over the decades when faced with the growing awareness that it was destined to be a small church, serving the colonial community as it expanded. Such a contraction in policy begged a theology, if only to warrant and even justify such a change in design. The Established Church became a small, predestined community, elect among the damned. Such attitudes were further reinforced as the Counter-Reformation movement in Ireland strengthened. Then the Established Church felt itself both saved and destined to live surrounded by all the signs of Antichrist. Articulation of belief in 1615 came from practical experience in Ireland and from the definite Calvinistic, Puritan influences which were prevalent in the Established Church at this time, particularly in Trinity College.

In addition to English Puritanism, the influence of the Scottish Reformation was present also within the Established Church.[5] At his accession in 1603 James I had imposed episcopacy on the Scottish church, thus creating potential for conflict in a church which had adopted a presbyterial form of government. Tensions came to a head in 1619 when the king, on his only visit to Scotland as James I, introduced the Articles of Perth and imposed conformity to the ceremonies of the Church of England. Such constrictions created tensions within the church in Scotland, and these were imported from Scotland when colonists came to settle in Ulster and required ministers to serve them.

In the early days of the plantation of Ulster Scottish ministers who came to Ireland found that they could rely on the support of lay patrons[6] and reach some accommodation with the Established Church regarding their ordination and exercise of ministry. Responding to their common need, both the Scottish Presbyterian ministers and the Established Church bishops achieved a certain *modus vivendi*.[7] Moreover, there was theological justification in the 1615 Irish Articles for accepting Presbyterian views on ordination and episcopacy, for the bishops and clergy of the Established Church were essentially either Calvinist in doctrine or at least tolerant of such views.[8]

Yet the practice of Scottish ritual and discipline in Ulster furthered controversy already present within the Established Church regarding the significance of ceremonies.[9] In a speech to parliament in 1613 the Archbishop of Armagh, Christopher Hampton, urged conformity to the ceremonies of the church even 'if I believe and am persuaded in mind and conscience . . . [that they] work nothing with God'.[10] Ceremonies were for order and peace, 'things indifferent', not matters of doctrine or belief. Both Puritans and Scottish Presbyterians thought differently, and by 1621 Hampton had become aware that in Ulster ministers from Scotland were 'entertaining the Scottish discipline and liturgy. They offer wrong to the Church here established and the rites of the administration of the sacraments.'[11]

James Ussher, who succeeded Hampton as Primate, viewed the situation differently and was at pains to point out the strong links between the ancient Celtic churches of Ireland and Scotland: 'I will not follow the evil example of those that have of late laboured to make dissension betwixt the daughter and the mother, but account of them as of the same people.'[12] Yet there were deep differences between the churches and in time these became very marked to the extent that Henry Leslie, Bishop of Down and Connor, accused Scottish Presbyterian ministers in Ulster of saying 'that the order of Bishops [is] Antichristian . . . that our ceremonies are damnable . . . that our service book is a heap of errors . . . that the sign of the Cross in Baptism and kneeling in the act of receiving the Communion is plain idolatry . . . that all festivals, besides the Lord's day, and all set fasts are Jewish and contrary to Christian Liberty'.[13]

Difference in ritual and discipline was clearly expressed in the Six-Mile-Water revival of 1625. This movement which was initiated by James Glendinning, minister at Oldstone, evoked a wide response from the people. To harness this religious fervour and control the excessiveness of Glendinning, several other Scottish Presbyterian ministers organised monthly meetings in Antrim, which began on Thursday evenings and lasted all day Friday.[14] Huge numbers attended, and this tradition developed over the years into large communion services which attracted people from far and wide, including some separatists from England.[15] A Catholic writer in Ireland at this time spoke of the 'rigid Puritans or Brownists [who] . . . will not enter under the roofs of any churches which they think were polluted . . . but assemble their sect and congregation in woods and forests and climb up trees to bleat out their harsh sounding Psalms and service'.[16]

When Thomas Wentworth was appointed Lord Deputy in 1633 he found the state of the Established Church, with its Puritan and Scottish Presbyterian elements, unacceptable. A firm supporter of Archbishop Laud, Wentworth set out to reform the Irish church on the model of the Church of England. While attending to much-needed reform of the church's financial basis and organisation, Wentworth attempted to impose doctrinal uniformity as well. He placed William Chappell, a known Arminian, as Provost in Trinity College. His chaplain, John Bramhall, was appointed Bishop of Derry in 1634. When he visited dioceses in Ulster he reported the clergy there as 'absolute irregulars'. In 1634, simultaneously with the sitting of parliament, Convocation met in Dublin and examined the state of the church. Wentworth forced the Established Church to abrogate the Irish Articles of 1615 and adopt the Thirty-Nine Articles of the Church of England.[17] It was an effort to contain and control a church that was far too comprehensive for the Laudian, Arminian model which obtained in England at this time. Certainly in a short time the whole tone and atmosphere had changed, and in 1636 Bishop Leslie of Down and Connor debated with the Presbyterian ministers on their difficulty in accepting the Book of Common Prayer.[18] This debate, significant in itself, also symbolised Presbyterian rejection of the Established Church as reformed in 1634 by Laud, Wentworth and Bramhall. Leslie tried hard to meet the Presbyterians at least half way in the debate, making several concessions; but the arrival of Bramhall during the course of the debate heightened the differences and polarised the two traditions acutely. The *modus vivendi* was over. When Wentworth imposed the Black Oath in 1639, requiring rejection of the Solemn League and Covenant, it was clear that there would be no place for Presbyterians in Wentworth's Ireland.[19] Ministers in Ulster were ejected progressively from their livings and fled back to Scotland or attempted to sail to New England.[20]

Despite such legislation and activity, the effects which Wentworth hoped to achieve eluded him, for by 1641 the whole country was in turmoil, the Irish rebellion was threatening to destroy the Established Church in Ireland, and parliament was in the process of achieving supreme power in England.[21] Some initial efforts were made by the Long Parliament to reform the Established Church in 1642 and 1643. However, in 1647 the Book of Common Prayer and the ceremonies of the church were superseded by the Directory of Worship and the Established Church was effectively proscribed. For thirteen years it lived through a period of suppression, and when the church was restored in 1660 it emerged into a radically changed situation in Ireland. For during the Interregnum several new, dissenting traditions had entered Ireland, and Scottish Presbyterianism had been refounded in Ulster.[22] The old days of Ussher and comprehension were over; diverse forms of dissent had evolved and were articulated and practised outside the frame and structure of the Established Church. In future the Established Church would have to contend with renewed Scottish Presbyterianism, with English Presbyterianism, Independents and Quakers. It only slowly grasped that each dissenting tradition could not conform to the Restoration ecclesiastical settlement.

This particular evolution of Protestant dissent in Ireland is the subject of this book: Scottish Presbyterians, English Presbyterians, Independents and Quakers.[23] Each dissenting tradition is studied firstly in its own right, particularly its origins, structures, forms of worship and discipline, as well as location and membership. Controversy was central to dissent at this time, either within each tradition, between one tradition and another, or with the Established Church. These controversies served to sharpen self-understanding and enabled each tradition to articulate its own belief and conviction in public. For it was a time of shifting views and perspectives, leading to new definitions and clarity. As controversies unfolded, developed and concluded new insights were gained and the positions of the several dissenting traditions in Ireland emerged more clearly.

Inevitably most of the controversies were religious by nature and content. This was the interest and context of those who debated in print and pulpit, and through this medium all aspects of life in seventeenth-century Ireland were discussed and evaluated. Certainly all believed in God and in the basic message of Christianity and took this for granted when they spoke or wrote. Despite the fact that the heretical freethinker John Toland was born in Donegal, there was no movement towards Deism, Socianism or even atheism in Ireland during this period.[24] Rather it was the content of Christianity and its practice which provided the scope for controversy under several headings: Deism, Socianism, Arminianism. Each tradition had its nuances and accents in theology which emerged in the course of debate. This in itself reflected the understanding each had of the concept of 'God' and of 'church', among the most central and crucial subjects for debate at this time.

The issue of predestination was common to the three presbyterian traditions in the country: Scottish, English and Independent. Based on the teaching of the Westminster Confession of 1649, the doctrine known as 'double predestination' taught that God had foreordained some to eternal life and some to damnation. Presbyterians took their election by God as the foundation of faith and practice. Robert Craghead assured his readers: 'The way you know your election is first to believe; and if you believe, you are elected; and if you be elected, you will believe.'[25]

Arminianism, on the other hand, taught that people can be saved, can correspond to God's grace freely, and that salvation is possible for all. In a sense, Arminianism was a conservative movement, moderating the extreme Calvinism of the earlier reformation in England. The established churches in Ireland and England were perceived by presbyterians as Arminian in both theology and practice. This fundamental difference between the traditions was the basic polarisation underlying debates during the period 1660-1714. Furthermore, the Arminianism of the Anglican churches was expressed in an attitude of comprehension towards Protestant dissenters, which as the century wore on developed into latitudinarianism. For the established churches the tendency to reduce the accent on theology and doctrine in favour of piety and Christian behaviour was preferable to toleration.

Indeed, during this period toleration was an impossible concept, especially for the Established Church in Ireland, as it implied recognition of other dissenting traditions as churches in their own right. Such recognition had wide theological and political implications. On the other hand, comprehension was an impossible concept for Scottish Presbyterians, since conformity would imply acceptance of the Established Church, whose theology and practice they could not accede to in good conscience. Instead they hoped for toleration and full religious freedom. English Presbyterians were prepared to consider some form of occasional conformity, while Independents for different reasons did not take that option. And for all the religious traditions Quakers were both theologically incomprehensible and considered beyond the scope of defined Christianity.

Furthermore, during this period precisely how a church or community of believers was constituted, ordered and disciplined, particularly how worship was expressed, became a source of endless discussion and prolonged debate. Such dimensions gave all dissenting traditions the inner coherence needed to survive. Each had specific forms of worship, as well as definite times of preparation and reflection, which reflected their theology and furthered their own sense of identity; all had systems of excommunication/disownment to implement when these broke down in individual or group cases. For none could allow internal dissent at a time when the Established Church and the government were watchful.

Dissenting traditions often had strong leaders, mostly clerical but sometimes lay, who were well educated and wealthy. This was crucial in the period after the Restoration, particularly for the smaller traditions: English Presbyterians, Independents and Quakers. Ministers travelled a great deal, not only in Ireland, but in Scotland and England and further afield. Apart from Scottish Presbyterians, the actual numbers of Protestant dissenters were small. Moreover, each tradition, except Scottish Presbyterians, were dealing with second-generation congregations and so had to maintain spiritual enthusiasm and momentum among the membership. That they survived after the Restoration was due to firm leadership and the loyal following of families which originated in Ireland during the Interregnum or came to Ireland after 1660.

In the absence of detailed studies of both the Established Church and the Roman Catholic Church in Ireland at this time, some of the conclusions in this book await further reflection.[26] What emerges clearly, however, is that four Protestant dissenting traditions became rooted in Ireland after the Restoration. One originated from the early days of the plantation of Ulster, the others during the Interregnum; all four evolved into definite religious traditions in the country. Each had their own particular theology, which sometimes led to differences and controversy. Debates with the Established Church and with the government further strengthened their own identity. The theme of all such exchanges was centred on the meaning of 'God' and 'church' and on what belief in both meant in practice. As each tradition evolved, differences and distinctions between them emerged more clearly and contributed further to the moulding of Protestant consciousness in Ireland. In the end Protestant dissenters in Ireland showed just how far those who separate themselves from institutions which no longer serve their needs can travel. In that unending search all are dissenters.

Notes and References

1 C. R. Elrington, *The life of the Most Rev. James Ussher* (Dublin, 1848), pp 32-3.
2 Ussher to Challoner, 9 Apr. 1613 (*The works of James Ussher*, ed. C. R. Elrington, 17 vols (Dublin, 1847-64), xv, letter xi); Luke Challoner was a fellow of Trinity College Dublin and became its Vice-Chancellor in 1612. His notebooks show his leanings towards Puritanism, especially with regard to centrality of preaching. Ussher married his daughter Phoebe Challoner in 1614. J. P. Mahaffy, *An epoch in Irish history, 1591-1660* (London, 1903), p. 86.
3 In that context, the advent of the Roman Church interrupted the progress of the Church of Ireland. Ussher found justification for such views in the history of the Celtic Church in Ireland. James Ussher, *An epistle concerning the religion of the ancient Irish* (Dublin 1622); later Ussher further documented his work on the Celtic Church in Ireland when he published *Sylloge veterun epistolarum Hibernicum* (1632) (both in *Works of Ussher*, ed. Elrington, iv).
4 The nine Lambeth Articles were cited in full, and Articles 6-9 of the 1566 Articles were included.
5 This originated when James VI of Scotland sent agents to Dublin in 1597, hoping they could gain the support of the Irish gentry in his bid for the throne of England. James Fullerton and James Hamilton set up school in Dublin, and James Ussher was one of their first pupils. They were also among the first fellows of Trinity College. R. Buick Knox, *James Ussher, Archbishop of Armagh* (Cardiff, 1967), pp 7, 16.
6 Patrick Adair, *A true narrative . . . of the Presbyterian Church in Ireland (1623-1670)*, with introduction and notes by W. D. Killen (Belfast, 1866), pp 7, 10, 12, 17.
7 John Livingstone, *A brief historical relation of the life of Mr John Livingstone,* ed. Thomas McCrie (Edinburgh, 1848), pp 58-9; Andrew Stewart, 'History of the Church of Ireland', in Adair, *A true narrative,* p. 313; Marilyn Westerkamp, *Triumph of the laity: Scots-Irish piety and the Great Awakening, 1625-1760* (Oxford, 1988), pp 20-23; Knox, *James Ussher,* pp 174-7; David Stevenson, *Scottish Covenanters and Irish Confederates* (Belfast, 1981), pp 12-13.
8 Christopher Hampton, *An inquisition of the true church* (Dublin, 1622), pp 24-5.
9 Henry Leslie, *A treatise tending to unity in a sermon preached at Drogheda in 1622* (Dublin, 1623).
10 Hampton, *An inquisition of the true church,* dedicatory.
11 Hampton to Buckingham, 25 June 1621 (Bodl. Carte MS 61, f. 110).
12 Ussher, *An epistle concerning the religion of the ancient Irish,* p. 3.
13 Henry Leslie, *A treatise on the authority of the church* (Dublin, 1636), p. 90.
14 Adair, *A true narrative,* pp 41-3; Westerkamp, *Triumph of the laity,* pp 28-35; Leigh Eric Schmidt, *Holy fairs: Scottish communions and American revivals in the early modern period* (Princeton, 1989), pp 29-32.
15 Adair, *A true narrative,* pp 27-8.
16 Luke Rochfort, *The genealogy of Protestants, or a brief discovery of the first authors, founders and parents of their religion* (Paris 1621), p. 161.

17   This was subject of long debate: Nicholas Bernard, *The judgement of the late Archbishop of Armagh* (2nd ed., London, 1659); Peter Heylin, *Respondet Petrus or the answer of Peter Heylin to so much of Dr Bernard's book, entitled 'The judgement of the late Primate of Ireland': an appendix* (London, 1658); Nicholas Bernard, *Clavi trabales or nails fastened by some great masters of assemblies confirming the king's supremacy* (London, 1661), p. 62ff; Peter Heylin, *Aerius redivivus or the history of the Presbyterians* (Oxford, 1670), pp 392-5; Richard Parr, *Life of James Ussher* (London, 1686), pp 42-3, 66; *The works of the Most Rev. John Bramhall*, ed. John Vesey (Dublin, 1676), introduction (no pagination) and pp 935-7.

18   J. S. Reid, *The history of the Presbyterian Church in Ireland*, 3 vols (Belfast 1867), i, Appendix 4, p. 523ff.

19   Adair, *A true narrative*, pp 95-101; Stevenson, *Scottish Covenanters*, pp 18-19, 21-2, 32; Westerkamp, *Triumph of the laity*, pp 36, 38.

20   Adair, *A true narrative*, pp 37-9, 43, 59-65.

21   Brian Mac Cuarta (ed.), *Ulster 1641: aspects of the rising* (Belfast, 1993).

22   Phil Kilroy, 'Radical religion in Ireland, 1641-1660' in Jane Ohlmeyer (ed.), *From independence to occupation, 1641-1660* (Cambridge, forthcoming).

23   Neither the Baptists nor the Hugenots have been included since their history would not lend itself to this type of study. For recent work on the Baptists: Kevin Herlihy, 'The Irish Baptists 1650–1780' (Ph.D. thesis, T.C.D., 1992); Phil Kilroy, 'Radical Religion in Ireland, 1641-1660' in Jane Ohlmeyer (ed.), *From Independence to Occupation, 1641-1660*, op. cit.

24   J. G. Simms, 'John Toland (1670-1722), a Donegal heretic' in *I.H.S.*, xvi, no. 63 (Mar. 1969), p 304-19. The 'Act for effectual suppressing of blasphemy and profaneness' of 1697 was not against atheism or the denial of God, but against denial of the Athanasian creed. David Berman, *A history of atheism in Britain from Hobbes to Russell* (Croom Helm, 1988).

25   Robert Craghead, *Advice to communicants* (Edinburgh, 1695), p. 116. See also Thomas Hall, *A plain and easy explication of the Assembly's Shorter Catechism* (Edinburgh, 1697), no. 38, p. 38.

26   For recent work in this field see T. W. Moody, F. X. Martin and F. J. Byrne (ed.), *A new history of Ireland*, iii: *Early modern Ireland, 1534-1691* (3rd impression, Oxford, 1991).

PART I

ORIGINS OF DISSENT

1

Scottish Presbyterians in Ireland, 1649 – 1714

> By our meetings God has been pleased to preserve us in great
> unanimity of judgement, unity of affection, uniformity in all our
> ministerial actings . . . in our darkest times and greatest dangers.
> John McBride, *A sermon preached at the provincial
> synod at Antrim* (1698)

The Belfast presbytery wrote, in February 1649, to the 'sectarian party' in England and denounced its actions:

> they have with a high hand despised the oath in breaking the Covenant
> . . . and likewise labour to establish by laws an universal toleration of
> all religions . . . [have] strong oppositions to presbyterial government
> . . . have proceeded to the trial of the King . . . and with cruel hands
> put him to death. . . . We cannot but declare our utter dislike and detesta-
> tion of such unwarrantable practices, directly subverting our Covenant,
> religion, laws and liberties.[1]

The presbytery's statement, entitled *A necessary representation*, was
made with confidence and with the expectation that it would be
both heard and obeyed. The tone and content of such statements
underlined the strong position Scottish Presbyterians felt they
held in Ulster. This was due not only to recent growth in strength
there on account of the war. Scottish Presbyterianism in Ireland

15

had come through severe testing during the deputyship of Went-worth. Ministers were ejected from parishes and benefices, especial-ly after the 1634 Convocation, and by 1637 nearly all the ministers had been silenced, deposed and banished to Scotland.[2] However, political circumstances played into their hands when a Scots army was needed to help subdue the rebellion in Ireland. Five chaplains came with the Scottish army to Ireland in 1642, and these ministers organised the soldiers into congregations and sessions, thereby establishing the first formal presbytery in Ireland. Soon former congregations asked for ministers to return and reside among them. Such requests were sent to the General Assembly in Scotland,[3] and gradually Presbyterian congregations re-emerged in Ulster. By 1653 there were twenty-four Presbyterian ministers, and by 1654 the original presbytery had divided into three presbyteries; by 1659 there were five in all.[4]

Moreover, by 1642 the entire political and ecclesiastical con-text had changed: parliament governed, and the Established Church was officially silenced. Such a situation radically changed the role and self-perception of the Scottish Presbyterian ministers in Ulster. Combined with the doctrine of predestination and the belief that it was their destiny to rule, they had real motivation for seeking and expecting a voice in all political affairs of the day. This stance was shown in February 1649 when the Belfast presbytery condemned parliament in England. As expected, this was not well received by the 'sectarian party' in England, who, furious at the criticism of the Belfast presbytery, instructed John Milton to write a reply.[5]

Milton berated these 'pretended brethren' of a small town in Ulster who took it on themselves to rebuke the party in England; they had no right to preach 'beyond the diocese of Patrick or Columba'.[6] He accused them of being worse than bishops, claiming 'absolute and independing jurisdiction, as from like ad-vantage and occasion . . . the Pope has for many ages done'.[7] These 'most grave and reverend Carmelites' denied their own founder, John Knox, who taught the doctrine of deposing and of killing kings:

> And thus while they deny that any such rule can be found, the rule is found in their own country given them by their own first presbyterian

institutor; and they themselves like irregular friars walking contrary to
the rule of their own foundation deserve for so gross an ignorance and
transgression to be disciplined upon their own stools. . . . so haughty
in the pontifical see of Belfast'.[8]

Two Scottish Presbyterian ministers, Jeremy Kerr and Jeremy
O'Quinn, refused to read the *Representation* to their congregations,
and they appealed to the General Assembly in Scotland.[9] The
fact that both ministers supported Milton's views reflected the
tensions within Scottish Presbyterianism, a tension between those
who adhered to the king and accepted royal authority in religious
affairs and those who rejected this as contrary to the Covenant
in all its purity. It became even more divisive in January 1651
when Charles II was crowned at Scone, having subscribed to the
Covenant. These two strands in Scottish Presbyterianism grew
side by side in Ulster, and in some other parts of Ireland, and
became a source of internal and external conflict. In effect this
discord was an extension of what was going on in Scotland at
this time between the Resolutioners (supporters of the king and
Covenant) and the Remonstrants (supporters of the Covenant
alone).

In view of this, in 1654 the presbytery felt it necessary to pass
the Act of Bangor.[10] By this act ministers who came to Ireland
were not to bring in or even speak of the divisions in Scotland.
No congregation was to send to Scotland for a minister without
first consulting the presbytery. The presbytery would write to
both factions in Scotland, and only those ministers recommended
by both would be accepted in Ireland. In this way it hoped to
maintain some control of ministers who came from Scotland.
However, the plan did not succeed, as the tradition of dissent
in Scottish Presbyterianism had been well established in Ireland
since the 1620s. Besides, contact with Scotland was natural both
theologically and socially, for both countries were geographic-
ally proximate as if lying on the opposite shores of a lake. Thus
both extreme and moderate forms of Scottish Presbyterianism
were destined to exist side by side in Ulster and seek expression
in different ways.

Scottish Presbyterianism in Ulster entered into a third phase
after the Restoration, and when records resume in the 1670s it

is clear that the Presbyterian way of life, worship and ministry were well settled. The five meetings already in existence in 1659, Antrim, Down, the Route, Laggan and Tyrone, were thriving. A general committee composed of delegates from the five meetings had been established and met on a regular basis. It did not call itself formally a synod and during this period sought to define its powers. In September 1672 the general committee asked the meetings to discuss whether it had juridical power to conclude matters before them. The Antrim meeting thought it best not to give the general committee such power then, possibly because it was too difficult to communicate freely in public.[11] In practice, however, the general committee assumed a great deal of business sent in by the meetings, and whatever it decided was considered binding on all.[12]

A good example of how the general committee worked is found in the Laggan minutes for August and September 1679. That autumn the Tyrone meeting demanded that all five meetings should act as a united body. It complained that fasts and thanksgivings were being held without other meetings being told; that the Down meeting had given in to the magistrate without the other meetings agreeing to this step; and that, according to rumour, the Down meeting permitted taking the Oath of Supremacy 'in some sense'. So the Tyrone meeting asked the Antrim, Route and Laggan meetings to set down 'an authoritative general committee to prevent separate actings in things of common concernment' in the interest of harmony and unity. The Laggan meeting agreed with all the points raised by the Tyrone meeting and asked that they be treated at the next general committee meeting at Ballymena.[13]

Detailed instructions were given to the two ministers delegated o represent each meeting on the general committee; delegates returned to their own meetings with detailed replies, opinions and suggestions.[14] While the general committee met once, or possibly twice, in a year, the five meetings met monthly. Substantial records exist for Antrim and the Laggan; there are also records of the kirk sessions of Burt, Carnmoney, Dundonald and Templepatrick. Minutes were taken at these monthly meetings which included the name of the meeting, the date, place and number present. While ministers and elders were almost always present at the Laggan meetings, elders were not present at the Antrim meeting until after 1687.[15] Records of those present and absent were noted; absences were frowned upon and 'juridically rebuked'.[16] Correspondence was dealt with in some detail, both what was received and what replies were made and by whom.

Other business could include maintenance of ministers, visitation of parishes, arrangements for communion services, public penance and discipline, the training and ordination of candidates for ministry, the call from other congregations in Ireland for visits of ministers or applying to Scotland for ministers to supply need in Ireland.

Maintenance of ministers was a serious concern after the Restoration, for the salaries they had received during the closing years of the Interregnum were withdrawn. The people had to pay tithes to the Established Church and yet support their own ministers as well. While the *regium donum* was granted after 1672,[17] it could not maintain the ministry, and so ministers were sent around regularly to the congregations to urge them to provide maintenance in a practical way. For example, those congregations which called a minister were responsible for building a meeting-house, and none were to call a minister unless they were prepared to maintain him. The Down meeting felt this should be dealt with seriously, otherwise the church would fail.[18]

Visitation of the kirk was carried out by the ministers and elders appointed by the meeting. One of the best examples of this dates from 1654. The visitation of Broadisland was held on 11 October that year,[19] commissioned by the Antrim presbytery, with a moderator, Patrick Adair, and two other ministers, Anthony Kennedy and Thomas Hall. Two elders were also present. The minister, Robert Cunningham, was sent out of the room, and the elders of the kirk were asked about 'the soundness and authority of his doctrine, his painfulness in catechising, visiting the families and sick persons and how they were satisfied with his life and conversation, with his impartiality in discipline'. The elders were also asked about maintenance and were told to warn the session that the minister would be removed if he was not paid properly.

This procedure was not possible publicly after the Restoration, but a muted form of it seems to have existed in that ministers censured each other at the meetings, though without the elders present.[20] The account of the Burt kirk session for 1678 tells how in April of that year, Robert Rule and Robert Campbell told the heads of families in Burt to provide the ministers' house with timber and money 'to the end he may employ workmen as he thinks fit'.[21] In 1686 Carnmoney session, aware that the people were ignoring their dues, decided that the minister was to be paid before he baptised children.[22]

The communion service was held in different parts of the country, and its organisation ensured visitation of the people, since members of the congregation had to be examined and deemed worthy to receive communion. Communion services were held in different places during the year, mostly between the summer and autumn, and were attended not only by the congregation in the area but also by vast crowds from neighbouring sessions, with their ministers. A fast-day was appointed on the Thursday before the communion Sabbath, and on the Saturday the congregation heard a sermon in preparation. On Sunday the service began at 8 a.m. and lasted until the late afternoon. The communicants sat on long forms; other forms, higher and covered with linen cloths, served as tables. Every full-standing member could communicate by right, yet none could be admitted without a token of admission from their session. This token was withheld from any who were in penance, had a bad reputation, or had not paid fines. During the service there were from eight to twelve tables for communion,[23] and a separate address was delivered to each party; one minister addressed the people in the church, and two or three other ministers addressed the crowd outside. Sometimes refreshments were supplied in a neighbouring field, with drink served, though this was frowned on by the ministers as it broke the Sabbath.[24]

Ministers and elders planned the communion services in some detail. The Burt kirk Session noted the following programme for July 1681:

> July 24, a.m. Mr Gordon of Glendermot preached on 2 Cor. 5. 7.
> p.m. Mr Hampton preached on Cant. 5. 1.

July 27   Wednesday, Day of humiliation before communion.
          a.m. Mr Gordon preached on 1 Cor. 5. 7.
          p.m. Mr Tailzor preached on James 8. 9-10.

July 30   Saturday, Mr Craghead of Donoghmore preached on John 4.14.

July 31   Sunday, Mr Craghead of Donoghmore preached 1 Cor. 11. 23
          'before the work of the tables began'.
          Mr Gordon preached on Col. 2. 6 and Mr Crooks, Ballykelly,
          on Gen. 6. 9.[25]

Thus in the course of a week six sermons were preached and the parish had three visiting ministers for the preparation period and the actual communion service itself.[26] Indeed, sometimes the service was prolonged until Monday, when a final sermon was delivered.

The tradition of having large communion services was well rooted in Ireland from the early seventeenth century. John Livingstone described them in detail.[27] This continued throughout the Commonwealth period and after. For example, in June 1647 the Templepatrick kirk session asked two men to go to Carrickfergus for forty bottles of the 'best claret and one bushel of French flour' for the communion service.[28] In May 1657 for another communion service three dozen bottles of wine and one bushel of flour were bought; again in June 1660 three dozen bottles and one bushel of flour were ordered; for a service in 1670 four flagons of wine were ordered, and in 1693 fourteen gallons;[29] in Burt for a communion service in July 1694 three dozen bottles were ordered from Belfast.[30]

Large communion services were rare between 1660 and 1670, — as the political situation was too difficult. However, in 1670 Templepatrick session decided to have a service on 26 June, indicating that this was the first in a long time 'because of the prelates'.[31] Robert Campbell told Thomas Wyllie in August 1674 that they had held a communion service in Derry the previous summer, adding that 'as for public matters I bless the Lord to continue our liberty'.[32] In 1679 the size of a communion service in Armagh caused great concern because of the political unrest then in the country. Indeed, these large meetings aroused suspicion, particularly at times of crisis.[33]

Discipline and penance were strictly enforced by the kirk

session. The minister and elders sat as a court and judged the behaviour of the congregation. The congregation was divided into districts each of which was the responsibility of a named elder, whose duty was to observe the moral conduct of those in his charge. Two elders were named by the session to visit houses during Sunday service to see who was missing, and especially to find out who were in the alehouses. The minutes of the Antrim meeting and of the Templepatrick session for the Commonwealth period show the activity of the elders to have been quite comprehensive: members of congregations were called to account for missing service on the Sabbath, drinking then and at other times in excess, adultery and sexual licence, wife-beating and child-beating on the Sabbath, allowing children to play on the Sabbath, murder, desertion, irregular marriages and bigamy.[34]

The most common correction by far was that concerned with sexual mores, and the Antrim minutes contains long lists of those who were discovered at fault.[35] Some failings could be amended by fines, but sexual faults had to be publicly acknowledged and punished, normally for three Sundays in a row, sitting on a stool in front of the pulpit and facing the congregation; sometimes those being disciplined had to wear a white sheet and even stand in a basin of cold water.[36] Sometimes other meetings were informed about the faults of a member. Such sinners were visited by one or even two ministers; when repentance was considered genuine the person was absolved and allowed back to full membership.[37]

It was not possible to exercise such discipline in public after the Restoration, but there are indications that it was exercised privately. In 1672 the Antrim meeting noted that it was not able to cite people, 'the case of the time being such that the brethren could not call such persons so frequently before them as usually'.[38] But it is evident from the Laggan minutes that private censures took place at the meetings,[39] though it was recognised as unsatisfactory and constrained. In 1676 each minister was advised to establish discipline gradually in his congregation, and was exhorted not to judge each other's pace in this regard. Moreover, it was recommended that before censuring a person in public (at the session) the meeting should be consulted first.[40] There is no doubt that discipline continued to be enforced, however quietly. For example John Will, minister of Glendermot, was deprived in September 1679 following an examination by elders of his behaviour and teaching which had given scandal. Burt kirk session exercised public censure from at least 1678 and by 1694 was censuring faults and settling disputes in the area.[41] The Antrim meeting seems not to have resumed public censure before 1687, for in that year they asked whether or not it could be resumed in view of the indulgence given by James II.[42]

Another form of discipline exercised by a meeting was the imposition of fasts on the congregations for different reasons. In 1672 a fast was appointed 'for excessive rains'.[43] This must have caused some problems, as the meeting asked John Hart to write to Mr Semple in Dublin for advice; the reply was that fasts were observed elsewhere to no harm. So in the following year another fast was set for four reasons: excessive rains; for the propagation of the gospel; for purging of the three kingdoms of popery and superstition; for the king and inferior magistrates.[44] Fast-days were a regular feature of church discipline; they were appointed in time of natural calamity, in times of stress in the community, for example the sudden deaths of two ministers,[45] and in times of political turmoil.

Imposition of fasts was normally the prerogative of king and government. When it became known that Scottish Presbyterians imposed fasts on their congregations, governments of the day could only be suspicious. Meetings were sensitive to this, and when, during the time of the Popish Plot, the Laggan set a fast for 28 November 1678, it agreed that if the magistrate set a fast, they would observe that date instead. The meeting also agreed that if a day of thanksgiving was set for the discovery of the Popish Plot, then they would observe that too.[46] On the whole, the fasts set by the meetings seem to have been held unhindered by the authorities. There is some evidence to show that fasts were appointed for a certain day in all the meetings.[47] However, the government became concerned when the Laggan meeting arranged for a fast to be held on 17 February, 1681. In the context of the time, particularly with so much unrest in Scotland spilling over into Ulster, such independence was seen as subversive by the government. Ministers who called the fast were summoned to trial in Dublin.[48]

The quality of personnel and of formation for ministry was given priority by the meetings. The Antrim minutes contain a lengthy description of the preparation necessary prior to ordination. Firstly, candidates should be admitted for trials only if sufficient testimonials were provided, not only concerning their knowledge of scripture but also to confirm 'their piety, peaceableness and prudence'. The rules for trials were full and exact: the candidate had to show skill in giving popular sermons, in disputes, in answering questions on scripture, cases needing judgement, chronology and languages. The candidate was tried by the meeting to which he belonged then, and also by delegates from former meetings. Ideally this examination should have been held in public; as this was impossible at this period, members of the meeting considering the ordination of a candidate should visit his former congregation to find out all they could about him. Trials of candidates went on during the regular session meetings, and reports were made on their progress until they reached the required standard for ordination.[49]

Ordination itself was held in secret, and only those trusted members of the church were present. Immediately before ordination the candidate was questioned both for soundness of faith and for views on popery, Arminianism, Prelacy, Erastianism and Independency. The candidate was to adhere to the Covenant and, 'considering the temper of the times', be peaceful and subject to his colleagues. The newly ordained minister left for Scotland as soon as possible and remained there until he could return to Ireland safely, giving the impression that he had been ordained in Scotland.[50] Moreover, the general committee decided that the newly ordained should subscribe to the Act of Bangor of August 1654, by which the church divisions in Scotland were not to be introduced in Ireland.[51]

Congregations could call ministers either from within Ireland or from Scotland.[52] When political events were difficult in Scotland, ministers came over to Ireland for refuge until the storms abated; this created an uncertain supply of ministers in

Ireland, for the Scottish congregations called their ministers back as soon as it was possible for them to resume their ministry.[53] Calls also came from Virginia and Maryland.[54] The Laggan meeting was very insistent that all calls should be channelled through it and should not be initiated by a congregation on its own. If this was not observed, the meeting refused to visit and inspect the congregation or take responsibility for it in any way.[55]

The actual numbers in any given congregation at this time are difficult to determine. In 1672 William Petty suggested that the population of Ireland lay somewhere in the region of 1,100,000: 100,000 were Scottish Presbyterians; 100,000 dissenters of other Protestant traditions; 100,000 were of the Established Church; and 800,000 were Roman Catholics.[56] Petty's population calculation has been critiqued in favour of a bigger estimate,[57] but at least his distribution of religious affiliation serves as a starting-point for discussion. Bearing in mind that complaints to authorities would necessarily stress numbers, especially at the communion services, there is some evidence to show that congregations could have had up to 300 active members. In 1673 Oliver Plunkett noted that in Down and Connor Scottish Presbyterians were more numerous than Roman Catholics and Established Church members together.[58] In 1681 Captain John Nisbett complained that between 6,000 and 7,000 Scottish Presbyterians met in Raphoe 'though distinct in their several parishes'.[59] At this time there were thirteen sessions in the Laggan meeting, which on the basis of Nisbett's information would have averaged about 200–250 in each session. On the other hand, the Route meeting complained in 1676 that eighty of their members were being summoned from each parish to the official courts.[60]

In 1689 a list of ministers and their congregations was sent to the General Assembly in Edinburgh.[61] There were seventy-two congregations/sessions in the five meetings of Down, Antrim, Laggan, the Route and Tyrone. If each session had even 250 members, then the numbers of Scottish Presbyterians could have been around 18,000. This certainly increased after the 1688 Revolution, when it was estimated that some 8,000 families came

over from Scotland.[62] In 1694 William King calculated that
there were 30,000 Scottish Presbyterians in his diocese.[63] Joseph
Boyse claimed in 1695 that sessions in Derry generally had between 600 and 1,000 members.[64] The returns for 1704 noted
that Scottish Presbyterians were in the majority in Ulster.[65]
Scottish Presbyterians were 30 per cent of the population of
Belfast in 1670; this had risen to 70 per cent by 1705.[66] In 1712
Richard Choppin claimed that congregations in the Laggan
numbered 600–700 members and that each minister there had
'1,000 examinable members' or even more in some cases.[67] In
the absence of numbers for both the Established and the Roman
Catholic Churches, it is difficult to know what percentage Scottish Presbyterians were within the total population. It is clear
that they were numerous in Ulster and were perceived as a
threat.[68] Such threats were potentially heightened when great
numbers gathered for communion services.

Services for individual sessions were held in houses, barns or
stables according to what was possible and available.[69] In the
course of the 1660s meeting-houses were built, and Primate
Margetson, no doubt exaggerating, claimed that by 1669 meeting-
houses had been built in almost every parish, especially in the
north.[70] Nevertheless, there is evidence that having a meeting-
house was being taken for granted; even Bishop Mossom of Derry
gave permission for one to be built in Urney in 1679.[71] An interesting case emerged in 1673 when Thomas Gowan was given
leave by the new bishop, Thomas Hackett, to preach in the parish
church at Antrim.[72] The difficult question was whether he
should do this at all; and, if he did, whether the people would
be trapped into accepting the liturgy of the Book of Common
Prayer. The alternative was for the people to miss worship on
Sunday.

As a way out of the dilemma, the Antrim meeting asked Lord
Massereene to build a meeting-house for the Scottish
Presbyterians, which he refused to do as it would have placed
him in an even more difficult position with regard to
Ormond.[73] Besides, the Massereene family, with that of Lord
Donegall, leaned towards English Presbyterianism and appointed
chaplains from within that tradition.[74] In 1678 Ormond

complained that only twelve went to the parish church in Antrim on Sundays and that the illegal meeting-house of the Scottish Presbyterians was better frequented. He blamed Massereene for this, accusing him of never attending the parish church but instead holding conventicles either in his own home or in his mother-in-law's house. Massereene defended his actions, protesting that he attended the church sometimes and found over a hundred there. He denied all responsibility for the illegal meeting-house, but remarked it was poor affair, a small thatched house outside the town. Ormond was not convinced and repeated the complaint in 1681.[75]

In fact, however, the Established Church had quietly undermined Ormond's position: shortly before Gowan's arrival in Antrim, Massereene's own chaplain, the English Presbyterian John Howe had been given permission by the then bishop of Down and Connor, Roger Boyle, and the Primate, James Margetson, to preach in the parish church on Sunday afternoons 'after the liturgy had been read'.[76] Margetson remarked

in a pretty full meeting of the clergy . . . that he would have Mr Howe have any pulpit (where he had any concern) open to him in which he at any time was free to preach.[77]

From the Scottish Presbyterian point of view, Sunday worship in the parish church in Antrim remained unacceptable. Gowan tried to get agreement by compromise, undertaking to ensure an interval between the Established Church act of worship and their own form of worship. Pressure must have been heavy, for he asked that his critics be treated as 'disorderly and scandalous' and disciplined accordingly. In the end Gowan threatened to return to to his former church at Glaslough if a meeting-house was not provided by the people. The controversy was resolved in 1676 when a small meeting-house was built outside Antrim, apparently by the people themselves.[78]

This enabled Thomas Gowan to remain in Antrim as a minister and teacher. He started a school in Antrim in 1666 which received approval from all the meetings. In December 1674 the Antrim meeting noted that Gowan was educating young men in philosophy for eight years, but that the school could be endangered by other schools being set up in Ulster.[79] In view of this, the meeting proposed that there be just one school for Scottish Presbyterians; that all ministers encourage parents to send their children there; that one of the meetings oversee the school, especially the matter being taught there; that the school be in Antrim, and that Gowan continue as teacher.[80] The Laggan meeting fully concurred with this and expressed great satisfaction with the school. A few months later it sent the general committee two recommendations suggesting that two or three of the nearer meetings be visitors to the school, and that there be some kind of graduation ceremony for those who completed the school course 'as some public declaring them to be fit to teach the liberal arts'.[81]

In March 1675 the Antrim meeting proposed that a divinity school be established in Antrim under the supervision of Thomas Gowan and John Howe.[82] This idea seems to have borne fruit, though under the leadership of William Legatt:

> Mr John Leask of Gillhall near Dromore testifies: that William Legatt (non-conformist) of Dromore teaches the course of divinity to 6 scholars, some whereof intend to be master of Arts, who lodging in the towns come twice a week to the said Mr Legatt's house to be instructed in divinity; which disputations are performed publicly whereto they invite others to come and be auditors thereof; and that the said Mr Leask was by one of the students desired to come thither and propose an argument in order whereunto he offered his thesis in writing which he refused to accept. He further testifies that Mr Legatt did debate with John Magill of Gillhall esq. both publicly and privately to contribute something to Mr Gowan of Antrim towards the maintaining of his college (as they call it) where he teaches the course of philosophy.[83]

This development in education was seen as a real threat to peace and stability:

> . . . by pamphlets and letters without any name or author they stick out to slander even the greatest persons in the kingdom . . . as long as they are suffered to brood young ones to supply the vacancies occasioned by the death of the old . . . have their nurseries where a kind of philosophy and the tongues are taught and generally grammar schools as well as those for the English tongue are kept by those whom they choose and their catechisms taught to children.[84]

Linked with the work of education, and also reflecting their sense of rootedness in the country, the meetings asked that the 'history of this kirk' be written. Thomas Hall and Patrick Adair were asked in April 1672 by the Antrim meeting to gather papers and send them to John Drysdale, 'the writer of histories'. Nothing had been done by October of the same year, so the Laggan meeting asked Thomas Drummond to write a history of the church before the wars, and William Semple and James Wallace to continue the account after the Commonwealth.[85] There was a constant search for material throughout the 1670s, and finally Adair was entrusted with writing the work.[86] Further encouragement for such writing was provided by Thomas Wyllie, minister at Coleraine, who was responsible for having Calderwood's *History of the Kirk of Scotland* published in Holland in 1678. By 1679 it was circulating in the north of Ireland.[87]

A strong and cohesive body of doctrine and practice held this church together during a period of great uncertainty and sporadic persecution. It had a clear and simple form of government by general committee, meeting and session. Each level of government had certain issues to deal with and standards to maintain; the three levels also ensured steady communication between the kirks and allowed policy to be developed and tested. The congregations were subject to the authority of the kirk sessions, which had power to impose censures on any breaches. The authority exercised by session, meeting and general committee seems to have been accepted generally with few exceptions.[88] Though the discipline was severe, it affirmed the authority of both sessions and meetings, and in particular of ministers and elders. It also provided a sense of belonging and security in a period of great upheaval and change. With a sense of their place in history and the need to write their story, Scottish Presbyterians at this time further rooted themselves in this island to which they believed they had been sent to bring the gospel. The strength they had built up among themselves had real impact and directly challenged the Established Church when Scottish Presbyterianism assumed a much more public profile after 1688.[89]

Notes and References

1 *A necessary representation of the present evils and eminent dangers to religion, laws and liberties arising from the late and present practices of the sectarian party in England . . . By the Presbytery of Belfast, February 15 1649* (n.p., 1649), pp 42-3.

2 Stevenson, *Scottish Covenanters and Irish Confederates*, pp 12-13.

3 'There are about twelve or fourteen waste congregations on this nearest coast' (5 Aug. 1643). *Acts of the General Assemblies of the Church of Scotland, 1638-49* (Edinburgh, 1691), p. 161. See also pp 148, 151, 159, 190, 214 and index; Livingstone, *A brief historical relation*, pp 37-8.

4 Minutes of the Antrim meeting, 1654-58 (P.R.O.N.I., D1759/1A/1); Templepatrick Session Book, 1646-1743 (P.R.O.N.I., CR4/12/B/1), partly published by W. T. Latimer, 'The old session book of Templepatrick Presbyterian Church, Co. Antrim' in *R.S.A.I. Jn*, 25, (1895); 31 (1901); Adair, *A true narrative*, pp 204-15, 217-8, 220-3; Reid, *History of the presbyterian Church in Ireland*, ii, 193-238; Westerkamp., *Triumph of the laity*, pp 47-51; Stevenson, *Scottish Covenanters*, pp 290-1

5 *Observations upon the articles of peace with the Irish rebels on the letter of Ormonde to Col. Jones and the representation of the presbytery at Belfast* [1649]. In July of the same year the presbytery issued a strong condemnation of Lord Montgomery of the Ards. *Declaration of the presbytery of Belfast, 7 July 1649* (n.p., 1649).

6 Ibid., pp 54-5.

7 Ibid., pp 55-6. John Bramhall called the General Assembly of Scotland 'Antichrist'. [John Bramhall], *A fair warning to take heed of the Scottish discipline . . . most injurious to the civil magistrate* (n.p., 1649), p. 32.

8 Ibid., pp 63-5.

9 *News from Ireland* (London, 1650).

10 Adair, *A true narrative*, ii, pp 209-18.

11 Minutes of the Antrim meeting, 1671-91, pp 59, 64 (P.R.O.N.I., D1759/1A/2). This was proposed again in 1679, and the Laggan meeting thought it inadvisable to give the general committee power over all the meetings. Minutes of the Laggan meeting, p. 333 (ibid., D1759/1E/1).

12 Laggan minutes, 10 Sept. 1673, p. 64; Antrim minutes, 11 Mar. 1673, p. 83.

13 Laggan minutes, ii, pp 17, 21-2 (P.R.O.N.I., D1759/1E/2).

14 Laggan minutes, pp 181, 209, 219, 333; ii, p. 48; Antrim minutes, pp 209, 217, 260-1, 298, 313, 372.

15 Antrim minutes, 3 May 1687, p. 298.

16 Laggan minutes, 19 May 1674, p. 112.

17 Reid, *History of the Presbyterian Church,* ii, 404-5.

18 Laggan minutes, 22 Dec. 1674, p. 151; cf. pp 93, 101; 2 Feb. 1675, Antrim minutes, Burt Kirk Session minutes, p. 165. 30 Apr. 1678, (Union Theological College, Belfast), no pagination; Laggan minutes, Apr. 1693, p. 188; ibid., May 1695, p. 282. (Inisowen asked for a minister in 1695; having asked three times, they got a probationer; in 1697 they were told to pay him properly or he would be removed. Ibid., pp 246, 307, 313, 420).

19 Antrim minutes, 1654-8, p. 1.

20 Laggan minutes, 11 Aug. 1680, p. 73
21 Burt Kirk Session minutes, 30 Apr. 1678.
22 Carnmoney Session Register, f. 1 (Presbyterian Historical Society).
23 Each table had *c.* 75 communicants. The communion service had 'nigh eight tables . . . almost 600 communicants'. Carmoney Session Register, 26 June 1698, f. 37.
24 Latimer, 'The old session book of Templepatrick Presbyterian Church, Co. Antrim', pp 259-60.
25 Burt Kirk Session minutes, July 1681.
26 Robert Craghead, who preached twice at the service wrote a tract, on the communion service: *Advice to communicants* (Edinburgh, 1695). This is not a controversial work and was written for those who had found heavier books incomprehensible.
27 Livingstone, *A brief historical relation,* p. 30.
28 Latimer, 'The old session book of Templepatrick Presbyterian Church, Co. Antrim', p. 265.
29 Templepatrick Session Book, ff 122, 162, 169, 171.
30 Burt Kirk Session minutes, 15 July 1694. Full details are given of the costs of transport, for grinding wheat and baking the bread; the cost of a communion ticket that year was 3s 6d.
31 Templepatrick Session Book, 26 June 1670, f. 169.
32 N.L.S., Wodrow MSS, Folio 26, no. 132, f. 229.
33 Lovell to Coghill, 6 July 1679 (Bodl., Carte MS 221, f. 196).
34 See also Burt Kirk Session minutes, pp 280-96.
35 Antrim minutes, 1654-58, p. 45 and *passim.*
36 Latimer, 'The old session book of Templepatrick Presbyterian Church, Co. Antrim', pp 130-4.
37 Case of Isobel Atchinson of Ballyclare. Antrim minutes, 1654-58, pp 12, 20, 27.
38 Antrim minutes, 1671-1691, p. 51.
39 Laggan minutes, pp 28, 42; ii, p. 73.
40 Laggan minutes, 9 May 1676, p. 222, 9 Jan. 1677, p. 244.
41 Laggan minutes, ii, p. 34; cf. pp 35, 59 for Will's acceptance and maintenance after deprivation, Burt Kirk Session minutes, 10 Mar. 1678, 10 May 1694, case of Janet and John Logan; cases of stealing, disputes over lands and animals, pp 280ff, at end of MS, 1698-1703.
42 Antrim minutes, 3 May 1687, p. 298.
43 Ibid., Oct. 1672, p. 63; Laggan minutes, Oct. 1672, p. 25.
44 Laggan minutes, 30 July 1673, p. 58.
45 Ibid., 22 Dec. 1674, p. 157.
46 Ibid., 13 Nov. 1678, p. 322.
47 Ibid., ii, 2 Feb. 1681, p. 85.
48 N.L.S., Wodrow MSS, Quarto 75, no.18: 'Some short account of the troubles Messrs William Trail, James Alexander, Robert Campbell and John Hart, ministers in the Laggan in the north of Ireland, met with upon account of fast appointed by the presbyterial meeting in that boundary'. Text also in Reid, *History of the Presbyterian Church in Ireland,* ii, Appendix 9, pp 574-89. See Chapter 8 below.

49 Laggan minutes, pp 54, 58, 69, 72, 97. See also John Stevenson, *Two centuries of life in Down, 1600-1800* (repr., Dundonald, 1990), pp 157-61.

50 Rules for ordination, drawn up in 1672. Antrim minutes, p. 32ff.

51 Antrim minutes, 13 Aug. 1672, p. 53; Laggan minutes, 21 Aug. 1672, ii, pp 7-8.

52 Call from Londonderry session to Thomas Wyllie (N.L.S., Wodrow MSS, Folio 26, f. 212).

53 The case of Londonderry calling Robert Rule of Stirling is a good example of the conflict of interests and calls for ministers. Laggan minutes, pp 25, 50, 110, 126, 170, 173; ii, p. 48.

54 Laggan minutes, pp 1-2, 7, 51, 107, 271, 284, 312; ii, pp 82, 85, 91, 119, 184, 202, 224, 228; Antrim minutes 1671-91, p. 169. Boyd S. Schlenther, *The life and writings of Francis Makemie* (Presbyterian Historical Society, Philadelphia, 1971), p. 13. John Hart kept up links with Increase Mather in Boston. Ibid., p. 249; 'The Mather Papers' in *Collection of the Massachusetts Historical Society*, viii, 4th series (Boston, 1868), p. 37.

55 Laggan minutes, pp 1-2, 25.

56 William Petty, *The political anatomy of Ireland* (London, 1769 ed.), p. 305.

57 For example, Raymond Gillespie suggests a population increase from *c.* 1.7 million in 1672 to *c.* 2.8 million in 1712. Raymond Gillespie, 'Explorers, exploiters and entrepreneurs, 1500-1700' in B.J. Graham and L.J. Proudfoot (ed.), *An historical geography of Ireland* (London, 1993), pp 142-3. See also David Dickson, Cormac Ó Gráda and Stuart Daultry, 'Hearth tax, household size and Irish population change, 1672-1821' in *R.I.A. Proc.*, 82C (1982), pp 125-81.

58 *The letters of St Oliver Plunkett, 1625-81* ed. John Hanly (Dublin, 1979), p. 394; also pp 443, 530.

59 Extract of Captain John Nisbett's letter, 8 Apr. 1681 (Bodl., Carte MS 221, f. 231).

60 Laggan minutes, 29 Feb. 1676, p. 209. In 1673 Essex told Arlington that 'now of the Scotch nation, by the best estimates I can make, there are not fewer than fourscore or an hundred thousand men fit to bear arms' (*Essex Papers*,) p. 125.

61 N.L.S., Wodrow MSS, Octavo 12, ff 1-4v. This MS also lists six ministers for congregations 'in and around Dublin', but numbers for these are difficult to assess. The MS is printed in Reid, *History of the Presbyterian Church in Ireland*, ii, Appendix 12, pp 589-91, with some inaccuracies.

62 Francis Brewster, *A discourse concerning Ireland* (n,p., 1697/8), p. 34. In 1690 families came over from Scotland, not only to Ulster but also to Cork, Kerry and Limerick. B.L., Sloan MS 2902, f. 218. The Scots had two-thirds of the trade in Ireland, and Belfast is the second largest trading place.

63 William King, *An admonition to the dissenting inhabitants . . . of Derry* (London, 1694), pp 3-4, 10.

64 Joseph Boyse, *A vindication of the remarks on the bishop of Derry's discourse* (n.p., 1695), pp 125, 131. He also noted that the Antrim meeting had thirty-one sessions, seven more since 1689 (p. 131-2).

65 19 Feb. 1704. 'They have exact returns of their numbers throughout Ireland

and compute they are 5 - 3 of the church.' This refers to the Synod of Ulster. (N.L.S., MS 3740, f. 175)

66 John Nelson, 'The Belfast Presbyterians, 1670-1830' (Ph.D. thesis, Q.U.B., 1985), p. 8.

67 Richard Choppin to Thomas Steward, 8 July 1712 (Magee College, MS 46, Correspondence of Thomas Steward, 1699-1749, ff 142-3).

68 James Bonnell to John Strype, 13 Feb. 1691 (U.L.C., Baum. Papers, Strype Correspondence, Add. 1, f. 68).

69 Hugh Montgomery gave his barn for services. 18 Dec. 1666, Rawdon Papers, p. 222; see also, 'An examination of Hugh Montgomery of Co. Londonderry' (Bodl., Carte MS 35, ff 80, 88). This still obtained in 1688. Antrim minutes, p. 365.

70 Margetson to Ormond, 4 June 1669 (Bodl., Carte MS 37, f. 39).

71 Laggan minutes, ii, p. 13; cf. Laggan minutes, 1672-9, pp 267, 273, 283, 335 for details. In 1672 Bishop Mossom had refused to allow a meeting-house to be built in Derry (B.L., Stowe MS 200, ff 235, 301). Lord Massereene reported that some agreement had been reached between the parties (f. 309).

72 Thomas Gowan was born in Scotland and educated at Edinburgh. He was ordained for Donnagh, Glaslough, in 1658 and deposed in 1661 for nonconformity. He continued to minister at Connor until 1671, when he was called to Antrim to minister there and run a school. He wrote several treatises in Latin. James McConnell, *Fasti of the Presbyterian Church in Ireland, 1613-1840* (Belfast, 1951), no. 44, p. 9; Thomas Witherow, *Historical and literary memorials of Presbyterianism in Ireland*, 2 vols (London/Belfast, 1879-80), i, p. 53.

73 In 1665 Ornond warned Massereene to 'retire out of Ulster' unless he conformed to the Established Church (2 Oct. 1665, Bodl., Carte MS 49, f. 201).

74 Alexander Gordon and G. K. Smith, *Historic memorials of the First Presbyterian Church in Belfast* (Belfast, 1887), p. 10; Edward Calamy, *An historical account of my own life, with some reflections on the times I have lived in, 1671-1731*, ed. J. T. Rutt, 2 vols (London, 1830), ii, 629. Since Massereene was originally from Devon, it was natural that he would have English Presbyterian chap-lains; besides, as Jeremy Taylor remarked in 1660, 'the gentry being little better than servants while they live under the Presbytery' [Scottish], Mass-arene would prefer to retain his independence. Taylor, *A sermon preached at the consecration of the two archbishops and ten bishops, 27 Jan. 1661* (Dublin, 1661), p. 34.

75 Ormond to Massereene, 12 Jan. 1678 (H.M.C., *Appendix to 6th Report*, p. 170); Ormond to Massereene, 5 Feb. 1681 (Bodl., Carte MS 147, ff 132, 134).

76 James Armstrong, 'An appendix containing a summary history of the Presbyterian Church in the city of Dublin' in *A discourse on Presbyterian ordina-tion* (Dublin, 1829), pp. 84-6; H.C. Waddell, *The presbytery of Route* (Belfast, 1960), p. 31.

77 Edward Calamy, *Memoirs of the life of the late Mr John Howe* (London, 1734), pp 53-4; J. T. Carson, 'John Howe: chaplain to Lord Massereene at Antrim

---

34   *Origins of Dissent*

Castle, 1671-1677' in *Bulletin of the Presbyterian Historical Society of Ireland*, no. 7 (Dec. 1977), p. 14. John Howe took the Oxford Oath in 1665. Calamy, *Memoirs*, p. 41.

78 Antrim minutes, pp. 74, 78, 83, 88, 96, 100.

79 An account of the public schools within the province of Ulster, (Apr. 1685) 'School at Strabane taught by a fanatical person' (B.L., Stowe MS 202, f. 330); Fulke White, Antrim minutes, p. 252; John Binning, ibid., Nov. 1687, pp 329, 404; Archibald Pettigrew, ibid., Oct. 1688, p. 403. This may have been due to the fact that the philosophy school at Antrim was unable to function after May 1686. Ibid., 4 May 1686, pp 260-1; George Fleming's daughter kept a school in Benburb, Co. Armagh, c. 1670. Patrick Walker, *Some remarkable passages in the life and death of Alexander Peden* (3rd ed., Edinburgh, 1728), p. 106; Armstrong, *Summary history of the Presbyterian Church*, pp 58-60. Archibald Maglaine had a school in Belfast in the late 1670s. Nathaniel Mather to Increase Mather, 2 Mar. 1681 ('The Mather Papers', p. 29). In September 1679 Archbishop Boyle complained that Scottish Presbyterians 'begin now to follow the methods and ways for discipline of their brethren the Jesuits' (H.M.C., *Ormonde MSS*, v, 207).

80 Antrim minutes, 1 Dec. 1674, p. 161; Canon 99 of the 1634 Articles decreed that logic and philosophy were to be taught only in Trinity College, Dublin, not in schools. R. D. Edwards, 'The history of the laws against Protestant nonconformity in Ireland fron the Restoration (1660) to the Declaration of Indulgence (1687)' (M.A. thesis, U.C.D., 1932), p. 62. Gowan published two educational works: *Ars sciendi, sive logica, nova methodo disposita* ([London], 1682); *Logica elentica* (Dublin, 1683).

81 Laggan minutes, 2 Feb. 1675, p. 157; 6 July 1675, p. 181, nos 6, 8.

82 Antrim minutes, pp 169, 171.

83 Bodl., Carte MS 221, f. 194 (n.d.).

84 29 Mar. 1679 (Bodl., Carte MS 45, f. 317).

85 Antrim minutes, p. 32; Laggan minutes, p. 26.

86 Antrim minutes, p. 71; Laggan minutes, pp 181, 191, 198, 225, 264, 306; ii, pp 28, 48, 71, 79, 80.

87 David Maxwell to John Coghill, 17 June 1679 (Bodl., Carte MS 45, f. 330); Julia Mullin, *History of New Row Presbyterian Church Coleraine* (Antrim, 1976), p. 8.

88 Case of William Liston and John Semple, Laggan minutes, ii, 2 May 1694, p. 236; cf. pp 241, 246, 254.

89 This is discussed further in Chapters 7 and 9.

2

English Presbyterians in Ireland, 1647 – 1714

> There are many windfalls in Christ's orchard. Be you like the
> remaining berries in the top of the uppermost bough, abhorring
> disunion and defection and resolving not to rent, though with a
> violent hand, from your renowned Root.
>
> Joseph Eyres, *The church sleeper awakened* (1659)

The Long Parliament, in 1647, passed the measure entitled
*The Form of Church Government to be used in the Church of England
and Ireland*. While it was never implemented in Ireland, it indicated
the type of church government intended for the country, basically
Presbyterian in tone and content: government by congregational,
classical, provincial and national assemblies; worship according
to a Directory of Worship without exception; each congregation
to elect elders and to have weekly meetings; classical assemblies
to meet monthly, provincial assemblies twice a year, and national
assemblies when summoned by parliament. Each assembly had
its own powers. The classical assembly was the basic instrument
of government, and very few powers were reserved to the provincial assembly. Rules and procedures for ordination were laid
down in detail, as well as the role of lay people in the church.
Disciplinary procedures were listed, as were those particular faults

needing correction; and close co-operation with the magistrate was assumed in matters of discipline. In all, it was a simple if comprehensive mode of church government.[1]

This *Form of Church Government* appealed to a number of the clergy in Ireland during the Interregnum, many of them former Established Church ministers. The Established Church had only recently accepted the Thirty-Nine Articles of the Church of England in the Convocation of 1634, thereby undermining the authority of the 1615 Irish Articles. These had been Calvinist in tone and content. In addition, Archbishop Ussher was a very influential figure, and his views on a modified episcopacy were well known.[2] Thus, even without the *Form of Church Government* being enacted in Ireland, there were some clergy who adopted its general thrust when the Book of Common Prayer and the ceremonies were abolished in June 1647.[3] For them it was a matter of expediency, as Edward Worth was to explain later in 1660.[4] Such clergy, particularly while Henry Cromwell governed Ireland (1655-9), were joined by others from England who were already sympathetic to the form of church government authorised by parliament. Whatever about their critics, both groups of clergy had to find ways of working together and strengthening their own discipline and organisation in order to prevent total breakdown into factions.

In view of the need for strong church government, for structure, order and discipline, an association of ministers in Cork underlined the urgent necessity of having a properly ordained ministry.[5] They saw that some form of agreement was needed to guarantee ministry, create unity among themselves, and prevent intruders and factions. They listed the consequences of non-ordination, sixteen in all, each of them contributing to the confusion and ineffectiveness of religion in Ireland.[6] They insisted on certificates of ordination which could be presented to the magistrates, who should only receive ministers legally ordained. To this purpose all were to

> seek ordination from our brethren, the Scots in Ulster; the inconveniences whereof (the present state of affairs considered) are too obvious to need our instances; or from our brethren in England.

This was essential, even though they recognised it could be difficult to achieve, for journeys were long and expensive; furthermore, certificates from such a distance could be forged.[7] They obviously did not think they had authority on their own to ordain, and they sought to belong to a wider body which aspired to be a national church. In view of this aspiration, the Cork ministers wanted to be linked with either the Scottish Presbyterians in Ulster or the London Presbyterians. This was something Edward Worth, leader of the Cork association, was working for, seeing in that connection the way forward towards a national church.[8] Indeed, Worth's colleague in Cork, Joseph Eyres, had belonged to a London *classis* and represented the Cork association in London in 1658.[9]

Henry Cromwell cultivated both the Cork association, under the leadership of Worth, and the Ulster Presbyterians. This was a move away from the influence of the Baptists and Independents, in the direction of a centralised church, a conservative movement and one that promised to be highly successful. To promote such a development Henry Cromwell issued a proclamation on 20 January 1658 against those ministers who had come seeking positions in Ireland, having been ejected from England and Scotland.[10] By such means Cromwell hoped to prevent unwanted and divisive elements entering the country, thereby promoting the type of church order he envisaged and so broadening the basis of Protestant consensus in Ireland.[11]

He further encouraged this growth by calling ministers to Dublin in April 1658 to discuss their differences and try to come to some agreement by which they could live and act in harmony.[12] The convention which met in Dublin in April 1658 recognised the need for

> some godly ministers of differing judgements [to] be as opportunity serves called together and advised with by the magistrate what may be fit to be done or further afforded in order to a Christian composure in the things complained of and to a union and accommodation among dissenting brethren.[13]

This convention faced a considerable agenda: maintenance of ministers; conversion of the Irish; healing of divisions; catechising and use of the sacraments; discipline and suppression of heresy; Sabbath observance. Its basic objectives were summarised as 'the planting truth by catechising; watering the earth planted by sacraments; and fencing both by discipline'.[14]

Scottish Presbyterian and English Presbyterian ministers were in the majority at the convention, and they neutered the power of the Independents. Tithes were reintroduced, a major victory for Worth and the Ulster Presbyterians. Edward Cooke, a Quaker, commented:

> The committee of old priests sitting at Dublin have approved of them
> . . . and challenge the 10th part of our goods which they say is now their
> own . . . [they] set themselves to roost in the old mass houses up and
> down the nation.[15]

Worth went to England to present the findings of the convention to the English Presbyterians in London, Oxford and Cambridge. He received full approval and told Henry Cromwell that those he met thought they could 'close with the congregational brethren on the terms humbly presented to your excellency by the Dublin convention'.[16] Thus, in his capacity as leader of the Presbyterians in Cork, Worth exercised real influence in ecclesiastical affairs in the country. Associated with him were such ministers as Joseph Eyres of Cork, Samuel Ladyman of Clonmel,[17] Claudius Gilbert of Limerick[18] and Daniel Burston of Waterford,[19] all sympathetic to the Presbyterian model of church government within Ireland and England. They belonged to the emerging number of ministers, not only in Cork but throughout the country, who were prepared to work for and support a form of national church on the lines proposed by the Long Parliament in 1648 but never actually implemented.

The promise of such a church being established was lost in the political upheavals of 1659. By then Henry Cromwell had left Ireland and the situation was volatile. When the Dublin Convention met in 1660 there were hopes that the process begun under Cromwell could be continued. The Convention requested:

> That godly, learned, orthodox and ordained preaching ministers of the
> Gospel (and no other as ministers and preachers) be settled and that
> as speedily as may be throughout this nation and that only in a parochial
> way and encouraged and supported by tithes, glebes and other legal
> maintenance.[20]

A committee of eight ministers was appointed to advise the Convention, and an English Presbyterian, Samuel Coxe, was named chaplain to the Convention. Preaching to the Convention in March 1660, he argued for a Presbyterian form of church government, excluding the Independents, Quakers and Baptists.[21] However, hopes were short-lived, for by June 1660 the commissioners appointed by the Convention to treat with the king recognised that the initiative had passed from their hands. Caught in a double bind, they gave the king a double message when they asked:

> That the church of Ireland be resettled in doctrine, discipline and worship, as it was in the time of your most royal father of blessed memory, according to the laws then and now in force in that kingdom, with such liberty to tender consciences as your majesty in your declaration dated at Breda . . . has been graciously pleased to declare, and that godly learned, orthodox and ordained preaching ministers of the gospel be settled there as speedily as may be in a parochial way and supported by tithes, glebes and other legal maintenance.[22]

By the autumn it was clear that the Established Church would be restored[23] and that ministers would have to decide whether they could/would conform to the new realities. Speaking for the English Presbyterians in Cork, Edward Worth wrote to Bramhall in December 1660 and told him that the ministers in Cork had met for over a week and had drawn up a paper of submission. They indicated that

> we shall observe duly in our respective cures those parts of the church liturgy or Common Prayer against which we know no just exception. Whereto we conceive ourselves more strictly engaged because we live in the midst of papists who are not distinguished by any other legal character but that of recusancy to the Common Prayer.[24]

They admitted that in difficult times they had let some of the ecclesiastical laws drop, but argued also that these were 'alterable and changeable and not to be equated with the word of God'. Some ministers 'conscientiously scruple' and there was genuine variety in practice owing to differing circumstances, 'yet that variety naturally flows from one and the same principle of truth and unity'. It was essentially a pragmatic move on the part of the ministers, a change in direction, based on the need to have a church and government which could guarantee organised and disciplined church order and protect ministers and their people from papists. However it was expressed, the ministers recognised that their project was a failed one, or at least that it had inherited a new context and focus: that of the Established Church. Thus several ministers conformed in 1661 and were allowed to continue holding cures as members of the Established Church.[25] Others could not in conscience conform, and they continued within the presbyterian tradition they had tried to develop in the south of Ireland, in communion with their colleagues in the north; they were joined by some who had not been in Ireland during the Interregnum and gradually formed themselves into separate churches.[26] It is important to note that all three dissenting churches in Dublin at this time were basically presbyterian in theology, and that although they were identified with a particular church or congregation, there was a great deal of exchange, especially between English Presbyterians and Independents. Nevertheless, Cooke Street and Wood Street congregations in Dublin gradually emerged as centres of English Presbyterianism in Ireland.

Cooke Street congregation originated in Winetavern Street in Dublin when the minister there, Edward Baines, was ejected in 1661. Baines had come over from Cambridge during the Interregnum and had served in the parish of St John's in Dublin until 1661.[27] When Baines died in 1670 he was succeeded by Thomas Harrison,[28] who also had been in Ireland during the Interregnum as chaplain to Henry Cromwell.[29] In 1673 this congregation moved to a new meeting-house in Cooke Street. Harrison, who returned to Ireland at the request of the congregation, had an effective ministry in Dublin and was 'admired by all the brethren above all the rest'.[30] His church was attended by Lord Massereene, the Countess of Donegall,[31] and Lady Cole of the Enniskillen family. John Howe, an English Presbyterian appointed chaplain to the Massereene family in 1671, preached regularly in Cooke Street until he returned to London in 1675.[32] Elias Travers who succeeded Howe as chaplain to Massereene in 1676, preached at Cooke Street and was ordained there by the Dublin presbytery.[33] As a church

Cooke Street did not enter into public controversy and lived quietly under the generally mild policy of the government. The early history of Wood Street is scant. It is known that the Independent John Owen preached there in 1647,[34] and from 1652 to 1661 Stephen Charnock, fellow of Trinity College, Dublin, and lecturer at St Werburgh's, ministered in Wood Street. In 1657 he was joined by Edward Veal, who had been ordained for Dunboyne and was also a fellow of Trinity College.[35] Samuel Marsden succeeded Charnock in 1662, having been ejected from Cheshire.[36] The church seems to have been unmarked by debate or controversy in the period before and after the Restoration, and gradually, from Charnock's time, its Independent character gave way to that of English Presbyterianism.[37] In 1667 Daniel Williams, chaplain to the Earl and Countess of Meath and pastor at Drogheda, was called to Wood Street. There

> he had an opportunity of public service for near twenty years, by his labours in the pulpit, by his prudent advice, by improving the interest he obtained in persons of the highest rank and by several other methods in which Providence chose to make him a general blessing.[38]

Although there is little written evidence regarding Williams's time in Ireland, its impact was reflected in his will. He left money for the poor of Wood Street congregation and for the French refugees in the country, as well as £1,000 in perpetuity for promoting the gospel in Irish, all to be administered by trustees from Wood Street and New Row congregations.[39] Williams became better known when he moved to London in 1687 and laboured closely with Richard Baxter. Later on Williams found himself at the centre of debate between Presbyterians and Independents in England.[40] In Dublin Williams was assisted by Gilbert Rule in the years 1682-7,[41] when Rule was seeking refugee from persecution in Scotland.[42] Both men tried to mediate between the Scottish Presbyterians in Dublin when Capel Street and Newmarket congregations were polarised. Williams did not enter into the debate, except to write to the general committee in the north to express concern over affairs in Dublin, an action which contributed to the eventual resolution of the conflict.[43]

The public profile of Wood Street changed when Joseph Boyse came to Dublin in 1683 as assistant to Daniel Williams. Boyse was born in Leeds in 1660 of a Puritan family and was educated at Stepney by Edward Veal, formerly of Wood Street. In 1662 Boyse went to Amsterdam and became chaplain to the Brownists there for some time. In 1679 he became chaplain to the Dowager Countess of Donegall in Lincoln's Inn Fields, London, and in 1683 came to Dublin. There he remained for forty-five years and in the course of that time built up a reputation as a writer of weight, entering into the controversies of the day and strengthening the links between the northern, Scottish Presbyterians and the southern, mainly English Presbyterians in Ireland.[44]

The number of English Presbyterian congregations in Ireland during this period is difficult to determine, but certainly there were no more than seventeen. They were divided into five presbyteries: Dublin, Athlone, Galway, Munster and Drogheda.[45] Since no registers of either baptisms or marriages have as yet come to light, it is possible only to say that the actual membership of these congregations must have been quite small. Even though 3,000 of 'great and small rank', including the Lord Mayor and aldermen, attended Faithful Teate's funeral in 1666, these numbers would have included Scottish Presbyterians and Independents as well as English Presbyterians.[46] Joseph Eyres hoped that numbers would increase in his congregation in Cork,[47] though by the turn of the century John Cook realised that this would not happen.[48] In 1702 Bishop Downes noted that Presbyterians in St Peter's parish, Cork, had a meeting-house to accommodate 400 people;[49] by 1729 Richard Choppin, speaking of Wood Street congregation, could speak of 'this declining congregation'.[50] The survival of English Presbyterianism depended as much upon the loyalty of several, probably very few, families and the capacity of ministers to be self-supporting.[51]

Both Wood Street and Cooke Street churches had wealthy congregations which supported their ministers. Indeed, some of the ministers themselves were wealthy in their own right or were patronised by wealthy families.[52] But there was a movement to establish the ministry of the churches on a more organised basis towards the end of the century. First- and even second-generation congregations needed to ensure their continuity, and the creation of a General Fund was mooted in 1696. The imposition of the Test Act in 1704 galvanised the congregations and ministers into action, and the General Fund was finally established in 1710.[53] This ensured that congregations could continue when the members themselves were unable to support a minister. The idea of such a fund was supported not only by English Presbyterians but also by Scottish Presbyterians and Independents in Dublin.

The aims of those who set up the fund was to safeguard liberty of conscience, attract ministers to poor, small congregations, provide for new congregations, and encourage students for the ministry. The 'inconvenience and difficulty of private applications from particular persons on particular occasions and emergencies' was recognised. At the same time it was pointed out that wealthy persons had both the capacity and spiritual obligation to promote the aims of the General Fund: 'Wealth is a stewardship.' Steps were taken to administer the fund correctly, and a deed of trust was drawn up.[54]

The first trustees, twenty-seven in all, were ten ministers and ten members of the congregations of Wood Street, Capel Street, New Row, Cooke Street and Plunkett Street (formerly Bull Alley), as well as seven donors.[55] So it was a shared fund between Scottish Presbyterian, English Presbyterian and Independent churches.[56] In addition to the fund, the English Presbyterians received the 'English Bounty' from Queen Anne in 1708, which must have helped the churches at this time.[57] Through the bounty and the General Fund these churches were given a guaranteed income; maintenance was secure, ministers were provided for, and the future of the churches was ensured.

When John Dunton visited Dublin in 1699 he commented that

> the dissenters in Ireland are a very considerable people, as well for their number as wealth . . . have several meeting houses . . . and these are supplied with sober and pious teachers, among whom the reverend Mr Boyse may justly be named as the chief; one who by continual and hard study every day fit himself with new acquisitions towards the happy discharging of his pastoral care.[58]

It is basically through Boyse's writings that the history of Wood Street and the English Presbyterians in Ireland can be traced.

Indeed, while English Presbyterians were much fewer in number than Scottish Presbyterians, they managed to maintain their congregations in the country. The diary of John Cook, written at the end of the seventeenth century, gives some useful details of how the English Presbyterian church in Ireland had evolved since the Restoration and provides information on the number of congregations in the south of Ireland. The diary also indicates how ministers were prepared for ministry, showing how much it was a shared task, at least in Dublin.[59]

For example, when Cook started his ministerial training in Dublin he 'began with several others a course of weekly exercise and disputation before the ministers of Dublin, Mr Robert Henry, Mr Nathaniel Weld, Mr Joseph Boyse, Mr Elias Travers, Mr Alexander Sinclare, Mr Thomas Emlin who held weekly meetings to this purpose'.[60] This group worked together on the formation of future ministers, even though they adhered to different Presbyterian and Independent traditions: Robert Henry belonged to Capel Street congregation (Scottish Presbyterian); Nathaniel Weld to New Row (Independent); Alexander Sinclare to Bull Alley (Scottish Presbyterian); Elias Travers to Cooke Street (English Presbyterian); Boyse and Emlin to Wood Street (English Presbyterian).

Boyse introduced Cook to the thinking of Richard Baxter and indicated that he 'had a very great veneration for him'.[61] Cook wanted to follow both men's teaching and develop a 'charitable latitude in matter of opinion'. In 1696 Boyse and Emlin accepted Cook as a candidate for ministry in Wood Street, 'both (and especially the latter) being of very great abilities and eminent preachers'.[62] By 1697 Cook had passed all his trials and was licensed to preach. In that capacity he was sent to different congregations in the south of Ireland. He preached in Carlow, Clonmel, Waterford, Cork, Kinsale, Limerick and Tipperary. In May 1700 he received a call from Andrew Roe, 'a wealthy man', and friends in Tipperary, a small congregation which met in Roe's house. They promised him £50–60 per annum with accommodation.[63]

In the following year the little congregation wanted him to be ordained for Tipperary so that they could have a communion service in their area instead of having to travel to Clonmel. The request was laid before 'the ministers of Dublin and afterwards before the Munster ministers',[64] and all agreed that Cook should be ordained for Tipperary. On 1 October 1701 he was ordained in Roe's house by ministers from Bandon, Clonmel, Waterford, Youghal, Cork, Mallow and Galway.[65] While there is no evidence to show how big congregations were in the various towns, and every likelihood that they were small, nevertheless they continued to exist and exercised their own authority to call and maintain a minister; the body of ministers in Dublin and in Munster, the Dublin and the Munster presbyteries, acted as overseers of these churches, and they ordained ministers as they thought fit and ready. It is also evident that such ministers were from the Scottish Presbyterian, English Presbyterian and Independent traditions. By dint of necessity and fewness of numbers, at least in the south of Ireland, they learned to work together.

Nevertheless, there were latent theological tensions which emerged in 1702. Instead of being solely a body of ministers engaged in the formation of ministers, this same group acted as a judicial body and demanded the removal of one of its colleagues. Indeed, a hint of some of the differences occurring at this time between dissenting ministers of differing traditions is caught in Cook's account of his examination prior to ordination:

> Some exceptions were for awhile insisted on, on account of my latitude in the Arminian and Unitarian articles, but in compliance with the more severe temper of the aged brethren with whom I had to do, and being unwilling to sacrifice the Church's peace and the usefulness of my life and labours, to words and phrases, (in which according to the present plan the controversy very much lay) I gave a moderate satisfaction and removed their scruples, I renounced the systematic phrases and did my Confession in expressions of the greatest latitude and clearness I could.[66]

Such latitude was tested in Dublin in 1702 when Thomas Emlin of Wood Street was accused of denying the divinity of Christ and was cast out of his ministry in Wood Street by his own association of ministers in Dublin. This incident revealed the active role of the laity, especially elders, in the churches at this time. While Emlin was exposed by a member of Wood Street congregation, he was also supported by others in the congregation, who felt his dismissal unjust and undeserved.

Emlin came to Ireland as assistant to Boyse in 1691. He had previously been chaplain to the Countess of Donegall in England and in 1684 had accompanied her to Belfast. There he became friendly with Claudius Gilbert, who had been overtly Presbyterian in Limerick during the Interregnum but had conformed at the Restoration.[67] Emlin attended service in the parish church on Sundays in Belfast, and Gilbert came to Emlin's sermons in the countess's house. Emlin often officiated for Gilbert in the parish church; in fact he had a licence to preach from the bishop, and most thought Emlin had conformed; he even wore the dress of an Established Church clergyman.[68]

In 1688 Boyse asked Emlin to join him in Wood Street on condition that he clarify his position in Belfast. Rumours had spread to Dublin that Emlin was preaching in the parish church without licence or ordination. Emlin replied that while he was prepared to preach anywhere, he had not compromised on the question of ordination or subscription (presumably to the Thirty-Nine Articles).[69] In any event, political circumstances did not allow Emlin to respond to Boyse's invitation. Instead Emlin went to England, where he became influenced by the thinking of William Manning, a Socinian. In 1690 Boyse repeated his request, and on this occasion Emlin agreed to come to Wood Street.[70]

By all accounts, Emlin was a popular preacher. The members of Wood Street congregation were wealthy and of rank; among them was Esther Bury, a widow and daughter of a Jewish merchant in Meath, David Sollom. Emlin married Mrs Bury in 1694 and settled down to what promised to be a long stay in Dublin.[71] However, by 1697 Emlin realised that he was

> convinced that the God and father of Jesus Christ is alone the supreme being and superior in excellence and authority to his son . . . who derives all from him.[72]

He decided to remain silent on the subject, and for a time his views were not noticed. However, in June 1702 a member of the laity, Dr Duncan Cumning, an elder and former student for the ministry, told Boyse he had doubts about Emlin's orthodoxy. They decided to visit Emlin and ask him to declare his views on the divinity of Christ. Emlin told them he did not believe Christ to be equal with God, calling into question the doctrine of the Trinity. Emlin offered to leave Dublin immediately and so prevent disturbance in the congregation. Boyse refused to accept this compromise and insisted that the case be brought before the Dublin presbytery, a coalition of Scottish Presbyterian, English Presbyterian and Independent ministers. This meeting consisted of Nathaniel Weld of New Row, Independent; Elias Travers of Cooke Street, Independent; Francis Iredell of Capel Street, Scottish Presbyterian; and Mr Tate, who was minister to Sir Hercules Langford at Summerhill.[73] They dismissed him immediately without further consultation.[74]

Writing some years later,[75] Emlin explained that he had difficulties with the doctrine of the Trinity for some years before the crisis in Wood Street. He was not alone in this and noted that John Howe, formerly Lord Massereene's chaplain, had put forward the idea of three infinite minds (tritheistical scheme) and no one had publicly dismissed and tried him. The instant dismissal offended Emlin, and he resented that none of his congregation had been either consulted or even told he was leaving. So he decided to call the deacons and chief managers of the church and told them that

> differences in opinions had rendered me offensive to some there and to the other ministers, so that it seemed best I should leave them; therefore I thankfully owned the kindness and respects they had shown me for so many years and desired their dismission.[76]

The Dublin presbytery gave Emlin permission to go to London, but told him not to preach there; they sent a special delegation to convey this prohibition to him before he left Dublin, even threatening to inform London ministers about it.

> To this imperious message, so full of affectation of authority and expressive of rigid presbyterian tyranny, (which yet was attended by an Independent minister [Weld] as one of the messengers) . . . they assumed too much in forbidding me to preach, who had no authority from them, nor owned any in them over me; that I had as much authority to forbid them to preach as they to forbid me. . . . And this I suppose is what

the northern ministers (in their address and apology to Queen Anne, in answer to the convocation) call my being solemnly deposed from my office by a presbytery (though I never knew any who owned themselves to be such in Dublin).[77]

Obviously Emlin resented the manner in which he was dismissed and the authoritarian attitude adopted by the Dublin presbytery. He accused the Dublin ministers of acting like the pope. When he reached London he set about publishing his own account of what happened in Dublin.[78] He sent several copies over to Dublin, but the Dublin presbytery withheld them from the public until Boyse had written his response to Emlin's account;[79] both were published together, around the time that Emlin had returned to Dublin to settle his affairs.[80] While in Dublin he was arrested and charged with the civil offence of denying the Trinity and was put on trial on 14 June 1703. The court was composed of two archbishops and five bishops, and Boyse was called to give evidence against Emlin. The court ruled that Emlin should be jailed and fined £1,000. The Archbishop of Dublin, Narcissus Marsh, in his capacity as Queen's Almoner, also charged him an additional shilling in the pound of the whole fine.

Discipline was exercised rigorously. All Emlin's former friends disowned him, especially those of superior rank in society; the dissenting ministers of Dublin ignored him, and none came to visit him while he was in prison.[81] In September 1702 the Munster presbytery declared against Emlin.[82] This must have disappointed him deeply, for he had tried to contact some of his former colleagues, among them John Cook, who had been sympathetic towards him. In 1702, at an ordination at Leap, Boyse told Cook that Emlin was about to be dismissed. On his return home to Tipperary, Cook received a letter from Emlin explaining his position and saying that he had decided to break from Wood Street congregation. A few days later Cook had another letter from Emlin saying that the break had been made and that he was returning to England. He particularly resented the sentence of the Dublin presbytery forbidding him to preach in England and intended to ignore it.

Emlin was clearly hoping for some understanding and support

from Cook and other ministers. Cook admitted that they had
treated him badly:

> In September last [1702] was an assembly of the southern ministers at
> Cork, where they joined in subscribing a protestation against Mr Emlin
> and his errors. This was done not with that exactness that a matter of
> that nature requires for it was upon a bare account in general which
> they had from the ministers in Dublin. However, for peace sake and
> for avoiding animosity and contention, which being usually attended
> with the greatest uncharitableness . . . I submitted to subscribe the same.
> I am not without very great doubts in this matter so much debated.[83]

Emlin resented the intolerance he received in Dublin from the
dissenting ministers and from the Established Church. Referring to the Dublin presbytery which dismissed him, he was angry
that

> men who dissent on principles of conscience and liberty and find so much
> indulgence from an Established Church, should yet domineer and im-
> pose on their brethren with such imperious, cruel severity, and even
> threaten them with the execution of those laws against which themselves
> once made such loud and uneasy complaints.[84]

He was equally disillusioned with the Established Church in
Ireland; he had enjoyed toleration in Belfast, but that was toleration from an absentee bishop, Thomas Hackett.[85] Emlin had
thought the Established Church would have allowed latitude to
discuss matters of religion, and he saw this as part of the Protestant tradition:

> Might not any Protestant then, all these things considered, venture upon
> a serious examination of modern creeds by the light of revelation, the
> words of Christ's own mouth and the writings of his inspired apostles?
> Or might not I, who had been brought up in a diligent study of the
> scriptures and admitted to be a teacher of others, justly expect the liberty
> of declaring what I judged to be the doctrine of the gospel though re-
> jected by others not more infallible than myself?[86]

Emlin was released from prison in July 1705 and went to
England, where he preached to a small congregation. He visited
Ireland from time to time and maintained contact with 'the mid-
dling sort of people', who always welcomed him. Many of them
felt that he had been treated badly and that a decrease in the
Wood Street congregation dated from his dismissal.[87] Certainly

the debate did not end there, either in Ireland or in England, but there was greater scope and toleration for Emlin in England, especially after the Salter's Hall decision in 1719 not to require subscription to any confession of faith.[88]

All dissenters were in a difficult position at this time. In 1697 it was declared in law blasphemous to deny the Trinity, to assert that there was more than one god, to deny Christianity to be true, or to deny the divine authority of the Old and New Testaments.[89] Emlin's stance became a test case and dissenters could not afford to be seen lenient with regard to the law of the land. No doubt there were many like Cook who probably either agreed with him or at least had doubts and queries. Most of all, Emlin himself knew that real freedom of debate was both impossible and yet vital to any possibility of harmony within and between the churches. He cited Chillingworth:

> This restraining the word of God from that latitude and the understandings of men from that liberty wherein Christ and his apostles left them, is and has been the only foundation of all the schisms of the church.[90]

English Presbyterian theology was further developed in the debates concerning the role of bishops in the Established Church. Such disputes helped English Presbyterians sharpen understanding of church order and authority, especially in the period after the 1688 Revolution. In 1709 Boyse preached at an ordination in New Row and in the course of the sermon denounced diocesan bishops as

> a grand and pompous sinecure, a domination over all the churches and ministers in a large district managed by others as his delegates but requiring little labour of a man's own and all this supported by large revenues and attended with considerable honours.[91]

In the sermon Boyse examined the role and function of leadership in the early church[92] and argued that elders or ministers were never mentioned as subject to a bishop; in fact the office of elder and bishop were one and the same.[93] In the sermon Boyse gave a summary of the evolution in English Presbyterian thought, especially since 1660, on the issue of authority and leadership. He pointed out that at the Savoy conference Ussher's model of episcopacy, offered as a compromise solution, was rejected by the Church of England. Indeed, some bishops had declared the ordinations and ministries of dissenters null and void because they lacked the authority and ordination of a diocesan bishop, an attitude which was most offensive to the dissenters.[94] Boyse's sermon became a source of controversy with the Established Church, first in Dublin[95] and then in Belfast,[96] where Scottish Presbyterians came to Boyse's defence,[97] declaring that bishops and presbyters had the

> same names, same work, same power in managing that work and the same qualification for it; they are the same persons and their office in every respect the same.[98]

This provoked a strong reaction from Established Church ministers who resented the fact that Scottish Presbyterians in particular held synods and exercised jurisdiction over their people independently of the government. This was a particularly sensitive issue at a time when Convocation had been summoned in 1703 but only licensed to act in 1711.[99] The debate continued for some time and Boyse had the last word, for in 1716 at another ordination he rejected

> a late set of writers that call themselves Protestants who cry up the absolute necessity of an uninterrupted line of succession by what they call episcopal ordination . . . and this line of succession they are forced to derive through the polluted channel of the apostate church of Rome. . . . Those reformed churches that have not retained the diocesan form of government, they reckon all their ordinations invalid and null . . . and all these pretended teachers . . . never sent by Christ, no better than lay intruders.[100]

During the Interregnum in Ireland clerics like Edward Worth and his associates had hoped for a national church based on the *Form of Church Government* enacted in 1648 but never implemented by parliament. When the Established Church was restored in 1660 this hope died. Contrary to the Scottish Presbyterians, who could count on real support from Scotland and on the long tradition and presence they had in Ulster, English Presbyterians had no such support or tradition in Ireland, except that of a few years of experimentation during the Interregnum. Through their own determination and good leadership, through their convictions

sharpened by debate and controversy, English Presbyterians survived in Ireland. Had Scottish Presbyterianism triumphed in
Ireland as it did in Scotland after 1688, then the history of English
Presbyterianism in Ireland might have been very different. This
was not to be. While English Presbyterians did not expand in
any great numbers or challenge the Established Church in Ireland
in any serious way, they were an embodiment of another tradition of Protestant dissent in Ireland.

Notes and References

1   U.L.C., *The Form of Church Government to be used in the Church of England and
    Ireland, 29 August 1648;* B.L., Stowe MS 155, ff 80ff.
2   James Ussher, *The reduction of episcopacy* (repr., London, 1687).
3   Bodl., Carte MS 21, ff 155, 176; St John D. Seymour, *The Puritans in Ireland,
    1647-1661* (Oxford, 1921), pp 2-7.
4   Worth to Bramhall, 3 Dec. 1660, in Seymour, *The Puritans in Ireland*, p. 227.
5   *The agreement and resolution of several associated ministers in the county of Cork for
    the ordaining of ministers* (Cork, 1657) (Copy in N.L.I.).
6   Ibid., pp 13-15. Quakers at this time queried the ordination and ministries
    of Independent and Presbyterian ministers. *To all the inhabitants of Youghal
    who are under the teachings of James Wood* (n.p., *c.* 1657/8). Wood was a newly
    ordained Independent minister at Youghal. Wood stayed in Ireland after
    the Restoration and seems not to have conformed; he ministered in
    Tipperary and was master of the Erasmus Smith school there.
    T. C. Barnard, *Cromwellian Ireland: English government and reform in Ireland,
    1649-1660* (Oxford, 1975), p. 192n. In 1680 Wood published *Shepardy
    spiritualised.*
7   *The agreement and resolution*, p. 17.
8   B.L., Lansdowne MS 823, f. 57. Worth was born in Cork and ordained
    in June 1641; he became Dean of Cork in 1645; by 1650 he was acting
    as minister in Cork, with Joseph Eyres and John Murcot, and was in con-
    troversy with the Baptists there; in 1655 he became minister at Water-
    ford and returned to Cork in 1658. In 1660 he resumed his office as Dean
    of Cork and became Bishop of Killaloe in 1661. John Power, 'Waterford
    clerical authors, from the work of Rev. Thomas Gimlette' in *Irish Literary
    Enquirer*, no. 3 (16 Dec. 1865), p. 28; Barnard, *Cromwellian Ireland*, pp 117-22,
    126-32. Philip Dwyer, *The diocese of Killaloe from the Reformation to the close of
    the eighteenth century* (Dublin, 1878), pp 317ff, 343.
9   Barnard, *Cromwellian Ireland*, p. 121. Joseph Eyres was born in Co. Cork
    and was educated at Trinity College, Dublin, with Worth. He worked in
    Cork with Worth. *Alumni Dublinenses,* pp 5, 354, 895; B.L., Add. MS 19833,
    f. 12; B.L., Lansdowne MS 823, f. 91. He wrote *The church sleeper awakened*
    (Cork/London, 1659), which gives a good picture of the strengthening

power of the association in Cork and the standards required of the congregation there.

10 *By the Lord Deputy and Council,* 20 Jan. 1658 (Trinity College Dublin, Printed Books, Press A 7, 19).

11 Barnard, *Cromwellian Ireland,* pp 117-22.

12 The problem was raised in 1657: 'Proposals humbly tendered in order to the preventing such inconveniences as they may arise . . . 1657' (B.L., Lansdowne MS 1228, ff 8-10).

13 B.L., Lansdowne MS 1228, f. 10. The convention noted the following religious groups in Ireland at this time: native Irish Catholics; those who professed to be Protestant for political reasons; Episcopalians; Baptists; Presbyterians; Independents. Quakers are not listed. Ibid., f. 8v.

14 'The humble address of the ministers by authority assembled out of the several provinces of Ireland', May 1658 (B.L., Lansdowne MS 1228, f. 14); William Urwick, *Independency in Dublin in the olden times* (Dublin, 1862), p. 25.

15 Edward Cooke, *A paper from Quakers shewing the wickedness of the young priests lately come over into Ireland and how the evil justices of the peace set up the old mass houses for them. And also the taking away of goods out of people's houses that cannot for conscience sake pay for mending of old mass houses* (n.p., *c.*1658) (copy in F.L.L.). For Edward Cooke see Chapter 4, n. 18. Edward Worth, *The servant doing and the Lord blessing* (Dublin, 1659), p. 30. Lord Chief Justice Pepys advocated tithes and fixed ministries; for tithes see also Barnard, *Cromwellian Ireland,* pp 155-60. 'We have gotten a cheap religion and therefore like it because it saves our purses though not our souls.' Thomas Harrison, *Topica Sacra* (Kirkbride, 1712), p. 150.

16 Worth to Henry Cromwell, 20 July 1658 (B.L., Lansdowne MS 823, f. 79). In June 1658 Henry Cromwell wrote to his father, supporting all that Worth was doing in Ireland but omitting to state that both he and Worth were against the Independents. *A collection of the state papers of John Thurloe,* ed. Thomas Birch, 7 vols (London, 1742), vii, 162.

17 Henry Cotton, *Fasti Ecclesiae Hibernicae* 6 vols (Dublin, 1845-78), i, 347; B.L., Landsdowne MS 823, f. 51. Ladyman conformed at the Restoration, and was appointed to a living in the diocese of Cashel (Bodl., Carte MS 221, f. 130; ibid., MS 160, f. 6).

18 See Chapter 6, n. 3. Gilbert conformed at the Restoration.

19 Burston conformed after the Restoration. John Power, 'Waterford clerical authors, from the work of Rev. Thomas Gimlette' in *Irish Literary Enquirer,* no. 3 (Dec. 1865), p. 28; James Coleman, 'Some early Waterford clerical authors', in *Waterford Arch. Soc. Jn.,* vi (1900), p. 178; Burston wrote *The evangelist evangelising* (Dublin, 1662), which was approved by Convocation in March 1663. T.C.D., MS 1038, f. 76v; Cotton, *Fasti,* i, pp 140, 156, 174. Burston was minister at Tallow in 1655 and was probably a member of the Cork association. In his book, (pp 23, 31, 272), Burston admitted receiving 'presbyterial imposition of hands' which he rejected later on in favour of episcopal ordination. He became Dean of Waterford in 1670.

20　'Instructions for Sir John Clotworthy and William Aston Esq., members of the General Convention of Ireland now employed into England by the said Convention', 30 Mar. 1660 (B.L., Add. MS, 32471, f. 82v).

21　Samuel Coxe, *Two sermons preached at Christchurch Dublin beginning the General Convention of Ireland* (Dublin, 1660). Coxe was minister at St Katherine's Church in Dublin and had been in Athlone before that; he was ejected in 1662. R.C.B., MS Libr. 14, Vestry Book of St Katherine and St James, 1657-1692, pp 3, 25, 31, 47; John Healy, *History of the diocese of Meath*, 2 vols (Dublin, 1908), i, 299; Adair, *A true narrative*, pp 230-7; J. I. McGuire, 'The Dublin Convention, the Protestant community and the energence of an ecclesiastical settlement in 1660' in Art Cosgrove and J. I. McGuire (ed.), *Parliament and community* (Belfast, 1983), pp 130-1; McConnell, *Fasti*, no. 44, p. 9.

22　'The further humble desires of the commissioners of the General Convention of Ireland appointed to attend your majesty (T.C.D., MS 808, no. 9, f. 156).

23　Loftus to Ormond, 1 June 1660 (Bodl., Carte MS 30, f 478).

24　Worth to Bramhall, 3 Dec 1660 (cited in Seymour, *The Puritans in Ireland*, p. 227).

25　By the Act of Uniformity (1666) all clergy had to give public assent to the Book of Common Prayer and the ceremonies of the Established Church by 25 March 1668; by 29 September 1668 they were to be episcopally or-dained and have taken the declaration against rebellion and in particular against the Solemn League and Covenant. (By 1682 taking of the declara-tion against the Solemn League and Covenant was to be discontinued. This application of the Act of Uniformity in Ireland indicated how English policy affected Ireland, seemingly unaware of the significance of continued unrest in Ulster. See Chapter 8).

26　Letter of Daniel Rolls, Thomas Parson, John Hooke and Noah Bryan, Dublin, 8 July 1667 (Dr Williams's Library, Baxter Letters, 3, f. 76). The first three mentioned had been members of the Established Church who did not conform in 1660: see Seymour, *The Puritans in Ireland*, pp 214, 218, 220. For Noah Bryan, see Edmund Calamy, *An account of the ministers . . . who were ejected or silenced after the Restoration in 1660* (n.p., 1713), p. 629.

27　'Mr Baines lately set up in a chamber near Christ Church'. (Bodl., Carte MS 45, f. 277, *c.* 1662/3). Baines was involved in Blood's Plot. Barnard, *Cromwellian Ireland*, pp 142-3.

28　Armstrong, *Summary history of the Presbyterian Church*, pp 83-4; Thomas Har-rison, *Topica sacra*, dedicated to Henry Cromwell (Kirkbride, 1712); Calamy, *An account of the ministers . . . who were ejected* , p. 121; William Urwick, *Early history of Trinity College, Dublin, 1591-1660* (London, 1892), p. 81; Urwick, *In-dependency in Dublin*, p. 18. Harrison preached in America, England and Ireland. McConnell, *Fasti*, no. 72, p. 39.

29　B.L., Lansdowne MS 821, ff 155, 164, 170, 174, 212, 218, 222, 332. Har-rison came to Dublin to escape his critics.

30　20 Aug. 1670 (Bodl., Carte MS 221, f. 174v).

31　Alexander Gordon and G. K. Smith, *Historic memorials of the first Presbyterian*

Church of Belfast (Belfast, 1887) p. 10. Laetitia Hicks, Countess of Donegall, was an English Presbyterian who had English Presbyterians as her chaplains: William Keyes, Samuel Bryan and Thomas Emlin. Keyes accepted the authority of the Scottish Presbyterians in the north and belonged to the Antrim meeting.

32   The bishop of Down and Connor as well as the archbishop of Armagh allowed Howe to preach in the parish church in Antrim every Sunday in the afternoon. Armstrong, *Summary history of the Presbyterian Church*, pp 84-6. Howe had been in Ireland before the 1641 rebellion and returned to England during the rebellion. He was favoured by Cromwell and ejected in 1662. In 1665 he took the Oxford Oath and in 1671 returned to Dublin. Edmund Calamy, *Memoirs of the late Rev. Mr John Howe* (London, 1734). For further detail on Howe see Chapter 1, n 76-7.

33   Travers was aided by a former English Presbyterian, since he stayed with Claudius Gilbert when he was preaching in Belfast. Armstrong, *Summary history of the Presbyterian Church*, p. 86; Urwick, *Early history of Trinity College, Dublin*, p. 77; Joseph Boyse, 'A sermon preached at the death of Mr Elias Travers, 5 May 1705, at Cooke Street under the care of Mr Travers in Boyse, *Works*, 2 vols (London, 1728), i, 430-1.

34   Armstrong, *Summary history of the Presbyterian Church*, p. 66.

35   Ibid., pp 68, 73; Charles Irwin, *History of Presbyterianism in Dublin and the south and the west of Ireland*, (London, 1890), p. 313; Barnard, *Cromwellian Ireland*, pp 117, 136-7, 143. Veal left Dublin after the Act of Uniformity was enforced and ran an academy at Stepney; Charnock had been Henry Cromwell's chaplain and was involved in the 1663 plot, after which he moved to England.

36   Armstrong, *Summary history of the Presbyterian Church*, p. 68.

37   Seymour, *The Puritans in Ireland*, pp 29, 88, 110, 111, 116, 135, 141, 178.

38   Daniel Williams, *Practical discourses on several important subjects. To which is prefaced some account of his life and character*, 2 vols (London, 1738), i, p. ix. Williams was born in Wales *c.* 1643/4 and came to Ireland soon after the Restoration as chaplain to the Countess of Meath and pastor at Drogheda. He married into a wealthy family; his wife was the Countess of Mountrath's sister and a convert of Edward Baynes of Cooke Street. Edmund Calamy, *A funeral sermon preached upon the occasion of the [death of]* Mrs Elizabeth Williams, *June 10 1698* (London, 1698), pp 72-3, 89; D.N.B; Witherow, *Historical memorials*, pp 60-5.

39   Armstrong, *Summary history of the Presbyterian Church*, pp 68-9; Edmund Calamy, *A continuation of the account*, 2 vols (London, 1727), ii, pp 968-98. For the Independent church at New Row see Chapter 3.

40   Michael Watts, *The dissenters: from the Reformation to the French Revolution* (Oxford, 1985), pp 294-7.

41   Alexander Smellie, *Men of the Covenant* (Edinburgh, 1975), pp 402, 478, 512.

42   Williams was influenced by Rule and his Scottish Presbyterianism. Alexander Gordon (ed.), *Freedom after ejection: a review (1690-1692) of Presbyterian and Congregational nonconformity in England and Wales* (Manchester, 1917), p. 384. Later Rule became Principal of Edinburgh University and adviser

to William of Orange in Scotland. Armstrong, *Summary history of the Presbyterian Church,* p. 69.

43 Antrim minutes, pp 255-6, 265. See Chapter 5 for details.

44 D.N.B; Armstrong, *Summary history of the Presbyterian Church,* p. 70; Irwin, *History of Presbyterianism,* p. 314; Witherow, *Historical memorials,* pp 79-87.

45 Irwin, *History of Presbyterianism,* (1860 ed.), pp 166, 169, 171, 188-9, 192, 199-200, 212.

46 Toby Bonnell to John Strype, Oct. 23 1666 (U.L.C., Baum. Papers, Add. 4, iii, pt. i, f. 20). Aldermen at this time were often dissenters. *Cal. S.P. Ire., 1663-5,* p. 499. See also St John D. Seymour 'Faithful Teate' in *R.S.A.I. Jn.,* 6th series, x (1920), 43.

47 Joseph Eyres, *The church sleeper awakened,* (London, 1659) epistle dedicatory.

48 'Diary of the Rev. John Cook begun 1696', Presbyterian Church in Ireland Historical Library, Belfast, pp 6, 12.

49 'In the lane near the wall is the meeting house of the presbyterians, a large room, the seats and gallery will hold about 400 people.' Visitation Book of Dives Downes, T.C.D., MS 562, f. 84).

50 Richard Choppin, *A funeral sermon: Mr J. Boyse* ([Dublin], 1728).

51 The Langford family in Summerhill, Co. Meath supported English Presbyterian ministers and built a meeting-house there for worship. In 1683 Bishop Dopping of Meath forbade baptisms to take place there; later, in 1714, Dean Swift threatened to close the meeting-house though this did not actually occur. Healy, *History of the diocese of Meath,* i, 313; Armstrong, *Summary history of the Presbyterian Church,* pp 104-6; David Nokes, *Jonathan Swift, a hypocrite reversed: a critical biography* (Oxford, 1985), p. 220. In his diary (p. 4) Cook mentions Mrs Peniel Roy [Toy?] , 'gentlewoman much known and respected among dissenters in Dublin for much of pious and christian spirit'.

52 Boyse's sermons indicate the number of wealthy members in his congregation. See *Works,* i, sermons, pp 311, 318, 430-1, 435-9. Richard Choppin came from 'an opulent Presbyterian family'. Armstrong, *Summary history of the Presbyterian Church,* pp 70; see pp 56, 58, 78. Boyse and Emlin were chaplains to the Countess of Donegall, and Travers was a nephew of Lord Robartes and chaplain to Massereene. From the evidence of his will, Williams was a very wealthy man through marriage and property acquired. Calamy, *A Continuation of the account,* ii, 983-89; Calamy, *A funeral sermon* (London, 1698), pp 72, 89; Calamy, *An historical account,* ii, 56-7; H.M.C., *Ormonde MSS, iv,* 26; Emlin too married into a wealthy Jewish family from Meath. Emlin, *Works,* i, p. xx.

53 Irwin, *History of presbyterianism,* p. 33. The idea of a General Fund was first mooted in 1696: Armstrong, *Summary history of the Presbyterian Church,* p. 58.

54 Ibid., pp 32-3.

55 For details on the trustees see Irwin, *History of Presbyterianism,* pp 34-5.

56 Wood Street was by far the greatest contributor to the fund, especially Sir Arthur Langford. Joseph Damer of Tipperary also gave substantial monies. The fund realised £1,500 in 1710 and by 1829 had risen to £7,670, of which £6,750 came from Wood Street. Damer had been a Cromwellian

soldier who fled to France in 1660 and returned in 1662. He bought lands in Co. Tipperary and through sheep-farming built up a money-lending business in Dublin. He was one of the executors for part of Daniel Williams's will. He died in 1720 leaving a fortune of £400,000. Swift wrote a satiric poem about him. P. C. Power, *History of South Tipperary* (Cork, 1989) pp 81-2; Dáithí Ó hÓgáin, 'An tÓr Buí: staidéar an ghné de sheanchas Thiobraid Árann' in William Nolan (ed.), *Tipperary: history and society* (Dublin, 1985), pp 146-7; Calamy, *Continuation of the account,* ii, 983.

57   Irwin, *History of Presbyterianism,* p. 22. The queen, under the influence of Calamy, gave 'out of her privy purse the sum of £800 a year for the support of the English Presbyterians in the south of Ireland'. Classon Porter, *Regium donum and ministerial maintenance* (Belfast, 1884), p. 13. But see J. C. Beckett, *Protestant dissent in Ireland, 1687-1780* (London, 1948), p. 115.

58   John Dunton, 'Some account of my conversation in Ireland in a letter to an honourable lady with her answer to it' in *The Dublin scuffle* (London, 1699), p. 331; also pp 336-7.

59   'Diary of the Rev. John Cook begun 1696' (Presbyterian Church in Ireland Historical Library, Belfast). Cook was born in Dublin 1677 and was baptised by Mr Chambers, 'minister of a congregation that used to meet in Francis Street' (p. 1). In 1688 he was sent away to Whitehaven for safety until 1690 and on his return had a tutor for three years until he was ready to train for the ministry.

60   'Diary of John Cook', p. 3.

61   N. H. Keeble, *Richard Baxter: Puritan man of letters* (Oxford, 1982); N.H. Keeble and G.F. Nutall (ed.), *Calender of the correspondence of Richard Baxter,* 2 vols (Oxford, 1991).

62   'Diary of John Cook', p. 4.

63   In the eighteenth century there were two Roe families in Co. Tipperary, one in Thurles, the other in Cashel. William Nolan, 'Patterns of living in Co. Tipperary from 1770-1850' in Nolan (ed.), *Tipperary: history and society,* pp 306-7. In April 1686 one of Andrew Roe's children was baptised in New Row. New Row Baptismal Register, f. 10.

64   The presbytery of Munster included Clonmel, Limerick, Summerhill, Co. Meath, Tipperary, Waterford.

65   'Diary of John Cook', pp 5-6.

66   Ibid., pp 6-7.

67   Witherow, *Historical memorials,* pp 130-46; John Nelson, 'The Belfast Presbyterians, 1670-1830' (Ph.D. thesis Q.U.B., 1985), p. 32.

68   Emlin, *Works,* 3 vols (London, 1746), i, pp v-ix. Emlin was born in Lincolnshire in 1663 and went to Emmanuel College Cambridge; his parents, though Puritans, were friendly with their local bishop.

69   *Ibid.,* x-xii; George Mathews, *An account of the trial of . . . Thomas Emlin for publication against the doctrine of the Trinity, with a sketch of his associates, predecessors and successors* (Dublin, 1839), pp 2-3.

70   Emlin, *Works,* i, p. xviii; Mathews, *An account of the trial of . . . Thomas Emlin,* pp 4-5.

71   D.N.B.

72   Emlin, *Works*, i, 17.

73   Healy, *History of the diocese of Meath*, i, 313-15; in 1683 Bishop Dopping of
     Meath forbade Tate to baptise or preach. For the Langford family see
     Armstrong, *Summary history of the Presbyterian Church*, pp 104-6; Nokes, *Jonathan
     Swift*, pp 111, 220.

74   Mathews, *An account of the trial of . . . Thomas Emlin*, p. 10ff; [Joseph Boyse],
     *The difference between Mr E[mlin] and Protestant dissenting ministers of D[ublin] tru-
     ly represented (n.p., 1702);* 'Diary of John Cook', p. 9. From at least 1682/3
     (and probably much earlier) dissenting ministers in Dublin met once a
     month to confer on matters of common interest. Urwick, *Independency in
     Dublin*, p. 30.

75   [Thomas Emlin], *A true narrative of the proceedings of the dissenting ministers of
     Dublin against Mr Thomas Emlin* (London, 1719), p. 12ff.

76   Ibid., p. 18.

77   Ibid., pp 19-20; 'Diary of John Cook', p. 9.

78   Thomas Emlin, *Humble enquiry into the scripture account of the Lord Jesus Christ*
     (London, 1702); 'Diary of John Cook', p. 9.

79   Joseph Boyse, *A vindication of the true deity of our blessed Saviour* (Dublin, 1703).

80   'Diary of John Cook', p. 9. Cook visited Emlin in December 1702 while
     Emlin was still in Dublin; Emlin gave Cook copies of his account, hoping
     no doubt for support from him.

81   Emlin, *A true narrative*, pp 23-31. Bishop Wethenhall of Kilmore visited
     him privately in jail and was friendly towards him (p. 29); 'Diary of John
     Cook', p. 11. Cook noted that the fine was reduced to between £60 and
     £70 after some time.

82   'Diary of John Cook', p. 10; D.N.B.

83   'Diary of John Cook', p. 10. Cook may have been suspected as sympathetic
     to Emlin, for he was passed over when Wood Street congregation asked
     for him to succeed Emlin as assistant to Boyse. Cook did not really want
     the appointment, considering the treatment Emlin had received. In any
     event, Richard Choppin was appointed in March 1703.

84   Emlin, *A true narrative*, Appendix, p. 66; Emlin recognised that Boyse was
     genuinely disturbed at his imprisonment and tried to help him then. Ibid.,
     pp 36, 40.

85   Thomas Hackett was Bishop of Down and Connor 1672-94 and for most
     of that time resided in London. Hackett was deprived in 1694, following
     examination by an ecclesiastical commission Bodl., Carte MS 40, f. 265;
     ibid., MS 220, f. 33; *Tanner Letters*, pp 465-6, 468, 486-8, 490; R.C.B, MS,
     Gg/2/7/3/27; Bodl., Rawlinson MS c 926; Lambeth Palace, Gibson Papers
     929, 946; B.L., Lansdowne MS 446; P.R.O., SP 63/256/29, 30, 32, 38,
     41 i-ii, 55 i; Robinson Library, Armagh, Dopping Papers, iii; Cotton, *Fasti*,
     iii, 208, 232; v, 235; i, 240, 466.

86   Emlin, *A true narrative*, p. 11.

87   Emlin, *Works* i, p. xlii.

88   Watts, *The dissenters*, pp 375-7.

89   David Berman, 'The Irish Counter-Enlightenment' in Richard Kearney
     (ed.), *The Irish mind* (Dublin, 1985), pp 121, 129, 137. In 1697 the 'Act for

effective suppression of blasphemy and profaneness' was passed. David Berman, *A history of atheism in Britain from Hobbes to Russell* (Croom Helm, 1988), p. 25.

90 Emlin, *A true narrative*, p. 58.

91 J[oseph] B[oyse], *The office of a scriptural bishop* (Dublin, 1709), p. 4. Boyse's argument here against bishops was basically what he had said in 1687: Christ never instituted diocesan bishops.

92 Ibid., p. 5ff. Neither were bishops fixed in geographical areas in New Testament times; thus no diocesan bishops were established at that time, or made any claims to authority; indeed, none of the Apostles ever made episcopal claims as such. The superiority of bishops over presbyters began early after the Apostles, when bishops in the large cities began to claim authority over lesser towns; this was a power struggle, not a question of a superior office or order in the church. As a human constitution, bishops of larger cities like Rome and Constantinople began to claim superintendence over several particular churches. Damage was really wrought when these bishops began to turn several churches into one church governed by a bishop, something not in the gospels and not intended by Christ.

93 Boyse, *The office of a scriptural bishop*, pp 13-17.

94 Ibid., p. 18.

95 Edward Drury, *A discourse occassioned by Mr Boyse's ordination sermon, entitled 'The office of a scriptural bishop'* (Dublin, 1709). Cotton, *Fasti*, ii, 163, 154, 143. Two other Established Church ministers replied to Boyse in the same year: Matthew French, *An answer to Joseph Boyse's ordination sermon entitled 'The office of scriptural bishop' and to its appendix* (Dublin, 1709) (see Cotton, *Fasti*, iii, 267; v, 247); [Charles Whittingham], *Remarks upon some passages in Mr Boyse's sermons, vol i, more particularly in the preface and the last sermon entitled 'The office of a scriptural bishop'* (Dublin, 1709) (see Cotton, *Fasti*, ii, 130, 154).

96 John Campbell, *Mr Campbell's letter to a parishioner* (Belfast, 1711). Campbell was an Established Church minister at Killead in Connor and Sego in Dromore. Cotton, *Fasti*, iii, 104, 106; N.L.S., Pamphlets, 2/97, No. 4.

97 Thomas Gowan, *The power of presbyters in ordination and church government without a superior asserted and proved from holy scripture* (n.p., 1711); McConnell, *Fasti*, no. 64, p. 37; no. 186, p. 78; no. 270, p. 103; Witherow, *Historical memorials*, pp 217-20.

98 Gowan, *The power of presbyters*, p. 40.

99 William Tisdall, *The nature and tendency of popular phrases in general* (n.p., 1713) pp 19-20.

100 'Sermon XXXVI, preached at the ordination of Rev. Mr John Leland, 1716 in Boyse, *Works*, i, 419

3

Independents in Ireland, 1651 – 1714

Once you leave the rule of the Word, the will of God revealed
there, and begin in a way of superstition, you will never know
where to stop or stay.
  Samuel Mather, *The figures or types of the Old Testament* (1683)

During the Interregnum Independent ministers came with
the Cromwellian army to Ireland[1] and by 1651 there were
two Independent congregations in Dublin, one in the parish of
St Nicholas-within-the-Walls and the other in Christ Church.
Samuel Winter, minister at St Nicholas, came to Ireland as
chaplain to the parliamentary commissioners. He was appointed
Provost of Trinity College, Dublin, in 1652 and held that position until 1660. His congregation tended to attract civilians, and
his practice of requiring a signed covenant for admission of new
members was modelled on that of New England.[2] On the other
hand, John Rogers, sent to Ireland by parliament in 1650,
preached in Christ Church and drew Cromwellian army officers
to his services. Rogers required a declaration of conversion and
faith, either through the medium of dreams, inner experiences
or sermons heard which confirmed their conviction of election.
Signature of a covenant was optional.[3]

While Rogers's congregation was dissolved in 1652-3 as a result of conflict with the Baptists,[4] that of Samuel Winter in St Nicholas continued, and in 1654 he was joined by Samuel Mather, who was appointed that year to attend Henry Cromwell in Ireland.[5] Born in England but educated in New England, Mather was ordained in St Nicholas's church in 1656 by Winter, Timothy Taylor of Carrickfergus and Thomas Jenner of Drogheda.[6] He was made a senior fellow of Trinity College and co-pastor with Winter in St Nicholas's parish, though he preached every six weeks in Christ Church. Mather was also a commissioner for the approbation of ministers in Cork in August 1655 and so he enjoyed a strong position in church affairs. Yet while convinced of his own way, Mather did not assume an aggressive stance towards other religious groups. When Cromwell asked him to displace Episcopalian ministers Mather refused to do so, saying he was sent to preach the gospel but not to hinder others from so doing.[7]

Although Independents and English Presbyterians worked together in the early period of the Interregnum,[8] the power and influence of the Independent ministers began to weaken from the time Henry Cromwell effectively replaced Fleetwood as chief governor in 1655. Cromwell wanted to develop a wider, more comprehensive church and so favoured Scottish and English Presbyterians, thereby undermining the power of the Independents.[9] In reaction to this and to the attitudes of their colleagues in ministry in England,[10] the Independent churches in Dublin and Leinster, under the leadership of Winter, published an *Agreement and resolution* establishing their own forms of discipline and order in February 1659.[11] They saw themselves as an association of ministers in the Dublin/Leinster area, and they defined the form of church order and discipline needed to live in the midst of many enemies: Popery, Prelacy, Arminianism, Socianism, Seekerism, Quakerism, Antiscripturism and Erastianism.[12] They opposed Popery and Prelacy in particular:[13]

> not only as it is described in the Solemn League and Covenant but also as it is cried up by some in these days under the specious disguise of moderated, regulated or primitive episcopacy, and all the inventions of man tending thereunto.[13]

This was an obvious rejection of Scottish Presbyterians and of Worth and the association of ministers in Cork. To survive in the midst of these and to counteract their influences, family worship was advocated in detail. This included reading of the scriptures, prayer, singing of psalms, repetition of sermons and observance of the Sabbath. The ministers underlined the need for catechising according to the shorter or larger catechism, though ministers were free to use a different text if they wished. In this way the basic tenets of faith were passed on. The Directory of Worship of 1646 was to be used for worship.[14]

Discipline and order was to be observed; those who failed to do so would be excommunicated, though they could be re-admitted on repentance. The offices of pastors and teachers, as well as those of ruling elders and deacons, were described in detail. Pastors and elders were called to ministry by the people and were to be prepared properly before ordination or appointment. A general meeting, or assembly, was to be established for the sake of unity and to resolve differences. Meetings were to be called in the city, county and province which would be attended by ministers and elders. At the first general meeting a moderator would to be chosen, as well as a registrar to keep the minutes and records. All affairs were to be kept confidential, and members were to have no involvement in civil and commonwealth affairs. Such a statement indicated how radically changed their position had become; it also introduced a note of realism which ensured survival in what emerged as a reversal of fortunes.[15]

These structures provided a framework for the Independent churches in Ireland for the rest of the century. The *Agreement and resolution* did not initiate anything that had not been tried and lived out in Dublin and in some other parts of Ireland.[16] It was a reflection of lived experience written when the Independents had gradually lost power and influence in Ireland. The *Agreement* tacitly recognised this, and the Independents saw themselves as the elect of God living in the midst of enemies, needing to support one another in order to survive. The Restoration interrupted this process for a time, but enough had been articulated to allow the Independents to continue and consolidate what had been expressed in the *Agreement* of 1659.

The Independent church at New Row in Dublin was founded when both Samuel Winter and Samuel Mather were deposed for nonconformity in 1661 and were forced to withdraw from St Nicholas-within-the-Walls.[17] Although Winter and Mather had to leave Ireland in 1661, Mather was able to return soon after and held meetings in his house in Dublin until New Row meeting-house was ready. Mather was disenchanted at the Restoration and expressed his disapproval of both restored episcopacy and the Book of Common Prayer, seeing in them the influence of Rome. The vehemence of his preaching caused Lord Justice Mountrath to forbid him to preach in October 1660. He was told to hand in his sermon notes, which he refused to do.[18] At this point he left Ireland for some time, but by 1664 had returned; in that year he was interrupted while preaching in Dublin and sent to prison for a short period.[19] Mather's sermon notes were published after his death by Nathaniel Mather, his brother, who succeeded him in New Row, and no doubt these were the substance of what Mather preached in the early days of the Restoration.[20]

Despite his initial aggressive stance, Mather settled into leading the congregation at New Row. Membership of that church was permitted according to the criteria laid down during the Interregnum. According to the practice of Samuel Winter in St Nicholas-within-the-Walls, all members were required to sign a covenant. This was a New England practice, and one no doubt followed by Mather too, for there was constant exchange and correspondence between ministers at this time. In 1662 the New England synod affirmed the permanent and personal membership of children baptised in the church, and of their right in turn to have their children baptised too. Voting in church matters and admittance to the Lord's Supper was reserved to the regenerate. This arrangement was known as the Half-Way Covenant, and it served to prevent decline in membership.[21]

John Rogers defined an Independent church very clearly in 1653, and gave a detailed description on how to form such a church and provide for the admission of new members. This was a format for the admission of adult members and did not envisage then the question of admitting children to the church.[22]

However, Rogers's church had dissolved during the Interregnum before development in thinking could take place. In any event, by 1665 it was clear that New Row followed the consensus reached in New England. In a document entitled *Irenicum*, 'an essay for godly union', Samuel Mather referred to the Independent practice of admitting 'such parents as besides the profession of Christian faith walk without offence and so are judged worthy of the Lord's Supper, and their children'.[23]

Nathaniel Mather published a larger collection of his brother's sermons in 1683,[24] and through them the essential traits of the Independent church in Dublin under his leadership can be gleaned. No doubt this reflected continuity from the Interregnum period into the new experience of being fully nonconformist.[25] In keeping with the theology of particular churches, Mather taught that hierarchy of any kind was contrary to the gospel:

> For one gospel minister to claim a supremacy of jurisdiction over another gospel minister, within his own charge and congregation, this is that for which we justly call the Pope Antichrist.[26]

This, of course, was aimed not just against the Roman Catholics but also against the Established Church, and even the Presbyterian churches of the English and Scottish tradition, if to a lesser degree. They all had forms of church government and jurisdiction that expressed hierarchy and dependence. In contrast to this, the congregational churches stood alone and governed themselves as a single, gathered church of Christ. Mather was particularly hard on the Established Church:

> There is a mongrel generation risen up, whom some have justly called Calvino-Papistas, Calvinian Papists, who are for the protestant doctrine and for popish worship. I refer it to everyone's conscience to judge whether it may not be fitly applied to our late innovators, who are for a 'linsey-woolsey' religion, a mixture of sound and wholesome doctrine with anti-christian popish worship. The wine is mixed with water. The protestant faith with popish ceremonies and superstitions.[27]

Such human ceremonies were opposed to divine ceremonies, and Mather saw the former as full of darkness, as 'the imps of Antichrist'.[28]

In the course of his sermons Mather outlined the discipline

of the gathered or congregational churches, based to a large extent on the 1659 *Agreement*. For example, the process of excommunication indicated the standards expected in an Independent
church. For private scandals suspension was imposed on the of-
fending party. This involved a temporary banning from church,
from the sacraments and from voting, though technically the person remained a member of the church. Full and immediate excommunication was imposed for public offences such as sexual
licence and incest.[29] The elders of the church played a significant role in the process. While the minister told the congregation 'what God would have them to do', it was the elders who
actually excommunicated the offenders. 'Somebody must do it,
and who better than the officers who have the government of
the church in their hands?' The congregation was expected to
shun the company of the excommunicated, and the leaders ensured that this was observed.[30] If a congregation became lax or
corrupt, the minister might have

> to close with the lesser but sounder part of the people. And this is the
> remedy that all godly ministers generally have taken: they have left out
> the ignorant and profane parts of the parish from the sacraments, especially
> the Lord's Supper.[31]

In his desire to have a fully regenerated church, Mather regretted that the early reformers had not totally abolished all
popish things, for in his view many divisions and conflicts could
have been avoided had this been done. Instead the Restoration
revived holy days, music in church and vestments at a time when
they had begun to disappear from church practice. No wonder
he was disappointed when episcopacy was restored in 1660; it
must have seemed a backward step. Yet Mather held that tithes
in some form were necessary and that Parliament should settle
this by law, an impossible demand in the context of the Restoration in Ireland.[32]

The discipline and church order observed in New Row congregational church in Dublin after the Restoration was very much
in line with the 1659 *Agreement*. It also survived its critics, notably
Samuel Coxe, who preached two sermons to the Dublin Convention, one in March and the other in May 1660.[33] Speaking
from within the English Presbyterian tradition, Coxe declared:

> The Anabaptists, the Quakers and even all those that have separated
> from the church of Christ in these nations have so interrupted our
> counsels, disturbed our Parliament and supplanted our laws and birth
> privileges. . . . I desire this, that none be permitted to gather churches
> (as they call them) out of our parochial congregations or to exercise acts
> pertaining to church government in any of their private meetings.[34]

While Coxe's criticisms were aimed at all types of separatists, the Independent tradition was included in his condemnation. He hoped for a presbyterian form of church settlement and saw the congregational way as fragmenting church presence and effectiveness. Ormond saw it differently and perhaps from a more pragmatic point of view. He proposed to give 'congregational men some more indulgence than the law does'. This was to encourage nonconformists in England to come to Ireland with their trade and stocks and so help to build and sustain the economy. Clear guidelines were issued whereby those who came had to profess full acceptance of the doctrine of the Established Church and the authority of the king and in return were freed from the penalties of the Act of Uniformity. They were allowed to exercise freedom of conscience, to build their own churches and have their own meetings as long as the bishop was informed and they met during the daytime. They could elect their own ministers and support them, though they were also obliged to pay the usual tithes in the parish. A register was to be established by the bishop and everyone over sixteen years of age was to be listed in it; those listed were required to sign an agreement to keep the peace and take the Oath of Abjuration.[35]

This arrangement gave Independents the possibility of settling down in Ireland with the assurance that they could worship in peace. This was conditional on their observing the guidelines given them; any hint of non-observance was therefore treated with suspicion. They had no legal guarantee of religious freedom and no protection from the law; it was toleration in return for peaceful behaviour, and there were many who even then believed they were not to be trusted. It was important for their survival and freedom that the Independent churches should avoid any hint of unrest or disquiet.[38]

In this context the crisis caused in New Row congregation in

1669 by the preaching of Jeremiah Marsden needed to be dealt
with quickly in order to protect both ministers and congregation.[37] In the hearing of friends and enemies Marsden had
omitted to pray for the king and had referred to all ceremonies
as contact with Satan's throne. This was inflammatory, and on
the day after the sermon Mather spoke to Marsden and told him
that 'the godly ministers that walk with this church together with
the elders and deacons desired a meeting within a week'. Marsden
never came to the meeting, so two votes were passed:

> The one concerning your sister, declaring her a non member (which
> I have given her in a letter to her dated Nov. 10 1669). And the other
> concerning yourself, viz. that this church declared its disapproval of those
> reflections and offensive passages to the civil authority in our brother
> Marsden's late prayer and sermon.[38]

Mather refuted the millenarian interpretation that Marsden
had adopted when preaching on the text Revelation 2. 13, which
conjured up memories of the Fifth Monarchists and the turmoil
of the civil war. Marsden's views had given real offence to the
magistrates and civil authorities in Dublin. While Mather agreed
with Marsden in substance, he could not accept his manner of
expression, which was too extreme. In fact Mather had gone to
jail for similar views nine or ten years earlier: 'Nor do I disown
the sober notion of the Fifth Monarchy but have preached it.'[39]
But Marsden wanted to pull down the magistrates and preach
the Fifth Monarchy, and he called the king a ruler of Sodom
and Gommorah. Mather made it clear that now he held that
good laws and good magistrates were in fact signs of the Fifth
Monarchy. He reminded Marsden that the scriptures called all
to pray for the king and magistrates. And while he accepted that
the sacraments, church ordinances and the power of the keys had
been abused, yet for all that the legal powers of magistrates were
not rendered invalid. The king had been restored against both
their wishes, but it had happened and they should accept this
as the reality of the situation and not dream of other times.[40]
In time all their hopes would be realised, 'by God's Providence'.
Mather's views so expressed indicated a marked difference in
tone and indeed a neutering of radical thought. No longer

aspiring to be an agent of change, Mather had compromised his more extreme views in order to survive.

Marsden's sermon put the church under suspicion. It was reported that he had preached against the king in Mather's house, and people in high office in Dublin expressed surprise that this should be tolerated by Mather. As a result, Mather's meetings were stopped and he was threatened with prison. There was a rumour that letters were sent to the king about it. This was serious, for, as Mather explained to Marsden, over the years the king had been generous with 'peaceable nonconformists' and especially with Mather himself; the church had been left in peace to operate its own institutions, exercise church discipline, ordain and excommunicate, and sing psalms during the Lord's Supper. In other words, they had a lot of freedom to worship as they wished.

Mather reminded Marsden that Dr Harrison, minister at Cooke Street, had warned him:

> When you first came over you told me Dr Harrison sent this message by you to your sister: Remember me to your sister and tell her I hear she is breaking off from the church. Tell her it is not good to walk alone. I hear the reason of her breaking off is because Mr Taylor and Mr Mather used to pray for the King . . . tell her that will do us no hurt'.[41]

Despite this, Marsden and his sister had brought the church into disrepute and put in jeopardy the religious liberty they had 'in Dublin in great measure now these nine years'.[42]

Nevertheless, the religious liberty enjoyed by Independents was not damaged by the Marsden affair. In fact there was an influx of dissenting ministers from England in the following year in the wake of the Conventicle Acts.[43] In any event, the overall number of Independents in Ireland was too small to warrant suppression. In 1695 Joseph Boyse stated there were only six congregations in the country.[44] These were: New Row in Dublin, Limerick, Carlow, Cork, Wexford and Tipperary. While James Wood in 1680 could say that 'God has blessed some of you with large flocks',[45] both Nathaniel Mather and John Baily were both lamenting how few they were in numbers.[46] When Baily was imprisoned in Limerick in 1683 he preached to one-seventh of his congregation each day; his total congregation must have been no more than 100, given that a large number of people would not have been tolerated in prison rooms.[47] The New Row baptismal register, covering the period 1653-1737, provides the most accurate information concerning the numbers of that congregation in Dublin:

	Baptisms	Parents	Totals
1653-61	33	55	88
1662-70	36	59	95
1671-78	67	104	171
1679-82	70	125	195
1683-88	82	134	216
1689-95	64	98	162
1696-1700	99	129	228
1701-05	94	125	219
1733	1	1	2

Thus at its height New Row could have had around 1,000 baptised members, given that the number of children in families tended to be 5.4.[48] But this seems to have been the largest of the Independent congregations in Ireland;[49] the others were probably very much smaller, comprising families who had come to Ireland in Cromwellian times and who remained loyal to their own tradition.[50]

Indeed, after the Restoration the Independent tradition enjoyed a degree of freedom in Ireland which its counterpart in England envied. When Faithful Teate died in Dublin in 1666 there were huge numbers at his funeral, including the Lord Mayor and aldermen and many of all ranks of society, about three thousand in all.[51] Whatever about their past, the Independents after 1660 in Ireland were not seen as a great threat to the government, particularly as they were single gathered congregations and not bound to others in any organisational way. As Toby Bonnell wrote from Ireland to John Strype,

> Our non-conformists I hear make a shift to meet privately oft and that quietly . . . ours it seems are not troublesome nor quarrelsome as those of Scotland lately were, which also makes our bishops connive the more.[52]

So Mather ministered unhindered in New Row, except for the period immediately after the Restoration and when Marsden threatened to preach up the Fifth Monarchy. At this time no dissenting church could afford to have fanatics or disruptive elements within its congregation. There was in fact no Fifth Monarchy movement in Ireland at this time which Marsden could have represented, but to even evoke the old fears and memories was danger enough. Mather seems to have calmed the situation, and nothing came of the threats to his congregation.

Mather's leadership in Dublin was a focus for unity, and it is clear that he tried to reconcile differences between the Independents, Presbyterians and Baptists.[53] In his *Irenicum* Mather affirmed the common ground between the three traditions: the Westminister Confession, prayer, preaching the Word, the Sabbath. Indeed, commenting on the Sabbath, Mather wrote:

> There is no scruple made of joining together in prayer and preaching and hearing one another, which accordingly is ordinarily practised amongst us in this city . . . for it was a thing much scrupled at in the former age before the late reformation by some whose name and sect have disappeared, being worn out by the further progress of the light and work of Christ amongst us.[54]

In the difficult area of church order and worship, Mather found uniting principles: the rule of scripture; ministry and ordinances appointed by Christ; careful admission to the Lord's Supper; rejection of episcopacy and the ceremonies of the Established Church. Even then he noted that they did not reject individual members of the Established Church. However, he recognised that they differed on the issue of the universal, visible church, for Presbyterians denied the validity of particular churches; they also diverged on whether ordination was for a definite congregation or 'sine titulo'; and there were differing views on the function and authority of elders and of the presbytery.[55] The question of baptism remained crucial, and Mather had to admit that reconciliation of views was most difficult with regard to it. Baptists held to adult baptism; Presbyterians administered baptism to all 'who profess the Christian religion and their children', while Independents added 'and are worthy of the Lord's Supper'. Mather recognised that while there was some ground for meeting

Presbyterian views, there was none for accommodation with the Baptists.

Changing his focus, Mather suggested that union and communion in Christ be the source of their unity, and within that perspective he proposed that they accept one another as true ministers of the gospel, help one another in ministry, and receive approved members of each church to the Lord's Supper. It was the basis for some common vision and shared communion, since they were in 'a suffering condition together, under the pressures and yokes of men upon their consciences'.[56]

However by 1668, on Mather's own admission, the pressure on their consciences was light. He wrote to his father:

> If any had told me in April 1660 that I should have exercised the liberty of my ministry and conscience, either in England or Ireland, and that without conforming to the corruption of the times, and this for seven or eight years together, I should not have believed it; I should have thought it next to an impossibility.[57]

Indeed, he wrote the same to Marsden in the following year:

> He [the king] has suffered this church to practise all the ordinances and to observe all the institutions of Jesus Christ . . . even church discipline and excommunication, yea the singing of psalms . . . this church has ever practised it, whensoever they celebrated the supper of the Lord, which . . . they did, even when things were at the worse, they have always concluded with the singing of a psalm, though it did expose them and their meeting to the more observation.[58]

Mather recognised that at least they had Protestant rule in the country and were allowed freedom of worship. The ideal for Mather would have been the purity and simplicity of the gospel, 'when the Lamb shall overcome the Beast' and all would be in the 'Kingdom of Christ in the 1000 years'.[59] The future looked promising, especially with the arrival of several dissenting ministers from England in 1670; so many came to Dublin that they had to be dispersed throughout the country.[60] But this did not last long, and by 1684 the situation had changed, at least for the Independents.

In that year John Baily, Independent minister at Limerick, noted that his church was in decline. The immediate reason was his imprisonment in Limerick since 1683 which led to his exile in 1684. Baily recognised that unless 'some godly young man might be had, whose charge is small and might be less taken notice of than I was', the church in Limerick would fail. From at least 1682 some of his congregation began leaving for New England, and Baily felt they had lost enthusiasm for and commitment to the church.[61]

The hazard for Independent churches, in terms of their future, was their particularity precisely as single, gathered churches. They had no formal, organisational links such as existed within the Scottish or English Presbyterian churches. This would have been alien to their theology and practice, for they were gathered churches, single congregations, having bonds of friendship with other churches but nothing more. In the absence of records, it can be surmised that such isolation contributed to their decline in Ireland. Moreover, there was no provision for training second-generation ministers for their churches. While congregations might hope for 'some godly young man', without definite planning for and training of future ministers, continued leadership could not be ensured. As Baily said,

> Could we but procure a magistracy . . . and a ministry, I know none
> might compare with us . . . Ireland has but few [ministers] it being but
> a planting, as it were, in that respect, though the north is very full.[62]

As it was, Baily could only exhort his congregation to live well, meet together and 'make your calling and election sure'. Their own theology worked against them; too much independence led to dispersion:

> I advise you not to be strangers one to another; this has been an old
> fault all along.[63]

To leave Limerick was not an easy decision, for Baily knew that his departure put the future of the church there in question.[64] Strictly speaking a congregation did not require a minister in order to be a church, but this situation was different in that the Limerick congregation was losing a minister and had little hope of another. This was important only if they wished to go into the future, since the theology and practice of the single, gathered church were directed towards immediate needs of a congregation, rather than planned for a permanent future.

In 1682 Nathaniel Mather wrote to Increase Mather:

> My maintenance falls short of what it was formerly and I fear is like
> to decrease. Few are added to us and the Devil has has stirred unhappy
> instruments, both to beget prejudices against us and sow ill seeds of
> dissatisfaction among us. . . . The Lord guide and help us.[65]

Evidently New Row church was in difficulty, and it was a significant admission on Mather's part in 1687 when he declared:

> I have long, and am still of opinion that it is as good for Protestants
> that are cordially so, to live under wise and just Popish governors as
> such Protestants as we have had many.[66]

This admission from within the Independent tradition was a
measure of the change that had occurred. Yet both the 1659 *Agreement and Resolution* and Samuel Mather in 1669 indicated a withdrawal of Independents from the political stage:

> We must wait on the Lord's time for it and keep His way, and in the
> meantime submit to his wise and holy Providence. . . . God has ways
> enough for the safety of his people besides that of making saintship a
> title to government. . . . For what is Antichrist but a minister intruding
> into the work of a magistrate?[67]

This attitude, unthinkable in the 1650s, indicated acceptance of
their inability as a church to influence political events. To try
to do so was to act as Antichrist. Strong words indeed, but they
were an adaptation to reality and a recognition of the need to
find ways to live within it. As the century wore on, it became
more and more difficult for the Independent churches to survive financially. Because of this it was hard to attract and maintain second-generation ministers and congregations, though the
establishment of the General Fund in 1710 ensured that some
resources were available for the future. Contrary to Wood Street
and Cooke Street churches, New Row does not seem to have been
wealthy; indeed, Nathaniel Mather complained of poor maintenance. Such a position, in the context of greater wealth and influence in the other Dublin churches, was potentially divisive,
something hinted at by Mather in 1682.[68] However, such a
situation was averted by the manner in which the General Fund
was organised and distributed.

Such co-operation became possible because Independents and

Presbyterians, both Scottish and English, had been co-operating with one another since the Restoration. And although English Presbyterians, in theory at least, and Scottish Presbyterians in practice, had a stronger sense and different understanding of ministerial association than the Independents, the three traditions worked together out of necessity and the need to survive. This was the communion that Mather had advocated in his *Irenicum*.[69] It was essential that the churches in Ireland act as a body and that disputes did not emerge publicly. There is evidence that some tensions between the English Presbyterians and the Independents lay below the surface and could not find expression in Dublin.[70]

However, this changed when Daniel Williams and Nathaniel Mather moved to London after 1687. Both Williams and Mather were candidates in 1688 for the ministry at Lime Street congregational church in London. The members of the church were hesitant about Williams's candidacy, even though he declared his acceptance of particular, organised churches, stating that such 'are the proper seat and subject of gospel ordinances'; that they had power within themselves for their own government, without any outside jurisdiction; 'that visible saintship is the qualification of adult members'; that synods were for unity, not government; and that the consent of the church was required for admission to membership and for censures. Williams also promised not to change 'the practice of this church'.[71]

In the event, Lime Street congregation appointed Nathaniel Mather, for 'we think a Presbyterian minister an unsuitable officer to a congregational people', though it was hoped that Williams could be an occasional preacher in the church.[72] Tensions did not rest there, and soon Mather and Williams clashed on the issue of predestination. With the movement towards some form of centralisation and proposed accommodation, especially in London, Independents and Presbyterians were bound to be at variance. This could not have happened in Ireland, especially in Dublin, for both traditions could not afford to entertain public disputes there. Indeed, it was Williams who helped keep the peace between the Scottish Presbyterians of Newmarket and Capel Street.[73] It is interesting that both Mather and Williams, who had spent a long period in Ireland, only contended in public when they had moved to London. There they had wider scope and the issue of the 1691 Heads of Agreement to grapple with, and a different context within which to debate.[74]

From the time of Henry Cromwell's arrival in Ireland the fortunes of the Independent churches changed. Cromwell's policy of widening the basis of church government to include Scottish and English Presbyterians robbed the Independents of their special status. And although Cromwell did not intend to suppress the Independents entirely, his policy in effect reduced their influence and power in the country. From 1660 onwards the Independent churches in Ireland, mainly through the leadership of the ministers at New Row, particularly Samuel Mather, survived and retained their particular theology. In addition to New Row, there was an Independent congregation in Limerick; Gideon Jacque was minister to an Independent congregation in Wexford; James Wood ran a school in Tipperary and presumably had a congregation there; another Independent, Thomas Jenner wrote his work against the Quakers while 'living in Carlow in Ireland'.[75] Because they were so few and therefore not a political threat, these churches were left unhindered except in a time of political crisis, as in 1682–3. Even then they acceded to Archbishop Francis Marsh's request that they meet at home and not in their churches. Their need to survive and present a common front in Ireland helped to prevent controversy splitting the Independents and Presbyterians. It also provided the basis for a sharing of financial resources which guaranteed their futures.

Notes and References

1   Independent ministers in Ireland numbered about thirty, most of them settled in garrison towns. Seymour lists thirty-one Independent ministers; however, some of them were closer to English Presbyterianism. Religious boundaries and affiliations were very fluid at this time. Seymour, *The Puritans in Ireland*, pp 206–24.

2   [John Weaver], *The life and death of Dr Samuel Winter* (London, 1671); William Urwick, *Independency in Dublin of the olden time* (Dublin, 1862), pp 10–11; New Row Baptismal Register, 1653–1737; St John D. Seymour, *Samuel Winter* (Dublin, 1941); Armstrong, *Summary history of the Presbyterian Church*, pp 78–80;

The register of Provost Winter, 1654-57, ed. H. J. Lawlor (Exeter/London, 1907); R. L. Greaves and Robert Zaller, *Biographical Dictionary of British radicals in the seventeenth century,* 3 vols (London, 1982-4), iii, 333. Edward Wale also implemented the same form of covenant practice in Waterford. Edward Wale to Henry Cromwell, [Nov.] 1658, (B.L., Lansdowne MS 823, ff 134-6.

3   Urwick, *Independency in Dublin,* pp 10-11. Rogers published the 'Covenant of the Church in Dublin'. John Rogers, *Ohel or Beth-shemesh* (London, 1653), Bk II, Ch. 7, pp 459-61: 'The Covenant of the Church in Dublin collected out of the word of Christ according to the order of the Gospel'. This was a format for the admission of adult members and did not envisage then the question of admitting children to the church. For Rogers see Edward Rogers, *Life and opinions of a Fifth Monarchy Man* (London, 1867), pp 27-37, 57-74; P. G. Rogers, *The Fifth Monarchy Men* (London, 1966), pp 20-7, 34-5, 43-55, 54-57, 63-67; Charles Lloyd Cohen, *God's caress: the psychology of human experience* (Oxford/New York, 1986), pp 139-40, 145, 152, 157, 159.

4   Seymour, *The Puritans in Ireland,* pp 22-4, 59. The Baptists opened a meeting-house in Swift's Alley in Dublin in 1653.

5   Mather was born in Lancashire in 1625; his family went to New England in 1634, and Mather graduated from Harvard in 1643. He returned to England and ministered in Oxford and Leith and then came to Dublin in 1654. Greaves and Zaller, *Biographical Dictionary,* ii, 228; D.N.B.; R.C.B., Seymour MS, p. 41; Bodl., Carte MS 45, f. 277; Armstrong, *Summary history of the Presbyterian Church,* p. 79; Urwick, *Independency in Dublin,* pp 16, 23; Urwick, *Early history of Trinity College,* p. 77; Barnard, *Cromwellian Ireland,* p. 149; A. G. Matthews, *Calamy revised* (Oxford, 1934), p. 344; Commonwealth State accounts, *Anal. Hib.,* no. 15 (1944), p. 295; Cotton Mather, *Magnalia Christi Americana,* 2 vols (Hartford, 1853), ii, 39ff; New Row Baptismal Register, ff 1-3.

6   Taylor was a Presbyterian and became an Independent. He occupied the former rector's residence in Carrickfergus. He was one of the examiners for ministers appointed in 1655. In the years 1668-81 he ministered in New Row, Dublin. Armstrong, *Summary history of the Presbyterian Church,* p. 80; Anthony Wood, *Athenae Oxonienses,* ed. Philip Bliss, 4 vols (London, 1813- 20), ii, A1, 682; Reid, *History of the Presbyterian Church,* ii, 213, notes 20-2; Bodl., Carte MS 221, f. 79; B.L., Lansdowne MS 823, ff 73,780; Thomas Birch (ed.), *A collection of the state papers of John Thurloe,* 7 vols, (London, 1742), iv, 287; Seymour, *The Puritans in Ireland,* pp 24, 57, 72-5, 91-2, 97, 100, 126, 138, 192. Thomas Jenner was educated at Christ's College, Cambridge, and was minister of Horstead and Coltishall in Norfolk before going to New England. From there he went to Ireland, first to Drogheda and later to Carlow. B.L., Lansdowne MS 821, f. 200. In 1670 he wrote a tract against the Quakers in Ireland, *Quakerism anatomised and confuted* (n.p., 1670). G. F. Nuttall, *Visible saints,* (Oxford, 1957), pp 30-1.

7   Seymour, *The Puritans in Ireland,* p. 91.

8   Richard Baxter, *Reliquae Baxterianae,* ed. Matthew Sylvester (London, 1696), pt ii, 169-171.

9   Barnard, *Cromwellian Ireland*, pp 112-17; Reid, *History of the Presbyterian Church*, ii, 560-2. See the signatures to the 1658 address of the ministers to Henry Cromwell (B.L., Lansdowne MS, 1228, f. 14). In this address it is evident that both Samuel Winter and Edward Wale were reluctant signatories; they indicated this by signing separately from the body of ministers and with a heading 'For the substance of the matter I subscribe to the premises'.

10 Ibid, p. 128.

11 *The agreement and resolution of the ministers of Christ associated within the city of Dublin and province of Leinster* (Dublin, 1659).

12 Ibid., p. 2.

13 Ibid., p. 3.

14 Ibid., pp 5-8.

15 Ibid., pp 9-12.

16 Edward Wale to Henry Cromwell, Oct. 1658 (B.L., Lansdowne MS 823, ff 134-6).

17 New Row boasted that it had never known division because they did not 'impose human inventions' and 'stuck to the Bible alone', keeping respect for each others religious rights. Armstrong, *Summary history of the Presbyterian Church*, pp 21-2.

18 Samuel Mather, *A testimony from the scripture against idolatry and superstition, in two sermons . . . The first witnessing in general against all the idols and inventions of men in the worship of God, the second more particularly against the ceremonies and some other corruptions of the Church of England. Preached the one Sept. 27, the other Sept. 30, 1660* (Dublin, 1672).

19 Seymour, *The Puritans in Ireland*, pp 90, 141; Urwick, *The early history of Trinity College, Dublin*, pp 41-6; Mountrath and Bury to Secretary Nicholas, 4 Oct. 1660 (*Cal. S.P. Ire., 1660-2*, p. 41); Edmund Calamy, *An historical account of my own life,* 2 vols (London, 1830), ii, 415-19.

20 [Samuel Mather] *A defence of the Protestant religion against popery, in answer to a discourse of a Roman Catholic. By an English Protestant* (n.p., 1672). The advertisement was signed by Mather: Dublin, July 31 1670.

21 Certainly children were baptised in New Row church from 1653 (New Row Baptismal Register); E. Brooks Holifield, *The Covenant sealed* (Yale, 1974), pp 169-71, 196.

22 Rogers, *Ohel or Beth-shemesh*, pp 137, 239ff; Rogers, *Life and opinions of a Fifth Monarchy Man*, pp 63-7. Rogers also taught that women should have voting and decision making rights in the church.

23 Samuel Mather, *Irenicum, or an essay for godly union wherein are humbly tendered some proposals in order to some union among the godly of different judgements* (London, 1680); pp 14-16. For the contacts between the two countries see 'The Mather Papers' in *Collections of the Massachusetts Historical Society*, viii, 4th series (Boston, 1868). Winter was influenced by John Cotton in New England. Greaves and Zaller, *Biographical dictionary*, iii, 333. Edward Wale in Waterford had strict conditions for reception into his congregation (*c.* 1658) (B.L., Lansdowne MS 823, ff 134-6); Urwick, *Independency in Dublin*, pp 11-12.

24   Mather preached two sermons on Sundays from 8 a.m. to noon and from 2 p.m. to 5 p.m.; he also preached on Thursdays from 2 p.m. to 5 p.m. (Bodl., Carte MS 45, f. 277).

25   Samuel Mather, *The figures or types of the Old Testament, by which Christ and the heavenly things of the gospel were preached and shadowed to the people of God of old* (n.p., 1683).

26   Ibid., p. 189.

27   Ibid., p. 189.

28   Ibid., pp 189, 261ff, 352ff.

29   Ibid., pp 366-84: 'The gospel of the leprosy', 12 Apr., 1665.

30   Ibid., pp 381-2.

31   Ibid., p. 384.

32   Ibid., pp 440, 595, 612, 649-50, 673ff.

33   Samuel Coxe, *Two sermons preached at Christchurch Dublin beginning the General Convention of Ireland* (Dublin, 1660).

34   Ibid., pp 7, 25-6.

35   'Certain proposals humbly offered to the removal of such persons from England as by reasons of nonconformity there' (Bodl., Carte MS 45, ff 243, 275, 293, 288); Price to Bramhall, 5 July 1662. H.M.C., *Hastings MSS*, iv, 134.

36   Bodl., Carte MS 45, ff 286, 288.

37   Samuel Mather, 'A friendly consideration of some of the mistakes about the Fifth Monarchy, 12 Nov 1669, Dublin' (Bodl., Rawlinson MS, D 1347). Marsden with two of his brothers had come over to Ireland during the Interregnum. Barnard, *Cromwellian Ireland*, p. 140; Greaves and Zaller, *Biographical dictionary*, ii, 214-15. Marsden had been in Ireland in 1657-59, in Armagh and Clonmel; he maintained Fifth Monarchist views until his death in 1684 in Newgate. Walter Wilson, *The history and antiquities of dissenting churches and meeting-houses in Westminster and Southwark, including the lives of their ministers,* 4 vols (London, 1808-14), ii, 464-7; Calamy, *A continuation of the account*, ii, 942-5; Calamy, *An historical account*, ii, 796; B.S. Capp, *The Fifth Monarchy Men* (London, 1972), pp 210, 212, 218, 221.

38   Mather, 'A friendly consideration', f. 46.

39   Ibid., f. 54.

40   Ibid., ff 47-50. In 1659 Marsden was chaplain to the Fifth Monarchist, Col. Robert Overton. G. F. Nuttall, *Visible saints* (Oxford, 1957), p. 33; Ronald Hutton, *The Restoration: a political and religious history of England and Wales, 1658-1667* (Oxford, 1985), pp 32, 51, 74, 86, 98, 136. In 1663 Marsden was accused of complicity in the Yorkshire Plot of October 1663; both he and his brother Gamaliel refused to ask for licence in 1672, in accordance with the Declaration of Indulgence. R. Tudor Jones, *Congregationalism in England, 1662-1962* (London, 1962), pp 66, 92, 99-100. Marsden did not renounce his views. In 1684 Richard Baxter wrote a tract against Marsden: *The second part against the schism, being animadversions on a book famed to be Mr Ralphson's* (London, 1684). Ralphson was a pseudonym used by Marsden to avoid harassment. *Cat. S. P. dom., 1683,* 374, 375, 380; *1683-4,* 332, 335.

41   Mather, 'A friendly consideration', ff 51-2.

42 Ibid., f. 18. The sister referred to was probably Hester Marsden. She married John Murcot, who ministered in Ireland for a short period during the Interregnum and died in Dublin. On his death Hester Marsden received a grant of land in Co. Dublin. Seymour, *The Puritans in Ireland*, pp 69-70.

43 20 Aug. 1670 (Bodl., Carte MS 221, f. 174).

44 Joseph Boyse, *The case of the dissenting Protestants of Ireland in reference to a Bill of Indulgence vindicated from the exceptions alleged against it in a late answer* (Dublin, 1695), p. 2.

45 James Wood, *Shepardy spiritualised* (London, 1680), dedicatory.

46 Nathaniel Mather to Increase Mather, 9 Nov. 1682 ('The Mather Papers', p. 41; see also p. 54); Thomas Baily to Cotton Mather, 6 June 1683 (ibid., p. 491).

47 Cotton Mather, *The life and death of . . . John Baily* (Boston, 1698), p. 38.

48 Richard Vann and David Eversley, *Friends in life and death: the British and Irish Quakers in the demographic transition* (Cambridge, 1992), pp 240, 173. This study estimates that during this period Quakers in Ireland tended to have 5.4 children in their families.

49 On the 14 Sept., 1727, the *Dublin Gazette* announced: 'The Presbyterian meeting-house lying in New Row without New gate Dublin, with all the pews, seats and pulpit, as enjoyed by them lately, and in good order, fit for such a congregation, is to be let.'

50 A book of sermons composed by a Protestant clergymen resident at Youghal 1676-87 (N.L.I., MS 4201). This MS shows that an Independent minister preached in family houses during this period, in Bandon, Youghal and Mallow.

51 Bonnell to Strype, 23 Oct. 1666 (U.L.C., Baum. Papers, Add. 4, iii, pt i, f. 20); St John D. Seymour, 'Faithful Teate', in *R.S.A.I. Jn.*, 6th series, x (1920), pp 39-45; B.L., Add. MS 36792, f. 34; B.L., Add. MS 15669, f. 15; Bodl., Carte MS 328, f. 82; H.M.C., *Hastings* iv, p. 123.

52 Bonnell to Strype, 25 Dec. 1666 (U.L.C., Baum. Papers, Add. 1, f. 1). For Bonnell see William Hamilton, *The exemplary life of James Bonnell, Esq., late Accomptant General of Ireland* (London, 1707); H. R. McAdoo, 'The religion of a layman' in *Search: a journal of the Church of Ireland*, 14, no. 1 (spring, 1991), pp 36-43.

53 Mather, *Irenicum*; T. J. Holmes, *The minor Mathers* (Harvard, 1940), p. 154.

54 Mather, *Irenicum*, pp 2-4.

55 Ibid., pp 4-13.

56 Ibid., pp 16-18. Ministers from other churches performed baptisms in New Row (New Row Baptismal Register, ff 1, 7, 8, 11, 12, 20). They also performed exorcisms together in 1678. Richard Baxter, *The certainty of the world's spirits* (London, 1691), p. 218.

57 Cotton Mather, *Magnalia Christi Americana*, ii, 52.

58 Samuel Mather, 'A friendly consideration', f. 52.

59 Ibid., f. 53.

60 Bodl., Carte MS 221, f. 174.

61 John Baily, *To my loving and dearly beloved Christian Friends in and about Limerick, 8 May 1684* (n.p. 1684); 'The Mather Papers', p. 488. John Baily was born

in Chester in 1643 and ministered in Limerick from 1669 to 1683, when
he went to New England. He was offered a chaplaincy by Ormond, and
was promised a deanery or even a bishopric, which he refused. When
he was jailed for nonconformity in 1683 he divided his congregation into
seven groups; one group came daily to the jail for a sermon. He was released on condition he leave Ireland, which he did in May 1684. Cotton
Mather, *The life and death of . . . John Baily*, pp 33, 37-8; 'The Mather Papers',
pp 486-91; James Holmes, *Increase Mather: a bibliography of his works*, 2 vols
(Ohio, 1931), i, 142, n. 1.

62   Thomas Baily (brother of John) to Cotton Mather, 6 June 1683 ('The
     Mather Papers', p. 491).

63   Baily, *To my loving and dearly beloved Christian friends*, p. 34.

64   Ibid., p. 5: 'I have peace in what I have done, whatever constructions
     at home or abroad may be put upon it.' Nathaniel Mather did not sup-
     port such decisions, seeing them as desertion of the cause. David Cressy,
     *Coming over: migration and communication between England and New England in
     the seventeenth century* (Cambridge, 1987), p. 51.

65   Nathaniel Mather to Increase Mather, 7 Nov. 1682, ('The Mather Papers',
     pp 40-1). Mather's final remark could refer to the friction between Capel
     Street and Newmarket congregations in Dublin. However, in March of
     that year, Mather refused to baptise in private, indicating friction within
     his own church (New Row Baptismal Register, f. 7).

66   Mather to Richard Lobb, 26 Feb. 1687 ('The Mather Papers', p. 66).

67   Mather, 'A friendly consideration', ff 23, 49.

68   'The Mather Papers', pp 40-1. He could have been referring also to the
     tensions within Capel Street congregation which led to a rupture in 1683.

69   Certainly Emlin felt betrayed by his colleagues in Dublin and thought
     that Wood Street congregation began to decline from that time. Richard
     Choppin, preaching at Boyse's funeral in 1728, referred to 'this declin-
     ing congregation'. Emlin, *Works,* vol. i, p. xlii; Choppin, *A funeral sermon,*
     (Dublin, 1728), pp 12-13.

70   'The Mather Papers', p. 41.

71   Robert Browne to James Ball, 27 June 1688 (Dr Williams's Library MS
     24. 67, no. 2; see also no. 1).

72   June-July 1688 (ibid., MS 24. 67, nos 3-5); Wilson, *The history and anti-
     quities of dissenting churches,* i, 212-50.

73   Alexander Gordon (ed.), *Freedom after ejection: a review (1690-92) of Presbyterian
     and Congregational nonconformity in England and Wales* (Manchester, 1917), p. 384.

74   Daniel Williams, 'Man made righteous by Christs's obedience . . . also
     some remarks on Mr Mather's postscript' (1694) in Daniel Williams, *Prac-
     tical discourses,* 2 vols (London, 1738), pp 169-275. Nathaniel Mather, *The
     righteousness of God through faith upon all without difference who believe* (London,
     1694); John Howe to William Taylor 18 Aug. 1694 (Bodl., Carte MS 80,
     f. 584). For an account of the debate and its context see Watts, *The dissenters,*
     pp 289-97; C. G. Bolam, *The English Presbyterians* (London, 1968), pp 113-25.

75   Boyse, *The case of the dissenting Protestants of Ireland*, p. 2. McConnell, *Fasti,*
     no. 167, p. 69; Magee College MS 29, ff 395-401; Mathews, *An account*

of the trial of Emlin, p. 80; Laggan minutes, p. 328; Barnard, *Cromwellian Ireland,* p. 192, n. 39; R.D. Edwards, 'The history of the laws against Protestant nonconformity in Ireland from the Restoration (1660) to the Declaration of Indulgence (1687)' (M.A. thesis, U.C.D., 1932), p. 36; Thomas Jenner, *Quakerism anatomised and confuted* (n.p., 1670), title-page.

4

Quakers in Ireland, 1653 – 1714

It is clearly seen that many who pretend to a Reformation are
come no further . . . in practice are keeping up and making use
of the Pope's institutions . . . we . . . bear our testimony against
them and their tithes . . . though it be through great sufferings.
            William Stockdale, *Great cry of oppression* . . . (1681)

George Fox and his companions began preaching in rural
areas of north England in 1652 and gradually moved south-
wards, increasing in numbers and impact.[1] They became
known as Quakers, a term of derision, and by 1655 were a force
to be reckoned with in England. In the disturbed and restless
society of this period, Quakers attracted people who were searching for ways to understand both their own lives and the events
happening all round them. Indeed, Quakers were bound to make
an impact, for they were a totally new group within the Protestant tradition. No doubt in some respects they mirrored several
of the sects common in England since the Lollards, but historic-
ally the Quakers belonged to and originated during the civil war
in England. While the personality of George Fox was very important, his companions were equally powerful and effective.
Many of them came to Ireland from the earliest period of the

movement and established themselves in the towns and cities, particularly the garrison towns of the country.

One of the first to come was William Edmundson, whose life-span paralleled the growth, development and reformation of Quakerism in Ireland. Edmundson came in 1653 and settled as a shopkeeper in Antrim. He began holding meetings in Lurgan, County Armagh, and even at this early stage was persecuted for refusing to take oaths and using 'plain language'.[2] In 1655 he met George Fox in England and was affirmed in his convictions; he returned to Ireland and founded meetings in Dublin and all over the north to such an extent that he was imprisoned in Armagh.[3]

By this time other Quakers from England began travelling in Ireland. In 1654 Miles Halhead, James Lancaster and Miles Batman preached in cities and towns throughout the country.[4] In 1655 Elizabeth Fletcher, Elizabeth Smith and Barbara Blagdon preached in Dublin, Youghal, Cork and Limerick, suffering harassment, imprisonment and finally expulsion.[5] Thomas Loe, already a prominent Quaker in England, also came to Ireland in 1655 shortly after release from prison in Oxford. He travelled in the south of Ireland, to Limerick, Youghal and Cork; he returned in 1657 and was reported to have preached 'through the Dublin streets from St James's Gate to Stephen Rich's house, that is from the extreme west of the city to the extreme east'. Loe also travelled to the north of Ireland, particularly in the Armagh area. At this time he began the tradition of writing letters to different towns and cities in Ireland, calling the inhabitants to repentance or encouraging the newly convinced.[6] Thus from the earliest period of the movement Quakers travelled in Ireland, creating a network of meetings and contacts and gaining converts.[7] These came from all walks of life: gentry, farmers, shopkeepers, and especially soldiers.[8]

At this period Quaker teaching was more in reaction to other known beliefs rather than a defined set of convictions. While members of the Presbyterian and Independent churches could presume on some beliefs held in common, Quakers had already moved beyond and outside this frame of reference. Although their convictions would be articulated more clearly after the Restoration, even at this stage it was evident that Quakers rejected the doctrine of predestination and taught that salvation was open to and possible for all. To reach salvation each one was urged to turn to the 'light within', the only true guide, above even the scriptures. It was a religion of inwardness which affected views on the Trinity, the Last Judgement and the resurrection of the body — topics of confessional interest and debate at this time.

Quaker behaviour was consequent on their convictions and inevitably led to conflict: they preached in market-places, interrupted sermons, refused to take oaths or pay tithes, insisted on using 'thou' to all, refused to take off their hats in church or in the presence of superiors, denounced the clergy and the powerful. In fact they questioned and rejected almost every aspect of life, both religious and secular. The bearers of such views inevitably drew the fear and anger of their hearers, unless, of course, they themselves had become convinced. Indeed, hostility towards the Quakers grew in Ireland in proportion to their increasing presence in the country.

Such conflict is seen in the lives of Edmund Burrough and Francis Howgill, who came to Ireland in 1655 and were openly critical of government and the several churches. For this they were both persecuted and imprisoned, and in response further admonished their opposers:

> Cease from all your idle temples. . . . Cease from all your idle worship and feigned praise, for God is not worshipped in vain traditions. . . . Cease from all your idol shepherds and priests of Baal . . . cease from them and wait upon the Lord who is now risen to teach his people by his spirit in his way of truth and righteousness.[9]

This was very strong, convinced language and in effect undermined the foundations of society. Yet from a stance based on an inner experience of God, Quakers felt called by God, much as the prophets of the Old Testament had been: they were duty-bound to admonish and even curse if necessary all those in Ireland who held power and authority in the country. For example, Burrough and Howgill exhorted judges in Ireland to do their duty, otherwise 'God will cast you out of the seat of judgement as he has done the power of kings and bishops before you'.[10] Henry Cromwell was admonished, and the city of Dublin cursed.[11]

As well as cursing and admonishing people in public, Quakers also offered to dispute in public with their opposers. The ministers in Dublin and elsewhere in Ireland were challenged to come to the city for a public debate.[12] Twenty-seven queries (or questions)[13] were circulated by the Quakers in preparation for the event, and these examined the beliefs and practices of the Christian churches and in particular asked:

> 13. What scriptures have you for infant baptism and for singing druids' experience in rhyme and metre, calling it an ordinance of God, and what scripture for a sacrament?

> 15. What scripture or example have you for having a set place and a set way and staying 20 or 30 years at one place and bargaining with them beforehand for so much a year; were these things exercised by the apostles or are they your traditions and inventions?

> 17. Are not your places of worship idols and temples and is it not hypocrisy for you to be against papists and yet to worship in their churches?

> 27. Whether they that say none can be cleansed from all sins while he be upon the earth do not make the power of the second Adam to be of less effect than the first to transgress?

It was clear that the Quakers were questioning the fundamentals of religion: sacraments, church organisation, places of worship, doctrine, particularly predestination and reprobation. They were also critical of outward behaviour, even of mode of dress and manners.[14] Indeed, in 1659 Quaker books teaching such views were impounded in Dublin:

> Quakers' books consigned to one Samuel Claridge found on perusal to have an erroneous untoward spirit, denying external reverence to magistrates, condemning and disgracing ministers as antichristian, not ministers of Christ, but dumb dogs, priests and hirelings; expressing much bitterness against learning, maintaining perfection and freedom from sin in this life, also Popish and other tenets contrary to sound doctrine. Books to be detained, not suffered to be dispersed.[15]

Quakers at this period tended to be confrontational, and all groups in society were liable to receive criticism. On 6 February 1656 Henry Cromwell wrote to Thurloe: 'Our most considerable enemy now in our view are the Quakers.'[16] Afraid that their influence among army officers was increasing, he ordered that

Quakers be ejected from the army; they were to be arrested if
they resisted tithes, preached or disturbed ministers and people.
As it happened, the Quakers were not a political threat, but the
fear that they could be ensured that they would suffer persecution. In 1659 they appealed to parliament[17] and listed their sufferings in some detail. On their own evidence, the treatment
meted out to them was severe and relentless; some of the details
are graphic. For example, Edward Cooke was

> put out of the army for owning the truth; and afterwards for speaking
> to a priest at Cork was almost murdered, and for speaking a few words
> in a steeplehouse at Dublin was imprisoned near a quarter of a year
> by the mayor there. And Robert Southwell of Kinsale meeting him in
> the street there sent him to prison and no cause given; and had his brass
> and pewter taken from him (worth about 30 shillings) for not paying
> to the repair of the steeplehouse in Bandon; and he being an inhabitant
> of that town, at whose house the servants of the Lord meet together every
> first day, had his windows broken by the people of that town and great
> stones thrown thereat, and had one of his children wounded, so that
> he and his family are in danger of their lives.[18]

This was typical of the punishment suffered by Quakers for
refusing tithes, speaking in public places, either in churches,
market places or graveyards. Their behaviour was disruptive and
was perceived as a threat to political stability. Their message and
the mode of its delivery created tensions in the country, since
Quakers stated their beliefs with great conviction and often with
vivid words and actions. This stance did not end abruptly in 1660,
and records show that Quakers continued to be harassed for
meeting together, refusing to pay tithes or pay for the repair of
churches, refusing to go to church, to take oaths, take off their
hats or stop work on holydays.[19] Neither did the eccentric
behaviour of Quakers disappear immediately. For example, John
Exham went through Cork in 1667, his head covered with hair-
cloth and ashes, exhorting repentance.[20] An English Quaker,
Solomon Eccles, visited Ireland in 1669, and in September he
walked naked from the waist up into a Catholic service in Galway
with burning coals on his head, declaring to the congregation:

> Woe to these idolatrous worshippers: God has sent me this day to warn
> you and to let you see that if you repent not what shall be your
> reward.[21]

A month later, on release from prison, Eccles moved on to Cork, and on 16 October he went to the cathedral and called out at the end of Benjamin Crosse's sermon: 'The prayer of the wicked man is an abomination to the Lord.' Crosse had been a Presbyterian and had sworn never to wear a surplice, but in fact he had done so, though Eccles had no knowledge of this background.[22] Other instances of unusual behaviour are recorded. In April 1670 Anne Wright, a Quaker from Wicklow, walked into Christ Church Cathedral in Dublin during a service, covered in sackcloth and ashes, and at the end declared: 'That was not the worship that God delighted in'; in the following June she went through the streets of Cork and admonished the mayor of the city.[23] In 1674 John Knight stood naked in a church in Cork during the service. John Workman in Ross fasted for forty days.[24] In 1678 Katherine Norton from Coleraine preached in Irish on market day in Lurgan, County Armagh, and in the following year Judith Boulby published 'a warning to the inhabitants of Londonderry', having tried to preach there and been jailed.[25] In the main, however, Quakers gradually settled into their way of life, creating a tightly-knit community which gave them great strength and stability. There seems to have been little controversy among themselves except on the subject of the Muggletonians in Cork and Dublin.

This issue served as a focus for articulating Quaker belief and practice. In 1672 William Penn wrote a tract against the Muggletonians, refuting their tenets.[26] These were a mixture of beliefs, based on the dreams of John Reeve and Lodowick Muggleton. Penn reduced them to six in all: that God is not an infinite spirit; that God did not create out of nothing; that the human soul is generated at conception and not before and separately by God; that soul and body go to dust and rise together in a general resurrection; that God incarnated in the shape of a man and died as God and man for three days; that God predestined some for salvation and some for damnation, and this could never be altered.

In May 1673 the Cork meeting sought the advice of the Half-Yearly Meeting.[27] George Gamble, who had been a fervent Quaker and had suffered for his convictions,[28] had become a

Muggletonian under the influence of Colonel Robert Phaire.[29] Gamble met Muggleton in London in 1671 or early 1672, and this meeting confirmed his decision; he was joined by Henry Flaggator, Andrew Vivors and George Webber. Thus the Muggletonians developed in Cork and drew some converts to them from the Quakers.[30] The Half-Yearly Meeting of Friends had a copy of Reeve's book, *Transcendent spiritual treatise* (1651). It examined and condemned the teachings of Reeve and Muggleton. In addition, the meeting heard a rumour that some Quakers had revived the teachings of the Muggletonians; in view of this, the findings of the Half-Yearly Meeting were published in Cork:

> [We] have very seriously and in the council of God weighed and considered the principles and doctrines of the aforesaid Reeve and Muggleton, and the spirit from whence they flow. And do in the name and authority of the holy spirit of truth judge and condemn that spirit as a spirit of error and blasphemy sprung from the bottomless pit of darkness and high presumption. And by this our testimony do deny and detest the same, as neither fit to touch, taste nor handle of. Warning and admonishing all people in the fear and dread of the Lord God of heaven and earth, both to turn from it and avoid it.[31]

Muggleton replied quickly to this testimony of the Cork Quakers, pronouncing the twenty-six Cork Quakers 'cursed and damned in their bodies and souls from the presence of God, elect men and angels, to eternity'.[32] This was nothing new, as Muggleton had cursed many prominent Quakers in his day, including George Fox, Edward Burrough, Francis Howgill, Thomas Loe and William Penn, all of whom were prominent in Ireland.[33] Indeed, Penn's own book had come out in 1672 and no doubt was a great help to the Cork Quakers in their resistance to the Muggletonians. In effect the Muggletonians in Cork seem to have been small in number, and they faded in importance with the passing of Gamble and his companions. However, until at least 1687 Muggleton kept in touch with his followers in Ireland; he wrote long letters of encouragement and advice to several families and sent them his books.[34]

Some of the teachings of the Muggletonians could have attracted Quakers to join them, and some in fact did even after the strong admonition of 1673.[35] They believed they were the elect of God, the predestined; their organisation was informal; there was no preaching, worship or praying together, no regular meetings. They were not required to take a public stand; at the same time the doctrine of predestination made contact with other religious groups in Ireland easier and more respectable theologically. They remained a small group in the country, and some Muggletonians seem to have existed in Dublin towards the end of the century.[36] Richard Lawrence, writing in 1682, felt that the only groups in Ireland which could not be included within a comprehensive church, in the tradition of Ussher, were Roman Catholics, Quakers and Muggletonians.[37]

Gradually Quakers in Ireland consolidated both their structures and their way of life. A good example of this growth is seen in the words of advice given by Joseph Sleigh to his children before he died in 1683.[38] He told them to wait on the Lord in stillness and find the light and spirit of God within their own hearts. 'False ministers' would try to persuade them that sin was impossible to overcome, but this was a lie; the 'light within' dispelled sin and darkness. Strengthened with these convictions, they were to watch over their behaviour: their conversation, manner of dress, language, and attitude to the world;[39] they were to keep to the company of Quakers. Should they decide to go into employment, they were to seek honest families; if they wanted to marry, they were to seek advice of wise persons and bring up their children according to Quaker values. In all their business dealings they were to 'behave yourselves upright and justly to all men, that so by your holy lives and conversations truth may be well spoken of which will cause the Lord to bless your endeavours'.[40]

Such was the expectation and testament of a Quaker parent in the 1680s in Ireland, and it indicated integration of personal and social values. This development had occurred slowly after the Restoration to the extent that William Penn wrote to the Yearly Meeting in London in 1698, impressed with the order and discipline of Irish Quakers and extolling their virtues:

> their simplicity, gravity and coolness in managing their church affairs, their diligence in meetings, both for worship and business, their dispatch in mending differences and expedients to prevent them, but especially

their zeal against covetousness and against indifference in Truth's service and exemplary care to discourage an immoderate concern in pursuit of the things of this life.[41]

It was this combination of personal convictions lived out in a
closed group, coupled with a strong social and business sense,
which enabled the Quakers first to survive and then to thrive
as a small, coherent and cohesive community in Ireland. Before
1669, when George Fox visited Ireland and established formal
structures, Quaker meetings were informal and dependent upon
Friends visiting an area and holding meetings as they travelled
the country.[42] This was an effective way to maintain communication between the Friends in a time when the movement
was very new and all were living through periods of great political
unrest. By 1660, despite opposition, persecution and the informal-
ity of their structures, there were thirty established meeting places
in Ireland,[43] and fifty-three by 1701.[44]

Quaker meeting-houses tended to be concentrated in a few
areas, rather than dispersed evenly throughout Ireland. In Ulster
they were situated around Lisburn, Lurgan and Armagh; in
Leinster around Mountmellick, Moate, Edenderry and
Newgarden, as well as Wicklow and Carlow; in Dublin, Cork,
Waterford and Limerick.[45] In 1680 the Great Book of Tithe
was signed by one member from each of the 798 Quaker families
in Ireland.[46] This book was a testimony of conscientious objection to the payment of tithes, signed by one adult householder
liable for church tithe. There were 340 testimonies from Ulster,
including 156 women; 163 from Munster, including 61 women;
295 from Leinster, including 59 women. Taking this into account,
with estimates that Irish Quaker women in this period 1650-99
tended to have 5.4 children,[48] the actual numbers of Quakers
in Ireland between 1660 and 1714 would have been approximately
5,500-6,500.

Between 1660 and 1668 William Edmundson had set up six-
week meetings in Munster, Leinster and Ulster. These meetings
dealt with registration of births, marriages and deaths; administration of relief for those suffering persecution; care of the
poor; and reproof of those who had become lax.[49] Further
developments took place in 1669, when George Fox came to

Ireland and with Edmundson established the Men's and Women's Meetings in the main cities in Ireland. These were held monthly, but in Dublin the Men's Meeting was held fortnightly, and it acted as a permanent committee for the country. The monthly meetings took charge of local matters and sent representatives to the Province Meetings, which met quarterly. A general meeting met for the first time in 1669 and continued to meet in spring and autumn for over a century. It was called the National or Half-Yearly Meeting and was composed of representatives sent from the Province Men's Meetings. The Irish Half-Yearly Meeting sent representatives to the National Meeting in London.[50] In 1678 the Cork Women's Meeting proposed to have a general meeting also. It was agreed that the women would meet yearly at the time of the National Meeting, and they were left to organise themselves as they thought best.[51]

The manner of life expected of the Quakers was demanding and was examined regularly. In 1679 the Province Men's Meeting in Cork asked the monthly meetings to name Friends who could inquire into the lives of the membership and visit meetings to see that all was running properly. These acted very much like elders in the Presbyterian tradition. They had to give good example in their own lives and see that parents educated their children properly. They were recommended to gather before the actual meeting of Friends and plan the agenda; they were responsible for seeing that minutes were taken and that records of births, marriages and deaths were up to date. During the visits to meetings elders were to note the faults of members and report them to the Men's Meeting, thereby establishing a system of inspection and discipline which covered all aspects of family and business life, even to extent of reporting who fell asleep at the meetings.[52]

This system was certainly in operation by 1671, very soon after Fox's visit.[53] Elders had to encourage Friends to resist pressure to pay tithes and admonish those who had done so. They looked into business dealings and rebuked those who lived beyond their means, broke their word or got into debt. Employers were examined to see if they acted justly towards their employees, particularly to check if they kept their word to pay with money rather than in kind. Shopkeepers were scrutinised to see if they sold 'goods as truth will allow' and did not overcharge their customers.[54] Similar issues were dealt with in the Province Men's Meeting in Limerick in 1679 with the added points of marriages, oaths and incidences of drunkenness.[55] The minutes of the Men's Meeting in Lurgan for the years 1678-89, refer to both Men's and Women's Meetings dealing with all manner of business: land, marriage, wills, the poor, business practice, sexual offences and drunkenness.[56]

Tithes constituted an ongoing problem for Quakers.[56] In 1680 William Morris wrote a tract against tithes, asking that Quakers be dispensed from them.[58] Morris had spent time in the consistory court and knew he would be there again, so this work was published in the hope of some redress. He maintained that in Old Testament times tithes were levied only within the lands of the twelve tribes of Israel, 'the Jewish national church'. So, Morris argued, tithes should be levied only on the members of the Established Church in Ireland and on no other religious group.[59] Besides, Morris pointed out that tithes were intended originally for sharing among the poor, the widowed and orphaned, and this simply did not happen in Ireland. Instead the clergy extended their claim on all, 'whether English or Irish, Protestant or Papist, true or false worshippers it matters not to them, or whether they are rich or poor, fatherless or widows, bound or free'.[60]

In order to protect themselves, the meetings arranged that where possible Friends attended the assizes and sessions of the courts to help those prosecuted for non-payment of tithes or indeed other breaches of the law.[61] Sometimes public figures like Penn were able to help. In 1669 he persuaded the Lord Lieutenant to release all the Quakers in jail, first in Dublin and then in the rest of the country. Fox also helped when Clarendon was appointed Lord Lieutenant. He gave him several names of Friends in Ireland, and told Friends to contact Clarendon on his arrival in Ireland and apply to him in case of need.[62] But if they were unable to prevent arrest, Quakers were instructed not to resist with violence.[63]

Non-payment of tithes was a matter of principle from the

beginning, and it was part of the body of convictions Quakers wished to pass on to their children. To this purpose, in 1680 the Province Men's Meeting drew up directives for education within the family. Friends were urged to abide by the 'ancient principles of truth', and eleven points were drawn up. Tithes and any form of maintenance of the clergy or the church, including the repair of churches, were to be refused. All were to speak and act peacefully and use 'sound language', that is 'Thou' in conversation. Men were to avoid taking oaths or removing their hats except when at worship. All worldly customs and fashions were to be rejected. Cursing and every form of worldly behaviour were to be shunned, as well as the worship and religion of the world. All were urged to make up their differences quickly and never betray anything negative about one another to outsiders.[64]

Between 1680 and 1694 the more specific needs of young children were addressed. Children were to be educated within the Quaker tradition and not with other 'rude or proud children, with masters and mistresses who are not Friends'. They should not be allowed luxuries in food or drink, especially 'strong liqueurs', nor too much money to spend or fine clothes. Parents were to be vigilant and see that some children did not spend too long at school. They should be put to work hard, though not encouraged to begin big business projects which often ended in debt.[65] To maintain control over their children and indeed the parents, Quakers needed their own schools, and some were founded from at least 1675 onwards. By 1681 a meeting had been established for Quaker schoolmasters, and parents were encouraged to send their children to these schools.[66] While parents were urged to give a good example at home, the meetings were to inspect the schools, and the corrections meted out were to be accepted by the parents.[67] Friends were not allowed to remove their children from school, nor were schoolmasters or schoolmistresses to close school without permission from the Men's Meeting.[68] Friends were encouraged to be teachers, and it was suggested that poor children could be trained as teachers.[69]

If children were to be educated in the Quaker tradition, adults had to continue to observe the values so hard won in the early

days. Again and again, at the meetings and in letters of exhortation, Friends were urged to live simply and plainly, in every way.
So they were to dress simply and without affectation. House furniture was to be simple, useful and without ostentation, as was
the type of materials to be used in the house. Plain speech was
to characterise all their dealings, and they were not to bargain
or get into arguments over purchases, especially in an alehouse.
They were not to go to fairs except on business, and were forbidden to take part in the sports and pastimes at the fair. In other
words, all their dealings and their manner of life was to reflect
a basic simplicity.[70] Alehouses and smoking were frowned on;
behaviour at funerals was to be plain and seemly; brandy, or
'strong water', wine, tobacco and pipes and cakes were not to
be taken to excess at burials.[71]

In 1688, a year of great political upheaval, the Half-Yearly
Meeting in Dublin felt that some reformation of life was needed
and decided:

> to advise all that profess the Truth to walk as becomes the gospel in their
> conversation, apparel, deportment and dealings etc. which advice has
> not been so fully observed (by some) as we desired.[72]

Friends were urged to keep to 'the pure language of Truth and
be careful not to degenerate into the confused language of the
world. They were not to cut their hair and 'get great ruffling
periwigs'; those who had to get their hair cut were to get 'such
borders or periwigs as are plain and decent which best suits our
principles'. The meeting expressed fear that some were growing
cold and that children were not receiving proper formation; nor
were meetings being attended:

> our ancient practice . . . the neglect whereof we fear brings a coldness,
> deadness and barrenness upon the souls of some and may cause them
> to lose that warmth, freshness and zeal that was upon their hearts in
> former times.

Three years later, at the height of the Williamite war,[73] Friends
were told to look after each other and see the war as an opportunity for them to live simple uncluttered lives. Again all were urged
to speak plainly and deal honestly, keep their word and give
good example to the children. All were to examine their mode of

dress and avoid 'costly attire, foolish dresses and new fashions, ruffling periwigs, needless buttons, wide skirts and long flag-sleeved coats which appears to answer the fashion rather than service'.[74] This stress on plain dress was insisted on from the beginning. Quaker tailors were instructed to have meetings once each half-year 'to prevent the making of garments not agreeable to the plainness of the truth'. This was first suggested in 1677 and repeated in 1695 and 1703. Quaker shoemakers were also given similar instructions.[75] Obviously some kind of consistent reform was demanded, and this continued throughout the years after the war of 1689-91.[76] Joseph Pike recalled that in 1692 William Edmundson and the elders wanted to a have a general reformation in dress, clothes and furniture; to enforce this each Province Meeting was to appoint 'cleanhanded and faithful friends' to inspect all the families. Pike responded by changing all his furniture and house decorations for plainer ones: 'in a word we thoroughly reformed our houses'.[77]

In order to keep together as a close-knit community, Friends who lived in the country were encouraged to settle near one another 'for the ease and benefit of meetings and educating their children in the way of Truth'. Neither were they to move house without telling the meeting and getting certificates from their meeting before departure.[78] Another way of maintaining unity was insistence that marriages between Friends be validated at the meetings. Friends were instructed not to be married by a clergyman, nor to a 'person of the world'. Marriage by a clergyman was considered a serious fault, and some were cast out of meetings for having married according to the rites of the Established Church.[79] Parents were urged to watch most carefully over this and to refuse the marriage portion to any of their children who would not obey; if parents could not enforce this within the family, the meeting was to be told.[80]

By 1680 the question of mixed marriages had become a problem and this was addressed by William Edmundson. He noted that some were marrying outside the Friends and were being married by 'the teachers of the world', the clergy. Through an examination of marriage in the Old Testament, Edmundson showed his people that

> A breach is made upon our youths to the wounding and grieving the
> spirit of the faithful that are Abraham's children and are of the same
> mind with Isaac and Rebecca and cannot give their children in marriage
> to her people upon any account.

By using biblical language and history, he depicted the Quakers
as God's chosen people, surrounded by false worshippers who
tempted the chosen ones to forsake the true way.[81]

Another way of not conforming to the world and retaining
their own value system was to work on holydays. Quaker
employers were not permitted to let their apprentices[82] off on
holydays, and shopkeepers were to have their shops open 'as much
as in them lies' on Christmas Day and other holydays. On those
days the shopowners were to stay in their shops all day, and traders
were to work all day too. Until 1724 Quakers in Dublin at
Christmas time requested the Lord Mayor's protection of their
shops and property.[83] This was a form of testimony to their
convictions, and the meetings were responsible to see that Friends
'keep up the testimony for truth against the observations of such
idolatrous times'.[84] However, some concession was made in
1691 when Friends were recommended to use the names of days
in the weeks and months, in conversation and writing, 'according to the heathenish manner generally used in the world'.

Friends were encouraged to settle disputes among themselves
and were urged not to take cases beyond their own meeting. To
facilitate this and settle differences between Friends, a group was
established, comprising six from Ulster, six from Munster and
twelve from Leinster, which sat after the Half-Yearly Meeting
in Dublin and judged disputes which had not been settled either
at the monthly or the province meetings. It was like a court of
appeal, and it ensured that differences did not spill over into 'the
world'.[85] So strong was the desire to maintain unity that those
who refused to settle differences within the meeting were disowned; yet, with a note of realism, those dismissed from meetings
could be pursued in law by the injured party.[86]

Just as disputes were not to go beyond the confines of the
meetings, so doctrinal differences were not to be debated in
public. To this purpose, Friends were forbidden to enter into
'public disputes with any about religion or in controversies in

writing' without the permission of the meeting; if anyone wrote a book or tract, it had to be submitted to the meeting before publication. Even those who possessed books critical of the Quakers were to tell the meeting how they actually proposed to use such books.[87] Those who held doctrines contrary to the teachings of the Quakers were severely cautioned and sometimes disowned. In 1682 four men were accused of false doctrine concerning the devil.[88] In the same year Joseph Arnold was called to account for saying he worshipped wherever he wished, 'any worship that suited at the time'; he was also suspect for his interest in astrology.[89] In 1697 Edward Bennet of Cork held views which were rejected by the Quakers. With the agreement of the Province Meeting, Bennet was required to answer questions on his theory that the soul dies with the body and is not capable of reward or punishment; he also claimed that heaven and hell had no existence beyond 'the consciousness of men while they are in this world'. He had ten days to respond, and when he failed to reply he was disowned.[90]

The system of correction and disownment was exercised consistently, and it kept the body of the Quakers closely-knit, with a set of criteria which all had to observe. Failure to do so could lead to disownment. If disowned a person could not be buried in the Friends' burial ground, nor were any Friends to go to their funeral.[91] The disownment procedure was measured. First a person was presented with the accusation which he or she either could explain or deny; if this satisfied the meeting, membership was not withdrawn. However, this was not always the case. In 1671 John Howard 'fell into the accursed principle of Rantism' and committed adultery. Although he apologised, the meeting disowned him.[92] Those who went to the Established Church service or were married by a clergyman or were married without informing the meeting properly were severely rebuked.[93]

Traders were rebuked for malpractice, as was Joseph Thomas, a miller, for wasting corn and malt in his mill and for feeding pigs and cattle out of the sacks.[94] Friends were rebuked for moving from one part of the country to another without knowledge and permission from the meeting;[95] others were rebuked for taking out suits in Chancery.[96] It was a source of sadness when Friends who had suffered over many years for their convictions decided to opt out and go their own way and had to be disowned by the meeting. This happened when Henry and Ellen Tatlock, who had endured a great deal of harassment in Waterford in the early days, broke from the Quakers in 1681. Henry Tatlock had been a tailor and then became a glazier; he glazed the windows of churches and even those of Cashel cathedral, something impossible for the meetings to accept.[97]

To avoid disownment a Friend had to make an act of abjuration. This William Stanley did in November 1678. He had taken an oath several times, tried to hide the fact but was found out and rebuked. To avoid being disowned he made an act of abjuration which echoes the opening verses of the Epistle to the Hebrews and is a good example of the use Quakers made of biblical language.[98] Sometimes cases went on for years. In Dublin Jane Pildren persistently disturbed meetings in the period 1668-79. Even Thomas Loe's reprimand had no effect, and it had to be delivered by letter as Pildren refused to meet him or come to a meeting. The Men's Meeting tried to contain Pildren's behaviour in Dublin, but to no avail. The Women's Meeting, established in 1677, was asked to see what it could do, but Pildren did not come to their meeting either. So the case was never solved satisfactorily, and her strange behaviour continued to embarrass the Quakers in Dublin.[99]

Records and minutes were kept from the beginning, and reminders as to their importance were noted regularly. Monthly meetings kept records of births, marriages and deaths, as well as wills and inventories, and gave an account of all to the Half-Yearly Meeting.[100] Someone was deputed in the meeting to take particular responsibility for wills, and all executors had to be Friends.[101] Orphans were be cared for by the meetings; trustees were appointed to look after their needs and ensure them some privacy regarding their affairs.[102] Towards the end of the seventeenth century meetings were encouraged to get the ownership of their meeting-houses and burial places legally settled.[103] Definite instructions were given as to how to keep records of the sufferings of Quakers. In addition, they were forbidden to take farm or glebe lands; if they did, they were cast out of the meetings.

Nor were they to buy even the tithe wool, lambs, corn, or hay from a tithemonger or anyone involved in the collection of tithes; again those who did so were to be ostracised.[104]

The sufferings of Quakers from the beginning in Ireland had been recorded and published and must have been a source of support and encouragement, much in the same way as the histories of the kirk heartened Scottish Presbyterians.[105] In 1698, in an effort not only to keep records but also to have a written account of their history, the Half-Yearly Meeting sent out a series of questions to all the meetings. These inquired in some detail into the origins of Quakers in each area. Thomas Wight of Cork was asked to put the material together, and this in turn was revised by William Edmundson and later on by John Rutty.[106] At this time there were fifty-three registered meetings in the country. Thus not only was an historical account needed before the first-generation post-Restoration Friends died, but the meetings needed to know their tradition and understand why reform of life was so insisted on by the leadership in the late seventeenth and early eighteenth centuries.[107] In 1704 further help was offered to the meetings. In that year a summary of all the Half-Yearly Meetings held since 1669 was made, in the hope this would help the meetings keep true to the original traditions and practices.[108]

These traditions and practices had served the Quakers well. Apart from the religious motivations underlying the development of Quakerism in Ireland, the actual system they created bridged the public and private aspect of their lives. They practised a rigorous form of self-discipline and withdrawal from 'the world' and in this way survived as a group. At the same time they did business with this 'world', while carefully maintaining their strict, upright values. But then, correct economic behaviour promoted their way of life; anything less would have reflected badly on the body of Friends. Maintaining this balance between rejection of the standards of 'the world', and yet involvement within it was the constant preoccupation of the leadership from the 1670s onwards, especially as Quakers became wealthy and influential. The number of calls for reformation of life reflected the growing prosperity of Quakers in Ireland. Indeed, the very success of the

Quakers was seen as a threat to the quality of life which was the basis of their growth.[109]

In September 1691 this threat was faced when Friends reflected on the effects of the war on their way of life. All were asked to take the opportunity, given them by losses in the war, to live up to the ideal of a simple, uncluttered life, both at personal and public levels. The values so inculcated over the years were recommended again in detail.[110] However, such words of advice were not strong enough, for at the Half-Yearly Meeting in Dublin in 1692 Friends were warned again to check their excesses. Some had huge farms and big businesses and their lifestyle was changing, becoming too much 'of the world'. Practical steps were taken to put a brake on this. All meetings were to be examined by elders and reports given to the next Half-Yearly Meeting.[111]

Such moves persisted,[112] and in 1701 William Edmundson wrote what must have been his strongest criticism and condemnation of many Quakers at that time. He railed against worldliness and the danger of making money: Friends came to the meetings, loved to hear the word of God, but did not keep it; he condemned those who surrendered to the fashions of the world, in dress, houses and furnishings, and was especially critical of women and children. He had all the tone of a prophet, almost out of tune with his time.[113]

It was a long journey from 1653, when Edmundson had come to Ireland. He had lived through several periods of great upheaval, not least the war of 1689–91. His life-span saw the gradual growth of Quakers from outcasts to grudgingly accepted members of society who were often resented less for their strange religious stance than for their wealth. They had certainly come a long road in a short time. With the range of experience that he had, and the memories of enormous changes throughout his time in Ireland, Edmundson fought to retain what had been won so painfully by the first generation of Quakers.

Thomas Upsher wrote to Friends in Ireland, supporting Edmundson:

> I am under a necessity to remind you of the late prophecy of that ancient, eminent and faithful messenger and minister of Jesus Christ, William Edmundson, in Dublin at this half year's meeting, the substance

of which was that a dreadful day of distress was hastening on apace and should surely come, in which the Lord would dung the ground in this and other nations with the carcasses of men, and that the Lord would shake the fair and lofty buildings of many with their pleasant things that they have delighted in.[114]

Upsher was hopeful that a remnant would hear the words of the prophet and go forward in the spirit of the early days.[115] Nevertheless, the end of the seventeenth century was the end of an era. A definite period of growth had occurred, and Quakers would have to try to live with what they had created through their own discipline and active presence in the country. The new journey would be different, for they no longer had to fight for a place or be concerned for survival. In the future they had to discover how to sustain what they had achieved since the Restoration.

Notes and References

1   Barry Reay, *The Quakers and the English revolution* (London, 1985), pp 8-15; Barry Reay, 'Quakerism and society' in J. F. McGregor and Barry Reay (ed.) *Radical religion in the English revolution* (Oxford, 1986), pp. 141-45.

2   William Edmundson, *Journal of the life of William Edmundson* (Dublin, 1715), pp 6, 9-13. Edmundson was born in Westmorland in 1627 and he died at Mountmellick in 1712. He came to Ireland with his brother who was a soldier in the Cromwellian army.

3   Ibid., p. 21.

4   Joseph Besse, *A collection of the sufferings of the people called Quakers*, 2 vols (London, 1753), ii, 457ff

5   Thomas Wight and John Rutty, *A history of the rise and progress of the people called Quakers in Ireland, 1653-1700* (Dublin, 1751), p. 81; O. C. Goodbody, 'Ireland in the 1650s' in *J.F.H.S.*, no. 48 (1956-8), pp 34ff.

6   Kenneth Carroll, 'Thomas Loe, friend of William Penn and apostle to Ireland' in J.W. Frost and J.M. Moore (ed.), *Seeking the Light* (London, 1986), pp 62-3; Richard Harrison, *Cork city Quakers, 1655-1939* ([Cork], 1991), p.1. In 1666, William Penn heard Loe preach in Cork, became convinced, and was imprisoned with other Friends.

7   F.L.L., Caton MS, ii, 3/71, 3/73, 3/92, 3/97, 3/133-4, 3/150, 3/154; Spence MS, iii, 3/41.

8   Kenneth Carroll, 'Quakerism and the Cromwellian army' in *J.F.H.S.*, 54, no. 3 (1978), pp 135-54.

9   *The visitation of the rebellious nation of Ireland and a warning from the Lord proclaimed*, F[rancis] H[owgill], E[dmund] B[urrough] (London, 1656), p. 8.

10   Ibid., p. 19.
11   Ibid., p. 20. Barbara Blagdon also visited Dublin at this time and asked
      to speak to Cromwell. Besse, *A collection of the sufferings*, ii, 458.
12   *The visitation of the rebellious nation of Ireland . . .*, p. 29; Francis Howgill, 'Some
      queries to you all who say you are ministers of Christ in Dublin and to
      the rest in Ireland, to be answered by you or by your upholders. From
      us who in scorn by your generation are called Quakers' (Swarthmore MS,
      v, 10; Trans. vii, p. 49).
13   This was a common practice at the time. Differing traditions circulated
      queries for debate. For example, Christopher Blackwood, a Baptist, cir-
      culated such queries which Claudius Gilbert referred to in his several ser-
      mons given in Limerick during the Interregnum.
14   George Fox, William Morris and John Perrot, *Several warnings to the Baptised
      people* (n.p., 1659).
15   Orders in Council, 30 Nov. 1659 (R.M. Young, *Historical notices of old Belfast
      and its vicinity* (Belfast, 1896), p. 107).
16   *Thurloe state papers*, iv, 508, 672, 698. Quakers were active in Cork, Water-
      ford and Kinsale in 1656 (R.C.B., Seymour MS, f. 334); Thomas Morford
      cried out and refused to sit while the Independent, Edward Bale, was
      preaching. Morford to Fox and Howgill, 6 May 1659 (F.L.L., Swarthmore
      MS, i, 26; Trans., ii, 781); Joseph Eyres complained of being disturbed
      by some of 'unsound principles and unsavoury practices'. Eyres to Henry
      Cromwell, 27 Aug. 1658 (B.L., Lansdowne MS 823, f. 91); Quakers and
      Baptists were reported as very active in Galway. Rueban Easthorp to Henry
      Cromwell, 11 June 1657 (ibid., f. 86).
17   *A narrative of the cruel and unjust sufferings of the people of God in the nation of Ireland
      called Quakers* (London 1659).
18   Ibid., p. 1.
19   Abraham Fuller and Thomas Holms, *A brief relation of some part of the suffer-
      ings of the true Christians, the people of God (in scorn called Quakers) in Ireland,
      1660-1671* (n.p., 1672); Besse, *A collection of the sufferings*, ii.
20   Exham was born in Kerry and went to England to join the army, return-
      ing to Ireland in that capacity. He became convinced in 1658 and was
      visited by William Edmundson and Thomas Loe. In 1698 he went through
      Cork repeating the same performance as in 1667. Half-Yearly Meeting,
      1692-1710 (F.L.D., QM 1 C1, f. 61). In 1710 he went to Orrery's house
      and called him and all in it to repentance. 'The names of friends deceased
      in the kingdom of Ireland' (F.L.D., YM Fl, f. 61); Thomas Lunham, 'Early
      Quakers in Cork' in *Cork Hist. Soc. Jn.*, 2nd series, x (1904), p. 104; Wight
      and Rutty, *The rise and progress of the Quakers*, pp 105, 273; Besse, *A collection
      of the sufferings*, ii, 466.
21   Fuller and Holms, *A brief relation*, p. 45; Besse, *A collection of the sufferings*,
      ii, 476; Solomon Eccles, *Signs are from the Lord to a people or a nation* (London,
      1663); Solomon Eccles, *The Quaker's challenge* (n.p., 1668); T[obias] C[risp],
      Babel's builders (London, 1681).
22   Fuller and Holms, *A brief relation*, p. 44; Lunham, 'Early Quakers in Cork',
      pp 104-5. Such pattern of behaviour was part of Eccles's stance in the

Quaker movement at this time. Solomon Eccles, [Begins:] *In the year 1659 in the 4th month the last day of the month being the 5th day of the week, the presence of God was felt within me*; Eccles, *Signs are from the Lord*. In 1668 he challenged Catholics and Protestants first to a fast for seven days and nights and then to keep awake for seven days and nights: *The Quakers' challenge*; Kenneth Carroll, 'Early Quakers and "going naked as a sign" ' in *Quaker History*, no. 67 (1978), pp 69-87.

23   'A brief and true relation of Anne, wife of William Wright of Castledermot in the County of Kildare, who deceased the 1st day of December 1670' (Mary Leadbeater, *Biographical notes of Friends in Ireland* (London, 1823), pp 56-9.

24   Edward Wetenhall, *A brief and modest reply to Mr Penn's scurrilous and unchristian defence against the Bishop of Cork* (Dublin, 1699), p. 15; Thomas Wright and Nicholas Harris, *Truth further defended and William Penn vindicated* (n.p., 1700), pp 101, 158. John Burnyeat, Penn and Eccles travelled together in Ireland from January to June 1670 and spoke at meetings; Penn showed every sign of approval of Eccles. William Penn, *My Irish journal*, ed. Isobel Grubb (London, 1952), pp 34, 38-43, 59. There is no evidence of Quakers in Ireland going naked as a sign before 1669.

25   Wight and Rutty, *The rise and progress of the Quakers*, pp 129, 130-1.

26   William Penn, *The new witnesses proved old heretics* (n.p., 1672); Christopher Hill, Barry Reay and William Lamont, *The world of the Muggletonians* (London, 1983), pp 20-44.

27   'Testimony of a general meeting of Friends for the province of Munster against the erroneous doctrines of John Rood and Lodowick Muggleton' (F.L.D., Testimonies of disunity, QM II F1, ff 1-3).

28   Besse, *A collection of the sufferings*, ii, 472, 475, 476, 477.

29   As governor of Cork during the Interregnum, Phayre had been an enthusiastic Quaker. D.N.B.; Barnard, *Cromwellian Ireland*, pp 110, 149; Hill, Reay and Lamont, *The world of the Muggletonians*, p. 47. Gamble was married to Phayre's daughter; Phayre's wife was known as 'the chief lady Muggletonian in the county'. Penn, *My Irish journal*, p. 74.

30   'Testimony of a general meeting of Friends for Munster' f. 4; Kenneth Carroll, 'Quakers and Muggletonians in seventeenth-century Ireland', in David Blamires (ed.), *A Quaker miscellany for Edward H. Milligan* (London, 1985), pp 49-56; Hill, Reay and Lamont, *The world of the Muggletonians*, pp 47-8; Augustus Jessopp, *The coming of the friars and other historic essays* (London, 1889), p. 332.

31   'Testimony of a general meeting of Friends for Munster', f. 3.

32   Alexander Delemaine, *A volume of spiritual epistles: being the copies of several letters written by the last two prophets and messengers of God, John Reeve and Lodowick Muggleton* (London, 1820), pp 379-98.

33   Ibid., pp 337, 367, 397; Carroll, 'Thomas Loe', pp 66-7.

34   Ibid., pp 372, 400, 462-3, 499, 513.

35   Ibid., p. 499, Charles Yeeles, Thomas Miller and John White converted to Muggletonianism (22 Aug. 1681).

36   Muggleton was in correspondence with Major John Dennison of Dublin

in 1678. Delemaine, *Spiritual epistles*, p. 457; Marsh to Tenison, 10 Apr.
1697 (Lambeth Palace, London, Gibson Papers, MS 942, f. 133). Marsh
mentioned four Muggletonians in Dublin. Amos Strettell and John
Burnyeat, *The innocency of the Quakers manifested and the truth of their principles
and doctrine cleared and defended from the . . . wicked slanders of James Barry* (Dublin,
1687), pp 16-7; F.L.D., Sharp MS, S.8, no. 5, f. 4; *A representation of the present
state of religion with regard to infidelity, heresy, impiety and popery, drawn up and
agreed by both houses of Convocation in Ireland, 1711* (Dublin, 1711), p. 7.

37   Richard Lawrence, *The interest of Ireland* (Dublin, 1682), Part ii, Ch. 2, p. 96.
38   Joseph Sleigh, *Good advice and counsel given forth by Joseph Sleigh of the city of
      Dublin in the time of his sickness to his children* (London, 1696).
39   The word 'world' was an expression used by the Quakers denoting their
      effort to remain distant from what they perceived as a materialistic, lax
      and over-indulgent society around them. They tried as far as possible to
      be self-contained in their 'world'.
40   Sleigh, *Good advice and counsel*, pp 8-13, 20.
41   Joseph Pike, *Some account of the life of Joseph Pike of Cork, who died in the year
      1729, written by himself, with preliminary observations by John Barclay* (London,
      1837), pp xxx-xxxi; Thomas Story, *A journal of the life of Thomas Story* (New-
      castle, 1747), p. 130. Penn was visiting Dublin at this time with Story
      and John Everett, and they wrote to the London meeting from there.
42   Edmundson, *Journal*, p. 23; 'Life of John Burnyeat', in *The Truth Exalted,
      J.B.* (London, 1691), pp 27ff.
43   G. F. Nuttall, *Early Quaker letters* (London, 1952), p. 403.
44   Isobel Grubb, 'Social conditions in Ireland in the seventeenth and
      eighteenth centuries as illustrated by early Quaker records' (M.A. thesis,
      Univ. London, 1916), p. 21.
45   Vann and Eversley, *Friends in life and death*, pp 47-48. See also D. E. C.
      Eversley, 'The demography of Irish Quakers, 1650-1850' in J. M.
      Goldstrom and L. A. Clarkson (ed.), *Irish population, economy and society: essays
      in honour of the late K. H. Connell* (Oxford, 1981), p. 61.
46   'A record of the testimonies of the people of the Lord scornfully . . . called
      Quakers' (F.L.D., A. 29/35). In the National Half-Yearly Meeting in 1682,
      William Williamson was instructed to record all the testimonies against
      tithes. Isobel Grubb has estimated that at this time there were no more
      than 750 Quaker households in the country. Isobel Grubb, *The Quakers
      in Ireland* (London, 1927), p. 89.
47   J. M. Douglas, 'Early Quakers in Ireland' in *J.F.H.S.*, no. 48 (1956), pp
      30-1.
48   Vann and Eversley, *Friends in life and death,* pp 240, 173; for Ulster Quakers,
      p. 53.
49   *Christian discipline of the Religious Society of Friends in Ireland* (Dublin, 1971), p. 8.
50   Grubb, *The Quakers in Ireland*, p. 29.
51   *Christian Discipline*, pp 8-9.
52   Half Yearly Meetings, 1676ff (F.L.D., Half Y.M. A. 10, ff 97, 177). See
      also Half-Yearly Meeting held in Dublin, 10 Jan. 1692 (ibid., QM I C1,
      1692-1710, f. 1).

53 Ibid. Half Y.M., f. 381 (1671).
54 From the Province Men's Meeting in Cork, 30 Apr. 1679, to the next Half-Yearly Meeting (ibid., QM II F1, f. 22). See also meetings of 1678 and 1695 (ibid., QM II Z1, 0).
55 Province Men's Meeting at Limerick, 30 Aug. 1679 (ibid., QM II F1, f. 23).
56 Lurgan Men's Meeting (P.R.O.N.I., T1062 45); Moate Meeting (F.L.D., MM IV M2, ff 1, 5, 6ff); testimonies of denial and condemnation: a general testimony (ibid., MM II F1, ff 1-5, 10-11, 15.
57 Besse, *A collection of the sufferings*, ii, 466-93; National Sufferings, 1655-93 (F.L.D., YM G1). Quakers suffered for non-payment of tithes most of all between 1660-70; after that harassment was less intense; after the 1690 wars tithes were demanded more widely again. (ibid., QM II F1, f. 76; QM II Z1, R; YM G1, 1688ff).
58 William Morris, *Tithes no gospel ordinance, nor ever instituted of God for the maintenance of a gospel ministry, but ended with the levitical priesthood and abolished by the offering up of Christ* (n.p., 1680). William Morris had been a Baptist and captain in the army in Ireland; he was convinced by William Edmundson and in 1659 wrote a pamphlet to parliament asking that the Quakers should not be persecuted, imprisoned and harassed for tithes: *To the supreme authority . . . the Commons in parliament assembled* (London, 1659); he lived in Bandonbridge after the Restoration. F.L.L., Biographies of Quakers; 'The names of Friends deceased . . . in Ireland' (F.L.D. YM F1, f. 2v); Besse, *A collection of the sufferings*, ii, 446; Wight and Rutty, *The rise and progress of the Quakers*, 115, 144.
59 Morris, *Tithes no gospel ordinance*, pp 3, 5-6.
60 Ibid., p. 10.
61 Half-Yearly Meetings, 1676ff (F.L.D., Half Y.M. A 10, f. 13. 1687); 'Summary of the proceedings of several half-years' meetings held in Dublin for the nation of Ireland or a breviat of sundry needful general minutes and epistles thereof recommended to the several Provincial meetings of this nation and thence to the monthly or particular meetings to stir up friends to a faithful, diligent perseverance in the truth that the testimony and discipline thereof may be duly kept up to in all its branches, 1704. Collected by order of the Munster Province Meeting' (ibid., QM II Z1, A, 1669-73, Copies of applications to Justices of the Peace).
62 Elia Buckley, 'William Penn in Dublin' in *Dublin Hist. Rec.,* vi, no. 3 (June-Aug., 1944), p. 85; 'George Fox to Friends in Ireland, 1685' in *J.F.H.S.,* vii, no. 4 (1910), p. 181; Story, *A journal*, pp 128-9. For Penn in Waterford and Cashel in 1697, see James Coleman, 'Some early Waterford clerical authors' in *Waterford Arch. Soc. Jn.,* vi (1900), p. 181.
63 'Summary of the proceedings . . . 1704' (F.L.D., QM II Z1, S, 1687).
64 Province Men's Meeting, 7 Aug. 1680 (ibid., QM II F1, f. 27). Also, 23 Aug. 1680, Anne Jones fell into dancing, swearing and cursing (ibid., MM II F1, Testimonies of denial and condemnation, f. 56; 23 Sept 1687, misbehaving at a wedding, f. 141; for using oaths, Half-Yearly Meetings, 1676ff (ibid., Half Y.M. A 10, f. 235).

65 Half-Yearly Meetings, 1676 ff (ibid., Half Y.M. A 10, f. 75).

66 'Summary of the proceedings . . . 1704' (ibid., QM II Z1, S, 1675, 1681, 1681-5). In 1702 Bishop Downes of Cork noted that adjoining the Quaker meeting-house in Cork there was 'a large room where a Quaker teaches school at present' (Visitation Book of Dives Downes, T.C.D., MS 562, f. 84).

67 Half-Yearly Meeting 1676 ff (F.L.D., Half Y.M. A 10, f. 79 ff, 97; also ibid., QM II F1, f. 70).

68 Ibid., Nov. 1687, f. 315.

69 Ibid., 1691-5, ff 316, 317.

70 Ibid., f. 55 (1682, 1692/3, 1697), ff 245, 287 (1671, 1676, 1677, 1686, 1699); also 'Summary of the proceedings . . . 1704' (ibid., QM II Z1, F, 1671-1694).

71 'Summary of the proceedings . . . 1704' (F.L.D., QM II Z1, B, 1697).

72 *A testimony of tender advice and counsel given forth from our Half-Yearly Meeting in Dublin, the 9th of the 9th month 1688* (Dublin, 1688) (signed by Alexander Seaton).

73 The journal of William Edmundson contains a detailed account of how he and many other Quakers fared during the Williamite war.

74 *From our Half-Yearly Meeting held in Dublin, 9, 10, 11 Sept. 1691* (signed by William Edmundson, Abraham Fuller and Amos Strettell), pp 2-4.

75 'Summary of the proceedings . . . 1704' (F.L.D., QM II Z1, T, 1677); Testimonies of disunity, 1695 (ibid., QM II F1, f. 70).

76 *An epistle to Friends, Leinster Province Meeting, 9-11 July 1698;* William Edmundson, *An epistle containing wholesome advice and counsel to all Friends* (n.p., 1701). William Edmundson's brother John (1625-1707) fell away from Quakerism in old age. Isobel Grubb, 'William Edmundson, 1627-1712' in *J.F.H.S.*, xl no. 40 (1948), pp 32-6.

77 Pike, *Some account of the life of Joseph Pike of Cork*, pp 59-66.

78 From our Half-Yearly Meeting held in Dublin, 9, 10, 11 Sept. 1691, p. 6; Half-Yearly Meetings, 1676ff (F.L.D., Half Y.M. A 10, 1691, f. 185; 1680, f. 295); Testimonies of denial and condemnation (ibid., MM II F1, f. 65).

79 'Summary of the proceedings . . . 1704' (ibid., QM II Z1, XYZ, 1680). Testimonies of denial and condemnation (ibid., MM II F1, ff 25-7); Testimonies of disunity (ibid., QM II F1, f. 9 ff).

80 Ibid., Half Y.M. A 10, 1680, ff 131, 134. This request was repeated in 1688 and 1691 (ibid., QM II Z1, B, 1688), and redress was to be sought from the government if co-operation failed on this point. Such was the relationship between the Established Church and the Quakers in the 1680s that bishops were asked not to grant marriage licences to Friends unless they were sure of the parents consent to the marriage.

81 Paper of William Edmundson against mixed marriages, May 1680 (ibid., Half Y.M. A 11, Appendix, f. 416); also epistle of William Edmundson approved by the Half-Yearly Meeting (ibid., QM II Z I, E).

82 Friends were encouraged to place their children as apprentices among Quaker families; the care given to apprentices was checked by the meetings (ibid., Half Y.M. A 10, 1676, f. 9).

83 R. S. Harrison, 'Dublin Quakers in business, 1800-1850' (M.Litt. thesis, T.C.D., 1988), p. 433; 1680, 1682, 1703, Half-Yearly Meetings, 1676ff (F.L.D., Half Y.M. A 10, f. 41 (1676), repeated in 1696, 1701, 1706). In 1671 shop windows in Dublin were broken on Christmas Day. National Sufferings, 1655-93 (ibid., YM G1 f. 49). For years in Dublin there were riots on Christmas Day to force Quakers to shut their shops; nevertheless, such shops were popular, as they had fixed prices. Buckley, 'William Penn in Dublin', p. 83.

84 'Summary of the proceedings . . . 1704' (F.L.D., QM II Z1, C, 1676).

85 Concerning appeals, 1676 (ibid., Half Y.M. A 10, f. 7; cf. f. 123 (1675), Friends to settle disputes at meetings; repeated in 1687).

86 Ibid., f. 45 (1676, 1677, 1696, 1697).

87 Half-Yearly Meetings, 1676 ff (ibid., Half Y.M. A 10, Nov. 1693, f. 15; admonition repeated in 1703).

88 Testimonies of denial and condemnation, 1662-1722 (ibid., MM 11 F1, ff 87-9). The four men were John Beckett, Thomas Smith, James Beckett and Christopher Marshall.

89 Ibid., f. 104.

90 Ibid., f. 8.

91 Ibid., QM II Z1, B, 1682.

92 Testimonies of denial and condemnation, 1662-1722 (ibid., MM II F1, f. 8).

93 Ibid., ff 23-7, 36-7, 49, 50, 53; also Mountmellick Monthly Meeting (ibid., MM V G1, ff 318-21). When a meeting was informed about the intention of persons to marry, letters were sent to other meetings to get information; sometimes such letters were sent to England or Scotland. Men's Meeting, Dublin, 1677ff (ibid., MM II A1, f. 275v. 1677).

94 Testimonies of denial and condemnation, 1662-1722 (ibid., MM II F1, f. 64).

95 Ibid., f. 65; also ff 157, 255.

96 Ibid., f 69ff. William Chaunders took out a suit in Chancery against his landlord.

97 Testimonies of disunity, 1 Apr. 1681 (ibid., QM II F1, f. 7).

98 Ibid., f. 38. Stanley began: 'In all ages of time the Lord has appeared to the sons and daughters of men in making a glorious discovery of himself which [he] has in sundry times and in divers manners and in these latter days he has more largely appeared by his son . . .'

99 Ibid., ff 6-7; Men's Meeting, Dublin, 1677ff (ibid., MM II A1, f. 63); Carroll, 'Thomas Loe', p. 66.

100 *From our Half-Yearly Meeting, held in Dublin, 9, 10, 11 Sept. . . . 1691.*

101 Those who had not got Friends as executors had taken oaths, and this was considered a serious offence. Testimonies of disunity, 1684-5 (F.L.D., QM II F1, f. 395).

102 'Summary of the proceedings . . . 1704' (ibid., QM II Z1, O, 1684). The poor were cared for by the meetings. Men's Meeting Dublin (ibid., MM 11 A1, f. 54).

103 'Summary of the proceedings . . . 1704' (ibid., QM II Z1, R, 1697). On

the death of Joseph Sleigh, who was a widower, the five children were divided out among his mother and four Friends.

104   Half-Yearly Meetings, 1676ff (ibid., Half Y.M. A 10, f. 327ff for 1671, 1672, 1673, 1678, 1695, 1698, 1699, 1706; also, ff 345-8 for 1677, 1687, 1693).

105   William Stockdale, *Great cry of oppression or a brief relation of some part of the sufferings of the people called Quakers in Ireland, 1671-1681* (Dublin, 1683); Abraham Fuller and Thomas Holms, *A compendious view of some extraordinary sufferings of the people called Quakers in Ireland, 1655-1731* (Dublin, 1731).

106   Thomas Wight and John Rutty, *A history of the rise and progress of the people called Quakers in Ireland, 1653-1700* (Dublin, 1751).

107   Half-Yearly Meeting, Dublin, 9 Dec. 1698 (F.L.D., QM I C1, 1692-1710, f. 16); Grubb, 'Social conditions in Ireland', p. 17.

108   Summary of the proceedings . . . 1704 (ibid., QM II Z1).

109   Testimonies of denial and condemnation, General exhortation, 1679 (ibid., MM II F1, f. 49). See also f. 93 (1682); 30 Apr. 1679, *Testimonies of disunity* (ibid., QM II F1, ff 22-3, 33, 39); *A testimony of tender advice and counsel . . . 1688*. For a discussion of how Irish Quaker wealth and property extended to North America at this period, see Audrey Lochhart, 'The Quakers and emigration from Ireland to the North American Colonies' in *Quaker History*, 77, no. 2 (fall 1988).

110   From our Half-Yearly Meeting held in Dublin, 9, 10, 11 Sept. 1691.

111   Half-Yearly Meeting, in Dublin, 8, 9, 10 Dec. 1692 (F.L.D., QM I C, 1692-1710, f.1); Testimonies of disunity (ibid., QM II F1, ff 33, 39, 62, 70, 72, 73).

112   Edmundson, *An epistle to Friends, Leinster Province Meeting, 9-11 July 1698.*

113   William Edmundson, *An epistle containing wholesome advice and counsel to all Friends* (n.p. 1701).

114   Thomas Upsher, 'To Friends in Ireland and elsewhere', Dublin, 15 May 1699 (B.L., Add. MS 39318, p. 7).

115   Ibid., p. 8.

PART II

CONTROVERSIES WITHIN
DISSENTING TRADITIONS

5

Tensions within
Scottish Presbyterianism

> I think the Lord has a special hand in my coming to this place
> [Dublin] for he has not suffered me to be idle . . . he has kindled
> a fire which I hope Satan shall not quench.
>
> James Renwick, Covenanter, Dublin, August 1683

Tensions in Ulster

Dissent was a fluid reality within each of the religious traditions,
and within Scottish Presbyterianism, particularly since its refoundation in 1642, there was continual interplay between
moderate and extreme views. Originating in Scotland during
the civil war period, tensions between Resolutioners (supporters
of the king and Covenant) and Remonstrants (supporters of the
Covenant alone) continued to be significant in both religious and
political spheres.[1] The extreme Covenanting tradition was
maintained in Ireland by itinerant ministers from Scotland, such
as David Houston. As early as 1671 the Antrim meeting noted
that Houston was in Glenarm 'exercising a ministry without consent of the meeting'. When told to leave the country for a while,
he agreed to do so on the condition that he was given a
testimonial.[2] However, this seems not to have happened, and a

111

month later the Antrim meeting noted that Houston had talked with the Route meeting and acknowledged in public his 'irregular carriage' at Ballymoney; he also asked leave to stay in Ireland.[3]

The 'irregular carriage' of Houston was his adherence to the Covenanting tradition and his rejection of any form of co-operation with the monarchy.[4] Ministers with these views refused to accept appointments from either presbyteries or patrons and became itinerant ministers with quite strong followings, especially in the west of Scotland. The situation became even more acute when the Declaration of Indulgence of 1672 was accepted by many of the ministers in Scotland, and from then onwards the Covenant was more and more invoked in a militant way. Both ministers and followers became a source and catalyst for deep religious and social unrest which caused in great part the successive revolutions in Scotland of 1666 and 1679 and provoked the 'Killing Time' of 1684-8.[5]

Within this context the Route was anxious to either control or eject Houston. However, Houston seems not to have complied with what the Route asked, for in February 1672 that meeting appointed Thomas Wyllie to preach on 10 March at Ballymoney on the Sabbath 'after forenoon to intimate the suspension of David Houston from all carriage of the ministry'. The people were advised not to hear Houston and were told that if they did, they 'would be deprived of the sealing ordinances' and marriage.[6] Since November 1671 there had been 'scandalous divisions' in Coleraine, obviously caused by Houston.[7] By February 1672 the Route had decided to proceed against him, and he was summoned to appear before the meeting at Coleraine on the last Tuesday in March. Their basic objection lay in his disorderly behaviour and unwillingness to heed the meeting. He was a licensed preacher at this stage, though not ordained nor even in trials for ordination. In any event, he was deprived by the Route for his 'stormy and boisterous' attitude towards the meeting, for dividing the parish of Ballymoney, and for affecting other congregations nearby by preaching at the borders of parishes on the sabbath and during the week at Macosquin.[8]

There is evidence that the Route meeting thought of trying to get Houston arrested by the magistrate. On 5 March 1672

William Semple[9] wrote to Thomas Wyllie from Dublin and suggested getting advice on whether depositions made on oath would be accepted by a magistrate.[10] This was done, as a Captain Hunstone warned Houston that he would be arrested if he continued disturbing the people. The officer remarked later that Houston knew well enough what he was doing and had decided to submit himself to censure by the ministry.[11] The fact that the ministers were prepared to go to law over the case indicates how much the general body of Scottish Presbyterians wished to dissociate themselves from the fanatical element in their own church. On their perceived loyalty to the king and government lay their hopes for toleration and for growth. Besides at this time the *regium donum* was being negotiated on their behalf by Lord Granard.[12]

The meetings acted in unison on the matter and in August 1672 ordered that the Act of Bangor (1654) be taken 'by the newcome brethren'.[13] The Laggan asked for details on Houston's case, and on receipt of them fully concurred with what the Antrim meeting decided.[14] In September 1672 the Antrim meeting recorded Houston's confession and recognised it as the best possible solution given the situation; the confession had been sent to all the meetings for their judgement. A month later, since Houston seemed in good faith, he was allowed to preach in the Route, except to the people he had disturbed originally.[15]

There the matter seems to have rested, at least for a time. However, there were developments in Scotland which encouraged Houston. In 1681, following the deaths of Richard Cameron and Donald Cargill, 'remnant' Covenanting congregations formed themselves into praying societies in order to support each other in times of persecution. They met at Lesmahagow on the 15 December 1681 and set up a union, with a fortnightly circular letter and quarterly meetings. They drew up a declaration in 1682, which was a mixture of the former declarations of Sanquhar and Rutherglen, repudiating all unconstitutional acts of the king and the acceptance of the indulgence by ministers. The government responded to the challenge of the United Societies (also known as Covenanters or Cameronians) by searching them out and having them executed summarily, especially during the

'Killing Time' of 1684-8.[16] James Renwick, who witnessed the execution of Cargill, joined the societies and became leader of the Cameronians until his own execution in 1688.[17] Houston contacted the Cameronians in Scotland, and there is evidence that the United Societies too made contact with Ireland during this period. Certainly Renwick visited Dublin in the autumn of 1683 on his way back to Scotland from Holland.[18]

The 'Killing Time' began in Scotland in 1684, when the Apologetical Declaration was issued in October by the Cameronians. This was an open declaration of war on the government and on all who supported it. It was no different in content from the Sanquhar Declaration of 1680, but the tone was more vehement. Repression followed which had repercussions in Ireland, for from October 1684 Scots began to arrive on the east coast of Ireland seeking refuge from persecution.[19] James Callwell from Belfast brought a copy of the Apologetical Declaration, spread it abroad and told the people not to heed the indulged ministers who prayed for the king. Callwell was a follower of the United Societies and had given hospitality to a preacher, James Wilson, when he stayed in the north the previous year.[20] Prisoners taken at Carrickfergus in November 1684 admitted that

> they had subscribed to a kind of engagement carried about by one Callwell amongst the Scotch in the north, the substance of which is to assist the brethren now persecuted for the cause of religion in Scotland. . . . when they were asked whether they would pray for the King or no the only answer that could be got from them to that question was that they would pray for the elect.[21]

In August 1686, although not at that time a formal member of the United Societies, Houston encouraged people in Ulster to join Renwick's party in Scotland.[22] It is clear that the people of Ballycastle, Aghoghill, Drumall and Ballymoney supported both Houston and Renwick. Major Montgomery of Coleraine may also have been involved, as he had kept a minister of his own and a meeting-place for 500 on his farm since the Restoration.[23] In any event, the Antrim meeting noted that Houston had returned, that both the Route and Down meetings complained that 'multitudes' were following him and that this 'schism and flame' needed to be repressed.[24] Houston was cited three times and witnesses were called, even though this was difficult to do at the time. Finally

Houston was formally suspended by the meeting.[25]

Sometime in the autumn of 1686 Houston asked to join the United Societies. Two of the societies' members travelled to Ireland and talked with Houston to discover his motivation and understanding of their cause. They also went to the places where Houston had preached and spoke to many people there, who testified verbally but refused to give written statements, probably out of fear. The visitors were satisfied with Houston, who answered all the complaints made about his ministry. Despite this, the United Societies discussed the case further, even holding a meeting of all the ministers who had been in Ireland, and then sending another minister to examine Houston further. In December 1686 Houston went to Scotland and was presented with the testimonies of the societies. Houston agreed with all their principles and judgements. He then asked to read some of his own testimonies to them which explained why he had not obeyed the meetings in Ireland; he also presented testimonies supportive of his ministry which had been collected in places where he had preached in Ireland.[26] He said that he refused to baptise children of those who paid tithes. He also rejected those ministers who either accepted the indulgence or co-operated in any way with the authorities:

> whensoever he knew of any transaction of the ministers with the so called magistrates he did quit the meeting house and refused subordination to those ministers, which was a little after Bothwell.

Renwick thought highly of Houston and wrote:

> For my own part, I thought he seemed to have a right state of the cause and a right impression of the case of the church, and to be tender-hearted and zealous in the frame of his spirit, particularly for the royalties of Christ and against the idol of the Lord's jealousy, the ecclesiastic supremacy and civil tyranny.[27]

Obviously Houston had been a Covenanting minister in Ulster for some years, had rejected his own meeting of the Route in 1679 and in 1686 turned to the United Societies. The societies accepted him and as sign of his severance with the Route sent someone to Ireland to bring his wife and family back to Scotland.[28] In March 1687 the Antrim meeting noted that Houston was forbidden to preach in Ireland and in fact had left for Scotland. In view of the delicate situation in the country, the meeting thought Houston should be deposed. Proof of Houston's activities was sent formally to the General Assembly of the Presbyterian Church in Scotland.[29] Houston returned to Ireland after the revolution of 1688 and settled in or near Newtownards, County Down, under the protection of Lord Mount Alexander of the Ards, who hoped to use him to keep peace in the area.[30] Not for long, however, for in 1694 he was accused by the bishop of preaching the Covenant to a congregation of 500 in Armoy.[31]

So, for the space of twenty-five years Houston encouraged and maintained a small, convinced number of people who rejected the Restoration settlement. These caused divisions and unrest among Scottish Presbyterians at a time when the majority of ministers and members were resolved to work with the government. By and large, the majority view held and moderate Scottish Presbyterians consolidated their structure and organisation. Such a project could be jeopardised by fanatical elements in both Ireland and Scotland, and so any threat was treated with severity. However much they may have been attracted to the call of the Covenanters, most Presbyterians knew it was unrealistic in their situation.

Thus within the Scottish Presbyterian church in Ireland the element of extremism was seen as a real threat to the freedom ministers enjoyed on the whole. It was essential that the meetings and the general committee controlled the formation and ordination of ministers, as well as the calls made to ministers by congregations. Through this they hoped to vet all their personnel and reject any who refused to come through the system. David Houston played along with the Route meeting, but never intended to conform to the moderate stance of the indulged ministers. For a time he stayed within the system, and at least the meetings had a way of trying to discipline him, even if it failed.

Wandering or itinerant preachers, who belonged to no meeting at all, did not come under any authority.[32] They were influential and held a certain attraction; they came and went and brought news of all that was happening in the country and indeed in Scotland. A number were on the run from the authorities in Scotland and found safe houses in Ireland. To many in Ireland such preachers were a welcome link with Scotland and in their travels would be assured of protection. They were seen as martyrs and prophets, suffering for the kirk and resisting the enemy's persecution. Such was Alexander Peden.

Peden was deprived of his ministry in New Luce, Wigtownshire, in 1663 and for ten years was a conventicle preacher in Scotland and Ireland. As an itinerant preacher he visited Armagh in the early 1670s and encouraged the Goodhall family there in their resistance to prelacy.[33] Peden was arrested in Scotland in 1673 and spent over six years in the Bass Rock prison. Although he was banished to America in 1679, Peden in fact made his way back to Ireland. There he berated the ministers who complied with the government's order that all Scottish Presbyterian ministers declare that they had no part in the battle of Bothwell Bridge nor approved of it. Peden accused those ministers who went to Dublin of being 'sent and gone the Devil's errand'.[34]

Peden stayed around the Antrim area in 1679, and was in Ireland again in 1682, 1684 and 1685. There he stayed in safe houses: in 1682 he stayed with Mr Steil of Glenarm; in 1684 with John Slowan of Conert, County Antrim; in 1685 with Mr Craig and Mr Venor, an elder of the kirk, and with Venor's father-in-law, Mr Kilpatrick.[35] Venor's own minister opposed Peden and resented the fanatical element Peden nurtured.[36] With the activities of Houston already disturbing the people, cultivating unrest and the spirit of rebellion, Peden was viewed by many of the ministers as a further nuisance and threat to the church. Although Peden never joined the United Societies, he had great admiration for their principal leaders, Cargill and Cameron, and in time learned to respect Renwick; he was very much within the Covenanting tradition, contributing to it by his way of life and resistance. His style of preaching was striking:

> Now, what is it that has carried through the sufferers for Christ these twenty-two years in Scotland? . . . It is the filling up of Christ's sufferings in Scotland according to the ancient decree of heaven. For my part I seek no more, if He bids me go. He bade many, from 1660 to the year of the Pentlands engagement, go forth to scaffolds and gibbets for Him, and they sought no more but His commission. They went and He carried them well through. Then in 1666 at Pentland, He bade so many go to the fields and die for Him, and so many to scaffolds and lay down

their lives for Him. They sought no more but His commission. They went and He carried them well through. Again, 1679, at Bothwell, He bade many go to the fields and scaffolds and die for Him. They sought no more but His commission and went. And afterwards in the year 1680, at Ayrmoss, He bade so many go to the fields and scaffolds for Him. They sought no more but His commission and went. This cup of suffering has come all the way down from Abel to this year, 1682, in Scotland.[37]

No doubt this is the type of sermon Peden preached in Ireland, full of fire and flame. He held meetings in the houses of friends at night and sustained the hopes of the hearers for the return of the Covenanting days. Convinced as this small following was of their cause, mainstream Presbyterians feared their potential to disrupt the entire church and have them all branded as fanatics. The Covenanting movement among Scottish Presbyterians in Ireland was sustained and nurtured by the ministry of itinerant preachers from Scotland. Indeed the role of lay people was developed and strengthened by the fact that such ministry and preaching was both precarious and sporadic at all times. This was not entirely new, for from the beginnings of Scottish Presbyterianism in Ireland the laity were involved in their own form of worship and prayer. This was due both to the scarcity and the harassment of ministers.[38] It created a tradition which found expression in a new context: maintaining the societies formed both in Scotland and Ireland in the early 1680s, Covenanting societies, which had rejected the moderate stance within their own tradition.

Tensions in Dublin

Such tensions were not contained within Scottish Presbyterianism in Ulster, but spread to Dublin, where moderate and extreme elements clashed. After the Restoration Scottish Presbyterians became responsible for Bull Alley congregation in Dublin. Originally this church belonged to the Independents and was served by Robert Norbury and Robert Chambers.[39] However, Norbury died in 1662/3, and Chambers, a former minister in the Established Church, had to leave Dublin because he refused to conform and had been involved in Blood's Plot.[40] From the time of Norbury's death and Chambers's departure from Ireland, William Jacque, a Scottish Presbyterian, ministered in Bull Alley. Jacque came from Scotland during the Interregnum, was ordained at Aghadowey in 1655, and received a salary of £100 from Henry Cromwell. When the people of Clongish and the adjoining parishes in Longford asked for a minister, Jacque was sent in 1659. In 1663 he was arrested for complicity in Blood's Plot.[41] Two merchants in Dublin, Thomas Boyd and John Wallis, went bail for him of £500, and Jacque continued in Bull Alley.[42] There he stayed for some years until, dismissed from Bull Alley in 1667, he gathered his own congregation in Capel Street in 1668.

No record survives to explain why Jacque was dismissed from Bull Alley, but this event remained a source of conflict and friction. Even as late as 1698 it was noted that Jacque had never been authorised to establish a congregation in Capel Street.[43] Certainly Jacque wavered between the Independent and Scottish Presbyterian form of church government and confused his own congregation in the process. Nevertheless, while Jacque had difficulty accepting the authority of the general committee, he sought for recognition and inclusion within the meetings and attended the Antrim meeting on several occasions. It was an ambivalent relationship and caused unease in Dublin, allowing factions to grow within the Capel Street congregation which were very difficult to resolve. William Keyes was sent to fill the gap in Bull Alley, on a short-term basis at first; later on he was made permanent minister there.[44]

When the Antrim meeting minutes resume in 1672 the correspondence between Jacque and the meeting was extensive. At this time the Tyrone meeting had responsibility for Bull Alley and the south of Ireland in general.[45] Jacque wanted the Capel Street congregation to be joined to the Antrim meeting, but the Antrim meeting was suspicious of Jacque's motives. The meeting asked Capel Street congregation to send their views to all five meetings in the north, so that the general committee, rather than just the Antrim meeting, could deal with them. 'Grievances and grounds of the difference' were sent to the meeting by the elders in Dublin, but nothing at all came from Jacque himself.

The general committee censured Jacque for gathering a congregation without its consent.[46] It suggested that Jacque accept a colleague, formed in the Scottish Presbyterian/moderate tradition, hoping in this way that the problem could be modified; if Jacque refused this offer, he should be dismissed.[47] William Semple, on business in Dublin on behalf of the general committee, admitted that the most difficult part of his work was trying to keep a semblance of unity between Capel Street and Bull Alley until a decision was taken by the committee.[48] In the same year the Tyrone meeting asked the general committee if they could be rid of the responsibility for Bull Alley and of having to send ministers to the south of Ireland; they were finding it hard enough to get ministers for their own needs. The Antrim meeting advised that before any decisions were taken Bull Alley should be represented at the next general committee meeting, hoping to solve the problems of Bull Alley and Capel Street at the same time.[49]

The solution lay in establishing a committee of Scottish Presbyterian ministers in Dublin who would 'join with the rest of the synod and to subject themselves to the rest of their brethren'. In the same year (1672) the Laggan meeting decided to send one of their ministers, Archibald Hamilton, to visit Dublin to examine the possibility of establishing such a committee. The meeting recognised that this would be difficult to achieve, owing to the differences between Jacque and Bull Alley. Significantly, the meeting referred to the Act of Bangor (1654), whereby the disagreements in Scotland were not to be brought into the church in Ireland.[50] This indicated that the tensions in the Dublin congregations were serious, and not limited to questions of church order: the issue of the Covenanters had arisen in Dublin.

Under pressure from the Tyrone meeting to resolve the differences in his congregation, Jacque asked the Laggan meeting for help. Rather than act hastily, the Laggan sent William Semple again to Dublin to find out the best way to deal with the situation. The meeting also insisted that Jacque agree in writing to observe whatever decision the Laggan took with regard to Bull

Alley.[51] In the following year (1673), the Laggan meeting tried to conclude the business with Dublin:

> This meeting makes the overture to all the rest of the meetings that the business shall be *de novo* recognised by the meeting of Antrim together with the correspondents for the rest of the meetings.[52]

At the same time another matter came up for discussion, linked with the Bull Alley/Capel Street situation. Two candidates in Dublin, William Cock and William Liston, were ready for trials and ordination. On account of the differences in Dublin, the Laggan meeting could not see their way to allowing these ordinations to go forward. The Antrim and Tyrone meetings wrote to the Laggan suggesting the ordinations should take place. Again the Laggan sent two ministers to Dublin with authority to decide what was best there and then and so end the affair. However, if the Dublin committee continued to disagree, no decision was to be taken and a report to be drawn up instead. The outcome of this initiative was a request from the Dublin committee that the Laggan ordain Liston and Cock.[53]

Almost immediately the Laggan received a letter of protest from Colonel Sankey, William Keyes and William Cock.[54] Keyes had already asked to return to Belfast, giving reasons which have not been recorded. However, the general committee asked him to delay his decision until a meeting could be arranged. Eventually Keyes was appointed permanently to Bull Alley, in spite of the opposition of his congregation in Belfast and in particular of the Countess of Donegall. This action clarified the situation in Dublin. In May 1673 Jacque declared that he was willing to conform to the Scottish Presbyterian form of church government and recanted anything that was considered erroneous. At his own request he was annexed to the Down meeting.[55]

With regard to the ordination of Cock and Liston, the general committee insisted on the following conditions:[56] candidates were to accept the Presbyterian confession; they were to be ordained 'with a primary relation to the church ministerial and only a secondary to the place in which he is to labour'; they were to own the work of reformation carried out against popery; accept subjection to Presbyterian government by sessions, presbyteries, synods and general assemblies; and subscribe to the Act of Bangor. This last point indicated the source of the tension, which the Laggan had already pointed out. It arose from an effort to contain the dissident elements in the church and prevent the spread of the Covenanting tradition in Ireland, especially in Dublin. Through such conditions for ordination it was hoped that ministers could be controlled and disciplined.[57]

Nor were the conditions thus stipulated to apply only to the particular situation of Cock and Liston. In 1675 when the Cork congregation asked for a minister and Mr Cock proposed settling Mr Barclay there, the Laggan meeting encouraged this move on the condition that

> as he is in his judgement a Presbyterian so he would really show himself to be such by testifying his submission to the advice of his brethren and of subordination to the courts and jurisdiction of Jesus Christ amongst us.[58]

Again, in 1679 Cock wrote from Tipperary and asked if he could ordain Mr Harding for Cork, with two ministers, Mr Wood and Mr Bernard. Cock was advised to see if Harding agreed to 'our confession of faith and catechism'. There seemed to be no objection to the two ministers named, one of whom was certainly of the Independent tradition.[59] It is clear that the general committee and the individual meetings in the north of Ireland sought to maintain Scottish Presbyterian church order and discipline over churches and ministers in the south of Ireland. In 1675 the general committee proposed that Keyes, Liston, Cock and Jacque be annexed to the same meeting in the north, as this would be better for 'planting in the south'. This would curtail the autonomy of the Dublin committee, which perhaps was intended. In any event, the Laggan meeting did not approve of the proposal, and nothing was done in this regard.[60]

Yet a year later Jacque and Keyes themselves asked that Scottish Presbyterian ministers in and about Dublin be attached to a meeting in the north. In response, the Laggan made two suggestions: that all ministers in the south be established as a committee and annexed to the Antrim meeting; and that when candidates were presented for trials for ordination in the south some of the Antrim meeting be present.[61] Significantly, Cock and Liston thought the plan would only work if 'the English godly ministers at and about Dublin concur and join with it'.[62] This seems to have happened, for in 1681 at the ordination of Jacque's brother, Gideon, ministers of the English Presbyterian churches in Dublin were allowed to assist at the trial and ordination, as well as

> the concurrence and assistance even of such ministers of the congregational way and judgement as have been ordained by a consistory of presbyters, as far as they can prudently seek and obtain it.[63]

By insisting that ordinations could not take place unless Scottish Presbyterian church order was accepted and all the meetings in the north had given their approval, the general committee was able to retain control over ministers in Dublin, and indeed wherever one was called in the south.[64] So the matter rested, and apparently the authority of the northern committee was recognised and established. Jacque too seemed to have accepted the structures laid down. For example, he was asked to go to Cork and examine the possibilities of the committee answering a call from there; it was also mooted that he answer a call himself to go to Longford, where he had been during the Interregnum. As a matter of course Jacque referred to the Antrim meeting for an assistant minister, as well as for clarification of certain matters. The relationship seemed harmonious.[65]

However, this was not to last, and some hints that all was not well came in May 1683 when the Dublin committee yet again, through the Antrim meeting, asked the general committee to be independent of the northern meetings. The only response to this request was to note that the Dublin committee had paid no fees to the general committee; a donation of 10s was imposed, to be paid at Candlemas each year. However, at the same meeting a petition was presented by James Martin, a Belfast merchant,

> from divers of the people of Mr Jacque's congregation, with another paper containing a call to Mr John Hutcheson to be colleague in the ministry with the said Mr Jacque.[66]

Jacque was present at this May meeting of the general committee and was asked then if he could agree to the petition. He rejected it on several grounds: the petition was from a section of the congregation only; it would be difficult for the congregation to maintain two ministers; it would be unwise to have two ministers in Dublin in view of possible suppression of religious liberty. On these grounds the meeting decided to write a letter to the entire congregation in Capel Street and asked William Keyes of Bull Alley to speak to the congregation on a weekday and read the letter from the Antrim meeting.

In the following month the Antrim meeting, again with Jacque present, heard that some in Capel Street persisted in their request to have John Hutcheson as assistant to Jacque. This time Jacque produced a counter-petition from sixty-six of his congregation, rejecting the request for another minister. It was clear that Capel Street was a divided congregation and that the Antrim meeting could not be sure how much Jacque was responsible for the problem. Thomas Boyd of Dublin wrote to the meeting and explained that he had withdrawn temporarily from Capel Street, but gave no reasons; the meeting asked him for proof of Jacque's guilt in this affair, proof 'of such irregularities, as if known, might seem to render him unfit for the ministry, at least in Dublin'.[67]

It is difficult to know if Jacque really was the centre of the problem. While it is true that he seemed to be ambivalent over the forms of church government expected by the northern committee, nevertheless he sat on the general committee and referred to it in case of dispute. The truth may lie in the motivations of the group that wished to have another minister to assist Jacque. It was evident that they were dissatisfied, and the source of their dissatisfaction may have been the stance that the ministers in general were taking with regard to the government and its policy. While there was no real persecution of Protestant dissenters in Ireland at this time, it was evident that hard times were ahead.[68]

If Boyd, who had been actively involved with Jacque in Blood's Plot in 1663, was so disillusioned as to withdraw from Capel Street congregation, it could well have been because he felt that Jacque had surrendered both freedom and principle. For in August 1683 Jacque accepted the government's restrictions regarding religious worship, along with the Independents and English Presbyterians.[69] In this context, Boyd would have been influenced by David Houston's visit to Dublin in January 1683.[70] He would also have welcomed the visit of James Renwick in August of the same year.[71] Certainly Renwick[72] felt he had an opening in Dublin:

> I think the Lord has a special hand in my coming to this place . . . He has kindled a fire which I hope Satan will not soon quench. For all the people of this place were following men who did not follow the Lord and thought these were right enough; yet now some of them are saying we have been misled, we never knew before this we were standing between the Lord's camp and the adversaries . . . I have the more patience here because of the Lord's doing great things.[73]

When Renwick reached Scotland he wrote to a friend, exiled in Holland, giving details of the visit to Dublin. The people he met there wished him to stay in Dublin and argued that their need was greater than Scotland's, so he had promised to return; however, he explained, he had encountered the opposition of Jacque:

> But, as the Lord stirred up some people to all this, their (so-called) ministers increased their malice, especially one Mr Jacque, the ring leader of the rest, who sought to speak with me, which I would not, nor could, without stumbling of the people, refuse; who, when we met, we reasoned upon several heads.

They met again, and Jacque asked why Renwick was drawing his congregation from him. Renwick

> denied him to have a congregation and did only labour and desire to draw the people from sin unto their duty; and for accepting his call to preach, that I ought not, nor would not, because I could not own him as a faithful minister of Jesus Christ.[74]

Jacque challenged the validity of Renwick's ordination, but Renwick refused to debate this matter, saying there were no true ministers to judge him and Jacque was 'not competent to require that of me'. Besides, Renwick did not recognise Jacque's right to a congregation, to the exercise of ministry, especially for 'his yielding it up at the enemies command'.[75] This no doubt referred to Jacque's harassment by the government in the summer of 1683. He was cleared in law for 'holding an unlawful assembly' and so continued to hold meetings in the city.[76] The fact that he went to court and accepted the law of the land was fault enough for Renwick and his supporters in Dublin.

Renwick and the United Societies[77] kept up correspondence with Dublin, and on 3 October 1683 they wrote a long letter 'From the anti-popish, anti-prelatick, anti-erastian, true Presbyterian church of Scotland, to those that desire to join with the cause of God at Dublin in Ireland'. They wrote to their 'friends and covenanted brethren' a full account of the betrayal of the true kirk by most and saw themselves as 'the remnant who keepeth their ground' and 'follow the good old way'.[78] They told the group in Dublin that it would have to choose between the United Societies and the Dublin ministers. Those ministers had been wrong to accept the indulgence, and they deserted 'their meeting-houses at the command and threatening of men'. The society in Dublin was urged then to leave 'the backslidden ministers altogether unfaithful to our wronged Lord and Master'.[79]

The United Societies commended the welcome Renwick received in Dublin. Documents in Latin and English proving Renwick's ordination were sent to Dublin. Assistance by correspondence was assured, as was the promise of help for anyone 'whom the Lord sends forth unto us, clothed with his commission'.[80] It seems reasonable to assume that the group in Capel Street that broke off from Jacque was linked with the United Societies. Jacque, who had been involved in Blood's Plot in 1663, no longer followed that path. While none of their names have been recorded, there were some in Dublin who belonged to Covenanting societies and were actively involved in promoting the cause of Renwick and the United Societies. They were active in 1687, and Renwick recognised that:

> There are sundry societies in Ireland come out of the defections of the time who are keeping correspondence with us; I am desired to visit them and I purpose God willing to do so. When Mr David Houston was there in the end of spring he was very free and considerable numbers attended his preaching.[81]

Such interest and involvement in the United Societies in Ireland continued, and information was exchanged as to their purpose and growth.[82] This had begun at least as early as February 1683 and fed into the ongoing Covenanting spirit, which was strong among Scottish Presbyterians since the early days of the Covenant. It also built on the tradition, established from the beginnings of Scottish Presbyterianism in Ireland, of having groups meet for worship or for preparation for worship. Such groups or societies were of necessity lay movements, served by travelling ministers, such as Renwick, Peden or Houston.

The year 1683, then, was a momentous year for Capel Street congregation, and the tensions between the two factions continued long after Renwick's visit in August. By December 1683 nothing had been resolved, and the Antrim meeting heard again from several of the Capel Street congregation. They asked that either John Hutcheson become Jacque's colleague or that they separate with him and form a new congregation. They also wrote to Patrick Adair explaining their case. The meeting noted letters from this group, from William and Gideon Jacque, from the Dublin committee, and from the pro-Jacque faction in Capel Street.[83] The contents of the letters were not noted down, so it is difficult to know where the source of division lay. The case wore on until March 1684, when the Antrim meeting agreed that Capel Street would have to divide, since every effort to heal differences had failed. This was a blow and damaged the church; it was 'a scandal to our profession in that eminent place'.[84]

By April 1684 the split had occurred, and the Antrim meeting received letters from the new congregation at Newmarket in the Coombe reporting that they were receiving new members and they asked for a preacher. At the same time a letter of protest signed by Jacque and his congregation was sent from Capel Street. The Antrim meeting decided to encourage the Newmarket congregation to get preachers themselves until something definite could be arranged.[85] The meeting was disturbed to hear that some ministers and people in Dublin were critical of the Antrim meeting's involvement in the Capel Street/Jacque/Newmarket affair. This was serious, and Patrick Adair was deputed to write to Daniel Williams of Wood Street English Presbyterian congregation and explain the case to him. The meeting also decided to try to discover the reasons why people had left Capel Street.[86]

It is clear that the Antrim meeting was either unaware of or deliberately kept in the dark about the issues which led to the split in Dublin. Weary of the difficulties, it asked that the Down meeting take responsibility for Dublin, 'it never as yet having had the charge thereof'.[87] This did not happen, for in June 1684 two members of the Newmarket congregation asked the Antrim meeting again for preachers until Hutcheson could be appointed. The meeting decided to send Alexander Sinclair to Newmarket and so stabilise the situation there.[88]

In June 1684 the Dublin committee once again asked to be free of the northern meetings, and the request seems to have been either refused or ignored, for in July the Antrim meeting reprimanded the Dublin committee.[89] In requesting freedom from the five meetings in the north, the Dublin committee may have wanted to be free of the tensions within the Scottish Presbyterians in the north of Ireland, because these had spread to Dublin and were causing division. In Dublin they had to contend and work with the English Presbyterian and the Independent churches, and the possibility of harmony was greater if they could act freely on their own authority. Yet their petition does not seem to have been taken seriously.

In August, on the advice of the Laggan and Route meetings, the Antrim meeting proceeded with the libel against Jacque.[90] This decision was confirmed when respected members in Dublin advised that the libel should be pursued to the end. Tension in Dublin seems to have heightened, and the meeting noted: 'Mr Jacque sent a letter wherein he seems to decline our authority as proper judges in his cause.' A member of the meeting, Mr Hall, was deputed to write to Jacque and find out if he really meant to cut himself off; if there was some hope that he would still obey, one or two ministers were to go to Dublin, join William Keyes and Robert Kelso and some other ministers, and examine the libel against Jacque.[91]

Little clarification was forthcoming from Jacque, though he talked of submitting to a 'lawful synod'. At the same time Thomas Boyd sent a signed libel to the meeting and a decision was taken to send two ministers, John Anderson and James Pitcairn, to Dublin to hear the case in secret.[92] Jacque managed to block this move by proposing his own process and refusing any other;

he threatened that 'he will be constrained to take such measures as will not be pleasant in the issue'.[93] This could have been a threat to expose the links between the United Societies in Scotland and interested persons in Dublin; such information would certainly have embarrassed the general body of moderate Scottish Presbyterians.

Thoroughly weary of the affair, the Antrim meeting asked again to be relieved of the responsibility of Dublin and the south of Ireland.[94] Again its request was not granted, for a year later the Antrim meeting received approval from the Down meeting for the manner in which it handled the Jacque affair. But it was not over by any means. Gilbert Rule, who had been sent to Dublin by the Antrim meeting was

> discouraged on the account of his being discountenanced and looked down on by Mr Jacque, the ministers of Dublin and several professors therein and particularly that separation of others without and before the meeting's allowance, as also the Chancery suit against Mr Jacque by Mr Boyd, and lastly the libel given in by Mr Boyd against Mr Jacque.[95]

The meeting wanted to keep Rule in Dublin, especially in his capacity as assistant to Daniel Williams in Wood Street, and so the Newmarket congregation was asked to acknowledge publicly that they had acted wrongly in withdrawing from Capel Street without permission, even though they had been provoked into doing it by Jacque. This was a decision taken in weariness, for the meeting also indicated that it was ready to drop the libel against Jacque if only to keep the peace. The case in Chancery had to be settled, but nothing was to be paid unless the law found in Jacque's favour. It was a way of forcing Jacque to show his hand while protecting the ministry of Rule and maintaining good relations with other ministers in the city.[96]

This policy proved wise, for in June 1686 Williams wrote from Dublin and told the Antrim meeting that, with great difficulty, he had healed the differences between the two congregations,

> on this condition that the meeting will destroy the papers sent from Dublin hither from Mr Boyd as matter of accusation against Mr Jacque.

The meeting welcomed this cautiously and asked that Boyd and Jacque confirm this decision in writing.[97] It is difficult to know

whether the matter really ended there, for in the following year
the Antrim meeting once again asked for help in dealing with
ministers and congregations in Dublin and the south of Ireland,
threatening to abandon all 'at the foot of the rest of the
meetings'.[98] In April 1688 the general committee suggested that
the Dublin ministers be annexed to the Tyrone meeting, though
it confessed little hope that this would be accepted. The problem
was solved through political events, for Jacque left Dublin in
1688/9 and ministered in Whitehaven, with other dissenting
ministers from Dublin.[99] In 1691 the Antrim meeting was still
supplying ministers for Capel Street, but after 1692 this responsibility was assumed by the General Synod of Ulster. [100] Finally,
by June 1698 Capel Street congregation was freed by the Synod
of Ulster from any responsibility towards Jacque, 'he never having
been fixed there by any presbytery'.[101]

So ended a turbulent career in Ireland. In 1668 Jacque had
gathered his own congregation in Capel Street, and from this
time conflict ensued. For Scottish Presbyterians the basic structure of the church at Capel Street was fundamentally suspect,
but the northern committee persevered with it, possibly in the
hope of reaching agreement with Jacque and so avoiding a public
breach in the capital city. The unrest created by Jacque's am-
bivalence regarding church order was complicated by the influence of the Covenanting movement in Dublin. Jacque and
Boyd, who had both been implicated in Blood's Plot in 1663,
certainly differed in later years, and this discord came to a head
in 1686. It is difficult to know to what extent Boyd was involved
with Renwick and the United Societies, since the evidence was
destroyed or lost. Boyd did represent his case to the Antrim
meeting and sought a resolution there. In that respect, he accepted the authority of the meeting. Indeed, through all these
exchanges the general committee emerged as the source of
authority and decision-making. The Dublin committee of
ministers often found this difficult to work with and asked to be
freed from the general committee's authority. Since the Restoration the three dissenting traditions, Scottish Presbyterian, English
Presbyterian and Independent, met regularly in Dublin to settle
their affairs. There was a conflict of authorities, then, in the

affiliation of the Scottish Presbyterian ministers in Dublin and the south of Ireland. In time it would be amicably resolved, but at this period it was a source of difficulty and strain, as all dissenters sought to find ways to maintain growth and stability.

Notes and References

1   Ian B. Cowan, *The Scottish Covenanters, 1660-1688* London, 1976); Rosalind Mitchison, *Lordship and patronage: Scotland, 1603-1745* (London, 1983); David Stevenson, *The Covenanters: The National Covenant and Scotland* (Edinburgh, 1988); W. T. C. Brotherstone (ed.), *Covenant, charter and party* (Aberdeen, 1989).

2   Antrim minutes, 8 Aug. 1671, p. 3. Houston was born near Paisley in 1633. He went to Glasgow University in 1648 and took his M. A. in 1654. He came to Antrim in 1660 as a licentiate and undertook to supply some congregations belonging to the Route meeting. Nothing is known of his training for the ministry, but presumably he was greatly influenced by the Covenant tradition. McConnell, *Fasti,* no. 163, pp 67-8; Adam Loughridge, *The Covenanters in Ireland* (Rathfriland, 1987), p. 11.

3   Antrim minutes, 5 Sept. 1671 p. 5.

4   At the Restoration Orrery informed Ormond that Scottish Presbyterians said that they themselves would proceed against any who advocated the Solemn League and Covenant. Orrery to Ormond, 2 Jan. 1661. (T. Morrice, *A collection of the state letters of Roger Boyle, first Earl of Orrery* (Dublin, 1743), p. 29).

5   Stevenson, *The Covenanters,* pp 59-69; Mitchison, *Lordship and patronage,* pp 68-92; Julia Buckroyd, *Church and state in Scotland, 1660-1681* (Edinburgh 1980), passim.

6   Route meeting minutes, 27 Feb. 1672, N.L.S., Wodrow MSS, Folio 32, no. 89 (P.R.O.N.I., T525, no. 16); Robert Allen, 'Scottish ecclesiastical influence upon Irish Presbyterianism from the subscription controversy to the union of synods' (M.A. thesis Q.U.B., 1940) p. 16. Thomas Wyllie was minister of Coleraine *c.* 1669. Hew Scott, *Fasti Ecclesiae Scotianae,* 7 vols (Edinburgh, 1920), iii, pp 49, 94; Reid, *History of the Presbyterian Church,* ii, 407; Robert Wodrow, *History of the sufferings of the Church of Scotland from the Restoration to the Revolution,* 4 vols (Glasgow, 1836), i, 326; N.L.S., Wodrow MSS, Folio 32, nos 110, 111. He was instrumental in having David Calderwood's *History of the Kirk of Scotland* published in Holland in 1678.

7   N.L.S., Wodrow MSS, Folio 26, no. 123, f. 215.

8   Ibid., MSS, Folio 32, no 89; P.R.O.N.I., T525, no. 16.

9   William Semple (1624-74) was born in Scotland. He studied in Glasgow and was ordained for Letterkenny in 1647/8. He was on the Commonwealth lists from 1654. He was ejected in 1661, but stayed on in

Donegal and ministered to congregations there. Arrested in 1663, he was jailed by the Bishop of Raphoe from 1664 to 1670. He helped to negotiate the *regium donum* in 1672. McConnell, *Fasti,* no. 103, p. 48; Scott, *Fasti,* iii, 157; A. J. Weir, *Letterkenny: congregations, ministers and people, 1615-1960* (Belfast, 1960).

10   N.L.S., Wodrow MSS, Folio 26, no. 124, f. 217; also 13 Mar. 1672 (ibid., f. 218).

11   Shaw to Wyllie, 14 Mar. 1672 ibid., no. 125, f. 219; also Adair to Wyllie, 20 Mar. 1672 (ibid, no. 127, f. 222).

12   Reid, *History of the Presbyterian Church,* ii, 404-5.

13   Antrim minutes, 13 Aug. 1672, p. 51.

14   Laggan minutes, 21 Aug. 1672 p.7; 23 October 1672, p. 23.

15   Antrim minutes, pp 57, 60.

16   [Alexander Shields], *A hind let loose or a historical representation of the testimonies of the church of Scotland* (n.p., 1687); Alexander Shields, *The history of the Scotch presbytery, being an epitome of 'The hind let loose'* (London, 1692); J. K. Hewison, *The Covenanters,* 2 vols (Glasgow, 1913), ii, Appendix 3: 'The united societies', p. 557; Cowan, *The Scottish Covenanters,* pp 110, 124; I. B. Cowan, 'The Covenanters: a revision article' in *Scottish Historical Review,* xlvii (1968), pp 47-52; J. G. Vos, *The Scottish Covenanters* (Pittsburgh, 1980), pp 95-127; Magnus Linklater and Christian Hesketh, *For king and conscience: John Graham of Claverhouse, Viscount Dundee, 1648-1689* (London, 1989), pp 65-8.

17   Thomas Houston, *The life of James Renwick* (Edinburgh, 1987), pp 10-11.

18   Ibid., p. 12.

19   Bodl., Carte MS 40, ff 182, 187, 188; also f.189 for the October declaration; ibid., MS 50, f 228; B.L., Lansdowne MS 1152A, ff 182, 176, 156, 330-1, 344, 347, 349, 354, 361.

20   Nov.-Dec. 1684 (Bodl., Carte MS 40, ff 190, l90v, l91, 191v, 192). Callwell was a bookbinder. H.M.C., *Ormonde MSS,* vii, 293- 4.

21   26 Nov. 1684 (Bodl., Carte MS 220, f. 64).

22   Antrim minutes, 1 Mar. 1687, 292.

23   Ibid., 5 July 1687, p. 365.

24   Ibid., 3 Aug. 1686, p. 272.

25   Ibid., 2 Nov. 1686, p. 274.

26   Ibid., 5 July 1687, p. 305. Houston's followers from Ballycastle, Aghoghill, Drumall and Ballymoney, about twenty-three in all, wrote a testimony in support of him.

27   Loughridge, *The Covenanters in Ireland,* p. 12.

28   'The principal acts and conclusions of the United Societies in the west and south from their rise in 1681 to their ministerial journey to the assembly, 1690' (N.L.S., Wodrow MSS, Quarto 38, ff 161, 170, 171, 173-4, 178; also f.182, 189; Bodl., Carte MS 40, f.190.

29   Antrim minutes, 1 Mar. 1687, pp 287, 292. At the same time his followers in Ireland had to be disciplined, and the Route asked the other meetings in Ireland for advice. Houston had flouted its authority, disowned it, and appealed from them and the meetings in Ireland to the first General Assembly of the Church of Scotland. This is a strange statement, for it

is clear that Houston appealed to the societies only in Scotland, and indeed invited his followers to join with James Renwick in Scotland.

30 Hill, *The Montgomery Manuscripts*, p. 274, n. 51. Houston gave Mount Alexander 'a bond of compliance'.

31 Bishops of Meath and Derry to Capel, 24 Mar. 1694 (P.R.O., SP 63/256/29); Hugh McHenry of Dumfries, follower of Houston, suspected of wanting to come to Ireland, 2 June 1698 (*Records of the General Synod of Ulster, 1691-1820*, 3 vols (Belfast, 1890-98), ii, 32); Notes at end of the Antrim minutes; Loughridge, *The Covenanters in Ireland*, p. 13.

32 In 1687 the Antrim meeting cautioned 'Let sessions and congregation . . . be warned against vagrant, pretended ministers.' Antrim minutes, p. 305.

33 Patrick Walker, *Some remarkable passages of the life and death of Mr Alexander Peden, late minister of the gospel at New Glenluce in Galloway* (3rd ed., Edinburgh, 1728), p. 106; John Howie, *Biographia Scotiana or a brief historical account of the most eminent Scots worthies* (Glasgow, 1827), p. 514ff; 'Mrs Goodhall's memoirs of her husbands residence and imprisonment at Armagh A.D. 1658-77' in Reid, *History of the Presbyterian Church*, ii, Appendix 8, p. 563; F. J. Bigger, 'Alexander Peden, the 'prophet' 'in *U.J.A.*, ix, no. 3 (July 1903), pp 116-27; Thomas Cameron, *Peden the prophet* (Edinburgh, 1981), pp 20-1; John C. Johnston, *Alexander Peden, the prophet of the Covenant* (Kilkeel, 1988), pp 83-5; Alexander Smellie, *Men of the Covenant* (Edinburgh, 1975), ch. 35.

34 Walker, *Some remarkable passages*, p. 55; Johnson, *Alexander Peden*, pp 109-10.

35 Ibid., pp 56-8, 112-4, 117, 57.

36 Ibid., p. 112; Johnson, *Alexander Peden*, pp 123-9.

37 John Howie, *Sermons delivered in times of persecution in Scotland* (Edinburgh, 1880) p. 567.

38 John Livingstone, *A brief historical relation of the life of Mr John Livingstone*, ed. Thomas McCrie (Edinburgh, 1848) p. 80; When Houston and Peden died the small groups in Ireland were served by John Macmillan, who came to Ireland in 1707 and 1715; people brought their children to Scotland for baptism by Covenanter ministers. Allen, 'Scottish ecclesiastical influence upon Irish Presbyterianism', pp 225-6.

39 Armstrong, *Summary history of the Presbyterian Church*, p. 90; Barnard, *Cromwellian Ireland*, pp 136 n. 1, 137, 143, 175-6, 192 n. 41, 203, n. 92; New Row Baptismal Register, ff 1-2; Chambers returned to Ireland in 1673. Essex to Arlington, 17 Apr. 1673 (*Essex Papers*, p.78). Chambers wrote 'An explanation of the shorter catechism of the Reverend Assembly of Divines', 'from my study in Golden Lane in Dublin, October 16 1679'.

40 For Blood's Plot, see pp. 228-29.

41 Conway to Ormond, 11 June 1663 (Bodl., Carte MS 32, f. 331). For Blood's Plot, see pp. 228-29.

42 Thomas Boyd was a Dublin merchant and M.P. for Bangor; he was expelled from the House of Commons in 1663 for complicity in Blood's Plot. Hill, *The Montgomery Manuscripts*, pp 237 n. 72, 139. He owned land in Dublin, bought from Sir William Fenton in 1656, in the area of Castle Street, Copper Alley, Glebe Alley, Sinock Alley and Scarlet Alley. He built

houses there and rented them, taking the Earl of Orrery to court for non-payment of arrears. National Archives, Records of the Irish Record Commission, 1810-1830, RC 6/2, 322, 324; RC 6/3, 29, 71.

43   *Records of the General Synod of Ulster,* ii, 8. From 1661 to 1667 Jacque was a member of the Laggan meeting. W. D. Baillie, *A history of congregations in the Presbyterian Church in Ireland, 1610-1982* (Belfast, 1982), p. 439.

44   Sermons of William Keyes in Dublin, 1672 (Magee College, MS 29, ff 479-91, 533-44; Armstrong, *Summary history of the Presbyterian Church,* pp 90, 95-6; Irwin, *History of Presbyterianism,* p. 9; McConnell, *Fasti,* no. 83, p. 44; Antrim minutes, pp 55, 60, 67, 69, 79, 83, 87; Laggan minutes, pp 35, 53, 72. R. M. Young, *Historical notes of old Belfast* (Belfast, 1896), pp 101-5; Bodl., Carte MS 159, ff 151-151v; J. W. Nelson, 'The Belfast Presbyterians, 1670-1830' (Ph.D. thesis, Q.U.B., 1985), pp 7, 9, 289. Keyes was an English Presbyterian who came to Glaslough *c.* 1658/9 and became chaplain to the Countess of Donegall from 1659 to 1673.

45   Antrim minutes, 3 July 1672, p. 48.

46   Ibid., Oct. 1672, p. 64.

47   Ibid., 9 Apr. 1672, p. 31.

48   William Semple for Thomas Fulton, 15 Mar. 1672 (N.L.S., Wodrow MSS, Folio 26, no. 126, f. 221).

49   Antrim minutes, 3 July 1672, p. 48. It appears that the Laggan took on responsibility for Dublin and the south at this time.

50   Ibid., 21 Aug. 1672, pp 7-8; Antrim minutes, 13 Aug. 1672, p. 53. Bishop Hackett of Down and Connor pointed out to Essex how active the Covenanters were in his diocese at this time. Hackett to Essex, 29 Oct. 1672 (*Essex Papers,* pp 37-8).

51   Ibid., 18 Sept. 1672, pp 18, 28.

52   Ibid., 14 May 1673, p. 53.

53   Ibid., pp 54, 57, 62; sermon, 26 Jan. 1673 (Magee College, MS 29, f. 18).

54   Ibid., Nov. 1673, p.72; Antrim minutes, pp 55, 60, 67; Laggan minutes, pp 35, 40, 52, 69, 72. There is no record of the actual content of their protest. Possibly they wanted a more formal recognition of their right to ordain without assumed permission of the northern committee, which implied acceptance of Scottish Presbyterianism. Hierome Sankey was a Baptist, active in Ireland during the Interregnum. In 1674 he was nominated churchwarden by the vestry of St Bride's and paid a fine to 'free him as if he had served'. The nomination caused division between the minister and some parishioners, and the case was sent to the Archbishop of Dublin. R.C.B., P 327/3/1, St Bride's, St Michael le Pole's and St Stephen's Vestry Acts, 1662-1742, ff 40-1. (Sermons of Sankey are recorded for 1674 (Sermons of W. Lamb and H. Sankey, 1674, T.C.D., MS A.6.13). During the reign of Charles II Richard Lawrence held Baptist meetings in his home in Kevin Street, Dublin. *A memoir of Mistress Ann Fowkes, née Geale . . . with some recollections of her family, 1641-1774, written by herself* (Dublin, 1892), pp 15-16.

55   Antrim minutes, pp 69, 71, 79, 83, 87, 88.

56   Ibid., 3 June 1673, p. 97.

57 The Act of Bangor was included in the rules for ordination operative in the northern meetings at this time. Candidates were to 'adhere to the Covenant' and be peaceful 'considering the temper of these times'. Antrim minutes, pp 53, 32-7. Such rules caused some tension over the question of Liston and Cock's ordinations; this was probably represented in the conflict between the Independent stress on particular churches and the Scottish form of church government. Laggan minutes, pp 72, 76, 173, 237.

58 Laggan minutes, 9 Mar. 1675, p. 162. The Laggan rejected William Patterson for exercising a ministry in Sligo without reference to the meeting. Ibid., 21 Aug. 1672, pp 1-2.

59 Ibid., 5 Feb. 1679, p. 328. James Wood was Independent minister at Youghal in 1657, where he disputed with the Quaker James Sicklemore on the question of ordination (Sicklemore, *To all the inhabitants of Youghal who are under the teachings of James Wood*, (n.p., 1657/8)). He did not conform and was schoolmaster at the Erasmus Smith school in Tipperary, which was exempt from episcopal visitation during Smith's lifetime. Barnard, *Cromwellian Ireland*, p. 192, n. 39; Edwards, 'History of the laws against Protestant non-conformity', p. 136. Wood wrote *Shepardy spiritualised* (London, 1680); it was dedicated to his 'beloved friends the sheepmasters and shepherds in the county of Tipperary and Ireland', and Timothy Taylor wrote a letter of recommendation for it.

60 Antrim minutes, 26 May 1674, p. 147; Laggan minutes, 6 July 1675, p. 181.

61 Laggan minutes, pp 242, 246. This proposal was not implemented then; in 1680 the Laggan repeated it, but agreement was never reached even though by 1683 the Antrim meeting was dealing with Dublin. Laggan minutes, ii, July 1680, p. 65; cf. p. 194. In 1686 the Laggan asked again that Dublin be established as a meeting. Antrim minutes p. 280.

62 Laggan minutes, p. 246.

63 Ibid., ii, 20 Apr. 1681, pp 93-4; Gideon Jacque was ordained for Wexford in 1681. Sermon, New Ross 5 June 1681, (Magee College, MS 29, ff 395-401); McConnell, *Fasti*, no. 167, p. 69. By this tine in Dublin Independent, English Presbyterian and Scottish Presbyterian ministers had formed a loose form of association and met monthly in the city. See Chapters 4 and 5.

64 Antrim minutes, pp 186, 188, 192. In 1710 the Synod of Ulster and the presbytery of Dublin reached an agreement on ordination rules. Irwin, *History of Presbyterianism*, pp 38-9; *Records of the General Synod of Ulster*, 238-40.

65 Antrim minutes, 26 May 1674, p. 147; Laggan minutes, 13 June 1677, p. 264; Antrim minutes, Jan. 1683, p. 194; June 1683, p. 196.

66 Antrim minutes, pp 192-3. John Hutcheson was the son of Alexander Hutcheson, minister at Saintfield. Before 1679 he conducted a philosophy school at Newownards, Co. Down. He was ordained in 1690. He did not go to Capel Street, but his father was there from 1690-1692. McConnell, *Fasti*, no 165, p. 68; no. 76, p. 40; H.M.C., *Ormonde MSS*, v, 125, 608; Scotts, *Fasti*, vii, 663. *Francis Hutcheson: a special symposium on the thought, career and influence in Ireland, Scotland and America of the Ulster-Scots philosopher and dissenter* (supplement to *Fortnight* no. 308, 1992).

67   Antrim minutes, 12 June 1683, p. 195. Boyd had gone bail for Jacque when he was implicated in Blood's Plot See note 40 above.

68   Phillips to Boyle, 23 Jan 1683 (H.M.C, *Ormonde MSS,* vi, 519-20). This mirrored the situation in Scotland, where members of the United Societies felt that the vast majority of ministers had surrendered to the state and so betrayed the kirk. In February 1683 they sent Alexander Gordon with a call to ministers in Ireland, naming Alexander Peden, Michael Bruce (at Killinchy) and Samuel Arnot. John Howie, *Faithful contendings displayed* (Glasgow, 1780), pp 49-50.

69   For the situation regarding religious liberty in Dublin at this time see 'The Mather Papers', pp 37, 44, 46-7, 54, 56, 65, 486; J. T. Gilbert (ed.), *Calendar of ancient records of Dublin in the possession of the municipal corporation,* 6 vols, (Dublin, 1889-96), i, 345. The Quakers continued to meet for public worship and were highly critical of the acquiescence of other Protestant dissenters. John Burnyeat, *The truth exalted* (London, 1691), pp 74-5, 78-91, 87.

70   Phillips to Boyle, 23 Jan. 1683 (H.M.C., *Ormonde MSS,* vi, 519-20)

71   Wodrow MSS, Folio 24, as recorded in Wodrow MSS, Quarto 109 (index to the MSS), is missing from the collection in the National Library of Scotland. Despite extensive searches there and elsewhere it cannot be found. The index lists several letters: Letter of the societies to their friends in Dublin, 3 Oct. 1683, f.98; Letter from some people in Ireland, f.98; *c.* 1685, f.177; Letter to friends in Ireland, 2 Mar. 1687, f.210; Paper from Ireland to the societies, 26 Dec. 1688, f.240; Societies' letter to their friends in Ireland, 24 July 1689, f. 252; Also ff 209 and 216 contain material on Houston and Renwick, Sept. 1686–Aug. 1687. Some of these letters were published in the eighteenth century.

72   James Renwick was born in Galloway in 1662 and educated at Edinburgh. There he joined the secret meetings of the United Societies and witnessed the death of Donald Cargill. Destitute of ministers after the deaths of both Cameron and Cargill, the United Societies sent Renwick to Holland to be prepared for ministry; he studied at the University of Groningen and was ordained there by a Dutch presbytery. This ordination was queried by the church in Scotland. Renwick returned to Scotland in September 1683, *via* Dublin. He led the United Societies in Scotland and Ireland until his execution in 1688. Thomas Houston, *The life of James Renwick* (Edinburgh, 1987), pp 8-12, 40-3; Alexander Shields, *The life and death of Mr James Renwick* (Edinburgh, 1724); Robert Simpson, *Life of the Rev. James Renwick* (Edinburgh, 1843); W. H. Carslaw, *Life and times of James Renwick* (Paisley, 1901); W.H. Carslaw, *Life and letters of James Renwick* (Edinburgh, 1893); Jean Lawson, *Life and times of Alexander Peden and James Renwick* (Glasgow, *c.* 1905); Thomas Houston, *The letters of Rev. James Renwick, with an introduction by Thomas Houston* (Paisley, 1845); Howie, *Biographia Scotiana,* pp 528-46.

73   James Renwick to Robert Hamilton, Dublin, 24 Aug. 1683 (*A collection of letters consisting of ninety-three, sixty-one of which wrote by Rev. Mr James Renwick, the remainder by Rev. Messrs John Livingstone, John Brown, John King, Donald Cargill, Richard Cameron, Alexander Peden and Alexander Shields. Also a few by Mr Michael*

Shields at the direction of the general correspondence. *From the years 1663-1689 inclusive* (Edinburgh, 1764), p. 52.

74 Renwick to Hamilton, 20 Sept. 1683 (ibid., p. 56).

75 Ibid., p. 57.

76 Arran to Ormond, 1 Aug. 1683 (H.M.C. *Ormonde MSS*, vii, 93-4); Bodl., Carte MS 40, f. 54.

77 For details of the United Societies, their organisation and conviction see Alexander Shields, *The history of the Scotch presbytery, being an epitome of 'The hind let loose'* (London, 1692); Alexander Shields, *An informatory vindication of a poor, wasted, misrepresented, remnant of the suffering, anti-popish, anti-prelatick, ant-erastian, anti-sectarian true Presbyterian Church of Christ in Scotland* (n.p., 1707); John Howie *Faithful contendings displayed* (Glasgow, 1780); Thomas Houston, *The life of James Renwick* (Edinburgh, 1987). Copies of Shields's *The Hind let loose* were found in the Custom House in Belfast in 1696/7. William Tisdall, *The conduct of dissenters* (Dublin, 1712), p. 67.

78 *A collection of letters*, p. 352. (This letter is listed in the Wodrow Index, Quarto 109, for Folio 24, f. 98.)

79 Ibid., pp 353-4.

80 Ibid., pp 356-7.

81 Renwick to Hamilton, 15 July 1687 (ibid., p. 179).

82 To friends in Ireland, 2 Mar. 1687; To friends in Ireland, 24 Jan. 1689 (pp 388-9, 421-425). (These letters are listed in the Wodrow Index, Quarto 109, for Folio 24, ff 177, 252.)

83 Antrim minutes, pp 203-5.

84 Ibid., p. 208.

85 Ibid., p. 212.

86 Ibid., p. 217-18.

87 Ibid., p. 219.

88 Ibid., p. 223. Sinclair did not go to Newmarket; he was sent to Waterford in 1686 and went to Bull Alley, and then to Plunkett Street in 1692. In 1687 Newmarket asked for Mr Osburn of Brigh, Co. Tyrone. Armstrong, *A summary history of the Presbyterian Church*, pp 58, 95-6.

89 The meetings' approval of the Dublin minutes had not been acknowledged by either Keyes of Bull Alley or Jacque of Capel Street, and the meeting wondered if the ministers were actually meeting at all. Antrim minutes, pp 222, 227.

90 Ibid., p. 231.

91 Ibid., 2 Dec. 1684, p. 236. Robert Kelso was born in Templepatrick and was educated in Scotland; he was sent to Wicklow in 1674. McConnell, *Fasti*, no 169, p. 69.

92 However, if Jacque disagreed with this procedure, then the ministers were not to travel. Antrim minutes, 6 Jan. 1685, p. 238.

93 Ibid., 3 Mar. 1685, p. 241.

94 Ibid., 14 Apr. 1685, p. 244. The request was renewed in the following year. Ibid., 4 May 1686, p. 261.

95 Ibid., 6 Apr. 1686, p. 255. Rule had come to Ireland to escape harassment in Scotland. Alexander Gordon (ed.), *Freedom after ejection* (Manchester,

1917), p. 304; Armstrong, *Summary history of the Presbyterian Church,* p. 69; Smellie, *Men of the Covenant,* pp 402, 478, 512; Calamy, *An historical account,* pp ii, 514-18. His appointment to Wood Street was possibly a way of retaining good relations with the English Presbyterians in Dublin.

96 Antrim minutes, 6 Apr. 1686, p. 256. By July 1686 Rule reported that Newmarket admitted their mistake and that his own ministry was going well. Ibid., p. 265.

97 Ibid., 8 June 1686, p. 263.

98 Ibid., 7 June 1687, p. 305. The general committee in May 1687 queried if there were openings in the south for ministers; perhaps the Antrim meetings felt it could not handle any more appointments. Ibid., p. 298.

99 New Row Baptismal Register, f. 11. Later Jacque returned to Scotland and ended his days in Biggar. McConnell, *Fasti,* no. 77, p. 41. Gideon Jacque went to Liberton in Edinburgh in 1692 and returned to Wexford in 1695. He refused the Oath of Abjuration. McConnell, *Fasti,* no. 167, p. 69; Laggan minutes, ii, pp 93-4.

100 Antrim minutes, pp 372, 481. Armstrong, *A summmary history of the Presbyterian Church,* pp 96-99.

101 *Records of the General Synod of Ulster,* ii, 8.

6

Controversies between Quakers and other Dissenting Traditions

God did commit to the care and faithfulness of Christ his shepherd
a certain particular number to be justified and saved by him, and
therefore not all the race of fallen mankind, as Papists, Arminians,
Quakers, Freewillers . . . vainly teach.

James Barry, *The doctrine of particular election* (1715)

Quakers and English Presbyterians

While Scottish Presbyterians, English Presbyterians and Independents agreed on the basic beliefs and practices necessary for
the life of a church (ordained ministry, use of sacraments, primacy
of the scriptures, predestination/reprobation), Quakers had rejected these in favour of a simpler form of Christianity. Inevitably
the two views clashed, several times and in several ways, during
the second half of the seventeenth century in Ireland, and during the Interregnum Quakers and English Presbyterians were
constantly at loggerheads. Indeed, Quakers were bound to conflict with those conservative clergy who then were searching for
a strong, national church, with tithes restored and a settled
ministry, capable of controlling religious groups and wandering
preachers.

The Quakers grew in considerable strength in Limerick, and Henry Ingoldsby, governor of the city, tried to stem their growth.[1] In the course of 1655 the city had a succession of visits from Edmund Burrough and Francis Howgill, Edward Cooke and James Sicklemore, Barbara Blagdon and John Perrott. While Perrott was imprisoned in Limerick he was forced to hear a minister, probably Claudius Gilbert, whereupon, 'he having quite ended, I being moved by the Lord stood up and spoke'.[2] The debates did not end there, for Gilbert saw the Quakers as a threat to the stability of the country and wrote several tracts against them.[3] Their danger to society had been proved to Gilbert's satisfaction through recantations of former Quakers and through the opinions of magistrates and ministers in Ireland. It was clear to him that Quakerism was

> driven on by numerous Jesuits, friars and other Romish engineers to make a distraction and party for to serve their own ends, that having lost our truth and peace we may be fitted for their will.[4]

He distrusted their way of speaking, acting and praying, especially their extreme behaviour:

> they fume and foam, they range and toss . . . first ranting, then quaking . . . the Ranters were merrily, the Quakers were melancholically mad.[5]

New groups were often seen in their antecedents, either in the history of the early church or in the early period of the Reformation, or indeed in other religions. Thus Gilbert linked Quaker behaviour with the dervishes of Islam,[6] with the saints of the Roman Church, Dominic, Francis, Benedict, Ignatius, Catherine of Siena and Bridget, all 'the great patrons of Quakers'. They were also reminiscent of the Anabaptists in sixteenth-century Germany. Certainly Quakers in Limerick required the firm hand of the magistrates:

> The crowding of Quakers into these parts, especially into this city, has been a great concern of these lines . . . the tumultuousness of the Quaking rout had several times disturbed both the worshippers of God and the public peace. They had ensnared many of our soldiers, infected divers of our citizens, gathered many disciples in the garrisons and country, and railed most vilely at the magistrates and ministers of Christ. They had spread multitudes of pamphlets, libels and papers . . . and by all possible ways laboured to gather a strong party. . . . Divers papists among

us began to like their way finding it so like the monkish course of their friars . . . The Quakers spoke out against the ordinances, the word, sacraments, prayers, the sabbath etc. . . . They molested us daily from several parts of Ireland and England. Being turned out, they returned with their old tricks renewed.[7]

Gilbert spent hours debating with Quakers who came to Limerick, and he read their books and papers.[8] He specified which teachings and views he found most difficult,[9] and he accused Quakers of being revivers of old, long-condemned heresies. In particular Quakers were presumptuous, perfectionist, slanderous and 'wild beasts' in terms of doctrine. For example, they attacked the reality of Christ's humanity:

> What shall we think of those quaking impostors, that own no Christ above but what's in them, that renew the Ranter's blasphemy of Gods being all things, their being Christed etc. . . . His humanity variously assaulted by notionists of an old and new stamp, by many Behemenists and the swarms of Quakers . . . casts them into strange dreams about Christ's manhood which they fancy to have been but a fiction and a figure, a phantasm and apparition, that vanished after a while, to represent that within them which they call Christ.[10]

Gilbert insisted on the humanity of Christ, for by attacking that Quakers undermined the centre of Christianity:

> Christ's incarnation, life and passion are with them but stories and shadows; the life and substance is all within them. There say they lies Christ very deep in every man's heart, covered with earth, to be born and raised up, to live and to die, to do and to suffer. As for the Christ that died at Jerusalem, many do slight him, and many that seem to own him verbally, yet renounce him effectively . . . Our late Quakers . . . have revived those rotten dregs from the Familists, adding a new dress and access thereto.[11]

Gilbert accused the Quakers of claiming or winning salvation by their own efforts and of either denying or ignoring Christ's grace: they 'pass it in silence as needless or useless'. This struck at the heart of the doctrine of predestination and election and so was theologically intolerable.[12] Claiming 'immediate revelations and infallible oracles . . . pretending extraordinary acquaintance with God and spirits' made Quakers dangerously similar to the Gnostics in the early church.[13] In addition, they denied the resurrection, 'own no Christ but what is within them', put scripture and their own 'pretended revelations' on an equal footing, 'giving to their pretended light within the infallibility which the papists give to their pope and council'.[14]

Gilbert specifically accused the Quakers of being influenced by 'Jesuits, friars and other Roman engineers to make a distraction and party fit to serve their own ends'. He suspected that the Roman Church worked to win toleration for all, and to this purpose Roman agents

> must therefore appear under a pharisaical monkish garb, pretending much to external righteousness and self denial that their plausible colours may disguise their horrid inside . . . What could not be done by Seekers, Levellers, Arminians and Ranters shall now be better carried on by Quakers, the sublimate of them all.[15]

Gilbert also accused Quakers, in their personal life and behaviour, of being 'conceited perfectionists . . . in their pharisaical monkish holiness'. This referred even then to the austerity of life which would become such a hallmark of the Quakers. He also hinted that Quaker claims to infallibility were similar to that of the pope, a charge that also would increase with the years.[16]

Gilbert grasped the significance of the Quaker movement and saw it as undermining the basic tenets of reformation theology and practice. He saw the Quakers as essentially a destructive and negative force in Ireland. Thus from 1655 there were radical differences between the Quakers and English Presbyterians regarding several issues: the nature and mission of Christ, the doctrine of predestination and election, the place and role of sacraments, the primacy of the scriptures, the value of church order and its enforcement by magistrates. Quakers undermined these assumed foundations of an ordered society in a way which could only be interpreted as sinister. Just as the German Anabaptists brought confusion in their day, so the Quakers were doing in Ireland and specifically in Limerick.[17]

Another conservative Presbyterian minister, Samuel Ladyman, also attacked the Quakers and, like Gilbert, compared them to the Anabaptists of Münster.[18] Ladyman criticised the Quaker insistence on freedom of conscience, which he called a subordinate rule, 'the understanding's echo'. He insisted that conscience needed laws; on its own it was arbitrary and uncertain; even scripture could be abused by conscience, and its uncontrolled interpretation could have disastrous results:[19]

> How easily, how often is it abused by the ignorance of some and the corruption of others? Were the application of this righteous law left to conscience, the Quakers' dreams might commence uncontrollable edicts. Some would leave their wives, children, their families, and our Saviour's words, Matt. 19:29, must both justify and commend them.[20]

The debate with the Quakers was continued by another minister, George Pressicke of Dublin. Although not recorded as a member of the association of ministers, Pressicke argued for a comprehensive church at the Restoration, asking in particular that former 'godly ministers' be allowed to preach in Ireland.[21] He wrote a tract in 1660 against Baptists and Quakers in Ireland repeating both Gilbert and Ladyman's accusations that Quakers were similar to the Anabaptists of sixteenth-century Germany.[22]

Pressicke's work was as much a political as a theological tract, for from February 1660 the position of the Baptists and Quakers in Ireland became progressively undermined. Pressicke rejected any tradition that did not resemble Presbyterian church order. In this context, he denounced the Baptists, Quakers and Ranters for rejecting infant baptism; for refusing oaths and the taking of offices as magistrates, while giving the power of the sword to ministers; for rejecting profane learning and claiming that the ignorant were able to expound scripture; and for asserting that there were no ministerial callings in the church, but that all were to speak as they were inspired:

> We may see the sad symptoms hereof among ourselves, some have not spared to say they hoped within a short time there should not be a minister in Ireland.[23]

These remarks were particularly relevant when Pressicke wrote, for in 1659 there was a danger, for a short period, that Independents and Baptists could seize power in Dublin.[24] Attacks such as Pressicke's were provocative,[25] and Edmund Burrough responded on behalf of the Quakers, making it clear that his reply defended the Quakers only. He refuted all Pressicke's accusations.[26] He claimed that Quakers were good neighbours and good traders, who dealt justly and honestly with all. Sensing that a new order was emerging and that, like the Independents in 1659, Quakers would have to seek a way of survival, Burrough declared:

> We do own and acknowledge magistracy to be an ordinance of God, instituted of him for the punishment of evildoers and for the praise of them that do well; and we acknowledge all just subjection to authority, magistracy and government. This is our principle and has been our practice known throughout these kingdoms, that we are subject by doing and suffering to whatever authority the Lord is pleased to set over us, without rebellion, seditious plotting or making war against any government or governor.[27]

Nevertheless, Burrough asserted that while Quakers were not enemies to the church, ministry or gospel ordinances, they did resist the corruptions of all churches. Moreover, any attempt to impose faith, doctrine and worship by force of law and penalties was contrary to conscience and was in fact the work of Antichrist, the work of the devil. In the same year Burrough wrote another tract, intended 'more particularly to the inhabitants of Ireland and all sorts of people therein'.[28] He outlined Quaker convictions in some detail.[29] This was not just a defence of Quakerism but a restatement of the motivations which underlay Quakers' refusal to pay tithes, repair churches, go to any church services or in any way support the church system. Burrough was well aware that persecution lay ahead, and he warned Quakers that meetings would be forbidden and that they would be expected to attend church services. In the times ahead, Burrough warned, no private preachers would be allowed. This would stamp out the power of men and women to speak of God. Only those ordained would be allowed to preach, and this was truly another mark of Antichrist, for the education of ministers was not known in the time of Christ. All the churches, Roman and Protestant, had the outer form of religion, but in fact they all lacked the power of God within them.[30] This was the mark of Antichrist, of Babylon the great of Revelation 17:

> We need none of your outward prescriptions of forms of prayers, for the spirit of God teaches us in all these things, when and where and how we should worship the Lord God, who is a spirit.[31]

This is very much a transitional document warning Quakers of the hard times ahead, with even more harassment from their critics. However, in the period immediately after the Restoration there is little evidence of controversy between English Presbyterians and Quakers in Ireland until the debate between Daniel Burges and James Parke in Dublin in 1673. In that year Parke, a Quaker, replied to a pamphlet which Burges, an English Presbyterian minister in Dublin,[32] wrote against the Quakers. Parke visited Dublin in 1673, came across Burges's pamphlet and

> for the clearing of truth and for the sake of them that have inclination after it in Dublin or elsewhere, I have written in answer to it.[33]

By 1673 Burges had moved from Cork to Dublin, where he was ordained by Dr Harrison of Cooke Street and 'some other ministers there'.[34] Burges's pamphlet criticised the Quakers on both social and theological grounds, indicating the perceived growth of the Quakers, both as an economic and religious group, in Ireland. For example, Burges accused the Quakers of pretending to be honest and decent business people, boasting their virtue. The Quakers, according to Burges, 'crow on the multitudes that turn to them in all parts, of which they seem proud with a witness', and yet they were composed of

> ignoramuses, melancholy conceited fools, decayed shopkeepers to get and hoist up a trade, stale girls to get a husband and others of the like brand.[35]

Parke, of course, rejected all these accusations and asserted:

> It is well known that many substantial tradesman of all sorts, seeing the folly, deceit and wickedness of such as thou art . . . have turned to us and received the truth in the love of it.[36]

But when Burges accused the Quakers of being as wealthy as the pope and the Turks, and of boasting about it, Parke did not deny their wealth, though he refuted that they boasted about it. Burges had several theological differences with the Quakers, especially on the question of predestination. It was another example of the polarisation between predestination/reprobation on the one hand and, on the other, the possibility of a free response to God.[37] Burges also accused Quakers of denying the doctrine of the Trinity, which Parke refuted, stating the Quaker view that the persons of the Trinity as such were not found in the scriptures. Burges objected to the Quaker form of worship, especially their silent meetings, calling them inventions not found in the scriptures. Such worship without Bible, order of service or use of the sacraments was alien to Burges, and indeed to all the formal churches in Ireland. However, Parke dismissed such criticisms[38] and saw them as basically self-serving:

> Some people in Dublin did extol him for his unrighteous work which is for the fire. Yet others did believe he did it only to obtain acceptance among the clergymen there who had some suspicion of his fidelity to that church.[39]

Further debates between the Quakers and English Presbyterians were resumed in the early eighteenth century, in the exchanges between Joseph Boyse and Samuel Fuller.[40] The content and extent of Boyse's criticism of the Quakers was wide-ranging and centred on the actual beliefs of the Quakers concerning the Bible, the creeds, the 'light within', the place of the scriptures with regard to the 'light within', the place of worship and sacraments, the significance of justification and redemption by Christ, and the resurrection of the body. None of these topics were new, but they occurred constantly throughout this period. What seemed to have aroused Boyse's antagonism even more was the different lifestyle of the Quakers and their pursuit of wealth:

> Whether such vile errors when joined on the one hand with extreme pride and self-conceit, with gross censoriousness and uncharitableness in unsainting all that differ from them, with a wretched neglect of all family prayer and an immoderate pursuit of the world; and yet joined on the other with such an affected needless singularity in speech, garb and behaviour as the scriptures nowhere require, be not a palpable instance of Satan's transforming himself into an angel of light.[41]

The Quakers were distinct in several ways from the accepted norms observed within all the Reformation churches. Being different from and even dismissive of other traditions, pursuing wealth with success, dressing differently and speaking a language that was singular, aroused anger and perhaps jealousy in society; to many of their critics Quakers were so alien that they were accused of being possessed by dark spirits. In reality their fault lay in being different.

Samuel Fuller was from Dublin, a writer and publisher in his own right.[42] In his *Serious Reply to . . . abusive queries proposed to . . . the Quakers* Fuller tried to meet Boyse's views as far as possible, yet it was clear that on some issues there could be no agreement. For example, the sufficiency of God's grace and light for all people was reasserted; predestination was rejected firmly as untenable. The Bible and the creeds held their place of importance, but not as central as the 'light within':

> With the primitive reformers we say the Bible is our creed, the Bible is the text, the Spirit is the interpreter and that to everyone for himself, thereby establishing the right of private judgement against all popish implicit faith, the very basis whereon the Reformation stands.[43]

Certainly this is the Reformation tradition pushed to its own conclusion. Moreover, Quakers insisted that they could not be judged or written off simply because they did not have the training or tradition of their opponents. Fuller pointed out that Quakers were not scholastically trained but 'a plain people' saying things simply, not going into words like 'substance' or 'essence'.[44] They were liberated from the burden of such learning and had built their own way of life, held to it, organised themselves to live it, disciplined those who fell away, and dismissed those who would not conform to their expectations. It was as coherent a form of religion as any other in Ireland at the time, as highly disciplined and motivated as any other, and succeeded in surviving through this discipline and commitment. Thus the Quakers persisted in living a form of Christianity which aroused the ire and condemnation of other traditions in the country. Controversy served to sharpen self-understanding and perception, and Fuller's *Serious Reply* of 1728 showed the positive institutionalisation that had taken place among the Quakers since 1660.

Quakers and Independents

While public debate between English Presbyterians and Quakers lessened in the period immediately after the Restoration, it increased between the Independents and Quakers, especially after 1670. George Fox visited Ireland in 1669 and travelled the country, establishing the Quakers on a more organised and purposeful basis. In the course of the visit he met many people of other persuasions and drew new converts to the movement. In his journal Fox recounted how he debated on predestination and election with 'many great persons' who came to James Hutchinson's house for the discussion. Fox made it clear that Quakers did not accept strict predestination; rather they believed that Christ died for all and that salvation was available for everyone and all nations without exception.[45] For the Independents such teaching was inadmissible, as well as the Quaker view on what Independents held to be the essentials of Christian belief: the doctrine of the Trinity, one God and three persons; the scripture; the deity of Christ; the immortality of the soul; the resurrection of the body. It is significant that these five points were the matter of debate with the Quakers at this time, and Quaker opinions regarding them were refuted in print in Thomas Jenner's *Quakerism anatomised and confuted* (with a preface by Timothy Taylor, published in 1670).[46] It is significant that this work was written at a time when the church at New Row was disturbed by the teaching of Marsden, as a result of which he had to be publicly rebuked by Samuel Mather. To refute the Quakers was a sure sign of orthodoxy.

In his work Jenner explained that he wrote in order to prevent 'the spreading gangrene of Quakerism in this kingdom and especially in these parts where the Lord has cast my lot'.[47] He set about refuting Quakerism and examined what he considered to be four key errors. Jenner claimed that Quakers made no distinction between the nature of God and the nature of the human being, believing that the human soul is part of the divine essence. To Jenner this was heretical, since it made men and women equal to God, as well as making God partake in sinful humanity.[48] For the Independent/Presbyterian tradition this was theologically impossible, since it admitted some human goodness and initiative in the work of salvation. Again, Jenner rejected Quaker views on the Trinity which denied that there was any proof in scripture that there were three persons in God.

Jenner reasserted the traditional doctrine of the Trinity as handed down through the centuries.[49]

Jenner accused Quakers of denying Christ to be both God and man in one person, or that Christ had a true human body. Jenner quoted Fox, who had declared, 'Christ has but one body and that is his church.' Jenner also cited another Quaker who wrote: 'The redeemer of man is not that person who died at Jerusalem but the Light which is in every man by which he is given to see sin and enabled by it (if obedient to it) to be redeemed from sin.' For Jenner this negated the mystery of redemption and gave the impression that people could save themselves. Again, this view struck at the heart of the doctrine of justification and allowed Quakers to claim inherent righteousness. This was heresy indeed.

Finally, Jenner accused the Quakers of denying that the scriptures had primary authority as the word of God and that they were necessary for salvation. He knew this from his own experience:

> Myself being in Carlow in Ireland [in] 1669 did there and then hear a Quaker (after a long oration of his) profess that if the Bible were out of the world, it were no matter, for there is no need of it to salvation, people might be as well saved without it as with it if they attend to the light within and the power of God within them, and that for his own part he was not at all beholding to it for any grace or good he gained from it.[50]

For having rejected the rule of scripture, Quakers had developed the theme of the 'light within' as central to their belief. They called it Christ, the Spirit, salvation, the Covenant of Grace and the rule of conscience, and said this light was in believer and unbeliever alike. Jenner knew that the Quakers claimed to use this 'light within' as a way of discerning the spirit of good and evil, of right and wrong, of God or Satan. To prove his point Jenner told the story of a Quaker woman in Dublin who in the course of preaching said she had discovered a new light denied to other Quakers; they rejected her light, but she in turn repudiated this judgement and said her light came immediately from God.[51] Jenner asked, how the Quakers could really discern between the two views, since they denied the scriptures and asserted that everyone had the light of God within them?

In the case of conflict Jenner would appeal to an outside authority and the Quakers to a personal, interior one. To Jenner the Quaker view could only lead to confusion, and he concluded that Quakers believed themselves infallible, and so open to pride and evil influences.[52]

Jenner connected the Quaker rejection of the primacy of scripture with their rejection of appointed preachers. Worst of all, Quakers preached from inspiration, not from a text, and even allowed women to speak, which Jenner ironically declared as 'contrary to the expressed word of God'.[53] They also ignored all church organisation, offices and regulations; they disapproved of university-trained ministers and tithes and even denied that the magistrates had a godly function in society — which Jenner saw as undermining order in society.

On a more practical, social level, Jenner objected to the Quaker way of life, lived so separately from others. The language they used was mere flattery:'elect of God; the perfect ones; the seed of God; the tender lambs of Christ; the new born'.[54] He also resented that Quakers only saluted their own, which was contrary to scripture; they insisted on addressing all as 'Thou' and took off their hats to no one, neither bowed nor observed the ordinary civilities of life. Jenner rejected the Quaker practice of going naked as a sign and called it a delusion by the devil.[55] He was sure that the silent meetings which Quakers held led to hysteria and generated an atmosphere in which strange things happened. Among examples, Jenner cited the case of Mrs Wright:

> The last summer the said George Fox (as I am informed) came to the house of Mr Wright, near Castledermot here in Ireland, whose wife for a long time refused to go to the Quaker meetings or to hear them; but as soon as the said George Fox was come thither and had spoken with her, taking her by the hand and she hearing of him, she withdrew any further arguments, immediately turns an absolute professed Quaker (notwithstanding much means used to the contrary by myself and others) . . .[56]

Jenner recounted the ministry undertaken by this woman in some detail and saw it stemming from the fatal meeting with Fox and the atmosphere created by this intense silence of waiting sustained during Quaker meetings. Such meetings were large and growing in numbers. Jenner cited a letter a friend of his had received regarding the growth of the Quakers both in Ireland and abroad, despite all the sufferings and hostilities they had endured. Thus on the grounds both of their convictions and practices Jenner accused the Quakers of heresy. All that was essential, not only to the Independents but also to the fundamental Christian tradition, was apparently modified or radically changed by the Quakers: the nature of God and the human being; the nature and historicity of Christ; the doctrine of the Trinity; the theology of justification by faith alone; the inherent unrighteousness of the creature and inability to attain perfection; the primacy of scripture as the word of God; the preaching of the word; the necessity of sacraments and church order and ministry, supported by the magistrate. The Quaker stress on the inner authority of the person over and against the received Christian tradition of the day was bound to cause controversy. What had been a sect during the Interregnum, very much in the melting-pot at that time, had emerged into a defined body of people in Ireland with its own coherence and way of life.

Jenner's work was an attack on this way of life and conviction, and so George Whitehead and William Penn wrote a reply. Indeed, in May 1671 Fox urged Penn to publish:

> Several friends newly come out of Ireland who inform of the great want of this book in answer to his [Jenner's], I desire thee speed it up, laying aside all other things till it be done . . . we understand that Jenner makes a trade of his books in sending and selling of them up and down.[57]

In 1671 Whitehead and Penn published their reply to Jenner, though by this time Penn was in Newgate prison.[58] By way of stating their loyalty to the government, they dedicated the book to the Lord Lieutenant, Robartes, and his council and all the magistrates in Ireland. They made the point:

> It will always appear partial and unmanly that in a country only maintained by English civil interest those who are themselves dissenters and esteem persecution against them unchristian, should express so much Romish zeal in exasperating the civil magistrate to our utter ruin, who are both English and dissenters, too.[59]

However, they did not wish to enter into debate 'with the sharp gusts of a Scottish-Presbyterian-directorian persecution', but rather to state their case moderately and leave the world to judge them. They knew the Quakers had been useful to the economy in Ireland, and for this alone Quakers had a right to be protected. The first part of the book was written by Whitehead, who prefaced his remarks by saying all that Jenner and Taylor wrote against the Quakers were old arguments dredged up, out of date and answered long ago; he could only conclude that both were trying to win favour with the government.[60]

Whitehead refuted Jenner's work and in the process showed the clarity Quaker beliefs had reached at this time. He insisted that Quakers recognised the difference between creator and created and did not claim equality with God. Some individual Quakers had exaggerated this point and had been rebuked for it, and Whitehead wished that Jenner had taken that into consideration.[61] With regard to the Trinity, Whitehead asserted that the Father, Word and Holy Spirit were God, but not distinct persons; the idea of three persons was merely an 'unscriptural invented distinction . . . managed by Jenner and some other of his brethren'. Whitehead declared that Quakers believed in the divinity of Christ and that Christ died not just as a figure but in truth, that his death and resurrection brought salvation to humanity. But while he rejected Jenner's doctrine of redemption, declaring that Christ died for all, and not just for a few elect, predestined men and women, Whitehead also insisted on the perfection of the creature now, in and through the power of God, as a direct result of Christ's death.[62]

With regard to the primacy of the Bible, Whitehead argued that too much weight was given to the text; the scriptures were an expression of the spirit of God, but the spirit could not be imprisoned in the text; indeed, this spirit reached parts of the world where the Bible was not yet known. Moreover, anyone who spoke from the depth of the spirit spoke the word of God. Although Quakers esteemed the scriptures, they did not set them above Christ or the spirit of God as Jenner did in practice.[63] In this connection, Whitehead acknowledged the emphasis Quakers placed on the 'light within'.[64] Whereas Jenner called the 'light within' the light of nature, Quakers in fact called it the light of divinity, contrary to the doctrine of predestination and election, which Whitehead called:

this pitiful, mean and narrow spirit of rigid presbyters which grounds
all this their opposition against the universal favour of God upon a supposed personal election.[65]

This refutation of Jenner's views absorbed the first half of *A
serious apology*, and it was followed by Penn's contribution written in prison.[66] Penn underlined some of the points Whitehead
made and developed others. In particular he explained Quaker
views on preaching, which came as a personal call, 'an anoint-
ing', and through this they were qualified to preach 'not in corners, or under protection of earthly powers, nor yet in set places
for large stipends, but freely with our lives in our hands'.[67]
Consecrated days and times were not set aside, although they
had established definite days and times set apart for meetings.[68]
Penn outlined Quaker views on the sacraments, particularly em-
phasising that all the signs Christ used before his death were
transformed at the resurrection and were no longer valid nor
necessary.[69]

Penn refuted some details of Jenner's stories about Quakers
in Ireland. He accused Jenner of asking the Bishop of Leighlin
for approbation of his book and called him a hypocrite; this ought
to warn the Established Church 'what they themselves ought to
expect from the spirit of Jenner and his brethren had they a power
suitable to the Scottish-Directorian-will'.[70] Timothy Taylor's
preface to Jenner's book was especially offensive to Penn. Using
the book of Revelation, Taylor traced the rise of Antichrist, that
is the Church of Rome, and he accused Quakers of being crypto-
Catholics. One of the devices used by the pope to further his
designs was to send Jesuits to infiltrate all religious societies and
so foster differences and divisions among Protestants. Taylor
pointed out how useful the Quakers were in this regard, since
they resisted church government and so offended the 'the very
canon of faith'. Indeed,

> If the Quakers could but remove the ministers of Jesus Christ out of
> the gap, the Jesuits would with ease hand in the Pope at the breach.
> . . . I do not say that one Quaker in a hundred is a dogmatical formal
> papist, but I am satisfied that many Jesuits are designedly Quakers, stalk-
> ing under them and ploughing under their heifer, that once more they
> may set the Pope's claim above the throne of Christ and his mitre above
> the crown.[71]

Penn confessed amazement at Taylor's accusations, suggesting that in reality Quakers were further from popery than the 'Independent Presbyterians'. Quakers

> disown a settled ministry, tithes, infant water baptism, swearing, steeplehouses, external and visible signs under a gospel administration, the compliments, fashions and customs of the world; all highly owned, venerated and conformed to by Taylor and his brethren.[72]

Indeed, Penn asserted that Taylor need not attack Quakers regarding their stand on church government, for the Scottish Covenant and Directory of Worship had been used to justify the execution of Charles I.[73] The tone of this section harked back to the old antagonisms between Independents and Quakers during the civil war. Then the lines of theological differences were not so clear, though Taylor would have been aware of their general thrust. Before he came to Ireland Taylor was in the parish of West Kirby with Samuel Eaton, with whom he co-authored a book on the Independent way. Eaton wrote several works against the Quakers, and no doubt Taylor would have been familiar with Eaton's arguments.[74]

A dispute in print did not satisfy Penn, and he asked for a public debate in Dublin with Taylor and Samuel Mather. Both expressed willingness to meet in private, but Penn refused this and demanded a public forum. No account of such an event has been recorded and it was probably impossible to hold it, given the situation at this time within the Independent church at New Row. However, it is evident that the differences between the Independents and Quakers were very real both in theology and practice, in particular those arising from the Quakers' independent stance and self-contained way of living, which was a scandal to those traditions which looked to exterior authorities and structures for validation of their beliefs. The Quakers' essentially optimistic view of human beings, their belief in an inner human goodness which all people shared, all over the world, was intolerable in every sense to those steeped in a heavy theology of sin. Whether or not the Quakers could allow themselves to enjoy their theological liberty in real life is one question, but the Independent tradition was unable even to consider this a possibility and so the differences between them were very deep and enduring.

Tensions between Independents and Quakers found further expression in the debate between James Barry, minister of New Row church, and two 'Quakers, Amos Strettell and John Burnyeat. By all accounts, Barry led a strained life, bedevilled always by doubts as to whether or not he was elect or damned. Some of this he worked out in his own writing, and some by polemics against the Quakers.[75] In 1699 Barry wrote his autobiography, in which he recalled his companions in Dublin: Noah Bryan, Timothy Taylor, Samuel and Nathaniel Mather. He was born in Ireland in 1641 into an Established Church family and escaped so many dangers that later his family were disappointed 'that I should live to be fanatic'.[76]

In 1666 he joined New Row congregation after years of struggling with the question of predestination, which no one in the Established Church could answer to his satisfaction. The turning-point came on Easter Monday evening in 1666 after a day of futile debate with his family, including his uncle the Lord Chief Justice Santry, and 'seven or eight of the ablest and most famed of the fathers of the church of England then in Dublin'.[77] Some time later, on his own, Barry experienced election and began to follow Samuel Mather, saying that he was 'protected by God's elective love and left to stand alone when popery and Quakerism were coming in like a flood'.[78] Strettell and Burnyeat indicated that several papers passed between the Quakers and James Barry 'an Independent priest'. Barry preached publicly[79] against the Quakers, particularly on two points: that Quakers denied the resurrection, and that salvation was from Christ. By way of reply to these accusations, the Quakers asked for a public meeting in Dublin to debate three points: the resurrection, justification (including election and reprobation), and perfection in sanctification. The Quakers offered their largest meeting-house in the city, but Barry refused, saying he would be laughed at by the Quakers. So Strettell and Burnyeat replied on paper.[80] However, the reasons for refusing the debate also lie in the serious political tensions in Ireland at this time, and particularly in Dublin, when Roman Catholicism was in the ascendant and the Quakers were being treated well.[81]

Barry's criticisms were not confined to the area of strict theology. Like Burges in 1673, he accused the Quakers of being rich, saying:

> I doubt not but that this is one of the most powerful engines by which the art of Quakerism has been propagated in the kingdoms of the earth.[82]

Strettell and Burnyeat rejected this accusation; they saw their wealth as honestly earned and as a blessing; they criticised Barry, who had collected a lot of money on the pretext of going to America, and said it would be far better if congregations were not charged.[83] They also asserted that Quakers suffered for their convictions,

> many to the losing of all, not having a bed left to lie on, nor cattle to till their ground, nor corn for bread, nor seed, nor tools to work with all; also whipping, stocking, stoning, imprisonment they have been treated with.[84]

However, this was not central to the debate, and the Quakers accused Barry of evading the issues he had treated in three papers:

> In his first paper he calls us persons who delight in brangling and stirring up the spirit of animosity and prejudice, and men of as little charity and religion as those we receive our idle stories from . . . In his second paper he charges our principles to be dark and uncertain but lays down no argument against them . . . In his last he charges Quakerism . . . to be made up and constituted of subtlety causes dark and rotten, applying Ps. 17: 14 and Ps. 73: 12 to them.[85]

Strettell and Burnyeat challenged Barry to prove his points. And in addition they cited other witnesses who heard Barry say in a sermon that Quakers were 'the spawn of the Jesuits and the Jesuits the spawn of the devil'. Barry admitted to this. Others said they heard Barry couple the Muggletonians and Quakers, and that he called the Quakers all kinds of names in public. Yet in all this time Barry refused to meet the Quakers in open debate.[86]

Since Barry refused to debate in public, Strettell and Burnyeat were forced to publish their defence as *The innocency of the Christian Quakers,* dated 20 January 1688. They asserted two points of Quaker belief: in the resurrection after death, but not with the same earthly body; and that the human person has inherent righteousness and some degree of perfection and holiness by virtue of response to God's grace. Barry would have none of this: 'James Barry will have no mixture, it must be a faith without righteousness or else a justification and salvation without faith.' But inherent righteousness was the constant teaching of Fox, Whitehead, Penn and Burrough. Strettell and Burnyeat asked how Barry could really know who was saved or not. Quaker truth was surer: that all were saved in Christ, and scripture upheld this. In view of all these accusations against them, the Quakers appealed to Barry's congregation in Dublin and asked them to consider the leadership Barry was giving them.[88]

The innocency of the Christian Quakers contained a postscript noting that Anthony Sharp had sent two letters to Barry which were acknowledged and an answer promised. Sharp and Thomas Aston in Cavan Street held copies of all the correspondence between Barry and Strettell and Burnyeat. In November 1687 and January 1688 Sharp had written to Barry. Like Strettell and Burnyeat, he refuted the accusations about Quaker belief in the resurrection of the body and clarified the Quakers' understanding of perfection. He insisted on the possibility of keeping God's commands:

> God is just and commands no more than he offers his grace to enable men to obey if they would be led by Him, contrary to that opinion [which] says that no man either by his own power or any grace he has received is able to keep God's commands and so making it that God commands unreasonable things and impossibilities.[89]

This was, of course, the heart of the debate; two views of human nature were in conflict, and some reply was awaited. Like Strettell and Burnyeat, Sharp asked for a public debate in Dublin, but neither a debate nor a written reply were forthcoming. Eventually in 1715 Barry published his views on the Quakers, originally voiced in 1688 but not printed at the time for reasons which he outlined in the work.[90] In the preface Barry explained why it took him so long to publish his work:

> In the time of the popish government when popery and Quakerism smiled so amicably on each other as the two religions . . . which are

nearest of kin of all the religions visibly professed in these kingdoms, the people called Quakers sent me a . . . challenge in writing, which was afterwards published in print, to prove from the scriptures of truth the four doctrines here following:

1. The doctrine of the resurrection of the fleshly body, which dies and turns to dust.
2. The doctrine of justification by the alone righteousness of Jesus Christ, freely imputed.
3. The doctrine of imperfection in sanctification in the most martyred believer, while in this world.
4. The doctrine of particular unconditionate election before time.

He explained that he had wanted to reply in print and indeed had promised his congregation that he would do so; paper had been bought and a printer chosen when 'the storm came suddenly on the protestants in Dublin, that we were soon scattered asunder'.[91] When he finally did publish Barry chose not to treat all four issues and concentrated on his own preoccupation, the doctrine of election. The argument was familiar: that God had elected a few to be justified and saved, 'and therefore not all the race of fallen mankind, as papists, Arminians, Quakers, Freewillers etc. vainly teach'.[92] He proceeded to show how a person would know of election: self-examination, temptation from the devil, determination to 'cast your soul at the foot of divine sovereignty', relying on the merits of Christ. This was sure doctrine:

> If John Burnyeat, or any of his friends, who oppose the doctrine of particular election, can prove by the scriptures that God has given, or is bound by any law to give, special saving grace to rebels, who have fallen by their causelessly abusing and losing the grace given in Adam . . . any other than what he bestows on his elect and that in the right of election, I will readily submit and yield the cause.[93]

With regard to the query posed by Strettell and Burnyeat (as to how a person knows he is elect), Barry replied that they simply knew by conviction. He based his teaching on particular election on the Thirty-Nine Articles; the Westminster confession, clause 3; the Church of Scotland; the Church of Ireland 'in Bishop Ussher's time, 1615'; the Church of France, Article 12; the Synod of Dort, 7th and 15th canons.[94] By citing so many confessions of faith, Barry tried to show the Quakers how out of step they were with the teaching of the reformed churches generally, particularly on the doctrine of predestination.

The debate on predestination from 1660 onwards highlights some of the areas of disagreement between Quakers and Independents. Yet the tensions stemmed also from the fact that by 1670 the Quakers were more than just a religious group. They had established themselves in the country and did not yield under harassment or persecution. They had become united and bonded by their strong organisation and mode of government. They had become wealthy and prosperous, respected and valued, and were somewhat resented and envied for their success. On a theological level, Quakers had put themselves beyond the accepted parameters of the Christian life, rejecting the assumed essentials of Christian commitment. In their lifestyle and in some of their practices and beliefs they resembled papists, and in fact were suspected of being either crypto-Catholics or certainly allies of the papists in Ireland and England. Taylor and Barry dealt with this latter point. So too did the Scottish Presbyterians in Ulster.

Quakers and Scottish Presbyterians

Scottish Presbyterians were convinced that Quakers were crypto-Catholics. From the resumption of their records in 1672 both the Antrim and the Laggan meetings pressed for something in writing against the Quakers. Apparently John Hart was appointed before 1673 to write such a tract, and he seems to have produced a draft which was circulated among the meetings.[95] In 1673 John Howe and Thomas Gowan were asked by the Antrim meeting to write a tract against the Quakers, and the Down and Tyrone meeting encouraged this work.[96] However, Howe returned to London in 1675, and so Gowan was left to write the book on his own.[97] By 1680 the Laggan meeting wrote to the Antrim meeting asking for Gowan's book. It seems to have been in manuscript, for the Laggan asked either to copy Gowan's work themselves or pay the Antrim meeting to have it done. In the same year Gowan sent over some of the treatise, which the Laggan minuted as important and to be read carefully.[98] It was a sign of the times when Gowan asked in 1683 that his work on the Quakers be omitted from the minutes; he was also at this time drawing up a further work, 'a compendious treatise against the Quakers'. [99] By 1684 Gowan was dead, and the Route meeting asked that someone be appointed to finish his work. Thomas Hall was approached, but was so hesitant that the whole matter was referred to the committee. [100]

Although nothing of Gowan's treatise is extant, a summary survives of the general approach to Quakers, who were seen as a real threat both in themselves and in their supposed collusion with Roman Catholics. [101] The Scottish Presbyterian ministers urged their people to pray not just to stop popery and Quakerism, but to uproot them entirely; ministers were recommended to preach in public and private on the errors of both, but not to get heatedly involved in debate or in personal animosity. The meetings were to be equipped with the Confession of Faith, the Larger and Shorter Catechisms, Mr Pool's dialogue between papist and Protestant, Mr Fergueson's manuscript on the errors of the time. Such background information should enable ministers and people to refute and defend their position. Meetings were to appoint some members to read Quaker pamphlets and confute the errors they found in them, and perhaps write a little tract for general use.

Scottish Presbyterians were convinced that Roman Catholics and Quakers were in collusion with one another:

> Satan's design and Antichrist's design especial in the black mystery of Quakerism which is 1. to loose all the foundations of religion; 2. to cast off Christ the chief cornerstone of the holy scriptures which are the doctrinal foundation from being a foundation at all; 3. to destroy a ministry and order in the house of God and so to bring in anarchy and confusion which is attended with endless suits and debates; that so, in the last place, they may fix upon the spirits of people of rooted persuasion of a necessity of wheeling about again in the bosom of the mother church of Rome where they allege but groundlessly the only order and peace is to be found.
>
> Brethren would inform the people that these wayfaring Quakers have no call from God . . . several of them have been discovered to be Jesuit priests and so Antichrist's pedlars. [102]

This was a constant accusation made against the Quakers in Ireland and elsewhere: they were covert Roman Catholics. Rome, it was claimed, was using confused dissenters, in this case the Quakers, to infiltrate the Reformation churches, in this case the Scottish Presbyterian church. This allegation of links between Quakers and Roman Catholics had already been propounded by Timothy Taylor in 1670. Thus both Scottish Presbyterians and Independents in Ireland in the 1670s were convinced that there was collusion between the Quakers and papists. This idea had long origins, reaching back to the Interregnum.

Since then, however, the tone and content of the debate had changed. For one thing, Quakers articulated their beliefs clearly, and these were better grasped by outsiders, however critical and negative they were about them. In a sense, Quaker convictions were more of a threat than before, since Quakers did not accept the approved norms of Christian churches. What had been a loosely held set of beliefs in the Interregnum had become, in a relatively short time, a rooted stance and mode of believing and acting in society. There was no question of their conformity to any church, for they had moved beyond that into their own space and intended to stay there. They organised themselves in such a way that this could be ensured, through their manner of life, regularity of meetings, and through setting down rules for family life and marriage, trade, dress, language and dwelling. They were a self-contained group, held together and nurtured by the intensity of their commitment and conviction. Many of them became wealthy and prosperous, evident fruit of their labours. Such achievements were bound to call forth criticism and antagonism from all religious traditions in the country.

Notes and References

1   31 March 1658 (B.L., Lansdowne MS 822 f.17). Claudius Gilbert, *The libertine schooled* (London, 1657), pp 55-7. See note 3 below for Gilbert.

2   1 June 1656 (B.L., Lansdowne MS 821, f. 12). Perrott was jailed some further days for such behaviour.

3   Claudius Gilbert was appointed to Limerick in 1652, at a salary of £150 per annum, soon raised to £200. In 1654, with eighteen laymen of the city, he wrote to Oliver Cromwell 'from the church of Christ at Limerick', asking for 'an able godly painful ministry'. St John D. Seymour, 'A Puritan minister in Limerick' in *North Munster Arch. Soc. Jn.,* iv, no. 3 (1919),

pp 3ff; *Thurloe state papers*, ii, 118. Gilbert conformed at the Restoration and ministered in Belfast. In 1682 he published *Claudius Gilbert, A preservative against the change of religion* (London, 1683). He also contributed to Richard Baxter's *The certainty of the world's spirits* (London, 1691), pp 214ff; 247ff; Gilbert was prebendary of Armagh in 1666. Cotton, *Fasti*, iv, 51; v, 208. Gilbert remained on good terms with English Presbyterians and was particularly friendly with the Countess of Donegall's chaplains, who tended to be English Presbyterians.

4   Gilbert, *The libertine schooled*, pp 18-19, 55. This work was written in response to a series of queries which had been distributed in the city, based on Christopher Blackwood's *The storming of Antichrist* (London, 1644); Samuel Winter and Edward Worth had refuted this work. The author of the queries had also pleaded for toleration of the Quakers in Limerick.

5   Gilbert, *The libertine schooled,* p. 25

6   'Quaker' was used as term of contempt. For example, Samuel Winter used it to describe Islam, calling it 'the doctrine of Mahomet, that great Quaker'. Winter, *The sum of diverse sermons* (Dublin, 1656), p. 176.

7   Gilbert, *The libertine schooled,* pp 55-6.

8   Apparently some Quaker 'queries' were sent to Gilbert which he decided not to answer. These could have been those contained in Francis Howgill, 'Some queries to you all who say you are ministers of Christ in Dublin and to the rest of Ireland'. Howgill was in Ireland in 1655 (F.L.L., Swarthmore MS v, 10; Trans vii, p. 49).

9   Gilbert, *A sovereign antidote against sinful errors, the epidemical plague of these latter days* (London, 1658).

10   Ibid., p. 100.

11   Ibid., p. 111.

12   Ibid., pp 105, 133.

13   Ibid., pp 107, 108, 110.

14   Ibid., pp 114, 115, 118, 123.

15   Ibid., pp 18-19.

16   Ibid., pp 3, 108-9, 115

17   Ibid., p. 145

18   Samuel Ladyman, *The dangerous rule or a sermon preached at Clonmel in the province of Munster in Ireland, 3 August 1657, before the reverend judges of that circuit* (London, 1658). For Ladyman see Chapter 2, n. 17.

19   Ibid., pp 28, 33, 57, 68-78.

20   Ibid, p. 71.

21   George Pressicke, *Certain queries touching the silencing of godly ministers* (n.p., 1661). Pressicke also entered into debate with Griffith Williams, Bishop of Ossory, over Williams's book *The great Antichrist revealed*, and argued that the Westminster Assembly was not Antichrist, that Presbyterians never acted like Rome and so were not Antichrist. Pressicke, *An answer to Griffith Williams, Lord Bishop of Ossory, his book entitled 'The Great Antichrist revealed, before this time never discovered'* (n.p., n.d.). Pressicke seems to have been an Established Church minister, although he is not listed in Cotton, *Fasti;* he had a long divorce case which he presented first to two bishops in

London during the Interregnum and then to the Archbishop of Dublin. Pressicke, *A case of conscience propounded to a great bishop* (n.p., 1661).

22 George Pressicke, *A brief relation of some of the most remarkable passages of the Anabaptists in High and Low Germany, 1521* (n.p., 1660). For a discussion of religious traditions at this time see J. I. McGuire, 'The Dublin Convention, the Protestant community and the emergence of an ecclesiastical settlement in 1660' in Art Cosgrove and J. I. McGuire (ed.), *Parliament and community* (Belfast, 1983), pp 124-32.

23 Pressicke, *A brief relation*, pp 8-16.

24 Ibid., pp 1-4; Barnard, *Cromwellian Ireland,* p. 132; McGuire, 'The Dublin Convention', pp 122-9.

25 Quakers took such accusations seriously. As early as February 1656 Francis Howgill, then in Ireland, wrote to George Fox and James Naylor that enemies 'seek our life and accuse us for Jesuits and say they will swear against us' (F.L.L., A. R. Barclay MSS, Transcripts, no. 61, p.69).

26 Edmund Burrough, *A vindication of the people of God called Quakers . . . being an answer to a book dedicated to them by one George Pressicke* (London, 1660). He denied that they had any authority to exercise power which could in any way be called tyrannical or rebellious; rather they had been persecuted from the beginning. Neither did the Quakers originate from the Roman Church; in fact the Reformation churches stemmed from Rome. Nor did the Quakers use Catholic agents among them, as Pressicke hinted. Burrough accepted that they had their own revelations from God; they discerned spirits and lived plainly and soberly; they did not take oaths, as this was contrary to the gospel, but for all that they were not against the magistrate or government or indeed ministers as such.

27 Burrough, *A vindication of the people of God called Quakers*, p. 22.

28 Edmund Burrough, *The everlasting gospel of repentance and remission of sins* (London, 1660).

29 Guidance of conscience from the 'light within'; out of this, and not from the practices of religion, ordinances and duties, came new life; in this way the image of God was born in the human person. In the light of this, the ministry of false teachers had to be rejected. Instead of outer buildings for worship, the person became an inner temple, and God was worshipped there without respect of days, times or places. This is what it meant to be saved and to live in the power of God; all forms of religion without this power had to be denied, including profession of scripture, ordinances, church membership, praying and preaching. Ibid., p. 16ff.

30 Burrough, *The everlasting gospel,* pp 27-32.

31 Ibid., pp 21-4.

32 D.N.B.; Daniel Burges (1645-1713), born in Middlesex, was educated at Oxford. In 1667 the Earl of Orrery took him to Ireland for seven years to be headmaster of Orrery's school at Charleville, Co. Cork. By 1673 he was in Dublin, and chaplain to Lady Mervin near Dublin. He left Ireland in 1674, and went first to Marlborough and then to London in 1685. No copy of Burges's work has been found, but in his reply Parke outlined its main thrust.

33 James Parke, *The way of God and them that walk in it, vindicated against deceit and lies, being an answer to a malicious pamphlet entitled 'A caveat against the cheat of the Quaker's chaff', written by Daniel Burges, priest at Dublin in Ireland* (n.p., 1673), p. 4; Parke, 1636-96, was born in Wales and was a prominent Quaker. He spent most of his life in England and published Quaker works. He was in Dublin, visiting Quakers, when he discovered Burges's pamphlet. He spoke at George Fox's burial. F.L.L., Biographies of Quakers; D.N.B.

34 Mathew Henry, *Funeral sermon for Mr Burges* (London, 1713), p. 32.

35 Parke, *The way of God,* p. 9.

36 Ibid., p. 9.

37 Ibid., pp 10-12.

38 Ibid., pp 12-15.

39 Ibid., p. 17.

40 Although Boyse's views on the Quakers were originally articulated in 1707, they were published in the year of his death, 1728. 'Some queries offered to the consideration of the people called Quakers particularly of those in Queen's County', printed in Boyse, ii, 398-400. Samuel Fuller, *A serious reply to twelve sections of abusive queries proposed to the consideration of the people called Quakers, concluding the works of Joseph Boyse yet alive, an aged and eminent preacher among the Presbyterians in Dublin* (Dublin, 1728). However, in 1707 John Moor published a paper against the Quakers under the same title, *Some queries offered* . . . but with the addition 'By an inhabitant there'; the paper is included in a work by Moor, *Three discourses concerning transubstantiation, invocation of the saints and angels, worship of images* (Dublin, 1707). Both papers are identical. For Moor see Cotton, *Fasti,* i, 272, 249; William King's Letter Book, 1696-8 (T.C.D., MS 750, f. 215); Narcissus Marsh, 'Mr James Moor of Athy in my diocese, a worthy person', 1695 (Lambeth Palace, Gibson Papers, MS 942, f. 79). From 1708 to 1716 Moor ministered in Dublin. Herbert Wood (ed.), *The parish registers of St Catherine's, Dublin, 1636-1715* (Exeter/London, 1908). According to the D.N.B., Boyse published a set of sermons in 1708. It is difficult to know who was the author of the queries; certainly Fuller assumed that Boyse was the writer, and noted in his book that few in Queen's County 'had either seen or read them since the author owned them'.

41 Boyse, *Works,* ii, 398-400.

42 Grubb, *Quakers in Ireland,* p. 91 Fuller wrote a book on astronomy and another called *Some principles and precepts of the Christian religion.* He died in 1736.

43 Samuel Fuller, *A serious reply to* . . . *abusive queries propided to* . . . *the Quakers* (Dublin, 1728), p. 36.

44 Ibid., p. 58. In fact, however, Fuller was well-read and, for example, cites Ussher several times in his text to prove a point: pp 17, 40, 127.

45 George Fox, *Journal,* 2 vols (London, 1901), ii, 112-13. Hutchinson was a Quaker who lived at Knockballymeagher in north Tipperary. Penn, *My Irish journal,* pp 20, 67.

46 Taylor was an English Presbyterian and became an Independent; during the Interregnum he was chaplain to Colonel Venables in Carrickfergus.

There he occupied the former rectors's residence and the rent was paid by the corporation. He was one of the examiners for ministers appointed in 1655. From 1668 to 1681 he ministered in New Row. New Row Baptismal Register, ff 2-7; Armstrong, *Summary history of the Presbyterian Church,* p. 80; Anthony Wood, *Athenae Oxonienses,* ed. Philip Bliss, 4 vols (London, 1813-20), ii, A1, 682; Reid, *History of the Presbyterian Church,* ii, 229 n. 16, 249-56; Bramhall to Lane, 28 Nov. 1660 (Bodl., Carte MS 221, f. 79); Inquisition 1657, Down and Connor (R.C.B., MS Gg 2/7/3/27, pp 6, 71) (these are the notes of Classon Porter); Extracts from the Commonwealth and Carte papers, P.R.O.N.I., T780, f. 12); B.L., Lansdowne MS 823, ff 73, 139; Thurloe, *State papers,* iv, 287. Thomas Jenner was educated at Christ College, Cambridge, and was minister of Horstead and Coltishall in Norfolk before going to New England and then to Ireland, first to Drogheda and later to Carlow; cf. title-page of *Quakerism anatomised;* Harrison to Henry Cromwell, 14 July 1656 (B.L., Lansdowne MS 821 f. 200).

47   Thomas Jenner, *Quakerism anatomised and confuted* (n.p., 1670). Jenner dedicated the work to the Earl and Lady Donegall, presented a copy to Robartes, the Lord Lieutenant, and asked the Bishop of Leighlin for approbation of the book. Robartes responded, saying he 'was sorry to hear the Quakers held such ill principles, but the tares and wheat must grow together until judgement'. M. R. Brailsford, *The making of William Penn* (London, 1933), p. 75.

48   Jenner, *Quakerism antomised*, p. 15ff.

49   Ibid., pp 30-3. He even asserted that angels were persons in their own right since they had reason.

50   Ibid., pp 52ff.

51   This was probably a reference to Jane Pildren. See Chapter 4, n. 99.

52   Jenner, *Quakerism anatomised,* pp 85-6, 138-47.

53   Ibid., pp 96ff.

54   Ibid., p. 186.

55   Ibid., pp 148-51, 15.

56   Ibid., pp 157-63; 'A brief and true relation of Anne, wife of William Wright of Castledermot in the County of Kildare in Ireland' (Mary Leadbeater, *Biographical notes of Friends in Ireland* (London, 1823), pp 52-78). Anne Wright was attracted to the Quakers in Dublin in 1656 but was persuaded by Samuel Winter not to join them (pp 52-3). See also 'Names of Friends deceased in the kingdom of Ireland' (F.L.D., YMF1, f.l).

57   Brailsford, *The making of William Penn*, p. 208; also p. 75 for Penn's account of Jenner, 'an Independent Presbyterian priest of Ireland'.

58   George Whitehead and William Penn, *A serious apology for the principles and practices of the people called Quakers against the malicious aspersions, erroneous doctrines and horrid blasphemies of T. Jenner and Timothy Taylor in their book entitled 'Quakerism anatomised and confuted'* (n.p. 1671).

59   Ibid., dedication.

60   This could have been a veiled reference to the Marsden affair in New Row Independent Church.

61   Whitehead and Penn, *A serious apology*, pp 23-5.

62   Ibid., pp 20, 32-42.
63   Ibid., pp 48-54.
64   Ibid., pp 13-18, 22-4.
65   Ibid., pp 55-63.
66   Penn's portion of the work was entitled *The second part of the serious apology for the principles and practices of the people called Quakers.*
67   Ibid., pp 80ff.
68   Ibid., p. 12.
69   Ibid., pp 123, 132 ff.
70   Ibid., pp 178-9.
71   Jenner, *Quakerism anatomised and confuted,* preface by Taylor.
72   Whitehead and Penn, *A serious apology,* p. 193.
73   Ibid., pp 191-3, 197. Penn pointed out that the Independents destroyed the true Republican model because the priests did not want to lose their tithes.
74   Sauuel Eaton, *The Quakers confuted* (London, 1653); see also *The perfect pharisee under monkish holiness* (London, *c.* 1653); Barnard, *Cromwellian Ireland,* p. 140.
75   William Huntington, *The coal heaver's cousin rescued from the bats: the works of James Barry* (London, 1788).
76   James Barry, *A reviving cordial* (London, 1699), p. 24.
77   Ibid., pp 51ff. Santry (then Sir James Barry) served as chairman of the 1660 Convention in Dublin and was a firm supporter of the Established Church. McGuire, 'The Dublin Convention', pp 133, 138; D.N.B.; Bernard Burke, *A genealogical history of the dormant . . . and extinct peerages of the British Empire* (London, 1883), p. 134; New Row Baptismal Register, ff 4, 5, 7.
78   Barry, *A reviving cordial,* p. 118. This refers to the time when Tyrconnell put £100 on Barry's head and he had to flee from Dublin in disguise. William Huntington got this information from Barry's daughter: *A few fragments of the life and death of the Rev. James Barry, intended as a supplement to 'The coal heaver's cousin'* (London, *c.* 1790), p. 7.
79   Anthony Sharp's witnesses noted that Barry preached in Thomas Court; one described him as 'a Presbyterian or Independent priest' and another as 'the Independent preacher in Thomas Court' (F.L.D., Sharp MS, S.8, no. 6, ff 3, 3v, 4v.)
80   Amos Strettell and John Burnyeat, *The innocency of the Christian Quakers manifested and the truth of their principles and doctrines cleared and defended from the loud (but false) clamorous and base insinuations and wicked slanders of James Barry* (n.p., 1688), pp 1-10. Strettell was a leading Quaker in Dublin and in 1672 travelled with John Banks; he went bankrupt in 1720 and the National Meeting lent him £1,000 interest free. Grubb, *The Quakers in Ireland,* pp 32-4.
81   See Chapter 8.
82   Strettell and Burnyeat, *The innocency of the Christian Quakers,* p. 11.
83   Ibid., p. 11.
84   Ibid., pp 12-13.
85   Ibid., p. 15.
86   Ibid., pp 16-17.
87   Ibid., p. 23.

88   Ibid., pp 18-31.
89   F.L.D., Sharp MS, S.8, no. 5, f.16; see also S.8, no. 6, f.1.
90   James Barry, *The doctrine of particular election asserted and approved by God's word, in answer to a challenge given the author to make good the aforesaid doctrine* (n.p., 1715).
91   Ibid., preface, pp i-vi.
92   Ibid., p. 19.
93   Ibid., p. 70.
94   Ibid., p. 84ff.
95   Laggan minutes, May-Nov., 1673, pp 48, 64, 68, 73.
96   Antrim minutes, Jan.-Mar. 1673, pp 73, 77.
97   *Memoirs of the late Rev. Mr John Howe, collected by Edmund Calamy* (London, 1734), p. 50.
98   Laggan minutes, ii, July 1680-Feb. 1681, pp 62, 79, 82, 85.
99   Laggan minutes, Jan. 1683, pp 187, 193.
100 Antrim minutes, 19 Aug. 1684, p. 230; see also pp 231, 233, 235, 244, 260.
101 'Overtures for guarding the people against popery and Quakerism to be considered', 1672 (N.L.S., Wodrow MS, Folio 32, no. 91; P.R.O.N.I., T525, 16-17). For examples of antagonism against Quakers by Scottish Presbyterians see Besse, *A collection of the sufferings*, ii, 472-3; also J. M. Douglas, 'Early Quakerism in Ireland' in *J.F.H.S.*, 48, no. 1 (1956), pp 25-6.
102 'Overtures for guarding the people', nos 3, 5. Alexander Peden once came upon a Quaker meeting in Ulster and denounced the Quakers as evil people. Walker, *Some remarkable passages*, p. 115.

PART III

CONTROVERSIES WITH THE ESTABLISHMENT: Church and State

7

Controversies between the Established Church and Dissenters, 1660–1714

> I could reckon that the episcopal order is the principle of unity
> in the church; and we clearly see it so by the innumerable sects
> that sprung up when episcopacy was persecuted.
> Jeremy Taylor, *A sermon preached at the opening of the parliament of Ireland*
> (1661)

William King and Presbyterianism

Controversies between the Established Church and the Presbyterian traditions in Ireland highlight the areas of disagreement which were for the most part impossible to resolve. In the clash of religious ideas, differences were expressed, based on theological and cultural insights, and a middle ground scarcely existed. While there was some possibility that English Presbyterianism could reach an accommodation with the Established Church, Scottish Presbyterianism could not concede any ground to an Established Church which saw itself as the only source of religious authority and the true church in the land. In the exchanges between the churches a great deal of the life and practice of the churches emerge, as well as the active role of ministers and people.

During the period 1660–86 theological debates did not take

171

place publicly in Ireland between the Established Church and
either the Scottish or the English Presbyterians. However, despite
growing alarm that Roman Catholicism could triumph under
James II, controversy broke out between the Established Church
and English Presbyterians in 1686. The occasion was the conversion of Peter Manby, Dean of Derry, to Roman Catholicism
and the subsequent publication of his reasons for taking such
a step then.[1] William King, then Chancellor of St Patrick's,
Dublin, replied to Manby and in the course of his work criticised all Protestant nonconformists in Ireland for their separation from the Established Church. Such separation created
disunion and deprived nonconformists of civic and ecclesiastical
rights, forcing them to 'proceed on their own heads in spite of
their lawful governors'; they were by their own choice private
persons, excluded from membership of the true church.[2]

Joseph Boyse replied to these remarks[2] and complained that
King bitterly censured the whole body of nonconformists', excluding them from the catholic church. For Boyse argued at length
that dissenters were part of the true catholic church and that they
could not be excluded from it. Boyse cited Article 68 of the Irish
Articles of 1615, which defined the catholic church 'to be the invisible body of elected saints in heaven and earth'. Out of this
catholic church all particular churches were founded and had
their validity by a common rootedness in 'the invisible body of
elected saints'. Boyse accused King of 'pure Bellarmine', for
Bellarmine had argued that a particular church, the Roman
Church, was the true catholic church.[4]

Boyse pointed out that it was precisely because of this stance
that nonconformists had to separate from the Established Church.
This was at a price: loss of promotions, loss of estates and
sometimes imprisonment. On another level, differences in
theology and practice between dissenters and Established Church
members were too great to breach. King had accused the
dissenters of being close to Roman Catholics by separation, but
Boyse rejected this:

> Is it that we bow to the east and to the altar? Do we use vain pageantry
> in consecration of churches and utensils, baptising them with saints
> names? Do we frisk from place to place in reading our service, use the

sign of the cross, kneel at the sacrament which never obtained in the church before transubstantiation? Have we absolution for sins to the uncensured? Is private communion our manner? Do we have organs, singing boys, unscriptural confirmation, preaching deacons, reading over the dead, holy days, surplices, responsals and twenty more appendants of worship? The Romish church has all these; whereas we worship God without all this stuff added to the gospel institutions and are content with that for decency.[5]

Boyse considered the terms laid down for unity with the Established Church both severe and unacceptable: ministers had to be re-ordained, solemnly declare the Covenant not binding, and agree not to change anything in either liturgy or church discipline. He argued that conditions for union between them needed to be placed on a much more comprehensive basis, such as the Irish Articles of 1615 and the doctrinal articles of the Church of England.[6] Besides, Boyse claimed that true basis for the catholic church lay in having lawful pastors, rather than lawful governors, which King maintained.[7] Lawful pastors were those who had the necessary qualifications for the office, who were ordained by presbyters, with the consent of the people they were about to serve. In this context, all bishops and ministers of the Established Church were actually illegal.[8]

Developing this point further, Boyse rejected the view that bishops were instituted by Christ as the centre of catholic unity. To accept that would be to 'unchurch all the established churches that want a diocesan prelacy'.[9] Indeed, confessions of various reformed churches were true parts of the catholic church, though Boyse excluded Quakers 'because we know not their opinions', and Fifth Monarchy Men because 'I know no distinct churches constituted of them'. Variety of confessions did not detract from the unity of the catholic church; besides, Boyse argued that so-called uniformity before the Reformation was marked by schisms and divisions.[10]

Speaking to the reality that obtained in Dublin, Boyse insisted that Presbyterians and Independents had lawful pastors:

Particular churches are the chief integrating parts of the church-catholic. These churches consist of one or more pastors and a christian flock associated under his or their oversight for personal communion in faith, worship and holy living. . . . But the people do not owe them them a blind obedience nor have pastors any power but for edification. Much less can such bishops pretend to an higher power whose very office Christ never instituted, whose pretended relation to their diocese is founded on the people's consent to it.[11]

Boyse called the pastors of both the English Presbyterian/Independent churches 'bishops' and rejected Established Church bishops for 'assuming the sole power of church government and depriving the pastors of particular churches of an essential part of their of their office'. While acting as the king's officers, bishops could command obedience to the law of the country, yet in the area of church law Established Church bishops should not claim authority. For authority within a church arose from its being lawfully constituted: a society of Christians, united under one or more pastors as Christ appointed, for personal communion in faith, worship and holy living. While the method of the pastor's appointment was in dispute, this in itself did not form part of true churchness, 'for that a particular church have a lawful pastor is not absolutely necessary to its being a church'. Such views indicated the very real disagreements between King and Boyse on the question of ministry and church order, particularly in the area of hierarchical authority.

Boyse was convinced that only a comprehensive view could express the real meaning of the catholic church. He suggested that all churches own each other as true churches and maintain occasional communion in order to witness to charity, and that pastors accept each other as true ministers of the gospel and rejoice in one another's work, help one another in their ministries, speak well of each other and band together to defend the reformed religion. Indeed, whatever their differences, Presbyterians and Independents in Dublin and the south of Ireland maintained unity 'by the amicable consultations of their associated pastors'; this was a rather loose form of unity, in contrast to the very defined church order and discipline of Scottish Presbyterians in the north and parts of the south of Ireland.[12]

These proposals reflected how English Presbyterians already exercised accommodation between different traditions in Ireland. While the Established Church tried to accommodate some of their views, this was based on the assumption that the underlying structures of the Established Church would not be changed, even if Ussher's model was to be used.[13] In the panic of the times, some form of accommodation was considered, if only to allow Protestants in general to band together against the danger from Roman Catholicism. But as Boyse pointed out, to ask nonconformists to take the Act of Uniformity, the Oxford Oath and the oath of canonical obedience and accept re-ordination, was to ask too much and would concede all their closely held convictions.[14] Boyse would write a great deal more in his time, but in this reply to King he set forth the basic arguments for acceptance as nonconformist churches in Ireland.[15]

After the revolution and the accession of William and Mary the situation in Ireland had quite changed and the efforts made at accommodation between the Protestant churches in the pre-1688 period in Ireland no longer held urgency.[16] King had lived through the 1688 Revolution, during which he was in effect the leader of the Established Church in Dublin, and had been imprisoned for a period by the Jacobite government. In 1690 he was appointed Bishop of Derry, a diocese where Scottish Presbyterians were by far the most numerous and were much more opposed to the Established Church than English Presbyterians. King chose to confront Scottish Presbyterians on the question of worship, an issue that had been sensitive in Ulster since the early days of the plantation, and particularly in 1636.[17] In his *Discourse concerning the inventions of men in the worship of God* (1694) he addressed five topics: use of the Book of Common Prayer; use of scripture in church; forms of worship; music in church; communion services.

King noted with disapproval that ministers, instead of using the Book of Common Prayer at services, prayed aloud, extempore, and that the congregation remained silent. He condemned this as contrary to the scriptures.[18] He also criticised the lack of scripture readings in the Presbyterian Church. Only short texts of scripture were used, and the rest of the time was given to preaching. This setting aside the scriptures in favour of preaching was wrong 'unless you call your sermons (as some Quakers are said to do) as much the word of God as the Bible'. Whereas there was an organised structure for readings in the Established Church throughout the year, with catechism and Sunday school classes, Scottish Presbyterians had no such organisation for scripture readings.[19]

King knew that Scottish Presbyterians claimed that reading of scripture was done at home, but he rejected this view, arguing that the scriptures were intended to be read in church and that some could not afford to buy a Bible; furthermore, he was sure that some could not read. And in a comment that condemned the Established Church itself, King claimed that the Reformation had succeeded in England and Wales because the people in church had the Bible read to them in their own language:

> I am persuaded that if ever the native Irish be brought to the knowledge of God's word it must be by having it read to them publicly in a language they understand and not by thrusting Bibles privately into their hand, of the ineffectiveness of which we have had an experiment 150 years.[20]

King then treated the long and vexed question of outward forms of worship in church:

> Sitting has crept into some of our churches, chiefly by the occasion and countenance of those who have miserably fallen from us. While we do not have to follow every external thing Christ did, we follow the general rules of decency and reason. . . . If other dissenters think bodily worship such as bowing, kneeling etc. unlawful and unnecessary, because they are acts of the body and unfit on that account to be offered to God who is a spirit, why may not the Quakers omit the sacrament and the words of the mouth which are outward things? . . . The principle and reasoning are the same in all these and will justify the silent meetings of the Quakers, the extravangaza of those that pretend to be above all ordinances, as well as the irreverence of other dissenters.[21]

King also criticised the form of music used in Presbyterian services, by which the minister led the congregation line by line, singing the psalms in metre form. The Established Church, on the other hand, allowed musical instruments, and this seemed 'more requisite in northern countries where generally people's voices are more harsh and untunable than in other places'.[22]

The Scottish Presbyterian practice concerning frequency of communion puzzled King. Whereas the Established Church held communions at least three times yearly, monthly if possible and even weekly in large cities and towns, Scottish Presbyterians had no such fixed times, leaving it to the minister and elders to decide when a communion service was to take place. So while Sabbath observance was obligatory, communion was a rare event.[23] King either did not know, or chose not to recognise, the long-established Scottish Presbyterian custom of large communion services, held in different parts of the north and attended by numbers of ministers and often thousands of people.[24]

While differences in forms of worship separated the Established Church and Scottish Presbyterians, King was also aware of the well-defined church order of Scottish Presbyterians and thought there was a possibility of some agreement in this regard between Scottish Presbyterians and the Established Church, for both had similar forms of church organisation: districts, provincial churches and national churches. The crucial difference between them lay in the fact that Scottish Presbyterians were governed by a college of equal presbyters, while the Established Church had presbyteries governed by bishops. English Presbyterians in Ireland were not strong enough numerically to aspire to a national church organisation. In Ireland they were in practice, though not in theory, Independent churches. From his time in Dublin, King knew that Independents believed that Christ only instituted single, particular churches. For them classical, provincial and national churches were human inventions; contact with neighbouring churches was only in terms of charity and good relations and not in any governing sense. In view of this, King thought that agreement would be easier to achieve between the Established Church and Scottish Presbyterians.[25]

King addressed his work to his own clergy in Derry.[26] Then he addressed the Scottish Presbyterian ministers of Derry, specifically asking them for agreement on use of the Lord's Prayer in service, kneeling at service, frequency of the communion service, and the reading of at least a chapter of scripture at service. He also asked them to consider occasional conformity, pointing out that English Presbyterians accepted this.[27] Although King hoped to win some form of compromise,[28] he seemed unable to recognise that the form of worship in both traditions was a source of profound disagreement, not a 'few indifferent ceremonies'. This was clearly shown when Robert Craghead, who had been a Scottish Presbyterian minister in Ireland since the Interregnum, wrote a firm, negative response to King's *Discourse*.[29]

Craghead maintained that the ceremonies enjoined by the Book of Common Prayer, as well as the role of bishops and church government, prevented Scottish Presbyterians from joining the Established Church for worship, even occasionally.[30] He defended the ministers' use of scripture both for reading and preaching, as well as the ability of the people to read the Bible, insisting that even the very poor had a Bible, and in fact 'will punish themselves rather than want a Bible'.[31] Forms of worship enjoined by the Book of Common Prayer were alien to Scottish Presbyterianism: bowing and kneeling at the Lord's Supper were not required by scripture, though it was permitted to kneel at prayer. Anything else was 'will-worship', a human invention.[32] King was critical of their form of music, but Craghead maintained that the singing of psalms in metre rather than in prose was correct and that the use of instruments in church expired with the Old Testament.[33] On the vexed question of frequency of communion services, Craghead explained the tradition of holding them once or twice a year, if there was a settled congregation. One of the reasons they could not have it more frequently was harassment of both ministers and families by the bishop's courts.[34]

Craghead ended his tract with comments on the theology and practice of predestination and 'God's previous concourse', as against free will and universal redemption. Pastors ministered to their people more than half a day every fortnight and in particular taught predestination and election.[35] Craghead admitted that people had doubts and attributed them to the 'innate atheism of our depraved natures' which led them to question: 'Is there a God, is there a Christ, is there an eternity, can there be a resurrection, is there a heaven and a hell?' The solution was to 'labour to have your calling and election made sure'.[36] In ending thus, Craghead used the opportunity to instruct his people and help them maintain adherence to the strict doctrine of predestination, and indeed to Scottish Presbyterian theology and forms of worship.[37]

Boyse also wrote a tract in defence of Presbyterian forms of worship, from the perspective of the English Presbyterian tradition.[38] He was known in Dublin as 'a good ingenious man . . . of some latitude'[39] and because of this was more able to offer some form of consensus. For example, Boyse affirmed that all Presbyterians used formal prayer for baptism and communion services and had a formal dismissal at the end of services. But if formal prayer alone was used, this would lead to dullness and sloth in both the minister and congregation.[40] Moreover, Boyse argued that the Directory of Worship was quite specific about what topic to preach on, and that it had more emphasis on the mysteries of religion than the Established Church. The latter quoted Seneca and Cicero more frequently than apostolic writings and stressed morality rather than religion. What amazed Boyse and all the ministers he spoke to was the view that King had of northern ministers:

> Perhaps the ministers in the north of Ireland and those in Scotland (speaking generally) outstrip all others that we know of in the christian world as to their unwearied diligence in catechising those under their charge.

They divided their parishes into communicants and examinable persons. The communicants were visited once a year and were examined for their progress in knowledge and practice before being admitted to communion. It was the custom for all dissenters both in Ireland and in England to catechise each Sabbath and once every summer go through the whole catechism. Boyse asked if the Established Church clergy did anything like this. Ministers in the north of Ireland read scripture to their congregation each Sabbath except in the winter:

> I am credibly informed by such as live in the north that most families of dissenters read the scriptures daily. On the Lord's day before and after public worship as well; that is why they can drop it in the winter.

The people brought the Bible to service and had it explained to them; but the Established Church congregation brought the Book of Common Prayer to service and so were near to practising popery.[41] Bodily worship was a contentious issue and was linked with Laudianism. Dissenters in England and in the south of Ireland did not sit at public prayers. Boyse learned from ministers in the north of Ireland that 'the better sort' generally stood; though ministers recommended kneeling, people travelled so far to come to meetings that it was not insisted upon; the meeting-house was often so crowded that it would have been impossible to kneel anyway.[42] Boyse accepted that the prose version of the psalms used in the Established Church was as much the word of God as the metrical version. He objected to the version of the psalms used in the Established Church rather than their use of prose. However, Boyse thought that organs should only be used in parish churches to help keep the congregation in tune; they should not be used at all in cathedrals.[43]

With regard to the frequency of the communion service, Boyse indicated there was great variety of practice, but generally in Dublin and in churches of the English Presbyterian tradition a service was held once a month or every six weeks to two months. In the north it was held once a year, perhaps twice in large towns. It was a special form of service, as two-thirds of the communicants were strangers from other parishes, and the services were big gatherings. Services were held in different parts of the north, and it was customary to travel long distances to them. Thus people could go to communion services between four and fifteen times a year if they so wished and were allowed. Although Boyse preferred his own church practice of monthly communion, he pointed out that either way both churches communicated more frequently than the Established Church. In view of this, Boyse hoped that King would urge his people to join Scottish Presbyterians for communion, in the same way as dissenters were urged to attend the Established Church occasionally for worship.[44]

Boyse proposed the 1691 Heads of Agreement as a basis for unity.[45] However, he acknowledged that in matters of church government there were differences between the Independent and the Presbyterian churches. For while English Presbyterians accorded synods a governing power, the Independents gave them a consultative power. In practice, however, someone excommunicated from one Independent church could not join another church, since the pastors were bonded together in association and supported one another's decisions. The same applied to excommunication by the bishop's court, at least among English Presbyterians, and in view of this Boyse asked that the bishop accept marriages solemnised by a nonconformist minister.[46]

Boyse suggested practical ways of achieving union and accommodation with the Established Church: the renewal of the Established Church, asking it to reconsider the stance of Ussher with regard to exercising power with presbyters in the diocese (using Ussher's *Model of Episcopacy*); better preparation for ordination; reform of the clergy in parishes, especially in Down and Connor;[47] and the suppression of pluralities and non-residence. He also asked that dissenters be relieved of the Act of Uniformity, since taking it led to ministers being forced to accept re-ordination. Instead he suggested that the obstacles to communion with the Established Church be removed, especially excommunication of those who attended religious meetings other than those of the Established Church, of those who rejected the Book of Common Prayer and the ceremonies of the Established Church, and of those who could not accept bishops as a different order in the church.[48] However valid such observations were to Boyse — and they were made in a spirit of moderation — they could not be accepted by King, or indeed any member of the Established Church at that time. Apart from the fact that they were theologically impossible, they threatened the position and survival of a weak and fragmented Established Church. King said as much in his reply to Boyse.[49]

Basic to King's reply was the conviction that as a bishop he had the right and responsibility to exercise authority over Scottish Presbyterians. He claimed that of the 30,000 Scottish Presbyterians in the diocese only one in ten went to church. There were nine meeting-houses in the diocese, and about three hundred attended each of them. What happened to the rest who worshipped nowhere?[50] This was the heart of the problem as far as King was concerned. He knew the Scottish Presbyterians had neither enough room nor enough ministers for all their people, and so he wanted them to come to the Established Church for worship.[51] King then went into some details about the number of meeting-houses in the diocese in comparision to the greater number of parish churches. He had gone to a good deal of trouble to obtain these figures from his curates,[52] though his friends advised him to be sure his facts were accurate.[53] Capel, the Lord Deputy, thought him too persistent and hotheaded.[54]

From his reply to Boyse, it was clear that King was unable to grasp the reality of the situation in his own diocese. He saw the Established Church as the norm to which the Scottish Presbyterians had to conform. There was no middle, negotiating ground. Within that tight framework, King could not accept Boyse's view that decisions regarding outward forms of worship could be left to different congregations and that no fixed form of liturgy was necessary. Matters of church discipline and order, such as the right of the people to choose their ministers, were devalued by King, who thought that if they worshipped together all would be solved gradually.[55] He underlined the duties he thought he had as bishop, giving him unique rights:

> Mr Boyse has no such relation to those he takes on him to advise. He has yet owned no proper church beyond his single congregation. He has owned no ecclesiastical jurisdiction to whom on earth he and his congregation are accountable by the laws of Christ. He can claim no authority over any other congregation than his own, or challenge so much as to be a minister of Christ to any other, if they please to question it, without a new ordination, as appears from those Heads of Agreement produced by himself.[56]

In the following year Boyse responded to King in a further work which he dedicated to the Scottish Presbyterians in Derry.[57] Boyse also consulted ministers and elders in the north and used their testimonies to refute King's *Admonition*.[58] At the same time, in an effort to reach some agreement, Boyse invited King to expand his view of the catholic church, a source of contention between them since 1687. Only this could bridge the gap between the several churches of different traditions and practices within the reformed tradition. However, Boyse did not hold out much hope for this, since King refused Scottish Presbyterians (and Roman Catholics) the right to build meeting-houses on his lands.[59]

Nothing daunted, King wrote a *Second admonition* in 1696 in reply to Boyse.[60] This admonition reworked the same themes of the previous one, with further details gleaned from his own clergy.

King was particularly critical again of the large communion services. The government saw them as a threat to peace. For this reason King refused to allow meeting-houses on his land, arguing that the huge meetings held there were a real drain on his tenants:

> Coshering and exacting of tenants by way of meat and lodging is against the laws of this kingdom; and the popish priests lived by such ways but were not near so oppressive to their neighbours as your meetings are. . . . Your sacraments especially are attended with a most oppressive coshering . . . 4 or 5,000 meet together from distant places and stay several days. And indeed none that live near the meeting house can call their meat or drink or grass or houses their own during these times or dare refuse them.[61]

Rather than have such large communion services, King wanted the Scottish Presbyterians to come to his church for worship. He could not see that this would not work, that it could never be a solution. He was asking for an impossible change; since their beginnings in Ireland Scottish Presbyterians were well used to large gatherings, saw them as minor revivals and part of their tradition. In any event, at the level of theology and practice, the Book of Common Prayer, even in a mitigated form, could never be accepted. It was strange that King, who came from a Presbyterian background, could not grasp this.

In 1697 Robert Craghead responded to King's second admonition, concentrating once again on the issue of worship.[62] Craghead insisted that Presbyterians had always objected to joining the Established Church for worship, and he reminded his readers that there were books written about this which were burnt in the recent war, 'at least in this part of the nation'. A book was needed now, he said, so that ordinary people could answer for themselves when asked why they did not come to the parish church for worship. Craghead hoped this would help his congregations as well as increase understanding with the Established Church, for 'we cannot see with their eyes, nor they with ours'.[63]

He explained in detail the two points of doctrine and practice which prevented Scottish Presbyterians from attending the parish church: use of the Book of Common Prayer for worship, and the role and authority of bishops in the Established Church. The Book of Common Prayer could never be used by Scottish Presbyterians because of its use of the Apocryphal books, saints' days, versions of scripture, formal prayers, doctrine of the catechism, over-participation of the congregation in worship, the sign of the cross at baptism, kneeling at communion, parts of the communion service, godparents at baptism, and the doctrine that children are regenerate by baptism.[64] These points were similar to those raised by Scottish Presbyterians in their debate with Henry Leslie in 1636[65] and represented a consistent stand taken by them throughout the 17th century with regard to the Book of Common Prayer. By 1696 they had become well-established and deeply held convictions.

Craghead insisted that the Apostles were of one ministerial order and cited scripture to prove that this was so in the time of Christ and in the early church. The difference between bishops and presbyters arose out of custom and not by divine law or appointment. Craghead admitted that at some point presbyters allowed bishops to emerge into positions of power; while he left this point unfinished in the text, the logical conclusion to his thought was that this power was taken back, as a necessary reform, at the time of the Reformation.[66] As for re-ordination, which the Established Church required of dissenting ministers,

> This we judge a rejecting of us altogether and a manifest injury to the church of God. For first our ministers of the presbyterian persuasion are elected and ordained to the rules of scripture, the people's electing and the Presbytery ordaining. It were good if you were able to say as much for yourselves.[67]

Craghead pointed out that, in the light of these points, a great deal more 'than a few harmless, indifferent ceremonies' separated them. In this respect, Scottish Presbyterians should not be forced to worship against their wills, and Craghead cited Jeremy Taylor's *Case of conscience* to support his case and exhorted King: 'Be not so tenacious of your own traditions, customs and inventions as to scatter the flock of Christ'.[68]

In 1697 Craghead wrote a further response on behalf of the Scottish Presbyterians in Derry and dedicated his work to the mayor of the city, James Lennox.[69] The book was written for his own people, to explain

> The necessity of undeceiving many poor weak people who are taught that the difference between the worship of others and ours is only some harmless ceremonies, but conceal from them that some ceremonies are made worship to God without his command and others that are religious worship tendered to creatures, which is due to God only and therefore are not harmless.[70]

Communion services were still a source of deep division. King had obliged people under pain of excommunication to come to communion at least three times a year. Apart from the fact that worship in a Established Church was unacceptable, Craghead thought this imposition was far too harsh, especially on doubting Christians. This highlighted a difference in theology, noted by one of King's clergy:

> not one in five of their flock ever received the holy communion, though [had] a competent knowledge . . . they have an odd notion that it is means of confirming the adult in grace but not of conveying it.[71]

Craghead also defended Scottish Presbyterian church order. This had been well established during the hard years since the Restoration and had served them well. Ministers helped each other out, either when one had to be away ministering to scattered congregations or when a communion service was being held. When a congregation could not have a service, this did not mean there was no worship; some worshipped at home, and others met in smaller groups within an area. Again this was a well-established tradition among Presbyterians in Ireland since the 1630s.[72]

Craghead stressed the significance of the communion service, and in particular the preparation for communion, which they took very seriously 'that they may know to whom they dispense those holy mysteries'. Craghead insisted that this preparation was necessary; catechising and preaching were needed beforehand, and people were examined carefully. This took time; so did the communion services, in view of the great numbers present. Had they small congregations, such as King had, then all this could be done more quickly. As it was, four or five thousand could be present at a service, and even though only five hundred might communicate, the rest had to be cared for, be preached to and so prepared for communion another day.[73] In this context, Craghead claimed that very few were deprived of worship,

> considering the pains the people take in the summer time to travel abroad for opportunity of worship; making the congregation so numerous that no meeting house can contain them and therefore the ministers are often constrained to preach in the fields lest the people should be disappointed.[74]

While King criticised the disturbance created by huge crowds at communion services, Craghead countered this with the view that people willingly gave hospitality to communicants, in fact 'freely invite them to their houses, observing the gospel rule not to forget to entertain strangers'.[74] He also explained that the infrequency of communion services was due to constant harassment of Scottish Presbyterians by the Established Church over many years:

> I have been for a long time that my nearest neighbour durst not come into my house to hear a chapter of the Bible read and expounded to them; and at length forced to leave the congregation, my habitation and family altogether, not knowing of any hiding place from the rage of persecution. Sometimes the sacrament was administered at night, in great danger; sometimes ministers were pulled out of their pulpits with the consent of the bishop. So infrequent communion was due to this harassment both before and since the revolution [1688].[76]

Boyse's views on occasional communion, which King misunderstood as ordinary and regular communion with the Established Church, could not be accepted by Scottish Presbyterians. Worship with the Established Church could not be accepted on any basis. The Book of Common Prayer and the ceremonies of the church were too alien to the Scottish Presbyterians, were too closely linked to Roman Catholicism, and so were theologically impossible for them to consider.[77] This was the view not only of ministers but also of the people who supported their ministers, in addition to paying tithes to the Established Church, and who were, in Craghead's words, free . . . to declare they cannot in conscience countenance a ministry obtruded on people, without a call or consent, nor a liturgy of men's devising.[78]

So ended the long series of debates in which the three parties sought to define and explain their point of view. In matters of theology and practice, the two strands of Presbyterianism, Scottish and English, had most in common, though they diverged on the matter of church government and occasional communion. The understanding between them allowed Boyse to enter into debate with King, yet the northern ministers felt he had not represented their view completely, and so Craghead responded to King twice. This contribution brought into relief the convictions Scottish Presbyterians had on predestination and election by God, a fact which directed and guided their consciences and persuaded them they had to stand fast against any diminution of this doctrine. This was not new. Scottish Presbyterian ministers had argued long and hard with Henry Leslie, Bishop of Down and Connor, in 1636. What offended them then in the Book of Common Prayer and the ceremonies of the Established Church had not changed. At the end of the seventeenth century those differences remained, and while English Presbyterianism could just about accept occasional communion, this was unthinkable within Scottish Presbyterianism.

King still had to come to terms with the fact that the Scottish Presbyterians in his diocese were not going to conform to the Established Church. They were a church, separate and defined, having gathered strength and organisational experience in the period 1660-88, in spite of harassment and suspicion from the governments of the day. They emerged after 1688 as a united force and began to take a more public stand, speaking with a confident voice. If the age of Ussher and his spirit was over, the age of self-confidence and assurance had come and convinced Scottish Presbyterians that they could grow and thrive. The struggles were by no means over, but the hesitancies of the post-Restoration period were over and the members of the church could look ahead with optimism. With a mixture of predestination energy, so to speak, and reaping the fruits of long and well-tried church organisation and discipline, Scottish Presbyterians in the north of Ireland faced further and more difficult hurdles.

The Sacramental Test

The Sacramental Test debate began after the 1688 Revolution when Protestant dissenters in Ireland sought full religious toleration. Although the Oath of Supremacy was abrogated in 1691 and replaced by an oath which Protestant nonconformists could take, they were still limited by the Acts of Uniformity of 1560 and 1666. For this reason nonconformists sought to have full toleration granted, and they fought the possibility of a Sacramental Test being linked to a Bill of Indulgence.[79] Boyse presented the case:

> There are two things desired by dissenting Protestants in reference to a Bill of Indulgence: First, that it give them a full security for the free exercise of religion according to their consciences. Secondly, that there be no such clauses annexed to it as may disable them from serving their King and their country.[80]

Dissenters contended that such a bill was necessary to preserve the Protestant interest in Ireland and claimed it could not threaten the Established Church, since all the church's revenues and privileges were enshrined in law:

> The dissenting Protestants of this kingdom have never expressed any unpeacable turbulency towards their neighbours, much less have they shown the least dissatisfaction to the government.[81]

Here Boyse was speaking very obviously of the English Presbyterians, for Scottish Presbyterians would not have been seen in such a positive light. Tobias Pullein, Bishop of Dromore, replied to Boyse,[82] and while accepting the right of nonconformists to the free exercise of religion, he argued that a bill passed without any restrictions would create a multiplicity of 'sects'. This was an old argument. The Established Church persisted in calling the nonconformist churches 'sects'; to have accepted them as churches would have undermined the position of the Established Church and made the Sacramental Test debate irrelevant. Besides, the fear of Roman Catholicism justified their stance:

> For a general Indulgence has always proved instrumental to the advancing the popish interest among us and has therefore been vigorously

promoted by popish emissaries in England and that by express orders from their superiors abroad who have experimentally found it to be the most effectual method of introducing popery into a country and have expended very considerable sums of money for the purchase of toleration to dissenters.[83]

In addition, an indulgence such as Boyse wanted would lead to an influx of Presbyterians from Scotland. 'If they are turbulent at home, will they be any better in Ireland?' Scottish Presbyterians were 'sworn to extirpate prelacy' and had treated the episcopal clergy in Scotland severely. Moreover, a general indulgence would mean that all control over dissenters in Ireland would be lost. Memories of how the Established Church fared during the Interregnum were still sufficiently alive to evoke fears of what an indulgence might introduce into the country. Pullein wondered why the dissenters were not content with what they had achieved since the revolution; this was a tacit permission to exercise their religion publicly, build meeting-houses, even in corporate towns, and receive the royal bounty.[84] The message was clear:

No motives ought to prevail on us to make such large concessions to them as will in all probability shake the very foundations of the established church.[85]

Boyse replied quickly to Pullein, rejecting his suggestion that sects would increase if the indulgence was granted with the Test. The three 'sects' involved were Presbyterians, Independents and Baptists, and among the latter two there were 'but about six congregations that I know of in the kingdom'. Thus the Established Church was really concerned about the Scottish Presbyterians in the north of Ireland. Boyse did not grasp this fact and simply asked for a spirit of tolerance; he even wondered if occasional communion between the churches could not be practised by those who were likely to be

the most judicious as well as the most moderate persons and most likely to be the happy instruments of healing those breaches which persons of narrower judgements on either hand do unhappily widen.[86]

Indeed, he argued that the Test should be applied only to Catholics, which was the original intention of all such tests.[87] On both counts Boyse missed the point. Scottish Presbyterians would not consider occasional communion, and the debate at this time had little to do with Roman Catholics. Scottish Presbyterians were viewed as the most serious threat to the Established Church. Nevertheless, in his reply to Boyse Pullein defended his views.[88] He argued from history that any toleration of sects led to their increase. Indeed, in 1672 the Catholics benefited from the indulgence.[89] In the light of this evidence, Pullein argued that only Catholics would gain, and nonconformists would advance their own cause and splinter the Protestant interest even more. Pullein cited the example of David Houston and his followers in the north of Ireland who

> in the times of the greatest danger most scandalously separated themselves from the main body of the Protestants in the north of Ireland and publicly owned their acting on a different bottom from them.[90]

In addition, since 1690 thousands of Scots had come over to Ireland and, with the exception of the Highlanders, all were Presbyterians, with ministers who were 'all zealous for the Covenant'. Since the Presbyterian Church had become the established church in Scotland, the threat of Scottish Presbyterianism in Ulster was very real to Pullein: if their power and numbers increased in Ireland, the Established Church could be in great danger. Pullein voiced this fear and claimed that Cameronians or militant Covenanters had landed in Ireland and were numerous in the country. He also accused Boyse of being unaware of the real situation in the north,[91] where tempers were turbulent and unpredictable. Episcopal ministers had received harsh treatment in Scotland, and Pullein cited a number of examples to prove his point.[92] The same happened in Ireland, in Letterkenny and Derry.[93] How could any government allow toleration for such people, 'bigoted covenanters' whose zeal against popery could not hide their hatred of episcopacy?[94] Pullein reminded Boyse that this was not new, for the Oath of Allegiance which debarred dissenters from offices had not been revoked. The fact that it was not enforced did not mean it was void:

> their present quiet enjoyment of employment is not so much owing to their legal qualifications as to the kindness and leniency of the ecclesiastical governors.[95]

Bishop Anthony Dopping of Meath joined the debate at this point.[96] He maintained that dissenters had freedom of worship and freedom to trade[97] and that this was as far as the church and government should go. Indeed, the Test was needed in order to have some definite legal control over dissenters, especially in the north:

> 'Tis well known that the British are already possessed of one fourth part of the kingdom, that they have spread themselves into other provinces and that there are frequent colonies coming out of Scotland to carry on the plantation of the party; that the commons are generally fond of the Solemn League and Covenant and retain affection for it (though the nobility and gentry are otherwise affected); that by the 2nd Article of the Covenant they are bound to endeavour without respect of persons the extirpation of prelacy as well as popery.[98]

Thus toleration was impossible and foolish to consider, and Dopping argued that the Sacramental Test was a necessary measure in contrast to the Covenant which had led to the civil war. Both good government and church order required this Test. Either way, the church could not lose: it could find out who its enemies were, or it could gain new members.[99]

As the debate developed it was clear that exchanges between Boyse and the Established Church would not make much progress on the issue of the Scottish Presbyterians in Ireland. Boyse, representing the English Presbyterian tradition in Ireland, had a spirit of latitude which created the possibility of some consensus. Boyse was quite open to the idea of occasional communion.[100] What was much more crucial was the stance of the Scottish Presbyterians in the north of Ireland with regard to the Bill of Indulgence and the Sacramental Test. Their attitude became clearer in 1697 when John McBride published his response to Pullein and to Edward Synge, another Established Church clergyman who had entered the debate.[101] It was an echo of what Craghead had told King regarding the impossibility of common worship between the Established and Presbyterian Churches in Derry.

McBride stated that Scottish Presbyterian doctrine conformed to the Irish Articles of 1615, 'declared in the Convocation anno 1615, excepting in what relates to prelacy and ceremonies'.

Although the Scottish Presbyterian church in Ireland had different forms of church government, doctrine and worship, this did not mean it was not a true Reformation church. In the light of their unity as true Reformation churches, McBride asked if a limited form of toleration could not be granted to the Presbyterians alone in Ireland. In this way they would be united against their common enemy, Roman Catholicism.[102]

McBride argued that the Sacramental Test was unjust on several counts. From the point of view of doctrine, it was 'will-worship':

> Know that the most part of Presbyterians and Independents in Ireland are otherwise minded, who all judge and declare that the table gesture in receiving the sacrament and not the adoration is the most agreeable to the first pattern given us by Christ and his apostles and practised in the primitive church.[103]

He exposed the inherent contradiction of asking Presbyterians to kneel at communion and yet deny transubstantiation:

> Not to kneel in receiving, by this test, is made equally criminal with believing transubstantiation, the idolatrous worshipping of the bread and all the abomination of the Mass with papists and with denying and condemning both ceremony and substance with the Quakers.[104]

In McBride's view, the contradiction went even further in that Quakers did not believe in sacraments at all, whereas Presbyterians had two sacraments, baptism and the Lord's Supper. Yet both were to be punished for not accepting the Sacramental Test.[105]

However, it was clear that the Established Church wanted the Sacramental Test for two reasons: to control the growing power of Scottish Presbyterians in the north of Ireland, and to control their access (and that of Roman Catholics) to offices in the state and the army. By 1695 the threat from Scottish Presbyterians was much more real than from Roman Catholics. It was an old problem which needed to be solved with new urgency and adequate legislation. The presence of dissenters in Ireland after the Restoration had posed problems continually for the government which wanted to ensure that dissenters could not gain control of the country. Indeed, Ormond had understood that the legislation already on the statute books was intended only for Roman Catholics, and that it was therefore debatable whether it could be applied to dissenters.[106] To have specific legislation on the statute book would solve that problem once and for all.

With the Sacramental Test no such confusion would obtain, and dissenters could either be drawn into conformity or easily identified as nonconformists. One solution to the difficulty lay in cancelling the proposed Bill of Indulgence and returning to the tacit agreements of the early years of the Restoration, when no formal toleration was granted but dissenters could practise their religion privately on the understanding that they would not seek to extend or increase their congregations. It was a policy of containment, but it could not work as simply as that, for congregations expanded and meeting-houses were built. Some recognition of this was made when, after the 1688 Revolution, dissenters were allowed to meet, to build meeting-houses in new areas, and were granted the royal bounty.

The Test, then, was trying to reverse a process that had been evolving for thirty years. English Presbyterians and the Independents had grown in self-definition but not in significant numbers; they were not a threat to the Established Church. On the other hand, Scottish Presbyterians in the north and in some other parts of Ireland had grown in numbers and organisational strength and were certainly as big a threat as Roman Catholicism — indeed, probably even more so then in the eyes of the bishops. Thus the Established Church neither wanted nor could afford to grant Scottish Presbyterians full toleration without the Test. The risk was too great and the position of the Established Church too precarious without the full protection of the law. This was granted in 1704, when the Sacramental Test came into force in Ireland as a clause in the Popery Act. From the manner in which it was introduced into the Popery Act, it was evident that the Test clause was intended specifically for the Scottish Presbyterians.[107]

The Marriage Controversy

Even before the 1688 Revolution the issue of marriage was a source of latent controversy between the Established Church and

Scottish Presbyterians. In the period immediately after the Restoration Scottish Presbyterians questioned the wisdom of publicly celebrating marriages. Jeremy Taylor complained in 1665 that 'illegal and scandalous marriages' were being celebrated in his diocese.[108] However, by 1673 the Laggan meeting expressed the wish to make marriages more public if only to counteract the Established Church's accusation that they were invalid:

> Because the prelates here call marriage by nonconformist ministers fornication and are persecuting some here on that account, they appoint Mr Robert Rule the moderator to write to the several meetings about this and to show them that this meeting inclines to solemnise marriage publicly and to proclaim publicly among ourselves, besides public proclamation with the curates; only we would be at uniform practice with our brethren in this matter.[109]

By this time the Route, Antrim and Tyrone meetings had begun to proclaim and solemnise marriages publicly and the Laggan followed their example.[110] The fact that marriages were not celebrated according to the Book of Common Prayer was an irritant to the Established Church and indeed to the government. Bishop Hackett of Down and Connor complained of the abuse of such marriages:

> These nonconformists likewise perform all parochial duties here and defraud the ministers of their dues (not content with preaching only as they are in England), and what is of most wicked consequence, after they have married persons, the couple on discontents part and pretend they were not legally married.[111]

Essex, the Lord Lieutenant, also was concerned about Scottish Presbyterian marriages and the unrest they could lead to if not checked. Even if such marriages could not be prevented, for they 'scruple to our ceremonies of marriage', yet he thought that Scottish Presbyterians should be required to give a formal account of how their marriages were contracted.[112] This arose at a time when nonconformists were allowed to worship in public on Sundays, so obviously the church and government felt some things had gone too far. In addition, the Established Church was bound to deny the validity of marriages; to do otherwise would amount to accepting Scottish Presbyterianism as a church, with the right in theory to legislate for itself and have its laws, including property and inheritance rights, recognised by the state.

After the turbulent period of the early 1680s and in the light of James II's indulgence, meetings asked in 1687 whether or not it was safe to proclaim marriages in public again.[113] Political events in 1688 overtook the issue, but the debate resumed in 1702 when John McBride published a tract[114] defending marriages celebrated by Scottish Presbyterians and asked that they be accepted as legal and valid:

> Our manner of marriage is both lawful and peaceable, seeing the civil magistrate has not for about eighty years found any disadvantage to the public thereby, and therefore has not evidenced their dissatisfaction with any upon that account; all our marriages hitherto having had the same effects in law, as if they had been solemnised according to the rites of the established church, which also has confirmed their marriages, by granting administrations and probates of wills.[115]

McBride indicated that this situation had changed, that bishops now challenged their right to celebrate marriages and were accusing the Scottish Presbyterians of holding clandestine marriages.[116] McBride refuted this old accusation, stating that marriages were proclaimed on three consecutive Sundays in church, and none went forward without full parental consent on both sides; normally marriages were celebrated in the meeting-house, but not at fixed times nor during a communion service. The Established Church asserted that marriages were clandestine if not celebrated before a curate and according to the Book of Common Prayer. For McBride this was pure Trent and so had to be rejected, as was the dispensation that could be bought from the Established Church; this was seen as simony and certainly popish.[117] He also pointed out that Quakers and Roman Catholics were not persecuted for celebrating marriages,[118] and that in Spain, France and Italy, all three Catholic countries, nonconformist marriages were accepted as valid.

Ralph Lambert replied to McBride on behalf of the Established Church.[119] He insisted that the Established Church had the right to require adherence to its laws; in Scotland the episcopal ministers there had to conform to what was set down:

> Now if the presbyterian ministers of Scotland do think this and other laws are a warrant to them to solemnise all marriages even of persons

differing from them in religion, sure our author will grant that we have as good a reason to insist on the laws of this kingdom for our warrant; for he who upon occasion finds so hospitable a refuge among them can never believe any of their practices unjust nor that church blameable which imitates them.[120]

He reminded McBride that English Presbyterians in Ireland observed the marriage laws of the country and assured him that Quakers and Roman Catholics were not being prosecuted simply because the law had not caught up with them.[121] The appeal to 'eighty years' in the country could not give Scottish Presbyterians the right to their own forms of marriage: 'That which was wrong from the beginning will not grow right or legal by any length of time, no not in eighty years.' Besides the Act of Uniformity passed in 1666 established the forms of marriage obtaining in Ireland, and nothing in this regard had changed. Good government as well as justice in society and within marriage required conformity to the civil law of the country.[122]

A year later Edward Synge also replied to McBride.[123] Weary of the accusation 'popish' which McBride used of the Established Church,[124] Synge accused Scottish Presbyterians of using vague language about his church out of ignorance and prejudice: 'obscure notions of mystical rites . . . significant ceremonies, sacraments of human institution . . . all of which they call popish'. This was a diversion from the real issue, which was conformity to the established laws of the land regarding marriage. This had nothing to do with Rome.[125] Church and state in Ireland saw it as their duty to enforce the marriage laws in order to retain an ordered society; rejection of such laws was a threat not just to the church but to the government, especially in the times they lived in. It was clear, then, that any marriages not celebrated according to the laws of the land were null and void.[126]

He repeated that the two Acts of Uniformity had enacted such laws and that bishops were merely executors of this law in the land. Synge pointed out, as Lambert had, that the English Presbyterians in Ireland

are for the most part married according to our established liturgy. And yet I am persuaded they are persons of as much conscience as those in the north.[127]

Quakers and Roman Catholic marriages were equally at fault; they were not being treated differently, but it was difficult to enforce everything all at once. However, Synge felt that a Roman Catholic marriage would be upheld in court over that of a Scottish Presbyterian.[128]

From the Established Church point of view, the basis of the debate on marriage was similar to that on the Sacramental Test: both were ways of controlling the Scottish Presbyterians in the north of Ireland, who were seen as a real menace. Besides, to accept Scottish Presbyterian marriages as legal would signal acceptance of the validity of ordination within that tradition, something contrary to the 1666 Act of Uniformity. Other dissenters in the country, English Presbyterians, Independents, Baptists, Quakers, and for the present even Roman Catholics, were not be considered a serious threat. Both the marriage and Sacramental Test controversies taught Scottish Presbyterians that they would get nowhere unless they could win toleration without the Sacramental Test. In 1708 a formal petition was sent to the Lord-Lieutenant.[129] in which they complained that some in the Established Church were trying to deprive them of

> what we have so peaceably enjoyed, as appears by them pursuing both ministers and people in their courts for their nonconformity to the rules and ceremonies of the church, ministers for solemnising marriage clandestinely as they please to call it, and make void such marriages by obliging persons so married to confess publicly themselves guilty of the damnable sin of fornication.

They argued from the length of time they had been in Ireland, that they were

> a considerable body of Protestant subjects in this kingdom now about eighty years, who though dissenting from the established church in some things yet in all revolutions continued loyal and peaceable, suffering for our loyalty in the the time of the usurpation.

The petition outlined the situation: conformity to celebrating the marriage service according to the Book of Common Prayer had not been required before 1688; courts recognised wills made by Scottish Presbyterians; and the Established Church minister had received 'his accustomed dues as if they were married by himself'. Since the revolution they suffered harassment from the civil magistrates who questioned the validity of their marriages, which in turn threatened family inheritances. Unless this attitude on the part of the Established Church changed, Scottish Presbyterians would be ruined and society in general would suffer, for there were many conformists, clergy and laity, 'descending of parents so married of whom we are well assured there be several in this kingdom'. Despite this appeal, the Lord Lieutenant gave them no hope since

> our northern dissenters resolve to adhere to the confession of faith of north Britain and the southern prefer the Articles of England as the dissenters in south Britain have done.[130]

Thus while English Presbyterians in Ireland took occasional communion and had their marriages celebrated according to the rites of the Established Church,[131] such accommodation was not possible for Scottish Presbyterians. They had neither the hope of having the Sacramental Test removed or of having their marriages recognised, which ensured that hostility between Scottish Presbyterians and the Established Church in Ireland continued unabated.[132]

Loyalty and the Appeal to History

Ever since their 'Necessary Representation' made to parliament in 1649 (protesting against the execution of Charles I) Scottish Presbyterians in Ulster were particularly sensitive to the issue of their loyalty to the monarch. This was challenged by William Tisdall, vicar of Belfast, when he responded to the 1708 petition to the Lord-Lieutenant.[133] It was also a ploy to try to prevent a Whig ministry from granting any leniency to dissenters in Ireland. Tisdall accused Scottish Presbyterians of being antiroyalist since the reign of James I, and he cast doubt on their allegiance to Queen Anne.[134] Tisdall used Scottish Presbyterian historical documents to prove his point. For example, he critiqued their policy of consistently representing grievances either in Dublin or Whitehall:

> Most evident to any person who is conversant in the histories of presbyterian policy that the manner of framing, subscribing, applying

and publishing their addresses either to the King or Parliament was the mainspring of their grand political machine . . . whatever the subject of their addresses were, there was constantly an occasion taken of insinuating their own great merit and unequal returns made to them, the trumpet of their loyalty sounded loud and shrill in the preamble to their address, that the soft notes of their persecution and grievances might sound the more mournful and moving to the people; their boldest demands were urged in submissive terms according to the notion they had of their own powers or the difficulties of the public, and they were represented sometimes so modest and reasonable that the granting of them might seem only a debt and the refusal of them a great injury.[135]

It is significant that Tisdall had historical accounts to call on. For Scottish Presbyterians had ensured that histories were written from the earliest days of the plantation of Ulster.[136] Indeed, after the Restoration there was a concerted effort to continue this process, and it took a persistent attempt on the part of all the meetings in the years 1672-7 to reach a decision to appoint Patrick Adair as their historian.[137] The meetings were urged to send all their records and written memories to Adair, and this formed the basis of his history of the church.[138] Thus by the end of the seventeenth century the Scottish Presbyterian Church in Ireland had a sense of its own origin, root and identity; it had written its own story and had lived through a long period of testing. It had not only retained its own organisation and way of life, but had also developed and strengthened them to such a degree that after 1688 a strongly built church emerged quite clearly. John McBride gave expression to this in 1698 when he preached at the first public synod held in Ulster since the Restoration.[139]

The Established Church rightly viewed this growth in strength with suspicion and fear.[140] It was evident to the Bishop of Down and Connor, Edward Walkington, that Scottish Presbyterians had resumed their way of worship and organisation, interrupted by the war, and 'not content to assemble themselves in their several meeting-houses . . . they proceed to exercise jurisdiction openly and with a high hand over those of their own persuasion'. They celebrated marriages, attended communion services in great numbers, held sessions and synods, and had a philosophy school at Killylea.[141] In all, it was a resumption of the way of life and government they had retained and developed since the Restoration, but now lived openly.

In face of this strong presence, Tisdall pursued the issue of loyalty to the king in the years before the accession of William III.[142] Tisdall recognised a change in tone and attitude after 1689, one which was both confident and daring. Before that Scottish Presbyterians kept a low profile and 'entered into plots and associations . . . wrought by night in their mines to come at the great pillar which supported our establishment'. But after the revolution Scottish Presbyterians held synods and courts, sent out ministers to new congregations, appointed elders from among the powerful trading families, celebrated their own marriages and established their own schools, interfered with Established Church burial services, circulated books, refused the Oath of Abjuration, and denied the validity of episcopacy.[143] Moreover, Presbyterian trading families employed their own members rather than people of other churches, and Presbyterians had become burgesses and aldermen as well as postmasters. He viewed this growing power with alarm.[144]

Tisdall claimed that the Established Church had allowed this to grow under its feet and had not perceived the potential strength of Presbyterian discipline and church order. He looked back on the history of Scottish Presbyterians in Ireland, to Calvin and Knox, to the Solemn League and Covenant, as well as the subsequent Covenants and Covenanting movements after 1660.[145] He noted similarity with Roman Catholicism, even comparing Calvin and Loyola, who both set out to subvert the Church of England:

> By the fundamental principles of both presbyterian and popish policy there is no allegiance due to any Christian prince who does not profess and will not maintain what either call the true religion.[146]

Tisdall argued that the authority and rights of the Established Church would continue to be weakened if the Scottish Presbyterians continued to flourish in Ireland;[147] he was convinced that Scottish Presbyterians, united in principle and practice, could overcome the Established Church if they were left totally free to practise their religion. In other words, the Established Church simply had not got the strength and unity to survive without the protection of the law.[148]

In 1713 McBride replied to Tisdall and defended the historical record of Scottish Presbyterians in Ulster.[149] He described the period in Ireland when Ussher was Primate as an idyllic time, when Scottish Presbyterians and the Established Church coexisted in peace and mutual understanding.[150] All this had changed with the advent of Laud, when Scottish Presbyterians were forced into dissent. But McBride rejected Tisdall's practice of calling all dissenters Scottish in origin, pointing out that during the Interregnum there were Baptists, Independents and Quakers in the country.[151] He particularly defended the stance taken by Scottish Presbyterians in Ireland during the Commonwealth period, claiming they had suffered for it on account of their loyalty to the king. Their record of loyalty was clear and well documented and continued after the Restoration.[152]

In the same year a more detailed refutation of Tisdall was published by James Kirkpatrick,[153] who was quick to point out that loyalty was not synonymous with conformity to the Established Church in Ireland. True loyalty was honouring and supporting the just authority and power of the monarch, 'the original compact between prince and people'. Church and state were two distinct powers, the keys and the sword. He cited Ussher's speech of 1622 and declared:

> I never read a presbyterian writer who made larger demands on behalf of the church than those mentioned by the learned Ussher in the approved speech, and who was not cordially satisfied to make the same concessions with him to the civil magistrate.[154]

Ussher was never accused of disloyalty 'for asserting the inherent power of the church'. Indeed, the Church of England, in the Second Book of Homilies, held that the church could excommunicate the civil magistrate; yet it rejected the Presbyterian Church's claim to do so. Nevertheless, Scottish Presbyterians were loyal to the king from the beginning, and Kirkpatrick cited both Livingstone and Adair to prove his point.[155] He also denied Tisdall's claims that Scottish Presbyterians were disloyal to the present monarch and sought only to increase their power and influence through holding synods and sessions, education of their own people, use of elders in the church, celebration of marriage, and accepting new congregations in different parts of Ireland.[156] While McBride declared that neither ministers nor elders took the Solemn League and Covenant, he reiterated that episcopacy was merely a human ordinance, and that there was no distinction of order between bishops and presbyters; he regretted that while Scottish Presbyterians accepted the validity of the Established Church's episcopal orders, the Established Church did not accept the validity of Presbyterian orders.[157]

Both McBride and Kirkpatrick claimed that the Scottish Presbyterians constituted a separate Church, rooted in the tradition of the Reformation as it had occurred in Scotland, and in communion with other true Reformation churches. But the Established Church, viewing itself as the lawfully established church of the land, and therefore rightfully requiring conformity, could not afford to accept this view. Besides, by this time the theological differences between the two churches were very great and comprehension was impossible. At a communion service held about 1709 at Anahilt, County Down, Alexander McCracken preached:

> The yoke of [the Book of] Common Prayer, of kneeling, the sign of the Cross, surplice . . . that is the Devil's yoke and they that bear it are in the way of hell.[158]

Such remarks summed up the real differences in theology and practice between Scottish Presbyterians and the Established Church, and these went very deep. Nevertheless, some bishops continued to describe the differences as exterior, over mere rites and ceremonies. But Peter Browne, Bishop of Cork, recognised that Presbyterians differed from the Established Church on almost every aspect of religion: theology, rites, sacraments, orders, discipline, government and jurisdiction.[159] The Archbishop of Armagh, Narcissus Marsh, realised that there were real differences within the Established Church itself, and he had to tread a path through their own divisions:

> But for the use of the surplice I confess 'tis not generally practised through this province nor does it yet seem seasonable to require it in all places at once but may be introduced by degrees as I endeavour to do it in

mine own diocese. For the parishioners will be apt to mutiny if the thought of paying for a surplice should be laid on them in these calamitous times.[160]

Perhaps the real price for insisting on the surplice would be defection from the Established Church and Marsh understood that well.[161] Better not to insist than risk division; better to seek comprehension than confrontation. It was an echo of Ussher and his spirit, but this time it applied to those within the Established Church only. Too much had happened since the early seventeenth century, and both Scottish Presbyterian and Established Churches were too well defined to allow the old spirit of moderation to prevail between them. That belonged to a former age which had gradually passed away since the Restoration.

Quakers and the Established Church

Quakers arrived in Ireland during the Interregnum at a time when the Established Church was suppressed, and by 1660 they had become sufficiently rooted in the country to enable them to survive the upheavals of the Restoration period. Certainly the Established Church inherited the suspicion that Roman Catholics and Quakers were in some form of collusion with one another for political ends. In the wake of the Popish Plot, such suspicions were renewed, and in 1682 Robert Ware accused the Quakers of being crypto-Catholics.[162] He claimed that the Quakers had been used by the Franciscans as a cover for their activities in Ireland. In a plot masterminded from London, they suppressed their own practices of mass, prayers to saints and images, the supremacy of the pope. They easily insinuated themselves with the Quakers, for both had similar ways of acting: they went around in twos or threes; they used coarse, plain clothes and they condemned luxury; they persuaded people to join them, pretending visions, revelations and prophecies, messages and 'new lights'; they were uncivil and saluted no one properly and showed no respect towards the magistrate; they taught that the saints are perfectly holy in this life and do not sin. Indeed, Ware claimed that just as the Baptists sprang from the Roman Church, so the Quakers originated from the Franciscans.[163]

In another work published in the following year Ware reworked the same theme, giving an account of how the Jesuits had worked within the several sects in Ireland during the Interregnum. But

> These jesuitical policies were not sufficient to distract this nation without the help of Ignatius of Loyola's new found religion which was Quakerism.[164]

However far-fetched such theories seem now, there is no doubt that ever since the Quakers' arrival in Ireland there had been controversy about their origin, membership and purpose. Quakers themselves admitted as much and were careful to distance themselves from Roman Catholics or from any suspicion of collusion with them. When Gerard Moor, a Carmelite, recanted in 1682 Ware asked him to be tutor to his son. Anne Harris, a Quaker, warned Ware to check carefully that Moor was really a convert, for she said the Quakers had been much deceived in this way.[165] In the same year a rumour was put abroad that Quakers were paying a man, Crosby, to preach, and that he had been seen coming out of a mass-house in Dublin. The Quakers rejected this, pointing out that in any case it was not their practice to hire preachers.[166] Anthony Sharp, a Quaker and a successful businessman in Dublin, was accused in 1674 of being a Roman Catholic simply because he hired Roman Catholics in his business.[167]

Their colleagues in England were similarly scapegoated.[168] In 1680 George Fox denied that Quakers were Catholics:

> We have been branded as being papists and Jesuits and popishly affected. But be it known to all the world that we are neither papists nor popishly affected; for our religion, way and worship, and the grace truth, spirit, faith and gospel of Christ, which we walk and live in, was before the Pope, papists and Jesuits and their religions and worships were.
>
> And we have suffered in the days of Oliver Cromwell and in his Long Parliament time; and before Oliver was Protector, we suffered by papists' laws and laws made in Queen Mary's time.
>
> And we suffered in the days of Presbyterians, Independents and Anabaptists and now the Episcopalians.
>
> And the chief cause of all our sufferings, that have been by all those that have had power was for denying and not joining to the popish and jesuitical ways and relics of the papists which they held up and allowed among them.[169]

Ware's writings seem to have done the Quakers little harm in terms of their treatment by the government. While antagonism may not have abated between the religious traditions, it is clear that by 1683 the Quakers were not considered a threat to the government.[170] But there was always the fear that Rome would use any ploy to gain power and influence in England and Ireland. Whether this was true or not did not matter, for the myth of popery was sufficient to whip up almost any story at any time at this period. And yet the instincts of the critics were surer than they thought, for Quaker teaching struck at the very heart of received Christianity as then understood. No church, either Rome or any of the established churches, could accept or even understand the stance of the Quakers with regard to their teaching on the nature of God, Christ, the scriptures, ministry, worship and order. They were all convinced that such views could not be right; some even concluded that Quakers were a cover for other and more sinister purposes.

However, the Established Church had more difficulties with the Quakers than merely the suspicion that they were hidden Catholics. In company with the other churches in the country, the Established Church, in sermons and tracts by bishops and clergy, attacked what were the unacceptable beliefs and practices of the Quakers. Preaching at the consecration of the Bishop of Kildare, Henry Jones made a strong case for episcopacy. In this context, he denounced the Quakers, particularly their stress on equality and the role of the community which he thought only led to confusion:

> Let Quakers and such see this, among whom (in divine things) is no distinction of offices or persons, no, nor of sexes . . . all with them depending (in divine duties) on uncertain impulses whensoever and from whomsoever . . . God is not the author of confusion . . . and what greater confusion than for a body to be all in a heap and lump without head or foot or distinction of members.[171]

The Established Church, of course, required obedience,[172] and Quakers refused to conform. Rather than the Book of Common Prayer, the Quakers had their own forms and styles of worship which the Established Church resented. Joseph Teate advised his congregation:

> Avoid all conceited tones . . . such as we meet with in the discourses
> of Jacob Behman and Van Helmont; in the inscriptions and pages of
> the books of the Quakers which they call the bosom of God, the out-
> ward openings of inward shuttings, Godded with God, Christed with
> Christ, beams of approaching glory, these swelling words of vanity are
> unknown to the scripture and contrary to the simplicity that is in
> Christ.[173]

Quaker language was rejected, since it was so contrary to the Book
of Common Prayer and because it harked back to the civil war
atmosphere and renewed old memories; it even engendered fear
that such turmoil could happen again.[174] Richard Berry, preaching in Christ Church, Dublin, referred to 'our new-quaking lumin-
aries, who do so highly magnify and extend the Light within
them'.[175] In the perception of the Established Church, Quakers
had cultivated an inner, personal conviction which refused to
acknowledge the primacy of exterior religious authority constituted
in law.

To curb such independence the Established Church harassed
the Quakers. In their history Holms and Fuller noted that Quakers
in the period 1660-71 were suffering for the following reasons:
meeting together to worship in their own way; pleading freedom
of conscience; refusing to pay tithes and maintenance of the clergy;
refusing to pay for the repair or building of the churches; refusing to go to church and for reproving the people either in church,
in the markets or streets; refusing to swear and take off their hats;
and working on holy days.[176] What the Established Church resented most of all was the Quaker refusal to pay tithes and the
dues necessary for the building and upkeep of churches, or
'steeplehouses' as Quakers called them. So while the Established
Church had basically the same theological difficulties with the
Quakers as the Independents and Presbyterians, it had these additional grievances.

Tension between the Established Church and the Quakers was
heightened in 1688 when John Burnyeat and John Watson
published a defence of Quakerism.[177] They claimed that
Quakers were 'truly reformed Christians', and they rebutted the
accusations made by an Established Church minister, Lawrence
Potts, when one of his congregation, Robert Lacky, became a
Quaker.[178] Apparently there was pressure also put on Lacky by

a 'J.T.' (possibly Joseph Teate) not to become a Quaker on the grounds that Quakers did not take oaths, did not believe in the Trinity and denied that the scriptures were the word of God. These points were refuted by Burnyeat and Watson, and they justified their stand on the three issues.[179]

However, they explained that the real reason Lacky became a Quaker was the inner light 'that let him see the evil or defects in himself and others'.[180] Potts wrote to Lacky telling him he had confused religion with the behaviour of some people; Burnyeat and Watson took this point up:

> Many of the people of your church are of a loose conversation . . . many of your clergy also . . . and yet they [are] suffered to abide in their places and offices without being either excluded or silenced. . . . We have often observed how that in your church there have been and still are both swearers, liars, drunkards and men given to other profaneness, and yet little zeal appearing to excommunicate or exclude them. But when any for conscience sake could not pay the priest his wages, though it were for some small matter, oftentimes such a one should soon be prosecuted and excommunicated; so that by your practices you are more zealous for your gain and interest than for excluding evil and promoting righteousness in your church.[181]

Burnyeat and Watson were unimpressed by the quality of life in the Established Church. Moreover, they rejected Potts's view that tithes were scriptural. And yet the Established Church ministers asked money of those 'for whom you do no work. . . . How many thousands do you compel in Ireland to pay you that are not of your work.'[182] This was plain speaking, for the Quakers asked to be judged by the quality of their lives (not by doctrine or theology) and to be relieved of tithes.

Potts argued that Quakers had no right to preach at all because they were not sent officially in the name of the church. This, of course, was quite alien to the Quakers, who asserted that their commission came from Christ and that they 'do wait upon him to receive our ability daily'. This touched the whole area of training for ministry, ordination and placement, all rejected by the Quakers as having no warranty in scripture:

> Prove your way of being bred up at schools and learning your tongues and taking your degrees there and observing your ceremonies in your ordination and coming forth according to your traditions and then

looking for a benefice the greatest you can get . . . and while you stay
in a parish take such lordship upon you that none of your church or
hearers may have licence to speak or preach but such as are so ordained
as you are.[183]

Another debate opened between the Established Church and
Quakers when Penn and the Bishop of Cork clashed in 1698.
In that year Penn was in Ireland visiting Quakers, inspecting
his Irish estates and encouraging Friends to go to Pennsylvania.
He was accompanied by his son William, and two friends,
Thomas Story and John Everett. In his journal Story tells of the
crowds who came to hear Penn, and of the tensions between
Quakers and the other churches in Dublin.[184] A Dublin Baptist,
John Plimpton, published at least three tracts that year against
the Quakers,[185] in which he accused them of denying the scriptures and the person of Christ in favour of the 'light within'. In
response to Plimpton's *Ten charges,* Penn, Story, Anthony Sharp
and George Rook issued a broadside in March 1698 entitled *Gospel
truths*[186] in which Quaker beliefs were summarised as follows:
belief in God and 'the three that bear record in heaven'; the in-
carnation; redemption and justification by faith alone; obedience
to the 'light within', which was the key to all spiritual growth
and worship, all other forms of outward worship 'being but formal and will-worship which we cannot in conscience join nor
can we maintain and uphold it'; this message taught by Quakers
'without money and without price'; all excesses in fashion and
customs of the world were rejected; while they did not practise
sacraments, neither did they judge those who used them; finally,
they honoured the government as an ordinance of God.

During the early part of that summer Penn visited friends and
estates in Cork. While there he called to see the Bishop of Cork,
Edward Wetenhall, and gave him a copy of the *Gospel truths*. The
bishop indicated that he would like another meeting to discuss
the tract. He was disappointed when Penn called to see him later
in the year while he was away on visitation, and he therefore
replied in writing.[187] Wetenhall felt that on the basis of *Gospel
truths* the Quakers could not be called Christian at all. He went
through the broadsheet and found so many doctrines absent that
he had to declare Quakers outside the Christian faith.[188]

At this time the Bishop of Cork was in a difficult position. He had suffered far more than the Quakers during the revolution, and doubts about his adherence to the new monarchy prevented his promotion to Cashel.[189] Doubts had also been cast about his orthodoxy, by his own Dean Pomeroy and by some members of the Church of Ireland.[190] Indeed, he had expressed doubts privately regarding the person of the Holy Ghost, and so he must have been interested in the Quaker approach to the Trinity.[191] In any event, Wetenhall was ready to enter into debate with the Quakers, perhaps in some measure to justify himself in public. There is no doubt that he admired the Quakers for their consistency and convictions,[192] and indeed he said as much in his *Testimony*. However, Wetenhall's work also demonstrated that the social jealousies aroused by Quaker success and wealth[193] could be just as potent in argument as doctrinal differences:

> 1. Is it not your main end and study, by pretended mortification and renouncing the world while there are no sort of men alive that more eagerly pursue it nor have more effective, wily or secret ways of getting wealth than yourselves? Is it not, I say, your main aim and end to make yourselves a party considerable and such to which for reasons of state peculiar privileges must be granted?

> 2. Are not, to this purpose, many of your distinctive characters such as your different garb (for it is plain, not a few of your people's clothes, as to material, are more costly than ours), your way of speaking, yes, even your looks and gestures, assumed rather to make yourselves remarkable and at first sight known to other people, than out of any persuasion, sense of duty or conscience or obligation?[194]

The bishop's work was published in July 1698, and Penn replied in the same year. He argued that the broadsheet *Gospel truths* was merely a summary of Quaker beliefs and in no way intended to include everything. Penn knew that Wetenhall had several books by Quakers in his library, in particular Penn's own works and those of Barclay, and so he confessed to be all the more surprised at the bishop's reply. For example, Wetenhall took Penn to task on how the Quakers were a divisive force and wounded the unity of the church. This Penn rejected and queried the bishop on the divisions within all the churches, especially just then on the question of free will and grace, Arminianism, and the doctrine of the Trinity.[195]

Penn expanded the scope of *Gospel truths* and refuted the bishop's accusations against Quakers on several issues: the resurrection of the body, the sacraments, and Quaker use of language. It was in every sense repetitious, and Penn acknowledged that all his points had been argued before. But he pointed out the real source of their differences:

> That which has affected our minds most and engaged us in this separation was the great carnality and emptiness both of ministers and of people, under the profession of religion: they hardly having the form of godliness but generally speaking denying the power thereof.[196]

Moreover, Penn contended that the Established Church's insistence that divine revelation was confined to the first age of Christianity also caused division. These differences convinced the Quakers that they were right, that they were a church 'with less pomp and gaudiness in our worship, as well as in our clothes, than is the custom of some other churches'.[197]

In the following year Wetenhall wrote a reply to Penn in which his tone became much more virulent.[198] The bishop had an unruly temper,[199] and certainly in this reply he expressed his anger and even contempt of the Quakers. He accused the Quakers of denying four key doctrines: faith in Christ, justification by faith, (citing Penn's answer to Jenner in 1671), the resurrection of the body and the return of Christ to judge the world.[200] Returning to a point made strongly in his *Testimony*, he was even more critical of Quakers' wealth:

> The bishop has long observed and all men may observe as notorious the Quakers' eager pursuit of wealth and their effective, wily and secret ways of getting it . . . minding worldly gain and being so intent on it day and night . . . most days in the week without a prayer to God, either in public assembly or family . . . flying in all directions to get and keep money. . . . There is nothing to be eaten which is better than the ordinary, that comes into our markets here, which the people observe not presently bought up by the Quakers. They are still the earliest and best shopmen every market day for such commodities.[201]

The bishop rejected the Quaker belief in the 'light within' and saw it as contrary to revelation and competent interpretation of the scriptures. He gave three examples from Cork, where Quakers had really shown how misguided this 'light within' was in practice. A man called John Knight went into a church in Cork and stood naked in the church proclaiming the truth; John Workman in Ross fasted for forty days, claiming it as a miracle; when Betty Wheadons spoke at meetings in Cork, it was known that even Penn had to hide his laughter. This sort of singularity was scorned by the bishop, as was the Quaker mode of dress and address.[202] The bishop's reply to Penn was much stronger in tone and criticism than his *Testimony*, but Penn decided not to answer it; perhaps it was too personal an attack. In any event, it was left to other Quakers in Ireland to respond to the bishop.

And so in 1700 two Quakers, Thomas Wright and Nicholas Harris, replied to Wetenhall.[203] Their work was essentially a point-by-point refutation of Wetenhall's arguments, and it was evident that the Quakers resented the bishop's tone of contempt, especially towards Penn himself. They acknowledged that before this debate the bishop and Quakers had enjoyed good relations generally and that he and Penn were on friendly terms, to the extent that Wetenhall had prevented publication of a tract against Penn. Indeed, the bishop allowed Quakers in Cork to register their marriages in the bishop's court in Cork and advocated concessions to dissenters in general.[204]

In this context, it was difficult to understand this new negative attack on the Quakers. Wright and Harris suggested that the antipathy between Penn and the bishop was due possibly to the bishop's own difficulties with his church; they recognised also that both were powerful personalities and had very definite ideas. Wright and Harris boasted that

> No bishop in these three kingdoms has the big and scornful look and deportment of Mr Penn especially when he is in the humour for it.[205]

They also objected to the accusation that Quakers were too wealthy:

> We appeal from the bishop, our partial judge, to our neighbours who know and are better acquainted with our way of dealing than he; and how may we not with much more reason return his charge of worldiness upon himself and that not without proof, as he has done by us; what else made him leave the old bishopric and friends of Cork for a new one and strangers in the north of Ireland was it not because the latter was worth some hundreds per annum more than the former?[206]

They defended the actions of John Knight (in 1674) and John Workman; both were true stories and within the Quaker tradition. Going naked and fasting, though not for everyone to practise, were found in the Old Testament, and it was right for some to follow this example. But they did not accept the story of Penn laughing at a meeting in Cork: 'We let the bishop know whatever the custom of laughing be in his congregation, we have no such in ours.'[207] In addition to these points, the two writers repeated the arguments of Penn on the theological issues raised by Wetenhall. They corrected the bishop's use of Penn's tract against Jenner in 1671, accusing him of misquoting Penn on the question of justification by faith.[208]

Wetenhall had chided the Quakers for being inarticulate in comparison with the writers of the Established Churches. However, Wight and Harris argued that Quakers never pretended to theological training. Rather they relied on the light and spirit within to instruct, which was to them a far more valuable education than 'arts, parts, wisdom and learning of this world'.[209] By the time this work was published Wetenhall had moved to the see of Kilmore and the debate was over.[210] The exchanges between Wetenhall and Penn showed just how impossible it was for both traditions to reach some form of understanding. Basically it was a question of toleration of different ideas, and Penn was better placed to be open:

> We believe Christ to be the end and substance of all signs and shadows under the gospel to his people . . . therefore in reverence to the substance and not in disrespect to the visible signs declined the use of them, though at the same time we do not condemn those that conscientiously practise them.[211]

Such a statement reflected the strong self-perception enjoyed by many Quakers at this time which evoked the antagonism of the Established Church. They were a religious tradition in the country which had neither the basis nor the theological possibility of conformity. For in the period after the Restoration Quakers in Ireland had gradually settled into a peaceful, well-organised and cohesive body, with increasingly defined convictions and modes of living, reinforced by a firm discipline and method of overseership. They were in their own way as much a church as any other in terms of organisation and discipline, but their convictions were outside the mould and so caused deep friction in society generally. Another factor was their success in trade and business which made them indispensable and yet envied. Indeed Quakers argued that they were a very important part of the economic establishment in Ireland and should not be expected therefore to prove their loyalty to the political establishment by taking oaths. In their representations they asked for the protection of the law without having to take oaths and suggested a form of words they could in conscience accept. In so doing they insisted they did not want places of honour or power in the state. They wanted to preserve their liberties and properties, maintain their families, pay just taxes and rents, 'support our poor', and improve and promote manufactures, and in this way 'strengthen the Protestant interest in this kingdom'.[212]

Notes and References

1 Peter Manby, *The considerations which obliged Peter Manby, Dean of Derry, to embrace the Catholic religion* (Dublin, 1687).

2 William King, *An answer to the considerations which obliged Peter Manby, late Dean of Londonderry in Ireland, to embrace what he calls the Catholic religion* (Dublin, 1687), pp 6, 29. King's autobiography in Latin was translated in C. S. King (ed.), *A great Archbishop of Dublin, William King, D.D , 1650-1729: his autobiography, family, and a selection from his correspondence* (London, 1906). King was born in 1650 in Aberdeen, of Scottish Presbyterian parents, and moved to Tyrone in 1658; he had very erratic schooling and went to Trinity College, Dublin, in 1667. He was ordained for the Tuam diocese in 1674 and moved to St Werburgh's in Dublin in 1679. In 1688 he was appointed to deputise for the Archbishop of Dublin, who had fled to London. He was named Bishop of Derry in 1690. Cotton, *Fasti*, ii, 23, 118, 102; iii, 308, 320-1, 329, 332; iv, 32, 24.

3 [Joseph Boyse], *Vindicae Calvinisticae, or some impartial reflections on the Dean of Londonderry's considerations . . . and Mr Chancellor King's answer thereto in which he no less unjustly than impertinently reflects on the Protestant dissenters. In a letter to a friend* (Dublin, 1687).

4 Ibid. 'To the reader' (no pagination).

5 Ibid.

6 Ibid.

7 Ibid., p. 2.

8 Ibid., p. 6.

9 Ibid., p. 10.

10 Ibid., p. 12.

11 Ibid., pp 17-18.

12 Ibid., pp 53-58, 63-4.

13 [William King], 'The present state of the church', [1688] (T.C.D., Correspondence of William King, MSS 1995-2008, no. 69a, ff 1-14); for the question of reordination and use of Established Church liturgy see ff 7, 13-14. See also, Edward Wetenhall, *The Protestant peacemaker, or a seasonable persuasive to all serious Christians* (London, 1682); Andrew Carpenter, 'William King and the threats to the Church of Ireland during the reign of James II' in *I.H.S.*, xviii, no. 69 (Mar. 1972), pp 22-8.

14 [Boyse], *Vindicae Calvinisticae*, p. 26.

15 King wrote a reply to Boyse, but James Bonnell would not let him print it (U.L.C., Baum. Papers, Add. 1, f. 78).

16 Feb. 1687 ('The Mather Papers', p. 66); Bonnell to Strype, 21 Jan. 1688 (U.L.C., Baum. Papers, Add. 1, f.64).

17 William King, *A discourse concerning the inventions of men in the worship of God* (London, 1694).

18 Ibid., p. 50. This was an old criticism. Henry Leslie, *A discourse of praying in the spirit* (n.p., 1659).

19 King, *A discourse concerning the inventions of men*, pp 67-85, 92. King thought their catechism was far too difficult.

20 Ibid., pp 87-101.

21 Ibid., pp 115-31.

22 Ibid., pp 17-18.

23 Ibid, pp 156-61.

24 John Livingstone, *A brief historical relation of the life of Mr John Livingstone,* ed. Thomas McCrie (Edinburgh, 1848), pp 78-9; Marilyn Westerkamp, *Triumph of the laity: Scots-Irish piety and the Great Awakening, 1625-1760* (Oxford, 1988) pp 66-7, 70-1.

25 King, *A discourse concerning the inventions of men*, pp 176-7. King thought they might even agree to observe the excommunications levied by the bishop's court.

26 Ibid., p. 163. He encouraged them to read their services well and try to win the people; they had the advantage in that their appointment was not made by the people, so they could speak out freely. King advised them to avoid disputes, and be aware that while the church was busy with Roman Catholics, Deists and Socinians the enemy within was hard at work.

27 Ibid., pp 169-74.

28 Bonnell to Strype, 26 Dec. 1693 (U.L.C., Baum. Papers, Add. 1, f.77).

29 Robert Craghead, *An answer to a late book entitled 'A discourse concerning the inventions of men in the worship of God' by William, Lord Bishop of Derry* (Edinburgh, 1694). Craghead was born in Scotland in 1633 and educated at St Andrew's; he was ordained for Donoughmore, Co. Donegal, until he was ejected in 1661; he stayed on in Derry, though moved to Glasgow during the 1688 Revolution and subsequent war; he died in 1711. McConnell, *Fasti,* no. 45, p. 9; Witherow, *Historic memorials*, pp 88-94. Craghead dedicated his work to the mayor, aldermen and burgesses of Derry.

30 Craghead, *An answer to a late book*, pp 91-4, 112-18, 133-4, 139.

31 Ibid., pp 78-9, 86.

32 Ibid, pp 112-13.

33 Ibid., pp 6, 17.

34 Ibid., p 118. Besides, Craghead was not sure that scripture intended there be a communion service each Sabbath.

35 Ibid., p. 140. Thomas Hall of Larne wrote a tract for his people: *A plain and easy explication of the Assembly's Shorter Catechism (Edinburgh, 1697)*. Since 1646 he had been catechising his congregation and preaching on 'God's previous concourse'; see pp 1, 38, 76, 79, 93; Witherow, *Historic memorials*, pp 95-101.

36 Craghead, *An answer to a late book*, pp 152-9.

37 In the following year Craghead wrote a tract on the same theme: *Advice to communicants* (Edinburgh, 1695).

38 Joseph Boyse, *Remarks on a late discourse of William, Lord Bishop of Derry, concerning the inventions of men in the worship of God (n.p., [1694])*. By this time Boyse was already involved in the Sacramental Test controversy and regretted that King's book had forced him to enter into an another debate. But they were old disputants, and Boyse felt that silence on his part indicated assent to King's views. Boyse, *Remarks on a late discourse*, preface.

39 Bonnell to Strype, 15 Mar. 1694 (U.L.C. Baum., Papers, Add. 1, f.78). Boyse, *Works*, i, 13.

40 Boyse, *Remarks on a late discourse*, pp 80-6, 112-13.

41 Ibid., pp 88-95.

42 Ibid., pp 97-99.

43 Ibid., pp 69-74, 77, 114. Boyse wrote some hymns for his congregation in Dublin: *Sacramental hymns* (Dublin, 1693). In the preface to this work Boyse cited the practice of the reformed churches abroad which 'seems to reproach our own, who exceed us in the frequency of this duty as they have the advantage of us in the variety and sweetness of their tunes, their skill in fingering them and their doing it without the interruption of reading every line'. Edward Wetenhall also was critical of line singing of the psalms: *Of gifts and offices in the public worship of God* (Dublin, 1678), pp 412, 422, 425. There is a symbolic aspect to Boyse's *Hymns*. He had two versions for each hymn. The first was set in common metre; the second allowed another metre. A. W. Godfrey Brown, 'Irish Presbyterian theology in the early eighteenth century' (Ph.D. thesis, Q.U.B., 1977), p. 152.

44 Boyse, *Remarks on a late discourse*, pp 104-8.

45 'An essay of accommodation', being a scheme for uniting Presbyterians and Congregationals, drawn up c. 1680, Occasional Paper no. 6 Dr Williams's Library, London, 1957; Watts, *The dissenters*, pp 290-1, 293. English Presbyterians and Independents agreed that for major issues ministers of several churches should meet and whatever they concluded should not be ignored lightly by particular churches with their elders and members.

46 Boyse, *Remarks on a late discourse*, pp 108-11.

47 Boyse was referring to the absenteeism of the bishop, Thomas Hackett. See Chapter 2, n. 85.

48 Boyse, *Remarks on a late discourse*, pp 117-20.
49 William King, *An admonition to the dissenting inhabitants of the diocese of Derry concerning a book lately published by Mr J. Boyse* (London, 1694). He did not want a wide debate and had intended his first book to be distributed in the diocese only; a reprint appeared in London without his authorisation and through this public debate had grown. Once this occurred, he had no choice but to reply to Boyse, lest silence imply either assent or defeat. Bonnell to Strype, 15 Mar. 1694 (U.L.C., Baum. Papers, Add. 1, f. 78).
50 King, *An admonition*, pp 1-4.
51 Boyse had given him some hope that this could be acceptable, but Boyse was of a different tradition from the Scottish Presbyterians, who could not accept occasional communion in any way or for any reason. Bonnell to Strype, 6 May 1695 (U.L.C., Baum. Papers, Add. 1, f. 81).
52 Correspondence of William King (T.C.D., MSS 1995-2008, nos 357, 358, 359, 369).
53 Foley to King, 10 Oct. 1693 (ibid., no. 302; Foley to King, 12 May 1694, (ibid., no. 354).
54 Bonnell to King, 29 Nov. 1694 (ibid., no. 397).
55 King, *An admonition*, pp 28-37. King was willing to omit the cross at baptism and having godparents at baptism of Presbyterian children. Ibid., pp 40-1.
56 Ibid., p. 38.
57 [Joseph Boyse], *A vindication of the remarks on the Bishop of Derry's discourse about human inventions from what is objected against them in the admonition annexed to the second edition of that discourse* (n.p., [1695]).
58 Ibid., pp 1-3, 124, 125-34, 139-44.
59 Ibid., p. 134.
60 William King, *A second admonition to the dissenting inhabitants of the diocese of Derry concerning Mr Joseph Boyse's vindication* (London, 1696).
61 Ibid., pp 28-30, 115-19.
62 [Robert Craghead], *A modest apology occasioned by the importunity of the Bishop of Derry who presses for an answer to a query stated by himself in his second admonition concerning joining in the public worship established by law* (Glasgow, 1696). Boyse had explained in his *Vindication* that he wrote then because a quick answer was needed and at that time the Scottish Presbyterians in Derry were not able to do this. Boyse, *A vindication of the remarks*, p. 134.
63 Craghead, *A modest apology*, 'To the Christian reader'.
64 Ibid., p. 48ff.
65 Reid, *A history of the Presbyterian Church*, i, Appendix 4, pp 523-43.
66 Craghead, *A modest apology*, pp 1-10, 15-16, 21-23, 30-34, 38.
67 Ibid., p. 82.
68 Ibid., p. 105. King did not reply to this tract, but in 1702 an anoymous episcopal minister from the diocese of Derry dedicated a reply to King: *Remarks upon the book called 'A modest apology'* (n.p., 1702).
69 Robert Craghead, *An answer to the Bishop of Derry's second admonition to the dissenting inhabitants of this diocese especially as to the matter of fact relating to the public worship of God, wherein his misrepresentations are again discovered* ([Belfast], 1697).

70   Ibid., dedication to the mayor.

71   Scott to King, 11 June 1694 (T.C.D., MSS 1995-2008, no. 359). Craghead wrote two tracts related to these points: *Advice to communicants* (Edinburgh, 1695); *Warning and advice both to the secure and doubting Christian or more diligence to be sure of salvation* (Edinburgh, 1701).

72   Craghead, *An answer to the Bishop of Derry's second admonition*, pp 1-11.

73   Ibid., pp 50-8.

74   Ibid., p. 12.

75   Ibid., p. 94.

76   Ibid., pp 29-33;

77   Craghead dealt with the office of elders, pointing out that vestiges of their role were found in the lay chancellors, church wardens and officials of the Established Church. The elders were essential for good government, assisting the minister while never usurping his office and authority. Ibid., pp 44-6.

78   Ibid., p. 14.

79   J. C. Beckett, *Protestant dissent in Ireland, 1687-1780* (London, 1948), pp 31-9, 40-52; J. I. McGuire, 'Government attitudes to religious nonconformity in Ireland, 1660-1719' in C. E. J. Caldicott, Hugh Gough and J. P. Pittion (ed.), *The Huguenots and Ireland: anatomy of an emigration* (Dublin, 1987), pp 273-4.

80   [Joseph Boyse], *The case of the Protestant dissenters of Ireland in reference to a Bill of Indulgence represented and argued* (Dublin, 1695).

81   Ibid., p. 3.

82   [Josias Pullein], *An answer to a paper entitled 'The case of the Protestant dissenters of Ireland in reference to a Bill of Indulgence represented and argued'* (Dublin, 1695). All the bishops, with the exception of Edward Wetenhall, supported the Sacramental Test, though William King said 'he thought a virtuous man of any profession would do less harm in office than a vicious man of our own church'. Bonnell to Strype, 18 Oct. 1692 (U.L.C., Baum. Papers, Add. 1, f.74).

83   [Pullein], *An answer to a paper* p. 1.

84   Ibid., pp 2-4.

85   Ibid., p. 6.

86   [Joseph Boyse], *The case of the dissenting Protestants of Ireland in reference to a Bill of Indulgence vindicated from the exceptions alleged against it in a late answer* (Dublin, 1695), p. 11. Boyse objected to dissenters being called sects; all dissenters saw themselves as churches in their own right. Ibid., p. 2.

87   Ibid., pp 2, 8.

88   [Josias Pullein], *A defence of the answer to a paper entitled 'The case of the dissenting Protestants of Ireland in reference to a Bill of Indulgence from the exceptions lately made against it'* (Dublin, 1695).

89   Ibid., pp 2-5. Pullein cited a letter from Bramhall to Ussher in 1654 on this point, and used it to justify his own view.

90   Ibid., p. 5.

91   Ibid., pp 8-9.

92   Ibid., pp 15-21.

93 Papers of Abraham Hill (B.L., Sloan MS 2902, ff 138, 218); Francis Brewster, *A discourse concerning Ireland*, (n.p., 1697/8), pp 27-8, 31, 33.

94 [Pullein], *A defence of the answer*, pp 22-4. Brewster, *A discourse concerning Ireland*, pp 24, 27-8, 31, 33; Papers of Abraham Hill (B.L., Sloan MS 2902, ff 138, 218).

95 [Pullein], *A defence of the answer*, p. 27.

96 [Anthony Dopping], *The case of the dissenters of Ireland considered in reference to the Sacramental Test* (Dublin, 1695).

97 Beckett, *Protestant dissent in Ireland*, p. 42.

98 Dopping, *The case of the dissenters*, p. 2.

99 Edward Synge, then rector of Christ Church in Cork, wrote a short tract which, although not published at the time, was certainly circulated in the north: *A peaceable and friendly address to the nonconformists written upon their desiring an act of toleration without the Sacramental Test* (repr., Dublin, 1732); D.N.B. Synge was born in Cork and educated at Oxford; ordained in Trinity College, Dublin, he served in Meath and Cork; Bishop of Raphoe, 1714, and Archbishop of Tuam, 1716. Cotton, *Fasti*, i, 264*, 342, 337; ii, 104*, 119; iii, 354*; iv, 16.

100 Some dissenters in Dublin did take occasional communion. John McBride to Robert Wyly, 7 July 1704 (N.L.S., Wodrow MSS, Folio 26, no. 186). Richard Choppin, preaching at the funeral of Boyse in 1729, said that Boyse had never taken communion in the Established Church. Choppin, *A funeral sermon: Mr J. Boyse* ([Dublin], 1729).

101 John McBride, *Animadversions on the defence of the answer to a paper entitled 'The case of the dissenting Protestants of Ireland in reference to a Bill of Indulgence'* ([Belfast], 1697); McConnell, *Fasti*, no. 180, p. 72; Witherow, *Historic memorials*, pp 109-25.

102 McBride, *Animadversions*, pp 5-7. Quakers were not included either.

103 Ibid., p. 87.

104 Ibid., p. 45.

105 Beckett, *Protestant dissent in Ireland*, pp 131-5. Quakers negotiated their own form of oath. 'The case of the people called Quakers' (Marsh's Library, Dublin, MS Z 1. 1. 13, f. 96). McBride also refuted Synge's work in some detail, to which Synge wrote a reply in 1698: *Defence of the peaceable and friendly address against the answer lately given to it* (Dublin, 1698).

106 Ormond to Boyle, 11 July 1682 (Bodl., Carte MS 50, f. 194).

107 2 Anne, c. 6 (Ireland); McGuire, 'Government attitudes to religious non-conformity in Ireland, 1660-1719', pp 272-76; H.M.C., *Buccleuch and Queensbury*, ii, pt i, 201, 209-10; Beckett, *Protestant dissent in Ireland*, pp 42-7.

108 Taylor to Ormond, 5 Nov. 1665 (Bodl., Carte MS 34, f.297).

109 Laggan minutes, Nov. 1673, p.73.

110 Ibid., 6 Jan. 1674, p. 86; Dundonald (Kirkdonald) Session Book, 1678-1716. Marriages were proclaimed from at least 1678.

111 Hackett to Essex, 29 Oct. 1672 (*Essex Papers*, p. 38).

112 Essex to Arlington, 12 Oct. 1673 (ibid., pp 124-5).

113 Antrim minutes, 3 May 1687, p. 298; also 1 Nov. 1687, p. 332.

114 John McBride, *A vindication of marriage as solemnised by Presbyterians in the north of Ireland* (n.p., 1702).

115 Ibid., p. 53.

116 Bishop King was impatient with the government for not declaring against clandestine marriages (T.C.D., Letters of William King, 1699-1703, MS 750/12, pp 44, 78, 85, 111).

117 McBride, *A vindication of marriage*, pp 47-50. McBride accepted that Presbyterians sometimes concealed their marriages because the Established Church courts hounded them.

118 Ibid., 'To the reader'.

119 [Ralph Lambert], *An answer to a late pamphlet entitled 'A vindication of marriage as solemnised by Presbyterians in the north of Ireland'* (Dublin, 1704); Cotton, *Fasti*, iii, v, 9, 121, 238, 241, 250, 274.

120 [Lambert], *An answer to a late pamphlet*, p. 53.

121 Ibid., pp 11-13, 57-8.

122 Ibid., pp 56-60.

123 [Edward Synge], *A defence of the Established Church and laws in answer to a book entitled 'A vindication of marriage as solemnised by the Presbyterians in the north of Ireland'* (Dublin, 1705). On 20 August 1703 the Irish bishops asked Synge to reply to McBride (B.L., Add. MS 6117, f. 7v.).

124 McBride, *A vindication of marriage*, pp 28-9, 31, 40-1. Lambert too had refuted McBride on this point. Lambert, *An answer to a late pamphlet*, pp 15, 20, 28-34, 43.

125 [Synge], *A defence of the Established Church*, preface.

126 Ibid., pp 17, 22, 29, 41.

127 Ibid., p. 55; also p. 198.

128 Ibid., p. 287.

129 'The humble petition of the Presbyterian ministers and people in the north of Ireland, 1708' (Wodrow MSS, Folio 51, no. 48; P.R.O.N.I., T525, no. 48). This has 1708 as the date of the petition, but see Reid, *History of the Presbyterian Church*, ii, 484; John Stevenson, *Two centuries of life in Down* (repr., Belfast, 1990), pp 161-3.

130 McBride to Robert Wodrow, 2 Apr. 1709 (N.L.S., Wodrow MSS, Folio 26, no. 190).

131 This led to them being further questioned as to why they would not conform entirely. *The Church of England defended, with the dissenters' reply or cases of conscience proposed to the dissenting ministers of Dublin by certain young students who were of their communion and have lately joined with the Established Church* (n.p., 1709); Benjamin Hoadly, *The reasonableness of constant communion with the Church of England represented to the dissenters* (Dublin, 1709).

132 While officially the debate continued, in practice there was some conformity. John McBride noted that many did marry according to the rites of the Established Church 'to prevent danger', though he noted that the rich tended to conform and the poor married in the kirk. McBride to Wodrow, Dec. 4 1712 (N.L.S., Wodrow Correspondence, 1709-14, xx, no. 113, 484).

133 William Tisdall, *A sample of true-blue Presbyterian loyalty in all changes and turns of government, taken chiefly out of their most authentic records* (Dublin, 1709) Daniel Defoe, *The parallel* (Dublin, 1705); D.N.B.; David Nokes, *Jonathan Swift, a hypocrite reversed* (Oxford, 1985), pp 64-70, 134, 178, 186, 217, 381.

134 Tisdall, *A sample of true-blue Presbyterian loyalty*, pp 4-5, 15, 17-19, 21-22.

135 Ibid., p. 23.

136 John Livingstone, *A brief historical relation of the life of Mr John Livingstone . . . written by himself*, ed. Thomas McCrie (Edinburgh, 1848); Andrew Stewart, 'A short account of the Church of Christ' (N.L.S., Wodrow MSS, Octavo 75, nos 2, 3); printed in part in Patrick Adair, *A true narrative of the Presbyterian Church in Ireland*, ed. W. D. Killen (Belfast, 1866), pp 213-321.

137 Antrim minutes, pp 32, 71, ; Laggan minutes, pp 26, 181, 191, 198, 225, 264, 306.

138 Laggan minutes, p. 306; ibid., ii, pp 28, 48, 71, 79, 82.

139 John McBride, *A sermon preached before the provincial synod at Antrim, June 1 1698* (n.p., 1698).

140 Tennison to Archbishop of Canterbury (Lambeth Palace, Gibson Papers, MS 930, f.200); [Theo Harrison] to John Strype, 16 July 1698 (U.L.C., Baum. Papers, Add. 5, f. 251); copy of petition from the bishop of Down and Connor to the Lords Justices in Ireland, Sept. 1698 (P.R.O.N.I., T525, no. 12).

141 Petition from the Bishop of Down and Connor, 1698 (P.R.O.N.I., T525, no. 12). The bishop got little response, other than a perfunctory examination of McBride by the Lords Justices in Dublin. The attitude of the Lords Justices could be explained not only by their moderate views of dissenters but also by the manner in which the petition came to them. The bishop appealed to the Lord Chief Justice of England, who then sent the petition to Dublin.

142 [William Tisdall], *The conduct of dissenters of Ireland with respect to both church and state* (Dublin, 1712).

143 Ibid., pp 10, 15-26, 30, 35-45, 46, 50, 52-79.

144 Ibid., pp 19, 96-100; Brewster, *A discourse concerning Ireland*, pp 24, 33-4.

145 William Tisdall, *A seasonable enquiry into the most dangerous political principle of the kirk in power* (Dublin, 1713), pp 3-4, 9.

146 Ibid., p. 7. This accounted for the fanaticism inherent in Presbyterianism, in Covenanters/Cameronians, 'the hope of the kirk militants'.

147 William Tisdall, *The nature and tendency of popular phrases in general* (n.p., 1713), pp 19, 24.

148 [Tisdall], *The conduct of the dissenters*, p. 28.

149 [John McBride], *A sample of jet-black pr[ela]tick calumny in answer to a pamphlet called 'True-blue Presbyterian loyalty or the Christian loyalty of Presbyterians in Britain and Ireland in all changes of government since the Reformation; most particularly of the Presbyterians in Ulster since their first plantation there'* (Glasgow, 1713).

150 Ibid., pp 11-16.

151 Ibid., p. 22.

152 Ibid., pp 87, 151-73, 193-203, 214.

153 James Kirkpatrick, *An historical essay upon the loyalty of Presbyterians in Great Britain and Ireland from the Reformation to this present year 1713* (n.p., 1713); McConnell, *Fasti*, no. 173, p. 70; Witherow, *Historic memorials*, pp 156-68.

154 Kirkpatrick, *An historical essay upon the loyalty of Presbyterians*, p. 39.

155 Ibid., pp 161-6, 225-55, 288, 371-8, 383-5.

156 Ibid., pp 393-406, 413-35, 488-94, 504-6, 512.

157 Ibid., pp 540-1, 544-8.

158 Tisdall, *The conduct of dissenters*, p. 41. For McCracken see McConnell, *Fasti*, no. 182, p. 77; Witherow, *Historic memorials*, pp 304-9.

159 Peter Browne, *The doctrine of parts and circumstances in relation laid open* (Dublin, 1715), p. 84; A. R. Winnet, *Peter Browne, provost, bishop, metaphysician* (London, 1974), pp 86-90. William Tisdall thought that the Established Church paid too much attention to doctrine and worship and not enough to discipline and church order. Tisdall, *A seasonable enquiry into . . . the kirk in power* (Dublin, 1713), p. 3.

160 [Narcissus Marsh], 'State of the province of Armagh', 1706 (Lambeth Palace, Gibson Papers, MS 929, f. 41); Thomas Croskery and Thomas Witherow, *Life of A. P. Goudy* (Dublin, 1887), p.8; William Sheridan, *St Paul's confession of faith*, (Dublin, 1685) p. 11.

161 Certainly Dives Downes, Bishop of Cork (1699-1709), noted in his visitation book that many parishes lacked the Book of Common Prayer and in particular that in Assadown parish there was a pulpit in the church but not an altar (T.C.D., Visitation Book of Dives Downes, MS 562, ff 27, 34v).

162 Robert Ware, *Foxes and firebrands or a specimen of the danger and harmony of popery and separation, wherein is proved from undeniable matter of fact and reason that separation from the Church of England is in the judgement of the papists and by sad experience found the most compendious way to introduce popery and to ruin the Protestant religion* (2nd ed., Dublin, 1682). John Nalson wrote Part I, and Ware Parts, II and III.

163 Ibid., pp 141-50, 195.

164 Robert Ware, *The hunting of the Romish fox and the quenching of sectarian firebrands, being a specimen of popery and separation* (Dublin, 1683), pp 232-5.

165 Ibid., p. 235.

166 13 Mar. 1683 (F.L.D., Testimonies of denial and condemnation, MM II, F1, ff 84-5).

167 Isobel Grubb, 'Anthony Sharp:, an unpublished memoir' in *Friends' Quarterly Examiner*, 59 (1925) pp 180-1.

168 Richard Baxter, *The Quaker's catechism* (London, 1655); William Prynne, *The Quakers unmasked* (London, 1655); Edmund Burrough, *The memorable works of a son of thunder and consolation* (London, 1672); John Faldo, *Quakerism no Christianity* (London, 1673).

169 George Fox, *The Protestant Christian-Quaker a sufferer by relics of popery* (London, 1680), p. 14. In 1704 the same accusation was made against Penn: 'Penn who is the chief director of the whole party [Quakers] is a papist.' (B.L., Add. MS 28948, f. 130).

170 For example, the Quakers had a school in Dublin in 1680 (F.L.D., MM II F1, Testimonies of denial and condemnation, 1662-1722, f. 53). In 1680 John Ray set up a printing-press in Dublin and became the first official printer to the city of Dublin in 1681. Ray 'was nearly, if not quite a Quaker'. Mary Pollard, *Dublin's trade in books* (Oxford, 1989), pp 8, 95. Ray was member of St Luke's Guild from 1678. Robert Munter, *A dictionary of*

the print trade in Ireland, 1556-1775 (New York, 1988), p. 227.

171 Henry Jones, *A sermon preached at the consecration of Ambrose, Bishop of Kildare* (Dublin, 1667), pp 4-5.

172 Jeremy Taylor, *A sermon preached at the opening of the parliament of Ireland, 8 May 1661* (London, 1661), p. 11.

173 Joseph Teate, *A sermon preached at the cathedral church of St Canice, Kilkenny, 27 Feb. 1669* (Dublin, 1670), p. 27; Cotton, *Fasti*, ii, 305, 295; *Athenae Oxonienses*, ii, 791.

174 Teate, *A sermon preached . . .* p. 28.

175 Richard Berry, *A sermon on the Epiphany, preached at Christ Church in Dublin* (Dublin, 1672), p. 24; Cotton, *Fasti*, ii, 205; v, 137.

176 Thomas Holms and Abraham Fuller, *A brief relation of the sufferings of . . . Quakers in Ireland, 1660-71* (n.p., 1672), p. 45; Besse, *A collection of the sufferings*, ii.

177 John Burnyeat and John Watson, *The holy truth and its professors defended in a letter written by Lawrence Potts, priest of Staplestown near Caterlough, to Robert Lacky a parishioner and formerly a hearer of the said priest, occasioned by his forsaking and embracing the blessed truth herein vindicated* (Dublin, 1688). Burnyeat was born in Cumberland in 1631 and became convinced in 1653; he visited Ireland in 1659, America in 1664-7, returning to Ireland in 1670-1, where he met Penn; he settled in Dublin in 1683, and was imprisoned there for two months that year. He travelled in Ireland and England and America and wrote tracts to the meetings he visited. An epistle from John Burnyeat to Friends in Pennsylvania (Dublin, 1685). He wrote his own auto-biography, *The truth exalted* (London, 1691); he died in 1690. F.L.L., Biographies of Quakers; 'The names of Friends deceased in . . . Ireland' (F.L.D. YM F1, f.6). John Watson (1651-1710) came to Ireland in 1658 and was convinced by John Burnyeat at the Friends' meeting in New Garden in the early 1670s. He held meeting in his own house from 1678 and was jailed in Nenagh for two years for non-payment of tithes; he visited Quakers in Ireland and England. F.L.L., Biographies of Quakers; Besse, *A collection of the sufferings*, ii, 481-2.

178 Lawrence Potts was Chancellor of Leighlin, 1687-1703. Cotton, *Fasti*, ii, 394, 402. He was proctor for the chapter during the Convocation of the Established Church in 1704 (B.L., Add. MS 4815, f. 77).

179 Burnyeat and Watson, *The holy truth and its professors defended*, 'Advertisement to the reader'.

180 Ibid., p. 1.

181 Ibid., pp 2, 5.

182 Ibid., pp 7-14.

183 Ibid., p. 16.

184 *The life of Thomas Story, carefully abridged by John Kendall* (Philadelphia, 1805). Story was born in Carlisle *c.* 1663 and was a member of the Church of England until 1689; he travelled in England, Ireland, Scotland and America. F.L.L., Biographies of Quakers. Penn wrote to the yearly meeting in London, telling of his Irish visit (*The papers of William Penn*, ed. Mary Maples Dunn and Richard Dunn, 5 vols (Pennsylvania, 1981), 456). See

also Joseph Pike, *Some account of the life of Joseph Pike of Cork*, pp xxx-xxxi. Little is known of Everett, except that he travelled to Ireland with Penn in 1698 (*The Papers of William Penn*, v, 454, n. 1).

185 John Plimpton, *Ten charges against the people called Quakers;* John Plimpton, *A Quaker no Christian* (Dublin, 1698). No copies of these works are extant. He also wrote *Quakerism the mystery of iniquity discovered in a brief dialogue between a Christian and a Quaker, by way of supplement to my former papers exhibited in Dublin against them* (Dublin, 1698). Penn, Everett and Story replied to these in the same year: *The Quaker a Christian being an answer to John Plimpton's disingenuous paper entitled 'A Quaker no Christian'* (Dublin, 1698), Penn, *Truth further cleared from mistakes* (Dublin, 1698).

186 Anthony Sharp and George Rook, *Gospel truths to clarify the orthodoxy of Friends* (Dublin, 1698). Rook was a timber merchant in Dublin. Grubb, *The Quakers in Ireland*, p. 29.

187 From the Bishop of Cork and Ross, 26 Aug. 1698 (*The papers of William Penn, iii, 556-7); The testimony of the Bishop of Cork.* No copy of this tract is extant, but a copy was printed in Penn's reply, *A defence of a paper entitled 'Gospel truths' against the exceptions of the Bishop of Cork's 'Testimony'* (London, 1698), pp 6ff.

188 Penn, *A defence of a paper*, pp 6-11.

189 Bonnell to Strype, 21 Feb. 1691 (U.L.C., Baum. Papers, Add. 1, f.67).

190 Pomeroy to Archbishop of Cashel, 9 Aug. 1697 (P.R.O.N.I., Pomeroy Papers, T2954/1/8); Bonnell to Strype, 6 Apr. 1693 (U.L.C., Baum. Papers, Add. 1, f.75); Wetenhall to Dopping, 13 Oct. 1690 (Robinson Library, Armagh, Dopping Papers, ii, no. 172)

191 Bonnell to Strype 1694 (U.L.C., Baum. Papers, Add. 1, f.77).

192 Edward Wetenhall, *The Protestant peacemaker or a seasonable persuasive to all serious Christians* (London, 1682), p. 9; Edward Wetenhall, *Of gifts and offices* (Dublin 1678), pp 165-7.

193 In 1683 the Quakers in Cork were described as 'the greatest traders in the town'. Longford to Arran, Cork, 30 Aug. 1683 (H.M.C., *Ormonde MSS*, vii, 121.

194 Penn, *A defence of a paper*, pp 16-17.

195 Ibid., pp 36-42.

196 Ibid., p. 97.

197 Ibid., p. 58.

198 Edward Wetenhall, *A brief and modest reply to Mr Penn's tedious, scurrilous and unchristian defence against the Bishop of Cork* (Dublin, 1699). George Keith had written an earlier defence of the Bishop of Cork: *Some of the many fallacies of William Penn detected in a paper called 'Gospel truths', signed by him and three more at Dublin, the 4th of the third month, 1698, and in the late book called 'A defence of the "Gospel truths" against the Bishop of Cork's "Testimony"'* (London, 1699).

199 Bonnell to Strype, 6 May 1695 (U.L.C., Baum. Papers, Add. 1, f.81).

200 Wetenhall, *A brief and modest reply*, p. 7.

201 Ibid., pp 9, 21.

202 Ibid., pp 15, 20, 24.

203 Thomas Wright and Nicholas Harris, *Truth further defended and William Penn vindicated, being a rejoinder to a book entitled 'A brief and modest reply to Mr. Penn's tedious, scurrilous and unchristian defence against the Bishop of Cork'* (n.p., 1700). Thomas Wright, (1640-1724), came to Cork in the 1650s and was convinced there by Edmund Burrough and Francis Howgill. Nicholas Harris (1663-1741) was convinced in Dublin *c.* 1691 and settled in Charleville in 1693. F.L.L., Biographies of Quakers.

204 Wright and Harris, *Truth further defended*, pp 174-7; O. C. Goodbody, 'Seventeenth-century Quaker marriages in Ireland' in *J.F.H.S.*, 50, no. 4 (1962), p. 248; Wetenhall, *The Protestant peacemaker*.

205 Wright and Harris, *Truth further defended*, pp 66, 4-15.

206 Ibid., pp 65, 138-9. Wetenhall was translated to the diocese of Kilmore in 1699.

207 Ibid., pp 101, 158.

208 Ibid., p. 15.

209 Ibid., p. 155.

210 A small contribution to the controversy was added in 1701 when Peter Hewit, Chancellor of St Fin Barre's in Cork, published a book refuting proposition no. 10 of *Gospel truths,* on the question of sacraments: Hewit, *A plain answer to that part of William Penn's book against the late Bishop of Cork, wherein he attempts to justify the Quakers' disuse of water baptism and the Lord's Supper, showing the weakness and error of all his objections and refuting them particularly page by page* (Dublin, 1701).

211 Penn, Everett and Story, *The Quaker a Christian*, p. 9.

212 Marsh's Library MS, Z. 1.1. 13, f. 96 (n.d., but after 1709, probably *c.* 1712-13).

8

Dissenters and the Government

> Our lawyers in Ireland do not agree that the laws in Ireland can
> be made use of against any dissenters but the papists for whom
> they were only calculated . . . I confess I did not like the stretch-
> ing of penal laws beyond their original intention.
>
> Ormond to the Primate, July 1682

On the 23 October 1661 William Lightburne preached in
Christ Church, Dublin, on the positive fruits of the
Restoration:

> Have we not been lately delivered from anarchy and tyranny and bond-
> age and vassalage and oppression? and very mushrooms of men that
> did more than King it over us. . . . We have worship and service of God
> restored and the priests again set in their order to praise God in the
> beauty of holiness instead of anarchy; we have our ancient monarchy
> instead of confused parity; we have our reverend hierarchy instead of
> arbitary power.[1]

At this time members of the Established Church hoped for a
return to its pre-1641 status, to an extension of Wentworth's policy
and thereby of the authority of the church. However, what had
happened during the Interregnum could not be wiped out, and
certainly dissenters provided a continuity with that period which

the Established Church would have willingly forgone. Both government and church recognised that a difficult task lay ahead in all parts, England, Scotland and Ireland with regard to dissenters, as a policy of conformity to the restored episcopal churches was proposed. Indeed, for dissenters in Ireland the Restoration settlement was a disaster both theologically and politically, and they made no secret of their disappointment.

Henry Cromwell was recalled from Ireland in 1659, and in December of the same year Dublin Castle was taken over by army officers and members of the old Protestant gentry. They called for a General Convention to meet in Dublin in February 1660. In the early days of the Convention hopes of dissenters ran high, for the Convention requested a religious settlement favourable to them.[2] An English Presbyterian minister, Samuel Coxe, was appointed chaplain to the Convention, and a committee of eight ministers was appointed to advise the Convention's committee on religion. At first these ministers and the members of the Convention worked together on a religious settlement in Ireland, even to the extent that Scottish Presbyterians hoped that the Covenant would be taken.[3] Such a possibility was not tested, for by June 1660 the commissioners appointed by the Convention to treat with the king recognised that the initiative had passed from their hands.[4] Indeed, episcopacy was in the ascendant, signalled by the appointment of a full Irish hierarchy in the autumn of 1660, with John Bramhall as Archbishop of Armagh and Jeremy Taylor as Bishop of Down and Connor. It became clear that religious policy and settlement in Ireland would emanate from Whitehall, not Dublin.

This was grim news for the Scottish Presbyterians, and the synod of Ballymena sent William Keyes, an English Presbyterian, and William Richardson of Killyleagh to London to plead their case with the king. Their mission failed.[5] A further representation was made in early January 1661, this time to the Lords Justices in Dublin, again to no avail.[6] The subsequent interaction between Scottish Presbyterians and the governments of the day indicated how the laws against dissenters were interpreted in Ireland and how they were applied at least until after the 1688 Revolution.

As early as October 1660 Lord Caulfield told Bramhall:

> Not many days ago it was hardly possible to find two of one religion. And therein are those unhappy northern quarters most miserable, abounding with all sorts of licentious persons; but those we esteem most dangerous are the presbyterian factions who do not like publicly to preach up the authority of the Kirk to be above that of the Crown. . . . I have myself discoursed with divers of their ministers both in public and private who have maintained that the Kirk has power to excommunicate their kings; and when the oath of allegiance and supremacy were administered here one of them told me we had pulled down one Pope and set up another.[7]

Taylor also reported that some ministers were preaching sedition, rejecting the monarchy and urging revolution. Others were prepared to accept the monarchy and even episcopacy, but hoped the king would not impose it in Ireland.[8] Certainly Scottish Presbyterians tried to discredit Taylor in the hope of getting him removed.[9] Some of the 'prime incendiaries' spread rumours that Taylor was an Arminian, a Socinian or a half-papist; they got copies of his books and 'appointed a committee of Scotch ministers' to examine them and send a report to the king.[10] Taylor tried to debate with them, but the ministers refused; Taylor then sent a summary of what was being spread abroad in the north of Ireland:

> A particular of such doctrines as are usually preached and taught by the Scotch ministers in the north of Ireland in the diocese of Down and Connor.
> — that the Covenanters first drew the bloody sword; and before they would submit to these oaths, viz. of allegiance and supremacy and to these popish ceremonies, they would draw it again.
> — that times of persecution are coming on, worse than in Queen Mary's days.
> — that they would do well to get the Bible by heart because they will not be suffered to keep a Bible in their houses.
> — that the times are now at hand when it should be safer to break the sabbath than a holy day.
> — that the King's concessions in his declaration are a little mite of favour and no more.
> — that the service book and the mass book were both hatched in hell by the devil.
> — that we have got a King and the King has brought the bishops and they will bring in popery and then farewell all; and yet you, without, be valiant for the truth.

— they pray that the Lord though he suffers these wolves the bishops
to come into his Kirk here on earth, yet that he would never let them
come into his Kirk in heaven.
And many more seditious and more ridiculous not fit to trouble any
person of honour with.[11]

In this context of great unrest and turbulence, the Established
Church, long before the formal Act of Uniformity, passed in June
1666, set about containing the ministry of dissenters.[12] In January 1661 all meetings of dissenters were banned:

Sundry unlawful assemblies in many parts of this kingdom held by
papists, by presbyterians, by independents, by anabaptists, by quakers
and other fanatical persons meeting in great numbers, divers hundreds
and thousands at an assembly convened and congregated, some by
foreign pretended jurisdiction, others by a pretended domestic authority from a presbytery, other under congregational churches and all of
them contrary to and in contempt of His majesty's royal authority and
the established laws of the land.[13]

This was followed in May 1661 by a parliamentary order instruct-
ing all towns in Ireland to burn publicly the Solemn League and
Covenant,[14] and by a declaration of both houses concerning the
ecclesiastical government of Ireland and use of the Book of Common Prayer. Certainly with the Elizabethan Acts of Supremacy
and Uniformity, as well as the 1634 Articles and canons, the
Established Church had adequate legislation to enforce conformity. Convocation exercised its authority when it met in May
1661. Those clergy who had taken the Covenant were required
to renounce it in public,[15] and individual cases against clergy
were heard.[16] Conformity was seen as particularly urgent in
Ulster, and bishops there set about enforcing their authority.
Further representations were made both to the king and to the
Lord-Lieutenant, the Duke of Ormond,[17] on behalf of Scottish
Presbyterians in Ulster, but to no avail.

Yet despite this failure, the response of dissenters in general
to Blood's Plot in 1663 (a conspiracy of discontented officers with
a few ministers, led by Thomas Blood) was very mixed. Generally
ministers were unwilling to be part of the movement in Ireland
at the time. Had Blood succeeded, their stance might have been
very different.[18] However, suspicion of complicity was enough
for Ormond at the time, and many ministers were arrested and

jailed for security reasons in Carrickfergus and Carlingford as well as Derry and Lifford.[19] It is clear that some ministers were considered highly dangerous to the state, even if nothing conclusive could be proved against them. It was known that Andrew McCormick, minister at Magheralin, Co. Down, had assured the plotters in Dublin that 20,000 Scots in the north were ready to join in the revolt which included the plan to kill both the king and Ormond.[20]

By the middle of June 1663 some Scottish Presbyterian ministers in Down and Antrim were under arrest and some were on the run. Among those arrested was John Drysdale, who had come from Scotland around the time of the plot; he had been ejected by Taylor, and this sudden return looked suspicious to the bishop.[21] Lord Conway told Ormond that there were plots of Scottish Presbyterian ministers both in Antrim and Down and in the Laggan area, one of which was to take Kilkenny; but he had no proof, and the arrested ministers could not be held indefinitely. He suggested that they could be scattered to remote places until they agreed to leave Ireland for good.[22]

For his part, the Bishop of Raphoe, Robert Leslie, arrested the suspected ministers in his diocese. He picked out the ringleaders, among them John Hart, who was considered 'the most dangerous of them', though he had refused to join if part of the plot was to kill Charles II; even so, it was clear he had a great deal of knowledge about the plot and contacts in Scotland about it.[23] Bishop Wild of Derry similarly arrested ministers in his diocese and tried to contain their influence, though he echoed what other bishops said in that he had no proper jail to hold all the ministers securely.[24] So, owing to inadequate evidence and accommodation, the suspect ministers could not be held indefinitely, though those held by the Bishop of Raphoe were not released until 1670.[25] Some received protection from patrons or friends; others were forced to leave the country or go to another part of Ireland.[26] In a move to discover and isolate the fanatical element in the country, a proclamation was issued giving indulgence to all nonconformists, from 29 June to 24 December 1663, because they did not rebel.[27] In this way Ormond hoped the country could be restored to some peace and stability.

Thomas Price, Bishop of Kildare, wrote to Ormond on 10 July 1663 to tell him that one of his clergy, a Scot though born in the north of Ireland and who spent a good part of his life there, had received visits from his countrymen and had found them

> very tumultuous and are very much engaged in that plot and that they have their meetings very frequently in an island in the county of Antrim called Rathry, where those of the north of Ireland are to meet others of the same gang out of Scotland the 22 of this instant July. They are determined to go there even if there is an embargo on shipping; they will go to Red Bay three miles from Rathlin.[28]

Unrest in the north did not cease when the plot had been discovered in Dublin, for the ferment was bigger and older than the immediate problem of rebellion. It had become clear gradually to the Scottish Presbyterians that there was no possibility of being the state church, that their situation had radically changed, and that they were quite impoverished in many ways, certainly economically and politically. Something similar was happening in Scotland, and this had repercussions among Scottish Presbyterians in Ireland, for communication between the two countries was frequent and easy. The north of Ireland was nearer to the west of Scotland than Dublin; families lived in both countries and were a short boat journey away from each other. News travelled quickly this way. Moreover, at this time ministers were trained and ordained in Scotland, and it was natural that contacts made there would be maintained.[29]

In 1665 the ministers who had been banished to Scotland on account of the the 1663 plot had begun to return. Jeremy Taylor, Bishop of Down and Connor, reported that those who had started to conform to the Established Church had joined the conventicles again.[30] In the following year news of the Pentland Rising in Scotland reverberated in the north of Ireland, and Arlington warned Ormond that it could be serious.[31] Ormond told Arlington that he knew that 'some come from Scotland who called themselves ministers . . . who have a great concourse of people that follow and hear them preach all manner of sedition'. [32] Three weeks later Taylor told Ormond that the rising in Scotland had a real effect in his diocese and that John Crookshanks, who was involved in Blood's Plot in 1663, had been in the north sometime before the rebellion.

For Taylor it was a mistake to allow the banished ministers to return, for now they received pensions from the people 'by the authority of some landlords or rather landladies'.[33] Anthony Kennedy of Templepatrick preached an inflammatory sermon praising the godly people in Scotland. The bishop heard that the people, when paying their tithes at All Saints, signed the bond with the phrase 'in case there be no war or public disturbance before that time'. Ormond asked for a list of the ministers who had returned, for the names of the landowners who forced the people to pay the ministers, and told Taylor to arrest Kennedy.[34]

The unrest was not confined to the north-east. Lord Dungannon told Sir George Rawdon to seize Major Hugh Montgomery, the horsebreeder, in County Londonderry. Montgomery had been watched for some time. It was well known that he had conventicles at his house, either in the kiln or the stables, where up to 700 could meet at one time. Montgomery had not been at public worship since the Restoration, and baptisms, fasts and the communion service were all held on his property. Anthony Kennedy preached there on 4, 9 and 11 September 1666.[35] Montgomery also received itinerant preachers into his house. For example, James Patrick, a minister from Scotland, came to Montgomery's house, preached and baptised, and then returned to Scotland before the rebellion.[36] In January 1667 Robert Mossom, Bishop of Derry, told Ormond:

> That the factious preachers which run out of Scotland (like wild boars hunted out of a forest and throw their foam of seditious doctrine among the people) and other itinerant preachers which wander out of other dioceses be seized. And to that end the bishops be entrusted with 2-3 blank warrants for the governor of Ulster which the bishop may use privately by his agents, to avoid the odium upon himself, the better to prevail in undeceiving the seduced multitudes.[37]

Unrest continued, and in the following year it was reported that meetings were being held all through Antrim and that the Covenant was being taken. Many from Coleraine, Belfast, Carrickfergus and the Route attended these meetings, and their length can be gauged from the fact that at one such recorded meeting five candles burned from dusk to dawn.[38] This was confirmed by the Lord Chancellor, Michael Boyle, when he wrote to Ormond in October 1668 indicating that the bishop had told him how bad the situation was in Down and Connor. Some of the assemblies went on all night, during which the Covenant was taken. Ormond replied:

> It is not strange that the non conformists in the north of Ireland when they are more numerous and united should assume more boldness in their meetings than in other places.

Yet he acknowledged that if the Covenant was being revived, the government would have to be very severe; otherwise it would be seen as 'stupid, negligent and miraculously infatuated'. Scottish Presbyterians needed to know 'that the liberty they have is from compassion to their misguided judgements and not from any apprehensions of their power'.[39] An extensive list of the ministers preaching in the north was sent to Boyle in November 1668, and it indicated just how strong the ministry was there, and how the links with Scotland were continuing and developing.[40] Lord Dungannon wrote to Ormond:

> I find great disorder among the Scotch. I wish it may not come to mischief. All those Scottish ministers that were silenced here and afterwards sent to Scotland by your Grace's command are now returned and in all places preach up the Covenant very openly and with a boldness in my mind very dangerous.[41]

Dungannon warned that people who formerly had conformed no longer did so; the congregations were full and met in barns and houses, while the parish churches were empty. If this continued, rebellion would follow. Both Ormond and the king took this warning from Dungannon seriously, even though the Chancellor had in fact told Ormond about the growing audacity of the Presbyterians in September 1668. On 29 December 1668 Ormond told Boyle:

> the preaching up of the Covenant so boldly and so frequently and in so many places is a degree beyond conventicling and is the next immediate step to active rebellion.[42]

The Archbishop of Armagh summarised the situation:

> We have been and are much disordered and the people perverted by the multitude of conventicles of different sects who are now arrived to

that boldness that there is scarce a parish where there is not a meeting house to that end and publicly owned, especially in the north where they are said to grow formidable by the vast numbers of those who meet together and (as far as I am informed by understanding persons) that have erected presbyteries, chosen elders, appointed salaries to the ministers who are for the most part either emissaries or banished out of Scotland.[43]

The only solution that the archbishop could suggest was to have the law put into action by the justices of the peace, forcing the people to come to church. However, it was not as simple as that, for the strength of the Presbyterians was very real, and they were held together by their conviction and organisation and by the leadership of their ministers. Archbishop Margetson's report indicates the power Presbyterian ministers had developed since the refoundation of the church in 1642. In the midst of harassment and uncertainty, Presbyterians had created a structure and form of church government that was firm and enduring. After the Restoration the church went on less overtly at first, but gradually it emerged strong and rooted, clear in its purpose and tried by persecution. While the bishops and the government were aware that the Presbyterians continued to meet, the strength of their growth and the consistency of their organisation evaded them.

In 1669 Ormond was removed from the government[44] and between 1669 and 1677 three Lords Lieutenant served in Ireland. Lord Robartes (1669-70) was sympathetic to Presbyterians, though outwardly conforming, and was given instructions not to proceed against dissenters unless specifically authorised by the king.[45] Lord Berkeley (1670-72) continued this policy, and in addition was an ally of the Duke of York and married to a Catholic. Neither of these Lords Lieutenant were inclined to proceed against dissenters in Ireland. Indeed, under Berkeley's rule Roman Catholics were positively promoted,[46] and in 1672 Scottish Presbyterians received the *regium donum* from the king, a small sum of money paid to ministers which served as a sign of legitimacy, though not a formal recognition of dissent.

The Earl of Essex was appointed Lord Lieutenant in 1672, and he too received instructions not to proceed against dissenters in Ireland.[47] However, the growing power and confidence of Roman Catholicism in Ireland and England at this time forced

Essex to change this policy.[48] Scottish Presbyterians too demanded the attention of Essex. Bishop Mossom of Derry wrote
to him, complaining that Scottish Presbyterians in Derry needed
a restraining order, as they had got very powerful and treated
the Established Church in a very high-handed way. The magistrates upheld the Established Church, otherwise 'we should have
been trod on as dirt and the whole ministry with us'.[49] Essex
had already warned Whitehall that the Presbyterians in Derry
were very factious,[50] but in recounting how the Bishop of Derry
reached an agreement with the Presbyterians, he reflected on
the wider issue:

> I have here enclosed a copy of the Bishop of Londonderry's letter by
> which your lordship will find the terms which those nonconformists are
> at present brought to, which I hope for a time may keep them quiet,
> but the cure of that evil must be by another course, for I find that almost
> all the seditious preachers of Scotland, who are so factious and turbulent
> there as the government will not endure them, do upon their banish-
> ment out of that kingdom repair hither, and these are the men who are
> most followed by the multitude.[51]

In the same letter Essex explained to Arlington that the Scots
in the inland counties of the north-east of Ireland conformed to
the church, whereas those Scots on the coast were 'a very factious and turbulent generation'. This concern was very real, for
the west coast of Scotland was the centre of unrest and had easy
and quick access to Ireland. Throughout this period there is constant reference to this and numerous instructions from Lords
Lieutenant and from Whitehall to guard the coasts of the north-
east from those rebels who wanted to evade arrest by either fleeing from Ireland to Scotland or more commonly, fleeing Scotland
for refuge in Ireland.[52]

The newly appointed Bishop of Down and Connor, Thomas
Hacket, bore out Essex's point and understood quickly that in
his diocese there were two types of Scottish Presbyterian: the
moderates who accepted the Restoration settlement; the moderates; and the 'Remonstrators', who rejected it. The latter, he
explained, were

> therefore driven out hither, who are mad, factious, preaching up the
> people's liberties, spreading seditious books printed in Holland since

this war, of which some are fixed and some they call itinerant preachers.
. . . These excite the people to outrages against their legal incumbents
. . . perform all parochial duties here and defraud the ministers of their
dues (not content with preaching as they are in England), and what is
of most wicked consequence, after they have married persons, the coupled
on discontents part, and pretend they were not legally married. . . . They
are but lately come, disowned by all the principal men and may be as
silently returned whence they come. . . .

    I do not altogether despair of bringing some of the moderates to a
fair treaty. . . . I hope likewise to divide them which I have essayed by
suggesting to them probabilities of kindness for those who are moderate,
and that the violent only hinder them from, and that therefore they will
discriminate themselves from that party.[53]

The government sought to use this tension within Scottish
Presbyterianism to its own advantage by granting indulgence to
those who accepted the Restoration settlement, thereby isolating
the more militant faction. Certainly the meetings in Ireland saw
the itinerant preachers and some of the ministers called to congregations in Ireland from Scotland as a real threat to their own
survival.[54] For their part, the government saw Presbyterian organisation and structure as a threat in itself. It was known that meetings were regularly held and that a committee held power and
authority over all the congregations; the formation of ministers
for ordination was recognised as a source of potential danger, as
were the schools and method of catechising in the community.[55]

To both government and the Established Church, moderation
within Scottish Presbyterianism was a matter of degree only.
Moreover, the extension of Scottish Presbyterianism into new
areas in Ireland dismayed the Established Church. So when the
Laggan meeting responded to a call from the people of Sligo and
sent two ministers there on a visit, the Bishop of Killala was
furious.[56] Yet the visit of the two ministers, Samuel Halliday
and William Henry, was really similar to visits of other ministers
to places that had no resident minister of their own. In January
1677 Thomas Otway, Bishop of Killala, complained to Essex
about 'the Scotch presbyters who ramble up and down to debauch
the people'. He arrested two of the ministers and discovered a
whole network of families who acted as safe houses for travelling ministers in Sligo and Roscommon. The bishop was sure
that his diocese was not isolated in this respect and complained:

some of this gang wander over all the provinces of Ireland; that your
Excellency hears not of them because most of the justices of the peace
of this kingdom are almost all presbyterian . . . many of the justices that
are not so yet are as bad by their laziness.[57]

But it was not merely juridical ineffectiveness or connivance
which allowed Scottish Presbyterians to grow and extend influence. At another level they had the sense of being a chosen
people in the midst of idolatry and sin. They believed that in
and through their election by Christ they could win through;
they always hoped to be the 'Church of Ireland' and were prepared to wait and suffer for that cause. There were some in their
midst who wished to push that cause hard and with violence if
necessary. This the majority could not accept, and they therefore
tried to contain the fanatical element in Ireland and its growing
influence from Scotland.

Ormond returned to Ireland as Lord Lieutenant in 1677, and
his first years of office were taken up with the effect of the Popish
Plot in Ireland.[58] However, he was well aware of the continued
unrest in Ulster, which only needed an incident to allow it to
surface.[59] This was provided by the murder of the Archbishop
of St Andrews, James Sharp, in May 1679. Later in the month
a Presbyterian in Derry, Henry Osborne, declared in public that
he was pleased that the archbishop had been killed.[60] Such
views were reported, and Presbyterian ministers were suspected
of being in favour of the rebels in Scotland who were defeated
in June 1679 at Bothwell Bridge.

The unrest in the north, generated by events in Scotland and
by the numbers who fled to Ireland for safety, was expressed by
increased meetings and more belligerent expressions of rebellion.
Thomas Nisbett wrote a long account of developments in
Ballymoney area.[61] Communion services were very numerous,
having at each one up to three or four thousand present. The
temper of such meetings was belligerent:

To be short, they all expect a sudden demolishing of the present established church in so much as hereabouts many refuse to take their tithes
to the clergy. A militia is here raised and arms put in the hands of very
many as malicious and bloody enemies of the church of England as any
Jesuits in the world; while the Jesuits are deservedly banished [from]

these kingdoms, 'tis strange the state should think it prudent or con-
venient to allow a sort of ministry of the same spirit and principle, in-
fusing into the rabble that if Christ will not help himself they must help
him. If some course be not taken, I assure you none of the established
church clergy shall be able to travel five miles in this country without
peril to his life.

Those Presbyterian ministers who tried to hold a moderate position were under pressure both to hold their congregations in check
and defend their ministry to the government. Robert Rule, minister of Derry, explained that while he was sorry that the Covenanters in Scotland 'are under such sad oppressions which provoked them to it', yet he could neither support the murder of Sharp
nor the use of violence, either in Scotland or in Ireland.[62]

With the defeat of the rebels in Scotland, the problems in
Ireland were increased. Some of the Scottish rebels had fled to
Ireland, and a watch had been set up for them at the ports. However, since many of the justices of the peace were Presbyterian,
it was suspected that many who should have been arrested entered
Ireland freely.[63] On the other hand, the general committee felt
it had to make a formal representation of its position to Ormond,
and accordingly they sent a petition to him through Lord Granard
on 5 July 1679.[64] This petition contained the usual points: that
they had been loyal to the king during the Interregnum and after
the Restoration, and that now they were much maligned and
misrepresented and wanted to declare in public that they knew
nothing about the rebellion in Scotland and had no part in it.
Ormond found this far too vague and thought it clarified nothing
in reality.

Ormond was particularly suspicious of the ministers of the
Laggan meeting; and because of this, Stewart, a former Presbyterian and a landowner in the area and now a member of the
Council of State, urged them to make a clear, public declaration of their complete loyalty. This they refused to do, saying
it had to be done in full synod, and such an assembly was not
possible for them to hold. However, the ministers promised to
try to deal with some resolutions in committee. The Laggan was
not in favour of an address to the king, but suggested writing
to Lord Granard and asking him to represent their loyalty. Finally

agreement seems to have been reached, as an address to the king was circulated for approval.

The rebellion in Scotland was over, but the movement of radical groups both there and in Ireland continued. Copies of the Sanquhar Declaration (1680), basically a restatement of the Solemn League and Covenant, were found in Ireland, and the government reprinted the document as an example of the sedition threatening both countries.[65] The declaration disowned the Stuarts and those ministers who accepted the indulgence offered by the king. It was militant in tone and defiant in its defence of Reformation principles as understood by the protesters. Moderate Presbyterian ministers continued to exercise their ministry and were not involved with the spirit of this declaration. However, with all the suspicions surrounding them, many of their actions and practices were seen either as seditious or potentially so.

For example, the Laggan meeting decided to call a public fast for 17 February 1681. There was nothing very unusual in this, as fasts were part of the congregation's discipline, and other meetings had held fasts that year and seem to have been left undisturbed afterwards. However, given the temper of the times and the fact that in law only the king could grant a fast, at the request of parliament, this action in the Laggan took on new significance. The causes for the fast were outlined in three parts: the sins of the people and of the times; the judgements of God on the people and the need to make petitions to God.[66] This looked innocent enough, and yet there was great unrest in the area, some of the soldiers refusing to take the Oath of Supremacy.[67] The ministers were blamed for this, particularly William Trail, James Alexander, Robert Campbell and John Hart. They were called to Dublin to defend their action in calling the fast in February.[68]

Trail in particular was suspected of substituting his own version of the Oath of Supremacy in place of the official version; he was also clerk to the meeting and held the minute book.[69] He was questioned carefully at the trial in Dublin and denied that he had ever taken the Solemn League and Covenant; he refused to take the Oath of Supremacy, saying that he was not free to do so, except in the sense understood in Article 58 of the Irish

Articles of 1615. Although he acknowledged the king's supremacy, Trail confounded and amused his questioners on what exactly that meant to Presbyterians and Episcopalians. He declared that he accepted all the 1615 Articles, with some exception regarding Article 77. That in itself was indicative of the stance held by the Laggan meeting and of the more moderate elements among Scottish Presbyterians in Ireland.[70] Trail also defended the fast of 17 February, saying it was 'a fast in a corner', not a national fast such as the king would have to authorise for the country. It was a good performance, and Trail seemed to have the sympathy of the court. Nevertheless, the ministers were imprisoned in Lifford for eight months, though in circumstances which allowed them to continue their ministry to the people.[71]

The trial of the Scottish Presbyterian ministers underlined a problem Ormond had in trying to prosecute dissenters:

> that which troubles me in that point is that our lawyers in Ireland do not agree that the laws in Ireland can be made use of against any dissenters but the papists for whom they say they were only calculated. I mean that the Act of Uniformity or any other regarding religion of the church. But that the law against riots and unlawful assemblies may possibly be interpreted to reach them is not denied by any I have spoken with upon the whole matter. I confess I did not like the stretching of penal laws beyond their original intention by subsequent construction, since it cannot be foreseen whom such a precedent may hurt.[72]

A few months later Ormond admitted the possible danger from Scottish Presbyterians who

> want but power to subvert the government. That they have presbyteries and do extend ecclesiastical jurisdiction I do not doubt, but as it is hard to convict them so I did not find by any of our lawyers that it could come within reach of any law in force in Ireland; nor had we power to suppress Jacque's conventicles though a meeting house was erected professedly for that use so near the council chamber.[73]

The government at least in theory had inherited legal power. Certainly the conditions of the Act of Uniformity, the Oath of Supremacy, the Oath of Allegiance, and attendance at church with use of the Book of Common Prayer and ceremonies of the Established Church, were all in place since the sixteenth century, intended originally for Roman Catholics. Nevertheless,

when the Book of Common Prayer was reissued in 1666 it was
clearly aimed at Protestant dissenters too. The requirement of
re-ordination by September 1667; rejection of all armed rebellion
and particularly of the Covenant; the promise not to change either
liturgy or discipline and to preach only with the authority of the
bishop — all these applied to Protestant dissenters in Ireland.[74]

On the other hand, Scottish Presbyterian ministers themselves
were not sure of their legal ground either and consulted lawyers
on several occasions.[75] At the same time they tried to contain
and deal with the fanaticical element within its own bounds and
authority. Events in Scotland always had repercussions among
Scottish Presbyterians in Ireland, especially the series of rebellions
and persecutions that occurred in Scotland after the Restoration: the Pentland Rising in 1666, the 1679 rising and the battle
of Bothwell Bridge, and the 'Killing Time' of 1684-8. These events
were marked in Ireland by unrest, Covenanting movements, and
some rebels seeking refuge in Ireland.

Thus both government and the Scottish Presbyterians were
unsure of their legal ground, and Ormond in particular tended
to deal with crises as they arose.[76] Scottish Presbyterians recognised and perhaps facilitated this procedure by carefully timed
representations of loyalty or protestations against harassment by
church officials, a tactic used by them consistently throughout
this period to real effect.[77] Ormond remained unimpressed:

> I think they are naturally more exalted and haughty in prosperity than
> dejected in adversity and therefore their acquiescence ought no less to
> be apprehended and provided against than their stiffness and obstinacy,
> and they can as easy find texts of scripture and precedents to recom-
> mend the one as the other to their people in due time and place.[78]

Perhaps Ormond was right in thinking that the Act of Uniformity should not or could not be applied to Protestant dissenters.
With a majority in the country firmly Roman Catholic, and with
Roman Catholicism evidently growing, a Protestant government
could find it very difficult to consistently apply the law against
members of Protestant traditions in Ireland. Besides, the English
laws against dissenters, especially the Conventicle Acts, were never
extended to Ireland, as Clarendon noted when he succeeded
Ormond.[79] In addition, the enforcement of laws against all

dissenters, including Roman Catholics, was always tempered by whatever foreign policy was being pursued at Whitehall.

In any event, throughout this period laws against dissenters were not applied in any continuous way. Both Samuel Mather and Nathaniel Mather bear this out.[80] Even in the critical times of 1682-6 only public meetings of dissenters were forbidden. In 1714 Arthur Langford, an English Presbyterian, spoke of the freedom to worship 'near these 40 years, by all the several governments under King Charles, King James, King William and Queen Mary, and Queen Anne'.[81] While the Scottish Presbyterians tested this approach severely, neither the Independents nor the English Presbyterians caused the government any undue concern throughout this period, with the exception of James Marsden in 1669 and possibly William Jacque in 1683.[82] Indeed, in the early years of the Restoration Ormond made a deliberate effort both to retain and indeed attract other congregationalists and 'Protestant strangers'.[83] In 1662 an 'Act for encouraging Protestant strangers and others to inhabit . . . Ireland' was passed,[84] in the hope of attracting business people to Ireland. There was a fine balance between promoting conformity and economy.

When Ormond was replaced by Clarendon in 1685[85] the political scene was changing rapidly in England and Ireland. In this atmosphere of foreboding, Protestants of all traditions in Ireland faced a political situation which for a short period forced a false unity against the common enemy, Roman Catholicism. However, this only postponed an inevitable confrontation which after the Glorious Revolution erupted between Scottish Presbyterians and the Established Church, with government procedure in Dublin dominated even more by policy in Whitehall.

Like the Independents and English Presbyterians, so too the Quakers in Ireland, after an initial period of harassment, enjoyed relative freedom to practise their beliefs. As the century wore on fewer and fewer were actually imprisoned for non-payment of tithes.[86] Quakers learned how to use representations[87] and the good offices of friends in high places, both in England and Ireland. By the 1680s Quakers had become accepted in the country and were not considered a threat to the government. Indeed, when John Burnyeat was jailed in 1683 he appealed to the Lord Deputy, the Earl of Arran, who said 'he had greater love for us than for any other dissenters because he believed we did men honestly'. In fact Arran wrote to Ormond at this time saying that only the Quakers held meetings in Dublin, and that as they had 'no particular teachers to give warning to, it is likely they may meet again; but I do not look on them as a dangerous sect'. The Earl of Longford wrote to Arran saying that in Cork papists and nonconformists had been suppressed, but that Quakers would be overlooked, 'most of whom are the greatest traders in the town and very peaceable men and submissive to the government'.[88] In fact at the Half-Yearly Meeting in March 1685 it was noted:

> to our public meetings abundance of other people came, even far more than could get into our house; . . . though the professors who shrink and hide, we are informed, do rail against the Friends; they do seem as if they were given up to hardness of heart and so set in their blindness and hardness . . . it appears they envy Friends good and are offended we do not fly into holes as they do.[89]

Penn himself urged Ormond to leave the Quakers in peace: 'Avoid troubling conscientious and quiet believing dissenters. They are best for the country and not worst for the church'.[90] William Edmundson told Fox in 1687 that Quakers were being treated very well:

> We have, several of us, several times been with the Lord Deputy of Ireland Richard Talbot, i.e. 1st Earl of Tyrconnell, and [the] Chancellor of Ireland, i.e. Sir Alexander Fitton and other chiefs in government and they are ready to hear us and [be] very kind but especially Lord Chief Justice Nugent who is ready to do anything he can for us. Several Friends in Dublin, Cork, Cashel and Limerick [are] made aldermen and in corporations some made burgesses, so such like to meet with trials in these places and I wish the truth suffer not in that case.[91]

Fox had misgivings about this and wondered if Quakers could hold office without having to take oaths and wear gowns; he asked: 'Will they let them sit among them with their hats on?' In the event, Anthony Sharp and Samuel Claridge took office as aldermen of Dublin, were excused the oaths, and wore no gowns.[92] When James II came to Dublin he gave his protection to the Quakers, 'well satisfied with the loyalty, peaceable demeanour and good affection of the Quakers'.[93] James Bonnell, writing after the 1688 Revolution in England and during its repercussions in Ireland, reflected:

> The Quakers at first took civil offices under King James and were looked upon by us and the Roman Catholics as the same with them; but latterly when they see how things were like to go, they sided once more with us; however even to the last they were favoured in all things by the government and truly we looked upon it to be reward from God to them for the peaceableness of their behaviour in all things.[94]

In fact William Edmundson felt that Quakers were too well accepted by governments of the day. The principal danger that Friends had to face as they entered the eighteenth century was not the threat of persecution but the lure of worldliness.

Notes and References

1   William Lightburne, *A thanksgiving sermon preached at Christ Church, before the Lords Justices and Council, 23 October 1661* (Dublin, 1661), p. 15.

2   'Instructions for Sir John Clotworthy and William Aston Esq., members of the General Convention of Ireland now employed into England by the said Convention' 30 Mar. 1660 (B.L., Add. MS, 32471, f. 82v).

3   Adair, *A true narrative*, pp 230ff; Samuel Coxe, *Two sermons preached at Christchurch, Dublin, beginning the General Convention of Ireland* (Dublin, 1660); J. I. McGuire, 'The Dublin Convention, the Protestant community and the emergence of an ecclesiastical settlement in 1660' in Art Cosgrove and J. I. McGuire (ed.), *Parliament and community* (Belfast, 1983), pp 130-1; McConnell, *Fasti*, no. 44, p. 9.

4   'The further humble desires of the commissioners of the General Convention of Ireland appointed to attend your majesty' (T.C.D., MS 808, no. 9, f. 156).

5   Adair, *A true narrative*, pp 241-4. Richardson was born in Scotland and ordained for Killyleagh in 1649. McConnell, *Fasti*, no. 98, p. 47.

6   George Hill (ed.), *The Montgomery Manuscripts, 1603-1706* (Belfast, 1859), pp 236-7, n. 76.

7   Edward Berwick (ed.), *Rawdon Papers* (London, 1819), 127-8.

8   Taylor to Montgomery, 27 Oct. 1660 (Bodl., Carte MS 31, f. 36).

9   This was not new. F. R. Bolton, *The Caroline tradition in the Church of Ireland* (London, 1958), pp 26ff; Barnard, *Cromwellian Ireland*, p. 132.

10 Taylor to Ormond, 19 Dec. 1660 (Bodl., Carte MS 45, f.25); Maxwell to Taylor, 3 Dec. 1660 (*Cal.S.P.Ire., 1660-2*, pp 115-16); Mountrath and Bury to Secretary Nicholas, 12 Dec. 1660 (ibid., pp 128-9).

11 Taylor to Lane, 19 Dec. 1660 (Bodl., Carte MS 45, ff 29, 28).

12 Besides former acts were available: the Elizabethan Act of Supremacy of

1560 (2 Eliz., c. 1 s.6), which included an oath of allegiance (28 Hen. VIII, c, 2); and 2 Eliz., c. 2, which required conformity to the Book of Common Prayer and ceremonies of the Established Church. R. Dudley Edwards, 'The history of the laws against Protestant nonconformity in Ireland from the Restoration (1660) to the Declaration of Indulgence (1687)' (M.A. thesis, U.C.D., 1932), pp 56-7.

13 22 Jan. 1661 (B.L., C 21, f. 1, no. 20).

14 Bodl., Carte MS 64, f. 442. The Mayor of Carrickfergus refused and was summoned to Dublin and fined £100; Edwards, 'The history of the laws against nonconformity', pp 82-3. Derry aldermen accepted the Oath of Allegiance but not the Oath of Supremacy (Bodl., Carte MS 45, f.72);

15 Bodl., Carte MS 45, f. 271.

16 Thomas Wilkinson, who ministered with Samuel Coxe, was proceeded against for not using the Book of Common Prayer, and James Knowles was ordered to attend Convocation for violating the authority of Convocation. T.C.D., MS 1038, ff 34v, 38, 41; Bodl., Carte MS 64 f. 271; R.C.B., MS Libr. 14, Vestry Book of St Katherine and St James, 1657-1692, p. 47; Barnard, *Cromwellian Ireland*, pp 1 46, 147.

17 H.M.C., *Hastings MSS*, iv, 104, 109-10; 'Paper from the Scotch ministers given me by the Lord Massereene, 30 Sept. 1662', signed P. Adair, A. Stewart, W. Semple (Bodl., Carte MS 45, f. 298-9); Adair, *A true narrative*, pp 256-7, 264-9; Robert and George Ross to Ormond, 25 Mar. 1663 in C. W. Russell and J.P. Prendergast, *The Carte MSS in the Bodleian Library, Oxford: a report* (London, 1871), p. 111; 1 Apr. 'A demonstration of the loyalty of the Presbyterian ministers of Ulster made out of many particular instances' 1663 (Bodl., Clarendon MS 80, f. 380); 'Reasons why the petitioned indulgence should be granted to the people of the north of Ireland' (Bodl., Carte MS 45, f.77).

18 Bodl., Carte MS 32, ff 412, 419, 437, 122, 123, 282, 328, 331, 393-4 ; Ibid., MS 45, ff 82, 85, 88 ; R. L. Greaves, *Deliver us from evil* (Oxford, 1986), pp 43-5; 135-57; Charles McNeill (ed.), *The Tanner Letters* (I.M.C., Dublin, 1943), p. 401ff.

19 T. W. Moody and J. G. Simms (ed.), *The bishopric of Derry and the Irish Society of London, 1602-1705,* 2 vols (I.M.C., Dublin, 1968, 1983), i, no. 149, p. 358.

20 R. M. Young *Historical notices of old Belfast and its vicinity.* (Belfast, 1896), p. 103; *Tanner Letters*, p. 404. Both McCormick and John Crookshanks were leaders at the Pentland Rising in Scotland in 1666. I. B. Cowan, *The Scottish Covenanters* (London, 1976), p. 64. For Crookshanks see McConnell, *Fasti* no. 48, p. 10.

21 Bodl., Carte MS 45, f. 82. Drysdale had been in Ireland from at least 1643 and preached sedition in Derry (Ibid., MS 8, f. 157).

22 Conway to Ormond, 8 July 1663 (Ibid., MS 32, f. 419; also ff 122, 123, 331).

23 *Tanner Letters,* 404; Bishop of Raphoe to Ormond, 3 July 1663 (Bodl., Carte MS 32, f. 398; also ff 412, 437).

24 Wild to Ormond, 7 August 1663 (Bodl., Carte MS 45, f. 85).

25 Adair, *A true narrative,* pp 283-8.

26 Ibid. pp 271-88; Bodl., Carte MS 45, f. 301.

27 Bodl., Carte MS 68, f. 596.

28 Ibid., MS 32, f. 328.

29 A proclamation had been issued in Dublin with the names of all suspects of the plot included; a copy of this had been sent to Scotland, where all who had come from Ireland within the previous ten days were to be examined. June 1663 (Bodl., Carte MS 71, f. 386); *The Registers of the Privy Council of Scotland*, 3rd series, i: 1661-1664, p. 371.

30 5 Nov. 1665 (Bodl., Carte MS 34, f. 297). In 1664 Taylor recalled all the copies he could of his *The liberty of prophesying* and burnt them 'as a protest against its use by non-conformists'. C. J. Stranks, *The life and writings of Jeremy Taylor* (London, 1952), p. 259.

31 Arlington to Ormonde, 24 Nov. 1666 (Bodl., Carte MS 46, f.192); also ff 160, 193-5; see ibid., MS 45, f. 109 for account of the rising in Scotland.

32 Ormond to Arlington, 8 Dec. 1666 (Ibid., MS 51, f. 174v).

33 26 Dec. 1666 (Ibid., MS 45, f. 116); Adair, *A true narrative*, p. 281.

34 Ormonde to Taylor, 29 Dec. 1666 (Bodl., Carte MS 45, f. 117; also f. 284 for list of ministers).

35 Dungannon to Rawdon, 18 Dec. 1666 (*Rawdon Papers* p. 222); An examination of Hugh Montgomery of Co. Londonderry (Bodl., Carte MS 35, ff 80, 88).

36 Bodl., Carte MS 36, f. 14; also MS 35, f. 80; MS 45, f. 284. In 1688 Major Montgomery still kept his nonconformist minister and a meeting-place for 500. Antrim minutes, p. 365; Hill, *The Montgomery Manuscripts*, p. 356.

37 Mossom to Ormond, 31 Jan. 1667 (Bodl., Carte MS 35, f. 87).

38 Sydenham to Page, 18 Sept. 1668 (ibid., MS 36, ff 330-2). The ministers involved were Patrick Adair, William Keyes, Thomas Gowan and Thomas Hall.

39 Boyle to Ormond, 26 Sept. 1668 (ibid., MS 36, f. 334); Ormond to Boyle, 20 Oct. 1668 (ibid., MS 49, f. 375).

40 A list of dissenting ministers in Ulster for the Lord Chancellor, 6 Nov. 1668 (ibid., MS 36, f. 345).

41 Dungannon to Ormond, 12 Dec. 1668 (ibid., MS 36, f. 404); Ormond to Ossory, 29 Dec. 1668 (ibid., MS 48, f.317).

42 Ormond to Boyle, 29 Dec. 1668 (ibid., MS 49, f.397); Boyle to Ormond, 24 Jan. 1669 (ibid., MS 37, f. 2).

43 Margetson to Ormond, 4 June 1669 (ibid., MS 37, f. 39).

44 J. I. McGuire, 'Why was Ormonde dismissed in 1669?' in *I.H.S.*, xviii, no. 71 (Mar. 1973); Ronald Hutton, 'The making of the secret treaty of Dover, 1668-70' in *Hist. Jn.*, 29 (1986); Ronald Hutton, *Charles II*, (Oxford, 1989), pp 260-1.

45 Instructions for Lord Robartes, (Bodl., Carte MS 37, f. 317).

46 David Dickson, *New foundations: Ireland, 1660-1800* (Dublin, 1987), pp 13-14.

47 Rules and instructions for Essex, 22 Sept. 1675 (B. L., Stowe MS 208, f. 283); Bodl., Carte MS 37 f. 484.

48 Dickson, *New foundations*, p. 14.

49 Mossom to Essex, 13 Sept. 1672 (B.L., Stowe MS 200, f. 235).

50 Essex to Arlington, 20 Aug. 1672, (*Essex Papers*, pp 14-16).

51 Essex to Arlington, 8 Oct. 1672 (ibid., p. 34).

52 In March 1675 the Archbishop of Glasgow complained that Galloway was infested with itinerant and vagrant preachers from Ireland (H.M.C., *2nd Report* (London, 1874), appendix, p. 203.

53 Hackett to Essex, 29 Oct. 1672 (B.L., Stowe MS 200, f.334); Hackett to Essex, 3 May [1673] (ibid., MS 202, f.1). In April 1673 the Laggan meeting suggested that Sir Robert Hamilton should act for them in Dublin and asked Lord Granard's opinion on this choice. Laggan minutes, pp 45, 64. Similarly in 1677 the Laggan meeting wrote to Patrick Adair and asked him to go to Dublin to represent their grievances. Ibid., p. 264.

54 Laggan minutes, 3 Aug. 1677, p. 276; ibid., 3 July 1678, p. 306.

55 Mar. 1679 (Bodl., Carte MS 45, ff 314, 317).

56 Laggan minutes, 28 Nov. 1676, p. 238; Otway to Essex, 22 Jan. 1677 (B.L., Stowe MS 211, ff 45, 47, 114, 120, 238); H.M.C., *Ormonde MSS*, iv, 17-18, 19-20, 25-6.

57 Otway to Essex, Jan. 1677 (B.L., Stowe MS 211, f. 120); also ff 45, 47, 114, 120; H.M.C., *Ormonde MSS*, iv, 17-20; W.G. Wood-Martin, *History of Sligo county and town*, 3 vols (Dublin, 1882-92), iii, 144; Oliver Plunkett also wrote about the increasing numbers and influence of Presbyterians in Ireland. John Hanly (ed.), *The letters of Oliver Plunkett, 1625-1681*, (Dublin, 1979), pp 373, 381, 387, 394, 443, 455, 530, 538.

58 Dickson, *New foundations*, pp 17-19.

59 In 1677 Archbishop Boyle told Ormond that 'the Covenant was much in vogue among them [Presbyterians] and publicly owned'. Edward MacLysaght (ed.), *Calendar of the Orrery Papers* (I.M.C., Dublin, 1941), p. 188.

60 Robson to Wilson, 23 May 1679 (Bodl., Carte MS 221, f. 195); Maxwell to Coghill, 17 June 1679 (ibid., MS 45, f. 330). James Russell, one of those involved in the assassination of Sharp, was found in Ireland, but he escaped. I. B. Cowan, *The Scottish Covenanters* (London, 1976) p. 95; J. G. Vos, *The Scottish Covenanters*, (Pittsburgh, 1980), pp 121, 123.

61 Nisbett to Crooks, 25 June 1679 (Bodl., Carte MS 45, ff 273-4. See also Richard Tennison, *A sermon preached at the primary visitation of Michael, Archbishop of Armagh* (Dublin, 1679), pp 4, 29, 32-33.

62 Rule to Stewart, 5 July 1679 (Bodl., Carte MS 221, f. 220). H.M.C., *Ormonde MSS*, v, 517; *Cal.S.P.Dom., 1683*, p. 73; Reid, *History of the Presbyterian Church*, ii, 99 n. 13, 339 n. 49.

63 Bodl., Carte MS 221, ff 196, 197, 199, 202, 200, 203, 210, 214, 217, 219, 223; 45, ff 314, 317, 319,, 331, 338-9; Ormond to Rawdon, 26 June 1679 (*Rawdon Papers*, p.262); Orrery to Essex, 24 June 1679 (B.L., Stowe MS 212, f 357). This problem was foreseen by Archbishop Margetson in 1664 (Bodl., Carte MS 33, f. 287.)

64 N.L.S., Wodrow MSS, Quarto 36, f.70; Bodl., Carte MS 45, f.345. The petition was signed by Michael Bruce, Killinchy, who was well known for his radical sympathies. Michael Bruce, *The rattling of dry bones*, (n.p., 1672) and *Six dreadful alarms* (Edinburgh, 1675); Bruce was born in Edinburgh in 1634 and came to Killinchy in 1657; deposed in 1661, he went

to Scotland until 1670, when he returned to Killinchy. McConnell, *Fasti,* no. 38, p. 7; Witherow, *Historic memorials,* pp 46-52; C. W. McKinney, *Killinchy* (1968), pp 22-5. Petition of several Presbyterian ministers in the north of Ireland, 5 July 1679. (Bodl. Carte MS 45, f. 345); also Ormond to Stewart, 8 July 1679 (ibid, f. 347).

65 *A true and exact copy of a treasonable and bloody paper, the fanatics new Covenant, which was taken from Mr Donald Cargill at Queensferry, June 3 1680, one of their field preachers, a declared rebel and traitor, together with their execrable declaration. Published at the cross of Sanquhar on the 22 of the said month after a solemn procession and singing of psalms by Cameron the notorious ringleader of and preacher at their field conventicles, accompanied with twenty of that wicked crew* (repr., Dublin, 1680); Ormond to Lauderdale, 16 July 1680 (Bodl., Carte MS 45, f. 361).

66 Laggan minutes, pp 85-6.

67 Bodl., Carte MS 45, ff 362-67.

68 N.L.S., Wodrow MSS, Quarto 75, no. 18; Reid, *History of the Presbyterian Church,* ii, Appendix 11, pp 574-89.

69 Bodl., Carte MS 45, ff 363, 365. The Laggan minutes stop in April 1681 and resume in 1690.

70 Article 77: 'Every particular church has authority to institute, to change, and clean put away ceremonies and other ecclesiastical rites, as they be superfluous or be abused; and to constitute other, making more to seemliness, to order, or edification.' (This is part of Article 34 of the Thirty-Nine Articles). The Westminster Confession was greatly influenced by the 1615 Irish Articles, and parts of the Confession are identical to some of the Irish Articles. A.I.C. Heron (ed.), *The Westminster Confession in the world today* (Edinburgh, 1972), pp 7, 45; John Thompson, 'The Westminster Confession' in J.L.M. Haire *et al., Challenge and conflict: essays in Irish Presbyterian history and doctrine* (Antrim, 1981), pp 8-9.

71 Trail went to America and eventually returned to Scotland. W.T. Latimer, *History of the Irish Presbyterians* (Belfast, 1902), p. 173; R.F.G. Holmes, *Our Irish Presbyterian heritage* (Belfast, 1985), p. 46; Boyd S. Schlenther, *The life and writings of Francis Makemie* (Philadelphia, 1971), p. 13.

72 Ormond to the Primate, 11 July 1682 (Bodl., Carte MS 50, f.194).

73 Ormond to Arran, 14 Nov. 1682 (H.M.C., *Ormonde MSS,* vi, 477); see also Arran to Ormond, 1 Aug. 1683 (ibid., vii, 93). On the 25 July 1683 Jacque preached in Dublin and was arrested; he was fined £40, which he paid immediately and so had to be released (Bodl. Carte MS, f. 54).

74 *Book of Common Prayer and administration of the sacraments and other rites and ceremonies of the church* (Dublin, 1666).

75 Laggan minutes, pp 296, 301, 331. Until further study is made of the lawyers who pronounced on these cases, it is hard to know whether the lawyers Ormond refers to were in fact dissenters themselves. For a discussion of law see T.C. Barnard, 'Lawyers and the law in later seventeenth-century Ireland' in *I.H.S.,* xxviii, no. 111 (May 1993), pp 256-82.

76 In 1666: Bodl. Carte MS 35, ff 80, 87, 88, 104; MS 36, ff 14, 16; MS 45, ff 116-17, 284-5, 286, 288; MS 46, f. 192, 194-5; MS 51, f. 174v. In 1668: MS 36, ff 330-2, 334, 345, 404; MS 37, ff 2, 11, 39; MS 48, 317.

In 1679: B.L., Stowe MS 212, ff 357, 361, 363-5, 367; H.M.C., *Ormonde MSS*, i, 55, 102; v, 112-3, 124-7, 206-8. In 1683/4: B.L., Lansdowne MS 1152A, ff 156, 176, 182, 330-1, 344, 347, 349, 354, 361; Bodl. Carte MS 40, ff 182, 187-92; MS 50, f. 228; MS 220, f.64, 73.

77   See notes 17, 63, 64 above. Further representations were made in: 1673 (Laggan minutes, pp 45, 64); 1677 (ibid., p. 264); 1679 (pp 23, 27-8); 1681, 'Humble supplication of the Presbyterian ministers of the north of Ireland to the king' (Bodl., Carte MS 45, f. 368); 1683 (Antrim minutes, p. 200); 1687 (ibid., pp 313, 324); 1689 (ibid., pp 414, 421); 1691 (Laggan minutes, p. 110); 1692 (ibid., p.139); 1693 (ibid., p. 175); 1695 (pp 298, 304); 1701, Representation to the Earl of Rochester (P.R.O.N.I., T525); 1708, 'Humble petition of the Presbyterian ministers and people in the north of Ireland' (ibid.); 2 Apr. 1709, John McBride to Robert Wodrow: petition in preparation (N.L.S., Wodrow MSS, Folio 26, no. 190); 1711, 'The humble address and apology of the Presbyterian ministers and gentlemen on behalf of themselves and the rest of their persuasion in the north of Ireland'.

78   5 Sept. 1683 Ormond to Mountjoy, (H.M.C., *Ormonde MSS*, vii, 124).

79   'Observations on the state of Ireland, 1684-5', S.W. Singer (ed.), *The correspondence of Henry Hyde, Earl of Clarendon,* 2 vols (London, 1828), i, 185-7.

80   'The Mather Papers', pp 13, 44, 46-47, 56-57, 62-63, 65-67.

81   'Arthur Langford to Dean Swift, 30 Oct. 1714 (Armstrong, *Summary history of the Presbyterian Church*, p. 105).

82   Even this incident involving Marsden remained more the concern of Samuel Mather than of the government, for by this time Robartes was Lord Lieutenant and sympathetic towards Presbyterians.

83   Bodl., Carte MS 45, ff 295, 293.

84   Ibid., MS 66 f. 487.

85   He too received instructions similar to those of Robartes and Essex: not to proceed against dissenters without first consulting Whitehall. Instructions for the Earl of Rochester, June 1685 (B.L., Lansdowne MS 1152A, f.314-314v).

86   For an estimate of the number imprisoned as well as the amount paid in tithes, during this period see Abraham Fuller and Thomas Holms, *A compendious view of sore extraordinary sufferings of the people called Quakers ... in Ireland 1655-1731* (Dublin, 1731), pp 123, 126-32, 135.

87   Douglas, Early Quakerism in Ireland, *J.F.H.S.* (48) 1956-8, pp 26-29.

88   J.B[urnyeat], *The truth exalted* (London, 1691), pp 78-91; Arran to Ormond, 4 Aug. 1683 (H.M.C., *Ormonde MSS*, vii, p. 95); Longford to Arran, 30 Aug. 1683. (ibid., vi, p. 121). Archbishop Marsh imprisoned Anthony Sharp and Abraham Fuller in Dublin in 1684. O.C. Goodbody, 'Anthony Sharp, wool merchant, 1643-1707, and the Quaker community in Dublin' in *J.F.H.S.,* 48, no. 1 (1956), p. 47.

89   Burnyeat, *The truth exalted*, p. 87. At this time in Dublin all nonconformists were forbidden to worship in public. 'The Mather Papers', pp 56-7. Quakers tried to avoid clashing with the government of the day. In 1675 they disowned Alexander Riggs for his disruptive behaviour in public,

fearing it would win Quakers a bad reputation. Testimonies of denial and condemnation (F.L.D., MM II F1, f. 19).

90   Penn to Ormond, 9 Jan. 1684 (Bodl., Carte MS 40, f. 128).

91   Edmundson to Fox, 12 Nov. 1687 (F.L.L., A. R. Barclay MS Transcripts, no. 103, p. 298).

92   Isobel Grubb, 'Anthony Sharp: an unpublished memoir' in *Friends' Quarterly Examiner,* 59 (1925), p. 181; Thompson to Ellis, 5 Nov. 1687 (B.L. Add. MS 28876, f. 39; *Anal. Hib.,* no. 32, (1985), p. 39); F.L.D., QM II Z1, O, 1688; Half-Yearly Meeting, Nov. 1687 (ibid., A. 10, f. 237); R.H. Murray, *Revolutionary Ireland and its settlement* (London, 1911), p. 65. Oaths had been dispensed with, for some Quakers, since at least 1672. *Cal. anc. rec. Dublin,* v, 12.

93   Protection for Quakers, 2 Aug. 1689 (T.C.D., MS 2203).

94   [James Bonnell] to John Strype, 5 Aug. 1690 (U.L.C., MS Mm VI 49, no. 8). In 1696 Quakers had difficulty in taking the oath offered them, but recognised that it tried to meet their sensitivities. Testimonies of disunity, F.L.D., QM II F1, f. 73ff.

Conclusion

We may expect some severe awakening stroke of the righteous
God which may sweep many of us off the face of the earth which
some apprehend to be near.

Robert Craghead, *Warning and advice* (1701)

Protestant dissenters in Ireland, in the course of the period
1660–1714, had developed a strong sense of identity, firmly
within the Reformation tradition, though separate from the
Established Church. While varying in numbers, all four traditions, Scottish Presbyterian, English Presbyterian, Independent
and Quaker had signalled that they were part of the evolving
Protestant consciousness, part of the Reformation project in
Ireland which had begun in the sixteenth century. They had
created structures, organisation and discipline which enabled
them first to survive after the Restoration and then become further rooted in the country. This reality was recognised in 1711
when the Established Church, meeting in Convocation, published
a statement on religion in Ireland.[1] Convocation had not met
since 1666, for none was convened during the parliamentary sessions of 1692, 1695-7 or 1698-9, and the *Representation* of 1711 was
the first public, formal and comprehensive examination of the

state of religion in Ireland for almost fifty years.[2]

It was of necessity a subjective view of a church which was threatened by the evident strength of dissenters, particularly in the north of Ireland. Although the Representation was cast in a pre-Interregnum mind-set and language, nevertheless it recorded the perceived growth of both Quakers and Presbyterians/Independents of all traditions in Ireland in the second half of the seventeenth century. Besides, the reaction such a statement evoked provided a forum for further debate and controversy, thereby articulating in particular the various strands of Presbyterianism and Independency in Ireland in the early eighteenth century.

Although the *Representation* made no mention of Presbyterians by name, they were in effect subsumed under 'Independents' — a term which covered Scottish Presbyterians, English Presbyterians and Independents. In no way could the Established Church recognise that these were or had become churches in their own right in Ireland. To them they were 'sects', originating at the time of the Interregnum, from the time of Cromwell, and Convocation used the emotive terms 'Independents, Anabaptists, Muggletonians, Quakers etc.', which certainly would have evoked old fears and old memories.[3] Recognition of corporate congregations, of churches, was an impossible step within the theological and political context of the period.[4]

The *Representation* voiced the conviction of the Established Church that all 'sects' had been treated too leniently and that the Scottish Presbyterians in particular were by far the most powerful group; as such they were singled out for detailed criticism. Indeed, in 1711 in a separate 'Representation', the Irish House of Lords protested that Scottish Presbyterians in Ireland had misrepresented the Established Church to the queen.[5] The Lords detailed the Established Church's grievances regarding Scottish Presbyterians; the measure and tone of the protest showed the strength of Scottish Presbyterians at this time. That they could so disturb the Established Church in 1711 was proof indeed of the tenacity of their hold in the north of Ireland.[6] The position of the Established Church was defensive, fearful that the 'schism which formerly in a manner was confined into the north has now spread itself into many other parts of this kingdom'.[7] The appointment by the Synod of Ulster of a minister to preach in Drogheda provoked a huge reaction from the Established Church, as would the proposed opening of a meeting-house in Belturbet, County Cavan, in 1712.[8] Fearing there was no possibility of either suppressing or indeed of forcing conformity on Scottish Presbyterians, Convocation urged a policy of containment, before 'presbytery and fanaticism' destroyed church and state. They asked that the *regium donum* be discontinued, suspecting that it was being used to finance new congregations.[9]

It was clear that Scottish Presbyterianism struck at the heart of the Established Church, for it condemned the doctrines and practices of the Established Church and judged its public worship popish and superstitious, its doctrines erroneous and unsound, and the Act of Uniformity unjust.[10] In addition, they exercised full presbyterial government, in sessions, presbyteries, classical synods and provincial synods; they executed ecclesiastical jurisdiction as in a court of law and gave sentence from which there was no appeal.[11] They had well-filled seminaries which, according to the Established Church, allowed them to evade having to take the Oath of Abjuration. Convocation complained that despite government censorship, Scottish Presbyterians published papers and pamphlets; in particular they had the Solemn League and Covenant and the Directory of Worship reprinted and circulated. No wonder all this grated on Convocation, for such behaviour would be considered a violation of *Praemunire* if any member of the Established Church so acted.[12] In this context, the Test Act was the only obstacle preventing Presbyterians from taking over the corporations and civil offices.[13]

Symbolically, indeed, Scottish Presbyterians had taken root in Ulster, as they had built meeting-houses 'in the form of churches' in many towns and cities and often not far from the cathedrals.[14] On its own evidence, Convocation betrayed a real fear that Scottish Presbyterians had the potential and desire to destabilise the Established Church.[15] And although the conditions for such an event did not really exist in Ireland at this time, the fear that what had happened in Scotland could occur in Ireland was enough to create alarm. It was disconcerting to be faced with the evident growth of Scottish Presbyterianism in the north of Ireland, the fruit of consistent and persistent adherence to church order, discipline and worship since the Interregnum.

Such strong criticism of Presbyterians in general on the part of the Established Church had to be countered, and so two addresses were sent to the queen, one from the Scottish Presbyterians and another from Presbyterians in Dublin and the south of Ireland. In each address the development of the churches can be perceived, as well as their differing contexts and traditions. The tone of the Scottish Presbyterian document was confident and strong.[16] Each point raised by the Established Church, in either the address from the House of Lords or the *Representation* from Convocation, was answered directly and shrewdly.

For example, aware of the position that Daniel Williams held in London as an English Presbyterian, the address pointed out that Williams had been minister in Drogheda. When he went to Dublin in 1667 he was succeeded by Mr Toy, who stayed there until 1688.[17] After the revolution, and in response to a request from the 'remains of that congregation', Scottish Presbyterians sent a minister to Drogheda.[18] Thus it was not a new area of ministry, but a continuation of one that had been interrupted by the war.[19] With regard to new congregations, ministers were sent to new places only at the request of the people; and new calls were a direct consequence of the war, when lands were taken by new families who wanted their ministers to settle with them in the new areas. In fact Scottish Presbyterians had been responding to calls from congregations since 1660, but because their organisation was secret in these earlier years this was unknown.[20]

Convocation had accused Scottish Presbyterians of harassing members of the Established Church. While accepting the fact on a small scale, Scottish Presbyterians argued that differing theologies meant inevitable indiscretions by 'some few of the meaner sort . . . while the clergy were performing the office for the burial of the dead, which practice is not approved by us'.[21] On the other hand, they complained that Scottish Presbyterians were harassed by the Established Church: leases were not renewed; in some cases leases had conditions, forbidding either the building of meeting-houses or the maintenance of those already built. They were forbidden to marry according to their own rites, nor did they have power over corporations, since this was claimed by the Established Church. They also denied that the Oath of Abjuration was an issue, for most took it; those who did not declared that their refusal was due to 'their scrupling some expression only, not the substance of the oath'.[22]

Most of all, the Sacramental Test was deeply resented, being so linked to the ceremonies of the Established Church. Their refusal to take the Oath of Allegiance was connected with this, for by taking the oath they could be forced to take the Test, or sent abroad without any guarantee of religious support within their tradition.[23] However, they denied that they had their own seminaries to train ministers; candidates had to be sent abroad to prepare for ministry. While there were a few schools (since 1660), they had nothing nearly sufficient for their needs. They denied that they had used the *regium donum* in any improper way, or that ministers took the Solemn League and Covenant at ordination.[24]

In their address the Scottish Presbyterians particularly defended their right to hold synods, arguing that they were for the good of the church, to preserve order and correct scandals. 'These meetings are commonly called synods and judicatories being so termed in these churches where they have civil sanction.' Since such were established by parliament in England, Scottish Presbyterians hoped for similar understanding in Ireland.[25] Indeed, on account of their being settled in Ireland for over a hundred years, and in view of their record in serving the crown, they asked for freedom and toleration to exercise their religion, without the imposition of the Sacramental Test.[26]

Central to the whole issue was the rejection of the model of episcopacy in the Established Church. Knowing this was insurmountable, Scottish Presbyterians asked for:

> mutual forbearance . . . with a spirit of moderation, free from all bitter invectives . . . being cordially agreed with all the Reformed churches at home and abroad in all doctrines held in common and in all that is essential to the Reformation.[27]

In other words, they asked to be accepted as a separate church, in its own right, fully within the Reformation tradition. But there was no possibility either theologically, economically or politically that this could be acceptable to the Established Church. In its eyes Scottish Presbyterians had to remain a sect and be led to conformity.[28] Only in this way could it be contained and controlled. They were too strong a body in the early eighteenth century to be trusted with toleration and freedom from the Sacramental Test.

Scottish Presbyterians also defended their own colleagues in Dublin, pointing out that it was a Dublin presbytery which had initiated the process leading to Thomas Emlin's removal from Dublin.[29] They also singled out the Independents, who were called heretics by Convocation, terming them 'sound Protestants . . . agreeing with the Established Church in the substance of her doctrinal articles and in all the fundamental points of Reformed Christianity'. And regarding their own relations with the Independents, they pointed out that

> the difference between us and them is so inconsiderable that there is not any minister commonly reputed to be of that persuasion but who cheerfully owns himself a member of some presbytery and who does not cordially join with us in the substance of our confession of faith.[30]

The Established Church had accused all Protestant dissenters of active hostility and in so doing had offended the English Presbyterians and Independents in Dublin and the south of Ireland. These made a separate representation to the queen,[31] quite different in tone and content from that of the Scottish Presbyterians. It was one of disappointment, for English Presbyterians and Independents considered they had enjoyed reasonably good relations with the Established Church.[32] Most of Convocation's criticisms simply did not apply to them: ill-treatment of members of the Established Church; ruining those who conformed; employing apprentices on certain conditions; filling corporations with their own members; imposing public penance on those who married according to the rites of the Established Church.

English Presbyterians and Independents could not be identified with Scottish Presbyterians, either in numbers, tradition or practice.[33] However, they insisted that all three dissenting traditions rejected bishops as anti-scriptural. For them bishops

and presbyters were one, not distinct orders; yet, contrary to the
Scottish Presbyterians, the dissenting ministers in Dublin and
the south refused to enter into conflict 'with the present episcopacy as it is part of the legal constitution or with those laws by
which it is established'.[34] In other words, they obeyed the law
of the land and conformed to the requirements of the Established
Church. In this context, they denied that they had called the
Established Church idolatrous or superstitious. Nevertheless,
Boyse had entered into prolonged conflict regarding the office
and order of episcopacy from at least 1687, and this debate was
carried on in Dublin and in the north of Ireland.

Clearly there was a split in their stance: in theory they did
not accept episcopacy as represented in the Established Church;
in practice they obeyed it as the lawful church of the land. It
gave them some latitude and the possibility of coexistence in the
country, but that their representation to the queen had to be so
muted and even neutered indicates the weakening position of
the English Presbyterians and Independents at this time. With
regard to new congregations, they explained that these were formed
only on request and were very few:

> And as those new congregations are few (not exceeding three or four
> in the three Provinces of Leinster, Munster and Connaght) so they were
> wholly occasioned by new families of Protestant dissenters fixing their
> habitation in such places.[35]

Such a statement from the English Presbyterians and Independents showed how unfounded the fears of the Established Church
were in their regard and how different in size and impact they
were from their colleagues in the north of Ireland. In its formal
Representation the Established Church considered all Protestant
dissenters of the Presbyterian/Independent traditions as one,
either to make their case sound even more alarmist or out of
actual ignorance.

The most trenchant criticism of the Established Church was
reserved for the Quakers. Whatever about the various Presby-
terian/Independent traditions in Ireland, they at least held some
basic beliefs and practices of Christianity in common with the
Established Church. But Quakers had gone beyond these boundaries and thereby put themselves outside the received tradition.

Since they had rejected the sacraments of baptism and the Lord's Supper, they were deemed to be no longer Christians; they rejected ecclesiastical authority and the authority of scripture and 'allow no Christ except that within them'.[36]

To the Established Church the Quakers, freed from the constraints of external religion, were able to band together and promote their common economic interests. Under the guise of annual and quarterly meetings Quakers set rates for goods and the rise and fall of commodities; the Established Church resented that Quakers were 'exempted from all those legal services both troublesome and chargeable to which those of our communion are liable'[37] and so were able to pursue gain unrestrainedly. With their agents in Ireland and England, they were able to anticipate anything that could affect them adversely. They were wealthier than any other religious tradition in Ireland, by common contributions, and so they were able to win exemptions and privileges. Since they were not pressurised to take oaths, many were attracted to join them.[38] All this apparent lack of religious belief and practice, linked with growing wealth and freedom, made the Quakers seem a real threat to the fabric of a Christian society. If allowed to prosper in Ireland, this would surely lead to infidelity and atheism.

The Quakers made no formal response to this trenchant condemnation of their beliefs and practices. Unlike the Presbyterians and Independents, they did not have a tradition of formal, public representation of their grievances to the monarch or the government. Rather they tended to use, as the Established Church pointed out, agents and contacts close to the monarch or government, a procedure developed by Fox and Penn.[39] However, the accusations of the Established Church underlined the steady growth of the Quakers as a strong, cohesive body in Ireland. Whatever interpretation was put on their structures and way of life, they had reached a place in Ireland which was specifically their own. It was similar to what the Scottish Presbyterians had achieved in the north of Ireland. Through organised meetings, discipline, worship and way of life, they had established themselves as a strong, if small, religious and economic force in the country.

The *Representation* served to outline the concerns of the Established

Church at this time; it had little practical effect on Protestant dissenters in Ireland. Debates continued, particularly between McBride/Kirkpatrick and Tisdall, but no further legislation was enacted against dissenters until 1714, when the *regium donum* was suspended (though renewed in 1715, after the accession of George I). There was a short period when the Tory ministry in Whitehall planned to extend the English Schism Bill to Ireland, but this collapsed in 1714 on the death of Queen Anne.[40] Indeed, by its criticism of the Quakers and the different Presbyterian and Independent traditions in Ireland, in particular the Scottish Presbyterians in the north, the Established Church acknowledged the position these groups had achieved in Ireland.[41]

From being small, hesitant groups in the mid-seventeenth century, Quakers, Independents and English Presbyterians had become rooted in the country by the turn of the century; Scottish Presbyterians had a longer history in the country, and after the initial setbacks under Strafford and Bramhall and later under Fleetwood, they rooted themselves slowly in the north and in a few places in the south of Ireland. In particular the Quakers and Scottish Presbyterians exercised firm discipline and organisation which enabled them to develop in a consistent and coherent way, to such a degree that it was basically these two groups which drew the greatest criticism from the Established Church in 1711.

English Presbyterians and Independents, however, were different. This was due partly to numbers, especially of the Independents, and partly to theology.[42] Whereas Scottish Presbyterians worked for some form of religious toleration, English Presbyterians in Ireland were hopeful of some form of accommodation within the Established Church, though they wanted to be themselves recognised as a church, separate and authentic.[43] Besides, with such small numbers, there was a great deal of overlap between Independents and English Presbyterians in Dublin and the south of Ireland. With so few churches they learned to exchange ministers, to co-operate with one another, and in practice English Presbyterians in Ireland were Independent churches.

It is evident that each of the four dissenting groups, Quakers, Independents, English and Scottish Presbyterians, rooted themselves in the country, and through controversies both within and between one another reached some clarity and definition about themselves. They developed a form of life, worship, discipline and theology within each of their traditions. And in addition to this, both the Scottish Presbyterians and the Quakers developed detailed organisational structures which they executed consistently. Lived sometimes from conviction and sometimes from social/internal pressure, such structures enabled the Scottish Presbyterians and the Quakers to become strong cohesive bodies in the country. Moreover, the political implications of a strong Scottish Presbyterian church in Ireland were very great for the government and for the Established Church in Ireland. On this point the Quakers differed, for they neither had the numbers to warrant any danger nor did they aspire to political power.

On the other hand, the English Presbyterians and Independents did not have the same approach to church order and structure. English Presbyterians hoped to be accommodated, as a church in its own right, within the Established Church. Theirs was the tradition of Ussher and Baxter, of moderate episcopacy within a spirit of wide comprehension. By the same token, they hoped for some form of agreement with the Independents and several times came very near to it in England. Certainly Samuel Mather was willing to work towards this; both churches recognised that they had to work together in Ireland anyway and mutually support one another. At the level of practice, they managed to reach consensus; at the level of theology, differences which lay under the surface needed only a different context for them to emerge into the open.

The period 1660-1714 was a highly formative, refining and defining time for the Quakers, Independents, Scottish and English Presbyterians in Ireland. In varying degrees of strength and influence, each of them witnessed to diverse forms of religious belief and practice in Ireland at that time. The pattern of this belief and practice gradually became more clearly perceived and articulated, and contributed to the formation and tradition of Protestant dissent in Ireland.

Notes and References

1   *A representation of the present state of religion with regard to infidelity, heresy, impiety and popery, drawn up and agreed by both houses of Convocation in Ireland* ([Dublin, 1711]).

2   T.C.D., MS 1062, ff 70v, 393, 451, 669. In 1703 the Irish bishops asked the queen for permission to meet, and after some time (to discover precedent and procedure) this was granted (B.L., Add. MS 36771, ff 1, 3, 15, 31); J.I. McGuire, 'Government attitudes to religious nonconformity in Ireland, 1660-1719' in C. E. J. Caldicott, Hugh Gough and J. P. Pittion (ed.), *The Huguenots and Ireland: anatomy of an emigration* (Dublin, 1987), p. 267.

3   *A representation of the present state of religion,* pp 7, 14.

4   R. D. Edwards, 'The history of the laws against Protestant nonconformists in Ireland from the Restoration (1660) to the Declaration of Indulgence (1687)'(M.A. thesis, U.C.D., 1932), p. 23.

5   'Representation of the Lords Spiritual and Temporal in parliament' (N.L.S., Wodrow MSS, Folio 35, no. 109; P.R.O.N.I., T525, no. 24); 7 Nov. 1711, ii, 1703-25. In 1708 the Presbyterians in the north of Ireland petitioned the Lord Lieutenant and Council (N.L.S., Wodrow MSS, Folio 51, no. 48; P.R.O.N.I., T525, no. 48).

6   Richard Choppin to Thomas Steward, 8 July 1712 (Magee College, MS 46, ff 142-3); Witherow, *Historic memorials,* pp 175-7, 324-7.

7   'Representation of the Lords Spiritual and Temporal'.

8   N.L.S., Wodrow MSS, Folio 35, nos 72-74; Folio, 26, no. 190; Bodl., Rawlinson MS, C. 984, f. 169 (*Anal. Hib.*, no. 2 (1931), pp 40-2); H.M.C., *Portland MSS,* v, 339-40; Beckett, *Protestant dissent in Ireland,* pp 54-58; Thomas Gogarty (ed.), *Council book of the Corporation of Drogheda,* 2 vols (repr., Cork, 1988), i, 302-3; David Nokes, *Jonathan Swift* (Oxford, 1985), p. 93.

9   'Representation of the Lords Spiritual and Temporal'. Both Representations asked that the *regium donum* be discontinued.

10 *A representation of the present state of religion,* p. 9.

11 John McBride's sermon in 1698 was well known, in which he had outlined the rights and duties of church assemblies. McBride, *A sermon preached before the provincial synod at Antrim, June 1 1698* (n.p., 1698), pp 7-15; Lambeth Palace, Gibson Papers, MS 930, f. 200; Petition of the Bishop of Down and Connor to the Lords Justices of Ireland (P.R.O.N.I., T525, no. 12).

12 Theo Harrison to John Strype, 16 July 1698 (U.L.C., Baum. Papers, Add. 5, f.251).

13 *A representation of the present state of religion,* pp 10-11; 19 Feb. 1704 (N.L.S., MS 3740, f. 175); 7 July 1704 (ibid., Wodrow MSS, Folio 26, no. 186); John McBride to Robert Wodrow, 2 Apr. 1709 (ibid., no. 190).

14 *A representation of the present state of religion,* p. 11.

15 Ibid., pp 12-13.

16 *The humble address and apology of the Presbyterian ministers and gentlemen on behalf of themselves and the rest of their persuasion in the north of Ireland* (n.p., 1711). Francis Iredell was sent to London with the *Humble address* and with detailed instructions. Witherow, *Historic memorials,* pp 151-4.

17 Toy went to Dublin in 1688. New Row Baptismal Register, f. 11. He signed and approved Boyse's *Sacramental hymns* in 1693. He had been in Dublin before his appointment to Drogheda. Bodl. Carte MS 45, f. 295.

18 *The humble address . . . north of Ireland*, p. 21.

19 The port towns of Derry, Portrush, Larne and Belfast were controlled by Presbyterians; a move to Drogheda, within that context, was viewed with suspicion. R.J. Dickson, *Ulster emigration to colonial America, 1718-95* (London, 1966), p. 4.

20 Laggan minutes, pp 1-2, 15, 50-1, 107 and *passim*; Antrim minutes, pp 169, 305, 398; N.L.S., Wodrow MSS, Folio 26, nos 121-2.

21 *The humble address . . . north of Ireland*, pp 22-3, 25.

22 Ibid., pp 22-4.

23 Ibid., pp 35-6.

24 Ibid, pp 26-7, 32-3.

25 Ibid., p. 28.

26 Ibid., pp 29, 37.

27 Ibid., p. 24.

28 Convocation wanted to send a letter to dissenters in 1709 'earnestly inviting them to unite with us and to declare on what terms they would be willing to join with us' Harrison to Strype, 14 Sept 1709 (U.L.C., Baum. Papers, Add. 5, f. 174).

29 *The humble address . . . north of Ireland*, p. 31.

30 Ibid., p. 32.

31 *The humble address of the Protestant dissenting ministers of Dublin and the south of Ireland* (n.p., 1711). This was signed by: Nathaniel Weld, Independent minister from New Row; Joseph Boyse, English Presbyterian minister from Wood Street; Richard Choppin, also from Wood Street; Alexander Sinclair, Scottish Presbyterian from Plunkett Street (originally Bull Alley); Ralph Norris, English Presbyterian minister from Cooke Street; Thomas Steward, also of Cooke Street.

32 Ibid., p. 40.

33 Ibid., pp 41-2.

34 Ibid., p. 43.

35 Ibid., p. 44

36 *A representation of the present state of religion*, p. 8.

37 Richard Caulfield (ed.), *Council book of the Corporation of Cork from 1609-1643 and 1690-1800* (Guildford, 1876), p. 306: 13 Mar. 1703. Richard Pike, son of Joseph Pike, asked to be dispensed from oaths. In view of 'several services done to this city (by his father, Joseph Pike and father-in-law Francis Rogers), Richard Pike junior is admitted free of this city as others of his religion and the oaths dispensed with'.

38 *A representation of the present state of religion*, p. 9.

39 Before 1660 Quakers did make representations to parliament. See *A narrative of the cruel and unjust sufferings of the people . . . in Ireland called Quakers* (London, 1659).

40 McGuire, 'Government attitudes to religious nonconformity', pp 274-6; Beckett, *Protestant dissent*, pp 58-63.

41   The *Representation* also dealt with the Huguenots (briefly) and Roman
      Catholics, pp 13, 15-17.
42   In 1695 Boyse said of the Independents that there were 'but six congrega-
      tions that I know of in the kingdom', whereas the English Presbyterians
      had seventeen congregations in five presbyteries. Boyse, *The case of the dissen-
      ting Protestants of Ireland* ([Dublin], 1695), p. 2; Irwin, *History of Presbyterianism.*
43   Joseph Boyse, *Sermon before the societies for the reformation of manners, Jan 6 1697*,
      p. 368.

Bibliography

Manuscript Sources

ARMAGH

Robinson Library

Dopping Papers

BELFAST

Public Record Office of Northern Ireland

D/1759/1A/1	Transcripts of the minutes of the Antrim Meeting, 1664-58
D/1759/1A/2	Transcripts of the minutes of the Antrim Meeting, 1671-91
D/1759/1E/1	Transcripts of the minutes of the Laggan Meeting, 1672-9
D/1759/1E/2	Transcripts of the minutes of the Laggan Meeting, ii, 1679-95, 1672-1700
CR4/12/B/1	Templepatrick Session Book, 1646-1743
T1062/45	Lurgan Men's Meeting, 1678-89
T780	Extracts from the Commonwealth and Carte Manuscripts
T525	Transcripts of the Wodrow Manuscripts (selected)
T2954/1/1-10	Pomeroy Papers
Mic. 1P/159/6	Session minutes and discipline, Lisburn Presbyterian Church, County Antrim, 1688-1709

Union Theological College
Burt Kirk Session Minutes, 1676-1719

Presbyterian Church in Ireland Historical Society Library
Agadowey Session Book, 1702-61
Carnmoney Session Register, 1686-1748
Connor Session Minutes, 1693-1735
Dundonald (Kirkdonald) Session Book, 1678-1716
Rev. James Alexander, book of sermons, Convoy 1678-1704
Diary of John Cook, 1696-1705

CAMBRIDGE

University Library

Baumgartner Papers	Strype Correspondence
Add. MS 711	Notebook of Anthony Dopping
Mm vi 49	Letter of Bonnell re Quakers, 1690

DUBLIN

Trinity College

MS 556	Acta de Synodo Ecclesiae, 1707-8
MS 562	Visitation Book of Dives Downes
MSS 668/1-668/3	Convocation, 1703-4
MS 750	William King's Letter Book, 1696-8
MS 750/2	Letters of William King, 1698-9 (microfilm)
MS 750/12	Letters of William King, 1699-1703
MS 808	General Convention, 1660
MS 865	William King's treatise on church government
MS 1038	Acts of the Irish Convocation, 1661-3, 1665-6
MS 1062	Convocation, from 1704 (Bishop Reeves Collection)
MSS 1995-2008	Correspondence of William King
MS 2203	Misc. Autographs, 59 Protection for Quakers
MS 2929	Transcripts of the Baumgartner Papers

Marsh's Library

MS Z 1.1.13	The case of the people called Quakers
MS Z 4.2.17	Dopping to Wetenhall, 1696
MS Z.3.1.1	Complaints against Samuel Winter
MS Z 4.4.8	Letters of Robert Boyle to Marsh

National Library of Ireland

MS 4201	Book of sermons, 1667-87

National Archives

RC 6/2-3   Records of the Irish Record Commissioners, 1810-30

Representative Church Body Library

MS Gg. 2/7/3/20	Seymour Manuscript
MS Gg 2/7/3/27	Inquisition, Down and Connor, 1657
MS Libr. 14	Vestry book of St Katherine and St James, Dublin, from 1657
MS J. 7	Survey of Killaloe, Edward Worth, 1661
MS Libr./23A	Visitation of Ossory, 1679
MS P 327/3/1	St Bride's, St Michael le Pole's and St Stephen's Vestry Acts, 1662-1742

Friends' Library

Half Y.M. A 10	Half-Yearly Meetings, from 1676
Half Y.M. A 11	Appendix: Paper of William Edmundson on mixed marriages
MM II A1	Men's Meeting, Dublin, from 1677
MM II F1	Testimonies of denial and condemnation, 1662-1722
MM III F1	Testimony of a general meeting, Munster
MM IV M2	Moate Meeting
MM V G1	Mountmellick Monthly Meeting
QM I C1	Half-Yearly Meetings, 1692-1710
QM II F1	Testimonies of disunity
QM II Z1	Summary of the Proceedings of Several Half-Year's Meetings held in Dulin for . . . Ireland, 1704
YM F1	The Names of Friends Deceased . . . Ireland
YM G1	National Sufferings, 1655-93
Sharp MSS	
A. 29/35	A Record of the Testimonies . . . of Quakers

Unitarian Church, St Stephen's Green West

Registers, Eustace Street Congregation: New Row Baptismal Register, 1653-1737

EDINBURGH

National Library of Scotland

Wodrow MSS	Folio, Quarto, Octavo series
MS 3740	Unrest in the north of Ireland, 1704

LONDON

Lambeth Palace Library
MSS 929, 930, 942   Gibson Papers

Dr Williams's Library
MS 24. 67   Letters re Daniel Williams, Nathaniel Mather
MSS Letters of Richard Baxter

Friends' Library

Caton MSS	Transcripts ii
Spence MSS	Transcripts iii
A. R. Barclay MSS	Transcripts
Swarthmore MSS	Transcripts ii, vii

British Library

Lansdowne MS 446	Commission for Down and Connor, 1693
Lansdowne MSS 821-3	Correspondence to Henry Cromwell, 1655-9
Lansdowne MS 1152a	Sottish rebels in Ireland, 1684-5
Lansdowne MS 1228	Proposals/addresses of ministers, 1658
Egerton MS 1762	Congregational churches in Dublin, 1654-5
Egerton MS 2168	Letters and papers of William Penn
Egerton MS 2429	William Penn's address to James II
Sloane MS 2902	Papers of Abraham Hill, 1697
Add. MS 4763	State of Derry diocese, 1670
Add. MS 4815	List of members of Lower House of Convocation, 1704
Add. MS 6117	Irish bishops, 1703
Add. MS 19833	Civil List, 1654
Add. MS 32471	Instructions for Sir John Clotworthy and William Ashton, 30 March 1660
Add. MS/34777	Resolutions of Convocation, 1711
Add. MS 36771	Irish Convocation, 1703
Add. MS 39318	To Friends in Ireland . . . T. Upsher, Dublin 1699

Stowe MSS 200, 202, 204, 206, 207, 208, 210, 211, 212, 228 Material concerning political and ecclesiastical affairs in seventeenth-century Ireland

LONDONDERRY

Magee College Library
MS 46   Correspondence of Thomas Stewart, 1699-1749
MS 29   (Kinnear MS) Sermons, 1658-1704

OXFORD

Bodleian Library
Carte MSS
Rawlinson MSS
Clarendon MSS

Printed Sources

PRINTED COLLECTIONS

Acts of the General Assemblies of the Church of Scotland, 1638-49 (Edinburgh, 1691)
An act for keeping and celebrating the 23rd day of October as an anniversary of thanksgiving, 27 Sept. 1662
The agreement and resolution of several associated ministers in the county of Cork for the ordaining of ministers (Cork, 1657)
The agreement and resolution of the ministers of Christ associated within the city of Dublin and province of Leinster (Dublin, 1659)
Airey, Osmund (ed.), *Essex Papers*, Camden Society, new series, xlvii, 167-79 (London, 1890)
Analecta Hibernicae, ii (Jan. 1931) (Bodl. Rawlinson MS c 984)
Athenae Oxonienses, ed. Philip Bliss, 4 vols (London, 1813-20)
Book of Common Prayer and ceremonies of the church (Dublin, 1668)
Book of Common Prayer with 1634 and 1711 canons (Dublin, 1795)
Berwick, Edward (ed.), *Rawdon Papers* (London, 1819)
Biographies of Quakers (Friends' Library, London)
Birch, Thomas (ed.), *A collection of the state papers of John Thurloe*, 7 vols (London, 1742)
Brady, John (ed.), 'Remedies proposed for the Church of Ireland (1697)' in *Archivium Hibernicum, xxii* (1959)
Bullingbroke, Edward, *Ecclesiastical law, statutes, constitutions and canons of the Church of Ireland*, 2 vols (Dublin, 1770)
Burke, Bernard, *A genealogical history of the dormant . . . and extinct peerages of the British Empire* (London, 1883)
Burtchaell, G.D., and Sadleir, T.U., *Alumni Dublinensis: a register of students [etc.] of Trinity College, Dublin* (2nd ed., Dublin, 1935)
Calendar of ancient records of Dublin, in the possession of the municipal corporation, ed. Sir J. T. and Lady Gilbert, 19 vols (Dublin, 1889-1944)
Caulfield, Richard (ed.), *Council Book of the Corporation of Cork from 1609-1643 and 1690-1800* (Guildford, 1876)
A collection of letters, consisting of ninety-three, sixty-one of which were written by . . . James Renwick (Edinburgh, 1764)

Constitution and canons of the Church of Ireland, 1634
Convention of Ireland, 1660
Correspondence of Robert Wodrow, ed. Thomas McCrie, 3 vols (Edinburgh, 1842-3)
Cotton, Henry, *Fasti Ecclesiae Hibernicae*, 6 vols (Dublin, 1845-78)
Declaration of the Presbytery of Bangor, 7 July 1649
Directions for preachers 1662 (repr. 1685)
Dunlop, R. T. (ed.), *Ireland under the Commonwealth, 1651-59*, 2 vols, (Manchester, 1913)
Eustace, P. B., and Goodbody, O. C., *Quaker records, Dublin: abstract of wills*, I.M.C. (Dublin, 1957)
The form of church government to be used in the Church of England and Ireland, 29 August 1648
Fox, George, *Journal*, 2 vols (London, 1901)
From our Half-Yearly Meeting held in Dublin, 9, 10, 11 Sept. 1691
Gogarty, Thomas (ed.), *Council Book of the Corporation of Drogheda*, 2 vols (repr., Cork, 1988)
Goodbody, O. C., *Guide to Irish Quaker records, 1654-1860*, I.M.C. (Dublin, 1967)
Grubb, Isobel, *Friends' books in Marsh's Library, Dublin* (Friends' Library, London)
Historical Manuscripts Commission:
  2nd, 4th, 6th Reports
  Hastings, ii
  Egmont, ii
  Portland, iii, v
  Buccleuch and Queensbury, ii
  Ormonde, i, ii, iv, v, vi, vii
Hanly, John (ed.), *The letters of Oliver Plunkett, 1625-1661* (Dublin, 1979)
Hill, George (ed.), *The Montgomery Manuscripts, 1603-1706* (Belfast, 1859)
Humble address and apology of the Presbyterian ministers and gentlemen . . . in the north of Ireland (1711)
Humble address of the Protestant dissenting ministers of Dublin and the south of Ireland (1711)
Ivimey, Joseph, *History of the English Baptists*, 2 vols (London, 1811)
Keeble, N. H. and Nuttall, G. F., *Calendar of the correspondence of Richard Baxter*, 2 vols (Oxford, 1991)
Latimer, W. T., 'The old session book of Templepatrick Presbyterian Church' in *R.S.A.I. Jn.*, xxv (1895); xxxi (1901)
McConnell, James, *Fasti of the Irish Presbyterian Church, 1613-1840*, revised by S. G. McConnell (Belfast, 1951)
MacLysaght, Edward (ed.), *Calendar of the Orrery state papers*, I.M.C. (Dublin, 1941)

McNeill, Charles (ed.), *The Tanner Letters,* I.M.C. (Dublin, 1943)

Mathews, A.G., *Calamy Revised* (Oxford, 1934)

'The Mather Papers' in *Collections of the Massachusetts Historical Society,* viii, 4th series (Boston, 1868)

Moody, T. W., and Simms, J. G. (ed.), *The bishopric of Derry and the Irish Society of London, 1602-1705,* 2 vols, I.M.C. (Dublin, 1968, 1983)

Morrice, Thomas, *Collections of the state papers of the 1st Earl of Orrery,* 2 vols (Dublin, 1743)

A narrative of the cruel and unjust sufferings of the people . . . in Ireland called Quakers (London, 1659)

The National Covenant and Solemn League and Covenant . . . renewed at Lesmahego, 3 March 1688

A necessary representation of the present evils and dangers to religion, laws and liberties. Presbytery at Belfast, 1649 (n.p., 1649)

News from Ireland (London, 1650)

Nuttall, G.F. (ed.), *Early Quaker letters* (London, 1952)

Observations upon the articles of peace . . . representation of the Presbytery at Belfast

Penn, William, *The papers of William Penn,* ed. Mary Maples Dunn and Richard Dunn, 5 vols (Pennsylvania, 1981)

The registers of the Privy Council of Scotland, 3rd series

Records of the General Synod of Ulster, 1691-1820, 3 vols (Belfast, 1890-98)

A representation of the present state of religion [Dublin, 1711]

Russell, C. W., and Prendergast, J. P., *The Carte MSS in the Bodleian Library, Oxford: a report* (London, 1871)

Scott, Hew, *Fasti Ecclesiae Scotianae,* 7 vols (Edinburgh, 1920)

Singer, S. W. *The correspondence of Henry Hyde, Earl of Clarendon,* 2 vols (London, 1828)

A testimony of tender advice and counsel . . . Half-Yearly Meeting (Dublin, 1688)

A true and exact copy of . . . the fanatics' New Covenant . . . taken from Donald Cargill at Queensferry, June 3 1680 (repr., Dublin, 1680)

Tudor and Stuart proclamations, calendared by Robert Steele, 2 vols (Oxford, 1910)

The visitation of the rebellious nation of Ireland and a warning from the Lord proclaimed, F[rancis] H[owgill], E[dmund] B[urrough] (London 1656)

Warner, G. F. (ed.), *The Nicholas Papers,* Camden Society, 4 vols (London, 1920)

Wood, Herbert (ed.), *The parish registers of St Catherine's, Dublin, 1636-1715,* Parish Register Society of Dublin, v (Exeter/London, 1908)

CONTEMPORARY/NEAR CONTEMPORARY WRITINGS

Adair, Patrick, *A true narrative . . . of the Presbyterian Church in Ireland (1623-1570)*, with introduction and notes by W. D. Killen (Belfast, 1866)

Baily, John, *To my loving and dearly beloved Christian friends in and about Limerick, 8 May 1684* (n.p.)

Barcroft, John, *A faithful warning to . . . Great Britain and Ireland* (Dublin, 1720)

_____ *A brief narrative of the life of John Barcroft* (Dublin, 1730)

Barry, James, *A reviving cordial* (London, 1699)

_____ *The doctrine of particular election asserted* (n.p., 1715)

Baxter, Richard, *The Quakers' catechism* (London, 1655)

_____ *The true history of councils enlarged and defended* (London, 1682)

_____ *The second part against the schism, being animadversions on a book famed to be Mr Ralphson's* (London, 1684).

_____ *Reliquae Baxterianae*, ed. Mathew Sylvester (London, 1696)

_____ *The certainty of the world's spirits* (London, 1691).

Bernard, Nicholas, *The farewell sermons* (London, 1651).

_____ *The judgement of the late Archbishop of Armagh* (2nd ed., London, 1659)

_____ *Clavi trabales, or nails fastened by some great masters* (London, 1661)

Berry, Richard, *A sermon on the Epiphany* (Dublin, 1672).

Besse, Joseph, *A collection of the sufferings of the people called Quakers*, 2 vols (London, 1753).

Blackwood, Christopher, *The storming of Antichrist* (London, 1644).

Boyse, Joseph, *Works*, 2 vols (London, 1728).

_____ *Vindicae Calvinisticae, or some impartial reflections* (Dublin, 1687).

_____ *Sacramental hymns* (Dublin, 1693)

_____ *Remarks on a late discourse of William, Lord Bishop of Derry* (n.p., [1694])

_____ *A vindication of the remarks on the Bishop of Derry's discourse* (n.p., [1695])

_____ *The case of the Protestant dissenters of Ireland . . . represented and argued* ([Dublin, 1695])

_____ *The case of dissenting Protestants of Ireland . . . vindicated from the exceptions alleged against it* ([Dublin], 1695)

_____ *The difference between Mr E[mlin] and the Protestant dissenting ministers of Dublin* (n.p., 1702)

_____ *A vindication of the true deity of our blessed Saviour* (Dublin, 1703)

_____ *A sermon on the death of . . . Elias Travers* (Dublin, 1705).

_____ *The office of a scriptural bishop* (Dublin, 1709)

_____ *A clear account of the ancient episcopacy* (London, 1712)

_____ *Remarks on a pamphlet published by William Tisdall* (n.p., 1716)

_____ *A true narrative of the proceedings of the dissenting ministers of Dublin against Mr Thomas Emlin* (London, 1719)

Bramhall, John, *A fair warning to take heed of the Scottish discipline* (n.p., 1649)

_____ *A sermon preached 23rd April 1661* (Dublin, 1661)

_____ *Works,* ed., John Vesey (Dublin, 1676)

Brewster, Francis, *A discourse concerning Ireland* (n.p., 1697/8)

Browne, Peter, *The doctrine of parts and circumstances* (Dublin, 1715)

Bruce, Michael, *The rattling of the dry bones* (n.p., 1672)

_____ *Six dreadful alarms* (Edinburgh, 1675)

Burnyeat, John, and Watson, John, *The holy truth . . . defended* (Dublin, 1688)

Burnyeat, John, *The truth exalted* (London, 1691)

Burrough, Edmund, *To the churches of Christ in Ireland* (n.p., 1656)

_____ *To you that are called Anabaptists in Ireland* (n.p., 1657)

_____ *A vindication of the . . . Quakers* (London, 1660)

_____ *The everlasting gospel of repentance* (London,[1660])

_____ *The memorable works of a son of thunder and consolation* (London, 1672)

Burston, Daniel, *The evangelist evangelising* (Dublin, 1662)

_____ *Christ's last call* (Dublin, 1666)

Calamy, Edmund, *A funeral sermon preached upon the [death] of Mrs Elizabeth Williams* (London, 1698)

_____ *An historical account of my own life, with some reflections on the times I have lived in, 1671-1731,* 2 vols (London, 1830)

_____ *An account of the ministers . . . who were ejected or silenced after the Restoration in 1660* (n.p., 1713)

_____ *A continuation of the account,* 2 vols (London, 1727)

_____ *Memoirs of the late . . . Mr John Howe* (London, 1734)

Calderwood, David, *The history of the Kirk of Scotland,* 7 vols (Edinburgh, 1849)

Campbell, John, *Mr Campbell's letter to a parishioner* (Belfast, 1711)

Campbell, Richard, *A directory of prayer* (London, 1696)

Chambers (Chambre), Robert, *An explanation of the Shorter Catechism of the Reverend Assembly of Divines* (Dublin, 1679)

_____ *The Church of England defended, with the dissenting reply, or cases of conscience proposed to the dissenting ministers of Dublin* (Dublin, 1709)

Cooke, Edward, *A paper from Quakers showing the wickedness of the young priests lately come over into Ireland* (n.p., [c. 1658]).

Corbet, John, *The ungirding of the Scottish armour* (Dublin, 1639)

Coxe, Samuel, *Two sermons preached at Christchurch, Dublin, beginning the General Convention of Ireland* (Dublin, 1660)

Craghead, Robert, *An answer to a late book* (Edinburgh, 1694)

_____ *Advice to communicants* (Edinburgh, 1695)

_____ *A modest apology occasioned . . . by the Bishop of Derry* (Glasgow, 1696)

_____ *An answer to the Bishop of Derry's second admonition* ([Belfast], 1697)

_____ *Warning and advice both to the secure and doubting* (Edinburgh, 1701)

C[risp], T., *Babel's builders* (London, 1681)

Defoe, Daniel, *Memoirs of the life and eminent conduct of Daniel Williams* (London, 1718)

_____ *The parallel* (Dublin, 1705)

Delemaine, Alexander, *A volume of spiritual epistles: being the copies of several letters written by the last of the two prophets and messengers of God, John Reeve and Ludowick Muggleton* (London, 1820)

Dopping, Anthony, *The case of dissenters of Ireland considered* (Dublin, 1695)

Drury, Edward, *A discourse occasioned by Mr Boyse's ordination sermon entitled 'The office of a scriptural bishop'* (Dublin, 1709)

John Dunton, *The Dublin scuffle* (London, 1699)

Eaton, Samuel, *The Quakers confuted* (London, 1653)

_____ *The perfect pharisee under monkish holiness* (London, [*c.* 1653])

Eccles, Solomon, [Begins] *In the year 1659 . . .*

_____ *Signs are from the Lord* (London, 1663)

_____ *The Quaker's challenge* (London, 1668)

Edmundson, William, *An epistle to Friends 1698*

_____ *An epistle containing wholesome advice and counsel* (n.p., 1701)

_____ *Journal,* (Dublin, 1715)

Emlin, Thomas, *Humble enquiry into the scripture account of the Lord Jesus Christ* (London, 1702)

_____ *A true narrative of the proceedings of the dissenting ministers of Dublin against Mr Thomas Emlin* (London, 1719)

_____ *Works,* 3 vols (London, 1746)

Eyres, Joseph, *The church sleeper awakened* (London, 1659)

Faldo, John, *Quakerism no Christianity* (London, 1673)

Samuel, Foley, *A sermon preached at the primary visitation . . . Dublin* (London, 1683)

_____ *Two sermons preached in . . . 1681, 1682* ([London], 1683)

_____ *An exhortation to the inhabitants of Down and Connor* (Dublin, 1695)

Fox, George, Morris, William, and Perrot, George, *Several warnings to the baptised people* (n.p., 1659)

Fox, George, *The Protestant Christian-Quaker, a sufferer by relics of popery* (London, 1680)

Ann Fowkes, *A Memoir of Mistress Ann Fowkes, née Geale . . . with some recollections of her family, A.D. 1642-1774* (Dublin, 1892)

French, Matthew, *A collection of Mr Boyse's several scurrilous and abusive reflections* (Dublin, 1709)

_____ *Mr Boyse's partiality detected* (Dublin, 1709)

_____ *An examination of Mr Joseph Boyse's postscript* (Dublin, 1709)

_____ *An answer to Joseph Boyse's ordination sermon* (Dublin, 1709)

Fuller, Abraham and Holms, Thomas, *A compendious view of some extraordinary sufferings of the people called Quakers, both in person and in substance, in the kingdom of Ireland, 1655-1731. In three parts.* (Dublin, 1731)

Fuller, Samuel, *A serious reply to twelve sections of abusive queries proposed . . . the Quakers, concluding the works of Joseph Boyse* (Dublin, 1728)

Fuller, Abraham, and Holms, Thomas, *A brief relation of the sufferings of . . . Quakers in Ireland, 1660-1671* (n.p., 1672)

Gilbert, Claudius, *The libertine schooled* (London, 1657)

_____ *A pleasant walk to heaven* (London, 1658)

_____ *A sovereign antidote against sinful errors* (London, 1658)

_____ *A preservative against the change of Religion* (London, 1683)

Gowan, Thomas, *Ars sciendi, sive logica, novo methodo disposita* ([London], 1683)

_____ *Logica elentica* (Dublin, 1683)

_____ *The power of presbyters in ordination and church government* (n.p., 1711)

Hall, Thomas, *A plain and easy explication of the Assembly's Shorter Catechism* (Edinburgh, 1697)

Hamilton, William, *The exemplary life and character of James Bonnell, esq. late accomptant general of Ireland* (London, 1707)

Harrison, Thomas, *Topica sacra* (Kirkbride, 1712)

_____ *Threni Hybernici* (London, 1659)

Henry, Mathew, *Funeral sermon for Mr Burges* (London, 1713)

Hewit, Peter, *A plain answer to . . . William Penn's book against the late Bishop of Cork* (Dublin, 1701)

Heylin, Peter, *Respondet Petrus, or the answer of Peter Heylin to . . . Dr Bernard's book* (London, 1658)

_____ *Aerius redivivus, or the history of the Presbyterians* (London, 1670)

Hollingworth, Richard, *Certain queries modestly propounded to . . . Samuel Eaton and Timothy Taylor* (London, 1646)

Howie, John, *Faithful contendings displayed* (Glasgow, 1780)

_____ *Biographia Scotiana, or a brief historical account of the most eminent Scots worthies* (Glasgow, 1827).

_____ *Sermons delivered in times of persecution in Scotland* (Edinburgh, 1880)

Huntington, William, *The coal heaver's cousin rescued from the bats: the works of James Barry* (London, 1788)

Jenner, Thomas, *Quakerism anatomised and confuted* (n.p., 1670)

Jones, Henry, *A sermon preached at the consecration of Ambrose, Bishop of Kildare* (Dublin, 1667)

_____ *A sermon of Antichrist, preached at . . . Dublin* (Dublin, 1676)

Keith, George, *Some of the many fallacies of Willian Penn* (London, 1699)

King, William, *An answer to the considerations which obliged Peter Manby . . . to embrace . . . the Catholic religion* (Dublin, 1687)

—— *State of the Protestants of Ireland under King James's governnent* (London, 1691)

—— *A discourse concerning the inventions of men* (London, 1694)

—— *An admonition to the dissenting inhabitants . . . of Derry* (London, 1694)

—— *A second admonition to the dissenting inhabitants . . . of Derry* (London, 1696)

Kirkpatrick, James, *An historical essay upon the loyalty of Presbyterians* (n.p., 1713)

[Lambert, Ralph], *An answer to a late pamphlet entitled 'A vindication of marriage . . . by Presbyterians'* (Dublin, 1704)

—— *A serious and humble address to the archbishops and bishops of Ireland* (London, 1705)

Lawrence, Richard, *The interest of Ireland* (Dublin, 1682)

Ladyman, Samuel, *The dangerous rule, or a sermon preached at Clonmel* (London, 1658)

Leslie, Henry, *A discourse of praying in the spirit* (n.p., 1659)

Lightburn, William, *A thanksgiving sermon* (Dublin, 1661)

Livingstone, John, *A brief historical relation of the life of Mr John Livingstone,* ed. Thomas McCrie (Edinburgh, 1848)

Loftus, Dudley, *Proceedings observed* (London, 1661)

[McBride, John], *Animadversions on the defence of the answer to a paper entitled 'The case of the dissenting Protestants'* ([Belfast], 1697)

—— *A sermon preached before the provincial synod of Antrim* (n.p., 1698)

—— *A vindication of marriage as solemnised by presbyterians in the north of Ireland* (n.p., 1702)

—— *A sample of jet-black pr[ela]tick calumny* (Glasgow, 1713)

Manby, Peter, *The considerations which obliged Peter Manby, Dean of Derry, to embrace the Catholic religion* (Dublin, 1687)

Mather, Cotton, *Magnalia Christi Americana, or the ecclesiastical history of New England, from its first planting in 1620 unto 1698* (London, 1702; reprinted 2 vols Hartford, 1683)

Mather, Samuel, *A defence of the Protestant religion against popery* (n.p., 1672)

—— *A testimony from the scriptures against idolatry . . . in two sermons* (Dublin, 1672)

—— *Irenicum, or an essay for union* (London, 1680)

—— *The figures or types of the Old Testament* (n.p., 1683)

Mathews, George, *An account of the trial of . . . Thomas Emlin* (Dublin, 1839)

Mathews, Lemuel, *A pindarique elegy upon the death of Jeremy Taylor* (Dublin, 1667).

Moor, John, *Three discourses concerning transubstantiation, invocation of the saints and angels, worship of images. Some queries offered to the . . . Quakers, particularly those in Queen's County* (Dublin, 1707) (copy held in GPA–Bolton Library, Cashel)

Morris, William, *To the supreme authority . . . the Commons assembled in London* (London, 1659)

_____ *Tithes no gospel ordinance* (n.p., 1680)

Murcot, John, *Several works of John Murcot* (London, 1657)

Parke, James, *The way of God and them that walk in it* (n.p., 1673)

Parr, Richard, *Life of . . . James Ussher* (London, 1686)

Penn, William, *The great case of liberty of conscience . . . defended* (n.p., 1670)

_____ *The new witnesses proved old heretics* (n.p., 1672)

_____ *A defence of a paper entitled 'Gospel truths'* (London, 1698)

_____ *My Irish journal*, ed. Isobel Grubb (London, 1952)

Penn, William, Everett, John, and Story, Thomas, *The Quaker a Christian* (Dublin, 1698)

_____ *Truths further cleared from mistakes* (Dublin, 1698)

Penn, William, Story, Thomas, Sharp, Anthony, and Rook, George, *Gospel truths to clarify the orthodoxy of Friends* (Dublin, 1698)

Pike, Joseph, *Some account of the life of Joseph Pike of Cork, written by himself* London, 1837)

Plimpton, John, *Ten charges against the people called Quakers* (Dublin, 1698)

_____ *A Quaker no Christian* (Dublin, 1698)

_____ *Quakerism the mystery of iniquity* (Dublin, 1698)

Pressicke, George, *A brief relation of some of the most remarkable passages of the Anabaptists in High and Low Germany, 1521* (n.p., 1660)

_____ *Certain queries touching the silencing of godly ministers* (n.p., 1661)

_____ *An answer to Griffith Williams, Bishop of Ossory* (n.p., n.d.)

_____ *A case of conscience propounded* (n.p., 1661)

Pullein, Josiah, *An answer to a paper entitled 'The case of the Protestant dissenters'* ([Dublin, 1695])

_____ *A defence of the answer to a paper entitled 'The case of the Protestant dissenters* (Dublin, 1695)

Ravaillac redivivus, being the narrative of the late trial of Mr James Mitchell, a conventicle preacher (repr., Dublin, 1678)

Remarks upon the book called 'A modest apology . . .' (n.p., 1702)

Richardson, John, *A short history of the attempts to convert the popish natives in Ireland* (London, 1712)

_____ *A proposal for the conversion of . . . Ireland* (2nd ed., London, 1712)

Rogers, John, *Ohel or Beth-shemesh* (London, 1653)

Rust, George, *A sermon preached at . . . death of Hugh, Viscount Montgomery of the Ards* (Dublin, 1664).

Sheridan, William, *St Paul's confession of faith* (Dublin, 1685)

Shields, Alexander, *A hind let loose, or a historical representation of the testimonies of the church of Scotland* (n.p., 1687)

_____ *The history of the Scotch Presbytery, being an epitome of 'The hind let loose'* (London, 1692).

_____ *An informatory vindication of a poor, wasted, misrepresented remnant . . . true Presbyterian Church in Scotland* (n.p., 1707)

_____ *The life and death of . . . James Renwick* (Edinburgh, 1724)

Sicklemore, James, *To all the inhabitants of Youghal who are under the teachings of James Wood* (n.p., 1657/8)

Sleigh, Joseph, *Good advice and counsel given forth by Joseph Sleigh* (London, 1696)

Smyth, Edward, *A sermon preached at Christchurch, Dublin* (Dublin, 1698)

Stanhope, Arthur, *The Bishop of Waterford's case* (Dublin, 1670)

_____ *Episcopal jurisdiction asserted* Dublin (1670/1)

Stockdale, William, *Great cry of oppression or a brief relation of some . . . sufferings of . . . Quakers in Ireland, 1671-1681* (Dublin, 1683).

Story, Thomas, *A journal of the life of Thomas Story* (Newcastle, 1747)

Strettell, Amos, and Burnyeat, John, *The innocency of the Quakers manifested* (Dublin, 1688)

Synge, Edward, *A peaceable and friendly address to the nonconformists* (Dublin, 1697; reprinted 1732)

_____ *Defence of the peaceable and friendly address* (Dublin, 1698)

_____ *A defence of the Established Church and laws in answer to . . . 'A vindication of marriage'* (Dublin, 1705)

_____ *An answer to all the excuses* (Dublin, 1697)

Taylor, Jeremy, *A discourse on the liberty of prophesying* (London, 1647)

_____ *Rules and advices* (Dublin, 1661)

_____ *A sermon preached at the consecration of two archbishops and ten bishops* (Dublin, 1661)

_____ *A sermon preached at the opening of parliament . . . 8 May 1661* (London, 1661)

Taylor, Timothy, and Eaton, Samuel, *The defence of sundry positions and . . . the congregational way justified* (London, 1646)

Teate, Faithful, *Nathaniel or an Israelite indeed* (London, 1657)

_____ *The soldier's commission* (London, 1658)

_____ *The uncharitable informer charitably informed* (Dublin, 1660)

Teate, Joseph, *A sermon preached at . . . St Canice's, Kilkenny* (Dublin, 1670)

Tennison, Richard, *A sermon preached at the primary visitation of . . . Archbishop of Armagh* (Dublin, 1679)

_____ *A sermon preached . . . Dublin* (Dublin, 1692)

The testimony of Abraham Fuller (n.p., 1687)

Tisdall, William, *A sample of true-blue Presbyterian loyalty* (Dublin, 1709)

_____ *The conduct of dissenters* (Dublin, 1712).

_____ *A seasonable enquiry into . . . the kirk in power* (Dublin, 1713)

_____ *The nature and tendency of popular phrases in general* (n.p., 1713)

Ussher, James, *The reduction of episcopacy* (London, 1687)

Vesey, John, *A sermon preached at Clonmel assizes* (Dublin, 1683)

Walker, Patrick, *Some remarkable passages of the life and death of Mr Alexander Peden* (3rd ed., Edinburgh, 1728)

Ware, Robert, *Foxes and firebrands or a specimen of the danger . . . of popery . . .* (2nd ed., Dublin, 1682)

_____ *The hunting of the Romish fox* (Dublin, 1683)

Weaver, John, *The life and death of Dr Samuel Winter* (London, 1671)

Weld, Nathaniel, Boyse, Joseph, and Choppin, Richard, *Seasonsble advice* (Dublin, 1722)

Wetenhall, Edward, *Collyrium, a sermon preached in . . . Dublin* (London, 1672)

_____ *Of gifts and offices* (Dublin, 1678)

_____ *The Protestant peacemaker* (London, 1682)

_____ *A practical and plain discourse* (Dublin, 1683)

_____ *A specimen of loyalty towards James II* (Dublin, 1686)

_____ *An earnest and compassionate suit for forbearance* (London, 1691)

_____ *Sermon touching divine right* (London, 1691)

_____ *The case of the Irish Protestants . . . sated and resolved* (London, 1691)

_____ *A sermon preached at Whitehall before the queen* (Cork, 1691)

_____ *Pastoral admonitions* (Cork, 1691)

_____ *A letter to a friend* (London, 1691)

_____ *A sermon setting forth the duties of the Irish Protestants* (Dublin, 1692)

_____ *A brief and modest reply to Mr Penn's . . . defence* (Dublin, 1699)

Whitehead, George, and Penn, William, *A serious apology for the principles and practices of the . . . Quakers, against . . . Jenner and . . . Taylor* (n.p., 1671)

[Whittington, Charles], *Remarks upon some passages in Mr Boyse's sermons, vol 1* (Dublin, 1709)

Wight, Thomas, and Rutty, John *A history of the rise and progress of the people called Quakers in Ireland* (Dublin, 1751)

Williams, Daniel, *Practical discourse on several important subjects,* 2 vols (London, 1738)

Williams, Griffith, *The great Antichrist* (n.p., 1660).

_____ *Seven treatises* (London, 1661)

_____ *The chariot of truth* (London, 1663).

_____ *A true relation* (London, 1663)

_____ *The persecution of John Bale* (London, 1664)

_____ *Several sermons* (London, 1665)

_____ *Four treatises* (London, 1667)

Winter, Samuel, *The sum of diverse sermons* (Dublin, 1656)

Wood, James, *Shepardy spiritualised* (London, 1680)

Wright, Thomas, and Harris, Nicholas, *Truth further defended and William Penn vindicated* (n.p., 1700)

LATER WORKS

Acheson, R. J., *Radical Puritanism in England, 1550-1660* (Longman, 1990)

Adamson, Ian, *The identity of Ulster* (2nd ed., Belfast, 1987)

Alexander, George, *Historic memorials of the First Presbyterian Church* (Belfast, 1887)

Allen, Robert, 'Scottish ecclesiastical influence upon Irish Presbyterianism from the subscription controversy to the union of synods' (M.A. thesis, Q.U.B., 1940).

Armstrong, James, *A discourse on Presbyterian ordination . . . with an appendix containing a summary history of the Presbyterian Church in the city of Dublin* (Dublin, 1829)

Atkinson, E. D., *Dromore, an Ulster diocese* (Dundalk, 1925)

Alymer, G. E., 'Unbelief in seventeenth-century England' in Donald Pennington and Keith Thomas (ed.), *Puritans and revolutionaries* (Oxford, 1978)

Bailey, Francis, (ed.) *An account of the the Rev. John Flamstead visiting Kilkenny in 1665* (London, 1835)

Baillie, W. D., *A history of congregations in the Presbyterian Church in Ireland, 1610-1982* (Belfast, 1982)

Barkley, J. M., *The Westminister formularies in Irish Presbyterianism, being the Carey lectures, 1954-56* (Belfast, 1956)

_____ *A short history of the Presbyterian Church in Ireland* (n.p., 1959)

_____ *The eldership in Irish Presbyterianism* (n.p., 1963)

_____ *Blackmouth and dissenter* (Belfast, 1991)

Barnard, T. C., *Cromwellian Ireland: English government and reform in Ireland, 1649-1660* (Oxford, 1975)

_____ *The English republic, 1649-1660* (London, 1987)

_____ 'Crisis and identity among Irish Protestants, 1641-1685' in *Past and Present*, no. 127 (May 1990)

_____ 'Reforming Irish manners: the religious societies in Dublin during the 1690s' in *Hist. Jn.*, xxv (1992)

_____ 'Protestants and the Irish language, c. 1675-1725' in *J.E.H.*, 44, no. 2 (Apr. 1993)

_____ 'Lawyers and the law in later seventeenth-century Ireland' in *I.H.S.*, xxviii, no. iii (May 1993)

Baumann, Richard, *Let your words be few: symbolism and silence among seventeenth-century Quakers* (Cambridge, 1983)

Berg, Joannes van den, *The idea of tolerance and the Act of Toleration* (London, 1989)

Beckett, J.C., *Protestant dissent in Ireland, 1687-1780* (London, 1948)

_____ 'The government and the Church of Ireland under William III and Anne' in *I.H.S.*, ii, no. 7 (1941)

_____ 'William King's administration of the diocese of Derry, 1691-1703' in *I.H.S.*, iv, no. 14 (1944)

_____ *Confrontations in Irish history* (London, 1972)

Benn, George, *History of Belfast*, 2 vols (Belfast, 1877)

Berman, David, 'The Irish Counter-Enlightenment' in Richard Kearney (ed.), *The Irish mind* (Dublin, 1985)

_____ *A history of atheism in Britain from Hobbes to Russell* (Croom Helm, 1988)

Bigger, F. J., 'Alexander Peden, 'the Prophet'' in *U.J.A.*, ix, no. 3 (1903)

Bolam, C. G., *The English Presbyterians* (London, 1968)

Bolton, F. R., *The Caroline tradition in the Church of Ireland* (London, 1958)

_____ 'Griffith Williams, Bishop of Ossory, 1641-72' in *Butler Society Journal*, ii, no. 3 (1987)

Bossy, John, *Christianity in the West, 1400-1700* (Oxford, 1985)

Brady, Ciaran, (ed.), *Worsted in the game: losers in Irish history* (Dublin, 1989)

Brady, Ciaran and Gillespie, Raymond, (ed.), *Natives and newcomers* (Dublin, 1986)

Brailsford, M. R., *The making of William Penn* (London, 1933)

Brooke, Peter, 'Controversies in Ulster Presbyterianism' (Ph.D. thesis, Cambridge Univ., 1981).

_____ *Ulster Presbyterianism* (Dublin, 1987)

Brown, A. W. Godfrey, 'Irish Presbyterian theology in the early eighteenth century' (Ph.D. thesis, Queen's University, Belfast, 1977)

Brown, Terence, *The whole Protestant community* (Field Day Pamphlet, no.7, Belfast, 1985)

Buckley, Elia, 'William Penn in Dublin' in *Dublin Hist. Rec.*, vi, no. 3 (June-Aug. 1944)

Buckroyd, Julia, *Church and state in Scotland*, 1660-1681 (Edinburgh, 1980)

Cameron, John C., *Alexander Peden, the prophet of the Covenant* (repr., Kilkeel, 1988)

Cameron, Thomas, *Peden the prophet* (repr., Edinburgh, 1981)

Campbell, John, *A short history of the Non-Subscribing Presbyterian Church of Ireland* (Belfast, 1914)

Capp, B. S., *The Fifth Monarchy Men* (London, 1972)

Carroll, Kenneth, 'Quakerism in the Cromwellian army' in *J.F.H.S.*, 54, no. 3 (1978)

_____ 'Early Quakers and "going naked as a sign"' in *Quaker History*, no. 67 (1978)

_____ 'Quakers and Muggletonians in seventeenth-century Ireland' in David Blamires, (ed.), *A Quaker miscellany for Edward H. Milligan* (London, 1985)

_____ 'Thomas Loe, friend of William Penn and apostle to Ireland' in J. W. Frost and J. M. Moore (ed.), *Seeking the light* (London, 1986)

Carpenter, Andrew, 'William King and the threats to the Church of Ireland during the reign of James II' in *I.H.S.*, xviii, no. 69 (Mar. 1972)

Carslaw, W. H., *Life and letters of James Renwick* (Edinburgh, 1893)

Christian discipline of the Religious Society of Friends in Ireland (Dublin, 1971)

Clarke, Aidan, 'Varieties of uniformity: the first century of the Church of Ireland' in W.D. Sheils and Diana Wood (ed.), *The churches, Ireland and the Irish,* Studies in Church History, 25 (Oxford, 1989)

Cohen, Charles Lloyd, *God's caress: the psychology of Puritan religious experience* (Oxford/New York, 1986)

Cole, Alan, 'The Quakers and the English revolution' in Trevor Aston (ed.), *Crisis in Europe, 1560-1660* (London, 1980)

Coleman, James 'Some early Waterford clerical authors' in *Waterford Arch. Soc. Jn.*, vi (1900)

S. J. Connolly, *Religion, law and power: the making of Protestant Ireland, 1660-1760* (Oxford, 1992)

Cressy, David, *Coming over: migration and communication between England and New England in the seventeenth century* (Cambridge, 1987)

Croskery, Thomas, and Witherow, Thomas, *Life of A. P. Goudy* (Belfast, 1887)

Cowan, I. B., 'The Covenanters: a revision article' in *Scottish Hist. Review*, xlvii (1968)

—— *The Scottish Covenanters* (London, 1976)

Dickson, David, *New foundations: Ireland, 1660-1800* (Dublin, 1987)

Dickson, R. J., *Ulster emigration to colonial America, 1718-95* (London, 1966)

Donaldson, Gordon, 'Covenant to Revolution' in Duncan Forrester and Douglas Murray (ed.), *Studies in the history of worship* (Edinburgh, 1984)

Dow, F. D., *Radicalism in the English revolution, 1640-1660* (Oxford, 1985)

Drummond, A. L., *The kirk and the continent* (Edinburgh, 1956)

Dwyer, Philip, *The diocese of Killaloe from the Reformation to the close of the eighteenth century* (Dublin, 1878)

Edwards, R. D., 'The history of the laws against Protestant nonconformity in Ireland from the Restoration (1660) to the Declaration of Indulgence (1687)' (M.A. thesis, U.C.D., 1932)

Edwards, R. D., and O'Dowd, Mary, *Sources for early modern Irish history, 1534-1641* (Cambridge, 1985)

Elliott, Marianne, *Watchmen in Sion: The Protestant idea of liberty* (Field Day Pamphlet, no. 8, Derry 1985).

Ellison, C. C. (ed.), 'Bishop Dopping's visitation book, 1682-5', in *Riocht na Midhe*, iv (1971)

Emerson, N. D., 'Christ Church Cathedral under the early Stuarts' in *Blotter, calendar and yearbook, Christ Church Cathedral* (Dublin, 1955-6)

Eversley, D. E. C., 'The demography of Irish Quakers, 1650-1850' in J. M. Goldstrom and L. A. Clarkson (ed.), *Irish population, economy and society* (Oxford, 1981)

Firman, N. 'Perceptions of the Quaker movement in the 1650s' (Ph.D. thesis, Univ. of East Anglia, 1985)

Fitzpatrick, Brendan, *Seventeenth-century Ireland: the war of religions* (Dublin, 1988)

Ford, Alan, *The Protestant Reformation in Ireland, 1590-1641* (Frankfurt, 1985)

Gillespie, Raymond, 'The Presbyterian revolution in Ulster, 1660-1690' in W. J. Sheils and Diana Wood (ed.), *The churches, Ireland and the Irish,* Studies in Church History, 25 (Oxford, 1989)

_____ 'The Irish Protestants and James II, 1688-90' in *I.H.S.*, xxviii, no. 110 (Nov. 1992)

_____ 'Explorers, exploiters and entrepreneurs, 1500-1700' in B. J. Graham and L. T. Proudfoot, (ed.), *An historical geography of Ireland* (London, 1993)

Gillespie, Raymond, and O'Sullivan, Harold (ed.), *The borderlands: essays in the history of the Ulster-Leinster border* (Belfast, 1989)

Goodbody, O. C., 'Ireland in the 1650's in *J.F.H.S.*, 48 (1956-8)

_____ 'Seventeenth-century Quaker marriages in Ireland' in *et al.*, J.F.H.S., 50, no. 4 (1962)

Gordon, Alexander (ed.), *Freedom after ejection: a review (1690-92) of Presbyterian and Congregational nonconformity in England and Wales* (Manchester, 1917)

Gordon, Alexander, *Historic memorials of the Remonstrant congregation of Templepatrick* (Belfast, 1899)

Gordon, Alexander, and G. K. Smith, *Historic memorials of the First Presbyterian Church of Belfast* (Belfast, 1887)

Greaves, R. L., *Deliver us from evil* (Oxford, 1986)

Greaves, R. L., and Zaller, Robert, *Biographical dictionary of British radicals in the seventeenth century*, 3 vols (London, 1982-4)

Grubb, Isobel, 'Social conditions in Ireland in the seventeenth and eighteenth centuries' (M.A. thesis, London Univ., 1916)

_____ *The Quakers in Ireland* (London, 1927)

_____ 'Anthony Sharp: an unpublished memoir' in *Friends' Quarterly Examiner*, 59 (1925)

Haire, J. L. M., *et al., Challenge and conflict: essays in Irish Presbyterian history and doctrine* (Antrim, 1981)

Harris, Tim, *Politics under the later Stuarts: party conflict in a divided society, 1660-1715* (Longman, 1993)

Harrison, R. S., 'Dublin Quakers in business, 1800-1850' (M. Litt. thesis, T.C.D., 1986)

_____ *Cork city Quakers, 1655-1939: a brief history* ([Cork], 1991)

Henderson, G. D., *Religious life in seventeenth-century Scotland* (Cambridge, 1937)

Herlihy, Kevin, 'The Irish Baptists, 1650-1780' (Ph.D thesis, Trinity College, Dublin, 1992)

Heron, A. I. C., (ed.), *The Westminster Confession in the church today* (Edinburgh, 1972)

Healy, John, *History of the diocese of Meath*, 2 vols (Dublin, 1908)

Hewison, J. K., *The Covenanters: a history of the church in Scotland from the Reformation to the Revolution* (Glasgow, 1913)

Hill, Christopher, 'Puritans and "the dark corners of the land"' in *T.R.S.H.*, 5th series, xiii (1963)

_____ *The world turned upside down* (Harmondsworth, 1978).

_____ *God's Englishman: Oliver Cromwell and the English revolution* (Harmondsworth, 1983)

_____ *The experience of defeat* (Harmondsworth, 1985)

_____ *A turbulent seditious and factious people: John Bunyan and his church* (Oxford, 1988)

Hill, Christopher, Reay, Barry, and Lamont, William, *The world of the Muggletonians* (London, 1983)

Hill, Jacqueline, 'Popery and protestation, civil and religious liberty: The disputed lessons of Irish history, 1690-1812' in *Past and Present*, no. 118 (1988)

Holifield, E. Brooks, *The Covenant sealed* (Yale, 1974)

Holmes, James, *Increase Mather: a bibliography of his works*, 2 vols (Ohio, 1931)

Holmes, R. F. G., *Our Irish Presbyterian heritage* (Belfast, 1985).

Houston, Thomas, *The life of James Renwick* (repr., Edinburgh, 1987)

_____ *The letters of James Renwick* (Paisley, 1845)

Howie, John, *Sermons delivered in times of persecution in Scotland* (Edinburgh, 1880)

Hutton, Ronald, *The Restoration* (Oxford, 1985)

_____ *Charles II* (Oxford, 1989)

Irwin, Charles, *History of Presbyterianism in Dublin and the south and the west of Ireland* (London, 1890)

Jessopp, Augustus, *The coming of the friars and other historic essays* (London, 1889)

Johnston, John C., *Alexander Peden, the prophet of the Covenant* (Kilkeel, 1988)

Jones, R. Tudor, *Congregationalism in England, 1662-1962* (London, 1962)

Jones, S. K., *Dr Williams and his library* (Dr Williams's Library pamphlet, London, 1948)

Keeble, N. H., *The literary culture of nonconformity in later seventeenth-century England* (Leicester, 1987).

_____ *'Loving and free converse': Richard Baxter in his letters* (Dr Williams's Library pamphlet, London, 1991).

Kelly, Patrick, 'Archbishop William King, 1650-1729' in Ciaran Brady (ed.), *Worsted in the game* (Dublin, 1989)

Kiernan, V. G., 'The Covenanters: a problem of creed and class' in Frederick Krantz (ed.), *History from below* (Oxford, 1985)

____ 'The later Covenanters' in Terry Brotherstone (ed.), *Covenant, charter and party: tradition of revolt and protest in modern Scottish history* (Aberdeen, 1989)

Kilroy, Phil, 'Women and the Reformation in seventeenth-century in Margaret MacCurtain and Mary O'Dowd (ed.), *Women in early modern Ireland* (Dublin, 1991)

____ 'Protestantism in Ulster, 1610-1641' in Brian Mac Cuarta (ed.), *Ulster 1641: aspects of the rising* (Institute of Irish Studies, Belfast, 1993)

____ 'Radical religion in Ireland, 1641-1660' in Jane Ohlmeyer (ed.), *From independence to occupation, 1641-1660* (Cambridge, forthcoming)

King, C. S., *A great Archbishop of Dublin, William King, D. D., 1650-1729* (London, 1906).

Knox, R. A., *Enthusiasm* (Collins, 1987)

Knox, R. B., *James Ussher, Archbishop of Armagh* (Cardiff, 1967)

Latimer, W. T., *History of the Irish Presbyterians* (Belfast, 1902)

Lawlor, H. J. (ed.), 'Diary of William King' in *R.I.A. Proc.*, xiii, 5th series (1903)

Lawson, Jean, *Life and times of Alexander Peden and James Renwick* (Glasgow, c. 1905)

Leadbeater, Mary, *Biographical notes of Friends in Ireland* (London, 1823)

Lecky, Alexander, *The Laggan and its Presbyterianism* (repr., Belfast, 1978)

Linklater, Mark, and Hesketh, Christian, *For king and conscience: John Graham of Claverhouse, Viscount Dundee, 1645-89* (London, 1989)

Lockhart, Audrey, *Some aspects of emigration from Ireland, 1665-1775* (New York, 1976)

____'The Quakers and emigration from Ireland to the North American colonies' in *Quaker History*, 77, no. 2 (fall, 1988)

Loughridge, Adam, *The Covenanters in Ireland* (Rathfriland, 1987)

Loupès, Phillipe, 'Bishop Dopping's visitation of the diocese of Meath, 1693' in *Studia Hibernica*, 24 (1984-8)

Lunham, Thomas, 'Early Quakers in Cork', in *Cork Hist. Soc. Jn.*, 2nd series, x (1904)

McAdoo, Henry, 'The religion of a layman: James Bonnell (1653-1699) in *Search: a Church of Ireland Journal* (spring, 1991)

MacCurtain, Margaret, *Tudor and Stuart Ireland* (Dublin, 1972)

McGuire, J. I., 'Why was Ormond dismissed in 1669?' in *I.H.S.*, xviii, no. 71 (Mar. 1973)

_____ 'The Church of Ireland and the "Glorious Revolution" of 1688' in Art Cosgrove and Donal McCartney (ed.), *Studies in Irish history presented to R. Dudley Edwards* (Dublin, 1979)

_____ 'The Irish parliament of 1692' in Thomas Bartlett and D. W. Hayton, *Penal era and golden age: essays on eighteenth-century Ireland* (Belfast, 1979)

_____ 'The Dublin Convention, the Protestant community and the emergence of an ecclesiastical settlement in 1660' in Art Cosgrove and J. I. McGuire (ed.), *Parliament and community: Historical Studies XIV* (Belfast, 1983)

_____ 'Government attitudes to religious nonconformity in Ireland, 1660-1719' in C. E. J. Caldicott, Hugh Gough and J. P. Pittion (ed.), *The Hugenots and Ireland: anatomy of an emigration* (Dublin, 1987)

McKinney, C. W., *Killinchy* (1968)

MacLysaght, Edward, *Irish life in the seventeenth century* (repr., Dublin, 1979)

McSkimin, Samuel, *History and antiquities of . . . Carrickfergus*, ed. E.J. McCrum (Belfast, 1909)

Marshall, Alan, 'Colonel Thomas Blood and the Restoration political scene' in *Hist. Jn.*, xxxii (1989)

Marshall, John, 'The ecclesiology of the Latitude men, 1660-89' in *Eccles. Hist. Jn.*, 36, no. 3 (July, 1985)

Matthews, A. G., *Calamy revised* (Oxford, 1934)

Maxwell, W. D., *A history of worship in the church of Scotland* (Oxford, 1955)

Millar, Patrick, *Four centuries of Scottish psalmody* (Oxford, 1949).

Miller, David, 'Presbyterianism and "modernisation" in Ulster' in *Past and Present*, 80 (Aug. 1978)

Mitchison, Rosalind, *Lordship and patronage* (London, 1983)

Mullen, Julia E., *History of New Row Presbyterian Church, Coleraine* (Antrim, 1976)

Munter, Robert, *A dictionary of the print trade in Ireland, 1556-1775* (New York, 1988)

Murray, R. H., *Revolutionary Ireland and its settlement* (London, 1911)

Nelson, John, 'The Belfast Presbyterians, 1670-1830' (Ph.D. thesis, Q.U.B., 1985)

Nokes, David, *Johnathan Swift, a hypocrite reversed: a critical biography* (Oxford, 1985)

Nolan, Willian, 'Patterns of living in Co. Tipperary from 1770-1850' in William Nolan (ed.), *Tipperary: history and society* (Dublin, 1985)

Nutall, G. F., *Visible saints: the Congregational way, 1640-1660* (Oxford, 1957)

Ó hÓgáin, Dáithí, 'An t-ór buí: staidéar an ghné de sheanchas Thiobraid Árann' in William Nolan (ed.), *Tipperary: history and society* (Dublin, 1985)

Peacocke, Irvine. J., 'Anthony Dopping, Bishop of Meath' in *Irish Church Quarterly* (1909)

Perceval-Maxwell, Michael, 'The adoption of the Solemn League and Covenant by the Scots in Ulster' in *Scotia: American–Canadian Journal of Scottish Studies,* ii (1978)

Phillips, W. Alison (ed.), *History of the Church of Ireland,* 3 vols (Oxford, 1933-4)

Pollard, Mary, *Dublin's trade in books* (Oxford, 1989)

Porter, Classon, *Regium donum and ministerial maintenance* (Belfast, 1884)

Power, John, 'Waterford clerical authors, from the work of Rev. Thomas Gimlette' in *Irish Literary Enquirer,* no. 3 (Dec., 1865)

Power, P. C., *History of South Tipperary* (Cork, 1989)

Reay, Barry, *The Quakers and the English revolution* (London, 1985)

‗‗'Quakerism and society' in J. F. McGregor and Barry Reay (ed.), *Radical religion in the English revolution* (Oxford, 1986)

Reid, J. S., *The history of the Presbyterian Church in Ireland,* 3 vols (Belfast, 1867)

Rogers, Edward, *Life and opinions of a Fifth Monarchy Man* (London, 1867)

Rogers, P. G., *The Fifth Monarchy Men* (London, 1966)

Rupp, E. G., *Religion in England, 1688-1791* (Oxford, 1986)

Schlenther, Boyd S., *The life and writings of Francis Makemie* (Philadelphia, 1971)

Schmidt, L.E., *Holy fairs: Scottish communions and American revivals in the early modern period* (Princeton, 1989)

Scott, Walter, *Old Mortality* (Harmondsworth, 1982)

Seymour, St J. D., *Succession of parochial clergy in the united dioceses of Cashel and Emly* (Dublin, 1908)

‗‗ 'Faithful Teate' in *J.S.A.I. Jn.*, 6th series, x (1920)

‗‗ 'Two letters relative to early Quakerism in Limerick' in *North Munster Arch. Soc. Jn.*, iv, no. 2 (1919)

‗‗ 'A Puritan minister in Limerick' in *North Munster Arch. Soc. Jn.*, iv, no. 3 (1919)

‗‗ *The Puritans in Ireland* (Oxford, 1921)

‗‗ *Irish Witchcraft and Demonology* (repr. London, 1989)

‗‗ *Samuel Winter* (Dublin, 1941)

Simpson, Robert, *Life of the Rev. James Renwick* (Edinburgh, 1843)

Smellie, Alexander, *Men of the Covenant* (repr., Edinburgh, 1975)

Stevenson, David, *Scottish Covenanters and Irish Confederates* (Belfast, 1981)

‗‗ *The Covenanters* (Belfast,1988)

Stevenson, John, *Two centuries of life in Down, 1600-1800* (repr., Dundonald, 1990)

Stewart, A. T. Q., *The narrow ground: aspects of Ulster, 1609-1969* (London, 1977)

Thomas, Roger, *Daniel Williams, 'Presbyterian bishop'* (Dr Williams's Library pamphlet, London, 1964)

Toon, Peter, *God's statesman: the life and work of John Owen* (Exeter, 1971)

Tyacke, Nicholas, *The fortunes of English Puritanism, 1603-40* (Dr Williams's Library pamphlet, London, 1990)

Urwick, William, *Independency in Dublin in the olden times* (Dublin, 1862)

_____ *Early history of Trinity College, Dublin, 1591-1660* (London, 1892)

Vann, R. T., and Eversley, David, *Friends in life and death: the British and Irish Quakers in the demographic transition* (Cambridge, 1992)

Vos, J. G., *The Scottish Covenanters* (repr., Pittsburgh, 1980)

Waddell, H. C., *The presbytery of Route* (Belfast, 1960)

Wallace, Dewey D., *Puritans and predestination* (Univ. of North Carolina, 1982)

Watts, Michael, *The dissenters: from the Reformation to the French Revolution* Oxford, 1985)

Weir, A. J. , *Letterkenny: congregations and ministers and people, 1615-1960* (Presbyterian Historical Society Library, Belfast, 1960)

Westerkamp, Marilyn, *Triumph of the laity: Scots-Irish piety and the Great Awakening, 1625-1760* (Oxford, 1988)

Wilson, Walter, *The history and antiquities of dissenting churches and meeting houses in Westminister snd Southwark, including the lives of their ministers,* 4 vols (London, 1808-14)

Winnet, A. R., *Peter Browne, provost, bishop, metaphysician* (London, 1974)

Witherow, Thomas, *Historical and literary memorials of Presbyterianism in Ireland,* 2 vols (London/Belfast, 1879-80)

Wodrow, Robert, *The history of the sufferings of the Church of Scotland from the Restoration to the Revolution,* 4 vols (Glasgow, 1836)

_____ *Analecta: materials for a history of remarkable providences, mainly relating to Scotch ministers and Christians,* 4 vols (Edinburgh, 1842-3)

Wood-Martin, W. G., *History of Sligo county and town,* 3 vols (Dublin, 1882-92)

Young, R. M., *Historical notes of old Belfast and its vicinity* (Belfast, 1896)

Index